To all our children, who inherit our history.

THE GOLDFISH BOWL

Cherie Booth, QC, is an eminent lawyer, married to the current Prime Minister, Tony Blair. Cate Haste is a writer and documentary film-maker whose previous books include the highly praised studies *Nazi Women* and *Rules of Desire*.

Contents

List of Illustrations

Clarissa Eden

1. Clarissa Churchill outside No. 10 Downing Street after her engagement to Anthony Eden, 12 August 1952. *(Getty Images)*
2. Clarissa and Anthony at their wedding reception at No. 10, 14 August 1952. *(Getty Images)*
3. At the Comedie-Francaise in early 1955. *(Countess of Avon Private Collection)*
4. On the election trail, April 1955. *(Countess of Avon Private Collection)*
5. At the Geneva Conference July 1955, with Mrs Eisenhower, Lady Dorothy Macmillan, Madame Faure. *(Countess of Avon Private Collection)*
6. Greeted by the Queen and the Duke of Edinburgh at Balmoral, October 1955. *(Countess of Avon Private Collection)*
7. Attending a film exhibition, summer 1956. *(Countess of Avon Private Collection)*

Dorothy Macmillan

8. Dorothy aged 20. (*Camera Press/Bassano*)
9. Dorothy Cavendish marries Harold Macmillan, 19 April 1921. *(Getty Images)*
10. Dorothy's appeal to the electorate at Stockton-on-Tees, 1923 general election.*(Macmillan Family Archive)*
11. Dorothy and Harold on their arrival at No. 10, January 1957. *(Crown copyright)*
12. At Birch Grove with nine of their grandchildren, 1956. *(Camera Press/ Harold Connold)*
13. Dorothy Macmillan at Birch Grove. *(Camera Press/Alan Clifton)*
14. In Ghana during their Africa tour, 1960. *(Conservative Party Archive/ Camera Press)*

Introduction

In 1994, when my husband was catapulted into the role of leader of the Labour Party, following the untimely death of his predecessor, John Smith, I had begun preparing myself for a change in his life. What took me completely by surprise was the effect that his new role was to have on my own, and that of our family. Because so many people saw him as the Prime Minister in waiting, we attracted the attention of the press and this gave me my first glimpse inside the goldfish bowl. Perhaps I was naïve in thinking that once Tony became leader of the opposition we could continue to live an entirely private life. If it was naïvety it was short-lived: I soon realised that life was never going to be the same again.

But despite that time of preparation in Islington, where we had lived since 1986, the move to No. 10 represented a transformation in our lives. I rapidly became aware that nothing prepares you for the reality of what awaits you behind that famous black door, and perhaps it is better that way. From the beginning, however, I was conscious that I was one of a long line of women – and one man – who had come into the house in similar circumstances.

The first prime minister's spouse I was really aware of was Mary Wilson. I was nearly 10 years old when Harold Wilson led the Labour Party to that narrow victory in 1964 and my father had been very active campaigning for that victory. Since Harold Wilson was also a Liverpool MP and I was living in Liverpool myself, I felt very interested in the new family at No. 10 and that interest increased when my father was invited to one of the Wilsons' famous parties. By the time Audrey Callaghan took over at No. 10, I was myself an active local party member in Westminster North Labour Party, as was my current boyfriend, a young barrister like me, Tony Blair. Later on in my life I met both Mary and Audrey and it was a strange feeling to meet in the flesh someone you had been conscious of from afar.

It was not until Tony had become leader of the opposition that I met both Denis Thatcher and of course Norma Major. Denis was always charming but our meetings were brief, while with Norma it was as if we were participating in parallel lives and seeing each other through the looking-glass. We had so much in common, yet we were on opposite sides of the political game.

The idea of this book first formed when, in 2002, we hosted a wonderful dinner party at No. 10 to celebrate the Golden Jubilee of Queen Elizabeth II. I wanted this to encompass not only the living ex-premiers and their spouses but also representatives of the families of all the prime ministers of her reign. So I met for the first time Clarissa Eden, along with Mary Soames, representing her parents Sir Winston and Lady Churchill, the Earl and Countess of Stockton representing Harold and Dorothy Macmillan, and the Earl and Countess of Home representing Alec and Elizabeth Douglas-Home. During the evening we talked of how it had been to live at No. 10, what had changed and what had not and I realised for the first time that there was a camaraderie born of shared experiences.

A few months later, I had a conversation with Dame Jennifer Jenkins about that Jubilee dinner and she lent me an American book she had just been reading. It was called *Hidden Power*[1] and each chapter was a short biographical account of the relationship between the twentieth-century presidents and 'first ladies'. I was fascinated by the book and started to wonder whether something similar could be done for the UK. I probably would have done nothing more about it, had I not become unexpectedly pregnant again in June 2002. Thinking that I might find myself with time on my hands, I thought that I could use that time to write a book. I had not written a book before and was anxious that it should be properly and thoroughly researched and written. My friend Cate Haste, I knew, had published a number of historical books about women in the twentieth century and I decided to approach her with the idea. We met and discussed it over a meal in the Lake District just after Tony and I had attended the closing ceremony of the Commonwealth Games and just before our proposed holiday in France. Cate was really excited by the idea and we agreed to pursue it on our return from holiday. Two days later I miscarried, so my idea of a maternity leave book was not to be. But the idea stayed with me. Cate and I decided we would do the book anyway, based on a series of interviews that I would conduct with Cate – so we would use my skills as a barrister and her skills as a writer and social historian.

For the next eighteen months, Cate and I interviewed together four of the living spouses, Clarissa Eden, Mary Wilson, Denis Thatcher and Norma Major, all of whom were generous with their time and memories. Sadly Audrey Callaghan was unable to speak to us because of illness, but Lord Callaghan kindly agreed to be interviewed. We also met with a long list of fascinating people who had in one way or another been involved with political and public life over the last fifty years. Some of them had known not one but several of the spouses and this reminded us just how close-knit the Westminster/Whitehall world can be. We also read all the major biographies of the prime ministers and were struck by how little space any of them gave to the character of the spouses or their relationship with the Prime Minister. It seemed as if the spouses were the invisible witnesses of history.

They all shared the experience of living in the two buildings that lie at the centre of the life of every prime minister: No. 10 and Chequers. No. 10 is primarily an office but an office which is also a home, and a unique historical building whose role at the centre of political life goes back to 1735, when Sir Robert Walpole secured the property as a residence for all future First Lords of the Treasury. Chequers is an Elizabethan manor house which was given to the nation as a place of 'rest and recreation for her Prime Ministers forever' in 1921. Situated in Buckinghamshire about an hour's drive from London, it is primarily a weekend home with a small office staffed by No. 10.

There was so much to find out. What sort of people were they, what were their backgrounds, hopes and aspirations? What experiences did they have in common and what things have changed over the years? Were they prepared for their role, or were they taken by surprise? How did they deal with life at No. 10? How intrusive was the press, and how has this changed? How did they find a way to live their own lives and conduct a marriage and a family life? How far did they feel caught up in the great events and crises of the day? Was there life after No. 10?

In the chapters that follow we hope to answer some of these questions, to allow these hitherto hidden voices to speak for themselves and at the same time to illustrate how their experiences throw light on the changing roles of men and women in the second half of the twentieth century.

Cherie Booth, 2004

Chapter One

Clarissa Eden

1955–57

Clarissa Churchill married Anthony Eden on a sunny August day in 1952. The engagement was announced only two days before. Neither of her parents was alive, and her closest surviving relations – her uncle, the Prime Minister, Winston Churchill, and aunt Clementine – had only a week's warning. 'I do so hope you will be pleased about this & give us your blessing,' Clarissa wrote to Clemmie. 'We have known each other for some time now, & we decided a few months ago that we would like to be together for always. I am terribly happy about it, & only wonder & hope that I will prove capable of being some comfort & help to him in his life.'[1]

Clemmie, on holiday in Capri, made immediate preparations to return. Churchill put No. 10 at their disposal for the wedding breakfast, and offered to give the bride away in place of his only brother John – Clarissa's father – who had died five years earlier. Clementine stood in for Clarissa's late mother, Lady Gwendeline Churchill. When Clarissa drove to Downing Street from her flat in Rossmore Court, she was greeted by a bank of press and photographers: 'It was daunting. I was alone in this building, and the press were all swarming around outside. I just sat there,' she remembers. This sudden jolt out of her carefully guarded private life felt like 'being in the path of a typhoon'.[2]

Two days later the Foreign Secretary – still glamorous at 55 – and his 32-year-old bride with her silk shantung dress, half-moon hat and large orchid spray, were married at Caxton Hall register office. Crowds lined the streets and waved from windows and balconies – as big a gathering as had cheered Elizabeth Taylor and her second husband Michael Wilding up the same steps only six months before. The marriage – dubbed 'Romance of the Year' in cinema newsreels – made headlines round the world.

Eden had planned a far more private event; the wedding was, he confided to his son Nicholas, *'an utter secret . . .* it will be as quietly as we can contrive & probably next month'.³ But, Clarissa recalls, he had misjudged press rhythms in British political life: 'He said we must wait until August, because August is the silly season and we won't get any publicity. But of course, it was exactly the opposite, because there wasn't anything else to write about.' The *Church Times* struck the only discordant note, pointing out that Eden was a divorced man, and warning that his behaviour made remarriage '"respectable" in the eyes of a pagan generation'. The criticism reflected the strict attitude to divorce that still prevailed in the Church and some sections of the Establishment which, three years later, forced Princess Margaret to choose between marrying the divorced Group Captain Townsend and renouncing her title to the succession. Clarissa was completely unperturbed by the fuss, despite having been brought up as a Catholic, though her friend, the writer and (Catholic) convert Evelyn Waugh, refused to speak to her from then on.

The marriage marked a dramatic change in Clarissa's life. Though she belonged to a family whose history had been entwined with the fortunes of the British state for centuries, politics had never interested her. She was chic and clever, with her own literary friends. Yet now she was thrown into the very heart of the political establishment, with no experience of the regular duties of a political wife, let alone the rigours and demands of life at the top.

Clarissa Churchill was born on 28 June 1920, the third child and only daughter of Major John ('Jack') Churchill, Winston's younger brother. Her father, who was 'very courteous, very good-looking and kind', according to Clarissa's niece, Sally Ashburton, had served in the Boer War and the First World War and then became a stockbroker, though the family was never well-off. Her mother, Lady Gwendeline ('Goonie') Bertie, daughter of the 7th Earl of Abingdon, was a renowned beauty, with 'wide-opened eyes . . . like blue flowers',⁴ cultivated and well read, an amateur artist with 'a puckish sense of humour which was devoid of any touch of malice', a 'sense of enchantment' and 'a rare power of sympathy'.⁵

It was not only her beauty she passed on to her daughter, but her intellect and her aesthetic tastes. From an early age Clarissa liked her mother's Liberal intellectual friends – the Asquith clan, the daughters of Liberal politician Archibald Sinclair, and the Bonham-Carters. She spent holidays at the Churchills' country home, Chartwell, and later Clemmie took her skiing in Austria. But the political atmosphere of the Churchill household hardly touched her. Of her uncle in the mid-1930s, rejected by his Conservative colleagues, out of office and at the nadir of his career, she remembers only that 'We would sit around the luncheon table endlessly listening to Winston telling us there was going to be a war and we would all get gassed.'

Like many girls of her class and generation, Clarissa received a patchy education. Moved from the rather competitive Kensington High School to a fashionable boarding-school where she was 'bored to death – very bad teachers', she soon managed to leave after complaining of unhappiness. She was restless, and though she admired her mother, she found her embrace stifling. The youngest of three children, with two much older brothers, she was brought up virtually as an only child. 'My mother loved me too much, and that's why I kept breaking out, going away. I just wanted to get out from under the whole thing of being loved too much.'

Her first escape came when she was sent to Paris at the age of 16 with a chaperon and two friends, Catherine Sinclair and Anne Powell, to be 'finished off'. Their intention was to paint: 'I went to a studio, and we all took ourselves very seriously. But I got a bit out of hand.' Her mother had asked the ambassador in Paris, George Clark, to 'keep an eye on Clarissa'. The outcome was not what Gwendeline had hoped. The dashing Embassy press secretary Charles Mendl and his wife Elsie de Wolfe, an interior decorator who had a pavilion at Versailles, took her up, and before long she was attending their regular Sunday events – 'dazzling parties, full of *café society* people', arriving in style in a huge green Rolls-Royce belonging to Hugo Baring, of the banking family.

When she eventually returned to London she enrolled at the Slade School of Art to study life drawing, but never wanted to pursue a career as an artist because, she says bluntly, 'I wasn't any good', though she had a deep interest in art and, on a trip to Italy in 1937, her friend, Julian Oxford, was 'struck by the confidence she always showed in her own judgements, and her caution in accepting the opinions of the fashionable critics of the time'. By 1938, she was impatient with the conventional London scene and refused to participate in the 'awful thing called "coming out" . . . I was fairly bolshie about that'. She declined to be presented at court or to have the traditional ball in her honour: 'I thought the whole thing was just nonsense. Boring to a degree.' As a *New Statesman* reader, she had left-wing friends who did not fit in with the débutante scene. Spurred by a romantic attachment, she returned to Paris.

When war threatened in 1939, Clarissa was staying in Romania with a writer friend, Marthe Bibesco. Oblivious to danger, she at first resisted her mother's urgent plea that 'Winston says there's going to be a war, you must come home' – perhaps because she'd heard it so often at Chartwell luncheons, and also because the 'very good-looking' Romanian Foreign Secretary assured her there would be no war. Luckily Marthe Bibesco's aviator husband flew her to Bucharest where she caught one of the last planes out before Romania fell to the German advance.

In 1940 she moved to Oxford after a friend, Roy Harrod, asked her what she wanted to do and she replied: study philosophy. It was an unusual choice as none of her women friends had been to university. Though not an undergraduate (she had left school without any quali-fications) she was tutored by philosopher A.J. Ayer and at the age of 19 found people who sparked her intellectual curiosity. 'My whole life changed,' she recalls. 'It was the most incredible thing that could happen to one. [It] was a revelation, terribly exciting.' She mixed with the pillars of Oxford's academic community – Isaiah Berlin, Maurice Bowra and David Cecil, who had been a friend of her mother's – and was 'the dons' delight because she was beautiful and extremely intellectual', says Antonia Fraser. The eccentric Gerald Berners, who Clarissa thought was 'a dilettante in the best sense', became a great friend: 'I'd never seen anything like him. He painted very nicely, he composed very nicely, he wrote very nicely, and his whole attitude to life was incredible. He also did the music for ballets with Diaghilev.'

At his house, Faringdon, she mixed with photographer Cecil Beaton (who thought her 'a most romantic character'), Violet Trefusis, John Betjeman and others on the literary and academic scene. Berners based a character in his novel *Far from the Madding War* on her: 'The first impression of her was of gentleness and modesty . . . she was extremely pretty [and her hair] was reminiscent of a cornfield at daybreak',[6] and she appeared in James Pope-Hennessy's *London Fabric* as 'swift and amusing, seeing things in silhouette and immensely capable of intelligent judgements', with a 'charming, evanescent shyness, smiling a private smile'.[7]

In the informal atmosphere of wartime Oxford, where she bicycled to and fro and nobody dressed up for dinner, her originality blossomed: 'She's basically a very private person,' says her friend Gay Charteris, who enjoyed her values, her fun and her unexpectedness. 'You never knew what she was going to say next, but it was always *her*. She was unusual, not at all running with the herd.' She had a natural style: 'Even when we were doing fire-watching duties together and slept in our clothes, she would get up looking as though she'd walked out of *Vogue*,' though her aloofness could be disconcerting to her contemporaries: 'She was hard to please. It was a sort of challenge to make Clarissa laugh. She didn't go out of her way with anybody much, and yet she had appeal,' diplomat Nicko Henderson, an undergraduate at the time, recalls.

Without quite knowing what she wanted to do, but concluding that she couldn't spend the whole war enjoying herself in Oxford, she took a job as a clerk at the Foreign Office decoding telegrams. Her friend Alfred Duff Cooper (Churchill's Minister of Information) arranged for her to live at the Dorchester Hotel – in cut-price rooms at the top because, with the danger from the bombing, 'nobody wanted to be at the top of anything'. Bombs never particularly frightened her, until the coming of the 'doodlebugs' – the V1s – in 1944, and later the V2 rockets, by which time nerves were a little frayed. She ate out at restaurants, although in 1942 there was 'nothing but fishballs', went to night-clubs, was courted by young men, and read voraciously, especially French literature. She worked briefly for the Women's Voluntary Service and in a factory where 'Alice and I sit [with] red hot irons soldering something'.[8] When the Dorchester Hotel arrangement ended she moved into a flat at Rossmore Court, in Regent's Park, a rather 'poor place to be' but all she could afford. It had a marvellous view over Hampstead and Highgate, and was just down the road from another friend, the writer Elizabeth Bowen.

During the war, her contact with Winston, then Prime Minister, and Clemmie was intermittent; she stayed with them at Chequers after the shock of her mother's death in 1941, and convalesced there after an illness when 'the house was icy & I slept in my fur coat' and 'W[inston]. was as loving, humorous, great and utterly seductive as ever in a series of quilted Chinese dressing gowns, & champagne for every meal', she wrote to Cecil Beaton.[9] She had her own circle of friends, including critic Cyril Connolly, editor of the literary magazine *Horizon*. 'People like Cyril had little gatherings in London and then one met all the other writers, and that is where I felt happy,' she remembers. Her first published article, in 1945, was a dispatch from Berlin for *Horizon* reporting on what remained of theatre and cultural life in the devastated city, and before that she worked briefly for a Ministry of Information newspaper directed at a Russian readership, called *British Ally* or *Britansky Soynznik*.

At the war's end, still with no clear idea of what she wanted to do and no private income, Clarissa landed a job on *Vogue*, reviewing theatre, music and art in the Spotlight column. Her articles were sharp and perceptive, but she never viewed this as a career. 'I'm completely idle by nature,' she declares, 'I never worked out of ambition. I just did it because I needed the money.' Career women were anyway regarded as 'rather peculiar' then. In 1947 she moved to a better-paid job at £25 a week doing publicity at London Films for the producer Alexander Korda. On the set of *The Third Man* she met Orson Welles – 'a modern version of those extrovert, creative, vital Renaissance figures' who became 'a pleasantly patient, polite and humane' dinner companion,[10] and a number of other stars who were less to her taste. Shy and often uncompromising in her judgements, she found actors, except Welles, 'not very interesting' and most of the films mediocre. Writing publicity coverage for *Anna Karenina*, *An Ideal Husband* and *Bonnie Prince Charlie* among others, she interviewed the 'always terribly grumpy' Cary Grant, and a temperamental Vivien Leigh, and escorted actress Paulette Goddard on a rather wild trip to Brussels.

Her life seemed to have gained its own momentum, almost despite herself, but for Clarissa, as for everyone else in Britain, life generally was pinched, with clothes rationing and shortages. So it was a high spot to be sent to publicise *An Ideal Husband* in New York, where she stayed at the Plaza Hotel and experienced a 'different world – very chic'. On her return to Heathrow airport, then a fairly small hut surrounded by grass, her current boyfriend didn't recognise her – she'd cut her hair short and had on 'the most incredible coat' which reached almost to the ground. She reflected the feelings of most women who longed for the end of austerity and rationing, and welcomed a new era of long flowing skirts, hourglass waists and feminine lines – a style that couturier Christian Dior had only recently unveiled with his 'New Look'. When someone gave Clarissa a smokey-orange Dior chiffon dress, she recalls, 'It was like a fire. It was beyond belief to have – absolutely wonderful.'

The gradual easing of wartime restrictions led to a new flowering of literary and cultural life. In 1949, Clarissa was offered a job as acting editor at Contact Books, a series on post-war Britain devised by the publisher George Weidenfeld. (The first of these, by a young civil servant named Harold Wilson, was called *A New Deal for Coal*.) Clarissa stayed for nearly a year and was, Weidenfeld remembers, 'a good editor. People liked her and she had very good contacts. She was a very, very interesting person – she still is.' When Contact folded she became an editor at Weidenfeld and Nicolson, where she remained until her secret engagement in January 1952. It was then expected of women that they would give up their work to take on the role of wife. Indeed in some professions, the Civil Service for instance, women were compelled to leave work on marriage.

On her engagement to Anthony Eden Clarissa was 31 and living an independent life – the proud owner of an early Morris Minor car, which was 'so rare that people used to stop in the street and look at me', and a cottage called Rose Bower which Cecil Beaton had helped her find in 1946 at Broad Chalke in Wiltshire. 'I am so excited I cannot sleep. I have never owned a bit of earth before,' she wrote to him.[11] The cottage released in her a passion for gardening which became a lifelong pleasure: 'I'd been in London for so many years and suddenly the whole idea of the country and a garden was intoxicating.' Though all her friends were married, she was not in the least concerned about still being single: her private life was very much her own. She seemed to Cecil Beaton 'so independent and capable of living by herself that one wondered at her ever deciding to "settle down"'.[12] In her eventful social and personal life, she moved easily between the country house set, fashionable society and the intellectual worlds of Oxford and London.

Clarissa had first met Eden when she was 16, at a country house party at Cranborne. He was the glamorous Foreign Secretary, a generation older than her, and she was a schoolgirl; he was, she says, 'a famous figure one looked at'. Ten years later, in 1946, she sat next to him at a dinner party given by Emerald Cunard. On his other side was a foreign lady 'who was very anxious to marry an Englishman at all costs so she monopolised him the whole meal'. It was only at the end that they had a brief conversation which, Clarissa recalls, 'ended with him saying in an undertone, "Perhaps we can have dinner." And I thought "Aha!"' She adds, 'You can tell the moment a man talks to you if they really like women, can't you? Just somehow the way they talk to you.' They went out to dinner together, and she went to weekend house parties at his country home, Binderton in Sussex. They were just friends, Clarissa says, for years. 'It didn't occur to me to marry him – he was a politician for a start. We weren't having an affair or anything, he just seemed a good friend.' But their relationship deepened.

In 1946, Anthony Eden was in the dying stages of his marriage to his first wife, Beatrice, with whom he had two sons, Simon and Nicholas. Beatrice found the life of a politician's wife lonely, and her isolation increased as her husband rapidly climbed the political ranks. He entered Cabinet at the age of 38 and within six months in 1935 became Britain's youngest Foreign Secretary for 150 years, establishing a reputation for skilful diplomacy which would be unshaken for two decades. His resignation in 1938 over Chamberlain's policy of appeasement towards Mussolini was a brief interruption in his ascent, and served more to enhance than damage his reputation. When Churchill took over in 1940, Eden was appointed Dominions Secretary, then Secretary for War in the Cabinet, and later Foreign Secretary. With the Conservatives' election defeat in 1945, Eden, who was by now seen as Churchill's 'heir apparent', shouldered much of the leader's burden as the Tory Party reshaped itself in opposition.

Divorce was out of the question for an ambitious politician, and Anthony, despite a number of dalliances, remained deeply attached to Beatrice. In June 1945 their eldest son Simon, aged 20, had been reported missing, shot down on a mission over Burma. His death shattered Eden, who never really recovered from the loss. For Beatrice it was devastating, and seems to have contributed to her decision finally to leave the marriage. In 1946, she sailed to America and in December that year they agreed to separate, leaving Eden free to pursue relationships but not to marry: his divorce did not come through until June 1950. Charming and courteous, he was attracted to clever and intelligent women and they to him, and though rumour linked his name to several women, nothing was made public.

What attracted Clarissa to Eden was the aesthetic side of his personality rather than his politics. He had a flair for languages, taking particular delight in Persian literature for 'the charm and melody of its verse, with its depths of dreams, richness, its descriptive and varied vocabulary'.[13] He was passionate about art; on trawls around Paris and other capitals he had built up an extensive collection of paintings, and he was widely read, like Clarissa, in the literature of several languages. Clarissa says: 'He had this extraordinary eye. He hated the word *intellectual*, but he read everything. He built up a library of three and a half thousand books and every single one is there because he actually read it. In the twenties he was buying paintings by Derain, Dunoyer de Segonzac, Marie Laurencin, and all these people for nothing – for £50, £20. And he would go to Zwemmers in Charing Cross Road and he built up a terrific collection; he had a Picasso drawing and a Braque, long before anybody was collecting them.'

When Eden proposed to Clarissa in January 1952, he was Foreign Secretary in the Conservative government which had returned to power in 1951. They kept their relationship so secret that all their friends were 'totally astonished'. Her friend Gay Charteris recalls, 'I knew she knew him, but it was a surprise to me', partly because of the age gap: 'in all our growing years he was very grand. We didn't think he was part of our generation.' There 'was a gasp' that a divorced man was marrying, Antonia Fraser recalls, and amazement that Clarissa, who was 'interested in the intellect and not in politics', was marrying a politician, albeit a cultured and handsome one. Clarissa had hesitated, first asking advice from Labour MP Woodrow Wyatt about the duties of a political wife on the national and international stage. Eden's Principal Private Secretary, Evelyn Shuckburgh, who only discovered they had any connection on the day of George VI's funeral in February, hoped solicitously that 'he can be induced to marry her. Nobody needs a wife more than he.'[14]

The marriage in August combined her youth and his glamour with the legendary Churchill name, and attracted worldwide attention. On their return from honeymoon in Portugal, Clarissa moved into 1 Carlton Gardens, the Foreign Secretary's official residence. It was daunting, she says, to enter this world being 'young and inexperienced in politics, and not really understanding'. Moreover: 'No one actually advised me at all, I just had to recognise what was good.' Anthony 'was no help at all. He just assumed one knew exactly how to behave, what to do, everything. I had to find out the hard way.' She had difficulty asserting herself at first – 'It was all so new to me and unlike anything I'd ever known in my life before.' She rarely had her husband to herself and was surprised at how often official business intervened in their daily lives. 'He was surrounded by private secretaries who had got used to him not having a wife. They'd really got their foothold in the whole thing and suddenly marrying me made it a bit awkward for them. I suppose they'd got so used to managing him, and being the ones who advised him, organised everything for him. Even his detective was bossy with me.'

Even so, she enjoyed being hostess at diplomatic receptions and official banquets for Foreign Ministers, because 'it was all done for you' by the Government Hospitality Service. She oversaw the menus and 'enjoyed sitting next to all these people who the dinner was being given for. Because, poor things, they always had to sit next to me. And it was interesting – or not, as the case may be.' One person who she did find engaging, and who became a lifelong friend, was Dean Acheson, American Secretary of State, whose wit and incisiveness she enjoyed – 'he was frightfully amusing, always making terribly funny jokes.'

She hosted regular teas for ambassadors' wives and was soon preoccupied with arrangements for a grand banquet which the Foreign Secretary was giving for the Queen at Lancaster House to mark the Coronation in June 1953. This included writing to various grand families of the land to ask for the loan of items for the occasion – the silver from Lord Harewood or from the Duke of Wellington's collection at Apsley House were suggested. The Duke of Buccleuch came up with gilt cutlery and several fruit stands; some people lent bowls, wine coasters and candelabra, while others offered furniture and carpets.[15] (The practice of begging and borrowing silver for official events continued up to Mrs Thatcher's day.)

Her new role as constituency wife was less demanding than it would be today, though she did her share of opening bazaars and fêtes. Warwick and Leamington, where Anthony had been an MP since 1923, were accustomed to not seeing him, she says: 'He went twice a year, once in August to make a speech – a speech not for them, it was for the public, the world – and then once at Christmas to make another speech. The constituents were delighted the more the Minister got up the ladder. It meant less time spent with them, but they didn't mind. They were frightfully proud that their Minister was doing well.'

Since Anthony had sold Binderton shortly after they married, they spent most weekends at Clarissa's cottage at Broad Chalke, where they had time to themselves. 'Raining and cold, Clarissa says this is the right way to run F.O. Lie in bed, direct office by telephone and read Delacroix. Very good too,'[16] Anthony wrote in his diary in December 1952. Their neighbour Cecil Beaton thought 'that she is very much in love with Eden, has great maternal feeling for him, and is perfectly content to devote her life to his welfare'.[17] Though the official boxes kept arriving, and phone calls often interrupted them, these were times for relaxation. 'We are very happy to be at the Bower – roses, sweet peas – lobster, strawberries and cream, Mersault – complete peace and enclosure from the world,' Clarissa wrote. Anthony shared her delight: 'Lovely sunny day. Made the most of it. Read & gardened & painted an indifferent watercolour of C's favourite view.'[18] Once when he was there alone, he wrote to Clarissa: 'Beloved, I must tell you that I love you very much & miss you very much. It is delicious here as ever but without you I cannot savour it somehow. However I will do my best but I do so wish that you were here with me.'[19]

One of Clarissa's passions was travel, and she had hoped, as Foreign Secretary's wife, to accompany him. But 'the whole thing of wives arriving and then being entertained and taken around – it didn't exist,' Clarissa recalls. 'Anthony always said, "you'd be in the way, we won't be able to have all-male dinners and get on with our work. There's no question of your becoming involved in them".' Eden was scheduled to visit President Tito in Yugoslavia shortly after they married: 'Anthony

said, "I certainly can't take you." I was pretty fed up about that. I
wanted to go, it would have been rather nice. I'd never seen Yugoslavia.'
Tito, a widower, had kept saying 'Will you bring your bride?' but
Anthony had demurred. He wrote to Clarissa from Belgrade declaring:
'The super excitement of the day was the sudden discovery of a Mrs
Tito!! Nobody knew she existed'[20] – moreover the bride was 28, which
only added to her sense of disappointment.

Clarissa's hope, expressed to Clemmie on her engagement, that she
would be 'some comfort & help to him in his life' was soon to be tested.
Only seven months into their marriage, Eden became seriously ill. The
series of operations he underwent would overshadow their lives. 'That
changed the whole thing,' Clarissa remarks. In April 1953, an operation for gallstones in the bile duct went badly wrong. Clarissa's friend
Ann Fleming recorded a visit to the clinic: 'Anthony was over three
hours on the operating table, I went to the clinic to be with Clarissa,
a grim day for her – sixteen doctors and Winston tampering with the
bulletins.'[21] Under a nervous surgeon badgered by Churchill with
warnings about the eminence of his patient, Eden lost massive amounts
of blood, and during further probing the bile duct was severed, putting
him in danger of his life. A further operation a few weeks later was no
less tense. He survived, but when the American specialist, Dr Richard
Cattell, heard about his case, he recommended yet another operation
later in Boston.

Eden's first convalescence was painful and slow. He was too ill to go
to Queen Elizabeth's coronation in June 1953, so Clarissa went alone.
When the Edens left for Boston on 5 June, waved off from a quiet
corner of London airport by Winston and Clemmie, the prognosis was
gloomy. Cattell gave Anthony Eden only a 50–50 chance of surviving,
a 20 per cent chance of regaining his earlier health, and a 10 per cent
chance of full recovery.[22] After an eight-hour operation, he warned that
Eden would need further treatment for the rest of his life.

From then on Clarissa was alert to his health: 'It was difficult for
her because she was young and Anthony was really always ill. But she
never, *never* wavered. She was wonderful with him,' Gay Charteris
observed. After a protracted convalescence, Eden and Clarissa flew back
to Europe where they spent September in Greece exploring temples,
swimming and picnicking by the sea.

On his return to the Foreign Office in October, Eden faced a crisis over the leadership succession. In June 1953, while Eden was away, Churchill had suffered a stroke. It was successfully covered up at the time and a caretaker government was set up under Eden's rival Rab Butler, who wrote to reassure Eden of Churchill's continuing support: 'I want you and Clarissa to know one thing, how brightly his loyalty to you burns & how we are holding the post for your return.'[23] Churchill made a remarkable recovery, but the voices calling for his resignation amplified.

Eden confided to Clarissa his growing frustration at Churchill's determination to hold on. She was not ambitious for him, but knew that *his* ambition was ultimately to be Prime Minister and she backed him 'because that was what he wanted'. At times, Eden was so irritated by Churchill's interference in foreign affairs, his meanderings in Cabinet, and his stubbornness that he even thought of leaving politics altogether. 'I cannot go on like this with this old man. I must escape somehow,' he wrote to Clarissa, but he was always courteous in public and restrained in Churchill's presence.[24] It was not in Eden's nature to plot with colleagues to hasten Churchill into 'graceful retirement'. The tensions appear not to have affected Clarissa's relations with her uncle and aunt, whom she saw at regular intervals.

A greater problem for Clarissa was Randolph, Churchill's unpredictable son, who had been her favourite cousin, but who harboured a deep dislike of Eden which he expressed at every opportunity, in private and in the press: 'We had friends in common and the same sort of humour and everything else, and we were very fond of each other. But he then of course became impossible,' Clarissa recalls. On her wedding day in 1952 he had told her, 'I'll give you two years to knock him into shape.' He kept his moratorium 'to the letter', suspending his attacks until their wedding anniversary in 1954, when they resumed. Which meant that Clarissa 'couldn't speak to him any more'.

Eden was often away. Clarissa did not go with him to the Bermuda Conference in December 1953, but he wrote to her daily about the difficult negotiations and his personal concerns: 'I am sad and tired, not so much about details as about this poor world and what I fear lies ahead.' The conference with the American and French leaders was 'hard going'. The weather was appalling: 'This room should be

lovely in fine weather but it is now pure *Wuthering Heights*', and
Churchill was: 'Amiable but completely vague. We are to dine together
tonight alone. I expect it will end up with [a card game] *Oklahoma*,'
Eden wrote. 'It is wretched to be without you, and I had no idea I
loved you and depended on you so much.'[25] In their personal life
there was sadness. Clarissa became pregnant, which made her feel
'extraordinarily unwell', and she miscarried in March 1954. Gay
Charteris visited her in hospital and expected her to say she felt
dreadful, 'instead of which she said, "Of course I feel well for the
first time for weeks." Well, it does sound heartless, but it wasn't, it
was just honesty. And she didn't tell me everything she was really
feeling. She's not that kind of person. I think she bottles up her
feelings a lot, she's so strong and reserved.'

Clarissa was able to go with Eden to the Geneva Conference on Indo-
China in April 1954. They stayed in a hotel overlooking Lake Geneva
but the Chinese delegation, armed with sophisticated bugging devices,
were lodged nearby, forcing Eden to accompany his conversations with
rather inefficient 'noises off' which consisted of banging on the table.
Exasperated, they moved to a villa called Le Reposoir loaned them by
a banker, where at first Evelyn Shuckburgh took charge of domestic
arrangements with 'only two German-speaking maids and a ritzy chef
who are assumed to do the catering, the shopping, the accounts, the
laundry, the housework, the cooking, pressing AE's trousers, answering
Clarissa's bells etc. etc. Everyone comes and asks me questions – who
is in to dinner? – what is to be done about wine?' He went 'on strike',
so Clarissa organised a housekeeper, which released him to do his
proper work, though he and the officials were promptly excluded from
the drawing room.[26] When Clarissa's friend Anthony Rumbold arrived
he chided her. 'At the first meal he said, "Well, I mean, where are the
fraises des bois? This is the time of year for *fraises des bois* – why don't
we have them?" And I was humiliated,' Clarissa chuckles, 'I had to pull
my socks up.'

When an official tour of the Middle East and Far East was planned
in early 1955, she was allowed to go because the Foreign Office team
hired a special plane and she could take up an empty seat: 'It was called,
rather inauspiciously, an Albatross – that was the make – you know,
four propellers going round.' The overall aim of the trip, at a tense

period of the Cold War, was to build up regional alliances as a defence against Soviet expansionism. Clarissa was given no briefing about the agenda by the team or by Anthony, and 'I hadn't the gumption to ask. Looking back on everything now, I can't believe how passive and hopeless I was. I never thought of saying "I want to know what's going on".'

Eden's fateful and only meeting with Egypt's President Nasser and his entourage took place in Cairo on 20 February, when they dined at the British Embassy – one of the more splendid of the imperial edifices, though for Arab nationalists it held unfortunate associations of British dominance. 'Nasser appeared to be very boisterous and happy and amiable,' Clarissa remembers, and her diary records: 'Great impression of health and strength – terrifically broad and booming . . . A. came up very late, having had a good talk with Nasser except regarding the Turco–Iraq pact, upon which he was very bitter.'[27] She and Anthony thought the meeting, aimed at persuading Nasser that it was in his interests to join the West-inspired Turco–Iraq alliance (eventually the Baghdad Pact) for Middle East security, went well. But 'apparently Nasser was slighted from beginning to end. He was slighted because Anthony spoke to him in Persian, he was slighted because he had the wrong clothes on, he was slighted because he was in the Embassy – that's what's now appeared,' Clarissa says. Nasser had exclaimed afterwards, 'What elegance! It was made to look as if we were beggars and they were princes!'[28]

By the time they arrived in Bangkok for the SEATO (South East Asia Treaty Organisation) conference, Clarissa was restless with the formalities: 'I said, "Do you mind if I go to Cambodia?" They were very polite, the poor Siamese, and they said "well, yes",' and arranged it. The other wives attending the conference joined in, though Clarissa feared it was 'the last thing they wanted to do'. They 'landed on this red earth strip – I didn't know they hadn't got an airport there – and all the ambassadors' wives had come up and they were fed up too. We were taken around the temple [Angkor Wat], and then we were shown into a huge hotel run by some French White Russians,' where they freshened up before dining on *poulet à l'estragon* in the middle of the jungle 'and then the wives all thankfully piled into the Dakota and got the hell out'. Clarissa, who felt it was a long way to come for one temple, stayed on with a charming Cambodian governor, and the former French cultural attaché took her round three more temples.

At a stop-off in India they were guests of the Indian President Nehru, with whom Clarissa struck up a friendship: 'I really liked talking to him. He had a great spirituality. He was a beautiful man, and a very, very shy man, very straightforward and without any spite or rancour.' Clarissa felt that their hostess, his daughter, Indira Gandhi, was less sympathetic: she was *farouche* – sullen and shy – and wary of them as British Conservatives who seemed at the opposite political pole to her.

The Edens arrived back in Britain to face renewed uncertainty about the leadership. Before his departure in February, Eden had several times pressed Churchill, who had intimated that he would resign in the first week of April.[29] Now, although opinion in the inner Cabinet had hardened in favour of his departure, Churchill found another excuse to hold on – the new Soviet leadership after Stalin's death had suggested Four Power talks at which he felt he must be present to ease the East–West stalemate.

He finally announced his resignation for 5 April, with Eden as his chosen successor. Clarissa's niece, Sally Ashburton, recorded in her diary: 'Uncle Winston's resignation and Uncle Anthony taking over.' A farewell dinner was arranged for Churchill on 4 April, to be attended by the Queen and the Duke of Edinburgh. The splendid occasion set a historical precedent – the first time the Queen was a dinner guest at Downing Street. But even at his departing moment Churchill was beset by doubts. Afterwards, he went upstairs, sat on his bed in his robes and medals and knee-breeches and, after a long silence, said 'with vehemence' to his secretary Jock Colville, 'I don't believe Anthony can do it.'[30]

The celebration was only slightly marred for Clarissa by the obnoxious behaviour of her cousin Randolph. Much the worse for drink, he advanced on her to announce that he was 'against the new regime' and had penned an article for *Punch* to say so. Clarissa was stung into writing him an angry but dignified reply: 'I am sad that you should value our friendship below the pleasure you get from your cheap and futile campaign against Anthony in clubs and, no doubt, in print. I cannot see what advantage it can possibly be to yourself, Winston or the Conservatives . . . I am genuinely amused and curious of all that the press write on A. but sustained attacks from *friends* I find impossible to take. You must understand that surely and appreciate my dilemma.'³¹ It was a dilemma she would learn to cope with often enough in the face of his – and others' – attacks on Anthony.

Clarissa moved into No. 10 Downing Street from Carlton Gardens with relative ease. Though her life as Foreign Secretary's wife had given her some sort of training, she was still largely unprepared for what she found there. She was very young, at 34, to take on such a role. But her habit of simply taking life as it came and looking for the interesting and the curious seems to have stood her in good stead, and was a kind of strength.

She had little time to settle before she was launched into the 1955 general election campaign, which advertised Eden as the man 'Working For Peace'. The outcome was uncertain. Polls in April showed only a small Conservative lead over Labour. Clarissa and Anthony travelled the country on a hectic schedule of open-air meetings, and speeches which promised continuing progress towards what was later termed 'the affluent society' and the fulfilment of Eden's vision of a 'property-owning democracy'.

With no previous experience of electioneering, Clarissa found it 'a revelation – all these flowers getting thrown at us all the time, and everyone screaming and yelling at us wherever we went'. On a visit to the notorious Gorbals slum area in Glasgow, 'there were all these people banging on the windows and saying "good luck" and all the rest of it. I thought that must be rather strange that they should be doing that. They were supporting *Anthony*. They were all going to vote Labour, but he was terribly popular with all sorts of people in England.' She admired his ease with ordinary people – 'He genuinely loved talking to the "man in the street",' – but it was a skill she did not share: 'I'd never done it. All I had to do was keep smiling.'

The press was politely interested in this stylish wife. An *Evening Standard* profile noting 'her natural and very genuine shyness' pointed out that she was 'the youngest Prime Minister's wife Britain has seen this century' and also 'the least conventional . . . Has any other Prime Minister's wife worked for a fashion magazine? Or as a publicist?'³² It seemed another sign of a dawning new age that a prime minister's wife brought to the job the experience of a separate working life, though it would be a further decade before another consort could claim to have worked for a living.

During the election Clarissa 'immensely eased the burden of the campaign', according to Eden: 'While she has no love of politics, or perhaps because of this, she was a firm, if sympathetic critic. More important still, she understood how to limit the strain by reducing the number of personal engagements outside the meeting halls and so, on the whole, I got through in better physical shape than I had expected.'[33] The Conservatives were returned with an increased majority – up from 17 to 60. It was a resounding vote of confidence for Eden, though the high tide of his personal success was soon to ebb.

The election over, Clarissa returned to No. 10 Downing Street to take up her duties. As all prime ministers' spouses have found, their role is not defined: each spouse makes of it what they can, fitting it to the expectations of the age. Like most young wives at that time, Clarissa believed her role was to support her husband: 'I felt I had to really spend all my time making everything as easy for him as possible. I'd never seen anybody working like that in my life before – working from dawn to two in the morning – and I just felt this is so awful, this life, that I must absolutely tailor my life to his.' Observers noticed an improvement in Eden's health and temper. He was 'a man more at ease with life than he ever was in the past. It is not often now that he runs impatient fingers through his silvering hair, and gives other signs of the nerve strains of an eager, restless temperament.'[34] Which was not to say that he did not have gusts of temper. 'He could certainly fly off the handle, no question,' Clarissa says, though she 'never took it very seriously'.

As she became absorbed into the Downing Street routine, Clarissa saw less of her own circle: 'I didn't have a life with them any more. Life was so full and I was so busy thinking about Anthony and looking after him and being sure that everything was just right for him. They used to come in for drinks sometimes. But [I thought] the last thing he wants to see, when he comes up to dinner is to find a lot of my friends lolling around on the sofas down in the White Drawing Room.' George Weidenfeld recalls: 'Only a few of her old friends were tolerated by Anthony Eden. He was very choosy about the people he liked.

Nothing to do with snobbery – he was a very ingrained sort of conventional Englishman.' Eden dropped everything to meet Greta Garbo when she visited Clarissa at No. 10, but he never met Cyril Connolly, nor the painter Lucian Freud, though he liked writer Antony Powell and his wife, Violet, who were neighbours in the country and Cecil Beaton, who admired Anthony's 'honesty, courage and fairness'.

'Home' at No. 10 is also an office which was, and still is, primarily geared to serve the Prime Minister. Living accommodation consists of the flat upstairs, though at that time they used some of the state rooms: Clarissa's sitting room was the White Drawing Room and they ate in the Small Dining Room. The flat was hardly private, however, since officials needed access to the Prime Minister at all hours in the course of business: 'We couldn't even share a bedroom without their presence, because they were there till late at night, and they turned up first thing in the morning. It was absolutely impossible – and all the [official] boxes all over the place.' Robert Allan, Eden's Parliamentary Private Secretary, recalled: 'I used to go to Downing Street quite early in the morning, and I would sit in the bathroom while he had a bath and shaved and I'd be with him while he dressed, and we'd talk about what was in the papers and what idiotic speeches had been made by friends or enemies over the weekend or over the last day or two.'[35] Anthony and Clarissa rarely had time to themselves. 'At every meal there was somebody. I don't remember ever having a meal alone with Anthony the whole time that he was in office. Because if there was nobody coming in, a foreigner or another politician to have lunch or dinner, then there was one of the boys from the Private Office who was coming to carry on working.'

The spouse's role, if considered at all, had to be fitted into that larger agenda. As hostess at No. 10 Clarissa oversaw one or two official functions a week, visits from heads of state, and she held regular receptions at Downing Street for Conservative Ministers, MPs and their wives. She had her own standards of entertaining, and one of her first brushes was with the Government Hospitality Service: 'They were very set in their ways. They had a caterer that they always had, and I immediately got across them by saying I didn't like that food. I was going to have my own and different caterer of some sort,' she says. She prevailed and was vindicated when Dulles, the visiting American Secretary of State, 'at one of these large dinners downstairs turned to his neighbour and said, "I'll bet you five pounds I know exactly what we're going to eat. It's always the same." And he lost because it wasn't at all what he was thinking it was going to be.'

Part of the spouse's role is also to oversee changes to the building. Clarissa 'loved the Downing Street house, I was terribly happy to live [there]', but she thought the state rooms could be improved. Up till then alterations by incumbents had been haphazard and confined to occasional colour changes. Clarissa conceived an ambitious plan to return the building's furniture and decoration to the original period style as designed for Sir Robert Walpole by architect William Kent in the 1730s: 'I thought it would be a saving in the end if they had it done in the right period, which wouldn't have cost all that much.' She researched the original damask patterns kept at Walpole's country home at Houghton, which 'they could have copied exactly, down to the right colours', and she went to the Soane Museum to establish the correct style of furniture and decoration – 'a creamy colour, and amazing red and crimson and a sort of spinach green, it was very odd' – which was used by architect Sir John Soane for the later addition in the 1820s of the State Dining Room and Breakfast Room. 'I asked Anthony if it would be OK, and he said "oh yes", and the Ministry of Works was sympathetic towards it too.' But as the economy faltered in 1955, financial constraints were more stringent and 'the whole thing got stamped on by the Credit Squeeze', though she did introduce some Kent furniture and paintings loaned from the National Gallery.[36]

As Prime Minister's wife Clarissa was not entitled to any staff. She paid for her own secretary who dealt with her increased correspondence and helped organise official visits with Anthony, which included accompanying the Queen when she laid the foundation stone for the new Coventry Cathedral, as well as her own agenda – opening fêtes, bazaars and fairs, launching ships and attending the annual Party Conference and the Conservative Women's conferences. The Edens paid for their own staff of a cook, kitchen maid, butler, housemaid for the flat upstairs, and Anthony's valet. For the first time Clarissa had a lady's maid, which she wasn't used to. Like the vast majority of women, she had grown accustomed to the wartime habit of making things last, so Clarissa 'used to get frightfully upset because [the maid] kept on changing the soap before I thought I'd really finished [it], which seemed to me a frightful waste'.

The maid also helped with her clothes. For a woman at the top of the social hierarchy in the fashionably formal 1950s, these could be elaborate: 'You were perpetually in evening gowns, tremendous evening clothes – tiaras and God knows what, and long gloves which had to be buttoned up.' Even though she was the most stylish of prime ministers' wives, the press, unlike today, took almost no interest in Clarissa's clothes. She favoured the couturier Worth, who produced 'very nice clothes' which she got at less than the full price. But even at that level of fashion, there were hiccups. 'We went to a reception at Buckingham Palace and the Mountbattens were in the receiving line, and as I approached I saw that Edwina [Lady Mountbatten] had got exactly the same Worth dress.' They managed to exchange pleasantries – 'how do you do?' and so on – but, says Clarissa, 'It was very silly of Worth. They must have known eventually there was going to be a clash. Well, I stopped going to Worth. I was furious.'

Downing Street officials were not always forthcoming about facilities available to the Prime Minister's wife – an aspect of life which has not changed since Clarissa's time: 'I think they were harassed, they didn't want to have to bother with the wife and what she wants and what she doesn't want,' she says. It was often up to her to ask what she was entitled to, and then 'they'd say "Oh yes of course. Have you not got it already?"' Nobody told her she was entitled to a car. All dressed up in her tiara and long evening dress, she would normally drive herself to Embassy functions in her own little car. On one occasion at the Jordanian Embassy in honour of the Queen of Jordan: 'I parked my Hillman Minx in front of the Embassy and went in. And when I came out, it was miles down the road and there were masses of huge cars and chauffeurs all in front. And they'd pushed my car right down the road. I complained to one member of the government [that] it was awfully awkward for me that they'd pushed it down the street, and they were outraged, and they said to Anthony, "She hasn't got a car and a driver, it's absolutely unbelievable!"'. She was offered the same car and driver that Clemmie Churchill had used – 'which they hadn't told me about at all'. But the saga didn't end there: it was 'immediately run into at the corner of Queen's Gate and Cromwell Road by an actress called Coral Browne. So then it was out of action for God knows how long,' Clarissa recalls.

Transport *was* available for official functions which she attended with Anthony, including those involving royalty. She enjoyed sitting next to the Duke of Edinburgh who was, like the Queen, almost her contemporary. 'He was always very outspoken. I rather enjoyed that. He didn't try to be tactful in any way. He was always saying rather surprising things.' With Anthony she visited Balmoral, usually staying one night, and remembers finding the rooms chilly.

Clarissa was also chatelaine at Chequers, the country house set in the Buckinghamshire hills which was made available for use by prime ministers after the First World War by Lord Lee, who foresaw that they may not automatically own a country retreat. Though Clarissa and Anthony still went for weekends to her cottage at Broad Chalke, they used Chequers for informal as well as formal functions. The great merit of Chequers is that it enables business to be conducted in more relaxed surroundings, while it offers leaders and their families respite from the bustle of Downing Street. Heads of state frequently stay there, and every two years, Chequers was the setting for retreat during the Commonwealth Heads of Government meetings.

Clarissa showed little interest in alterations – 'I didn't really like Chequers. It's not a period I like' – though she admired the setting: 'The park was one of the most beautiful I know – the lie of the land and the way the trees are planted I thought was absolutely ravishing.' She used the White Parlour as her sitting room as have so many spouses, past and future, and if there'd been a swimming pool, she would have been 'completely happy'. It was not until 1971, when Edward Heath was in power, that a pool was installed as a gift from the American Ambassador, Walter Annenberg.

Her main interest was the gardens. She eliminated bedding-out, introduced a range of fragrant old-fashioned damask, hybrid musk and Bourbon roses to replace herbaceous beds, and directed that more fruit – plums, apricots and peaches instead of only morello cherries – be grown in the kitchen garden. She had a running battle with the Estate to prevent the felling of trees and shrubs near the house. Friends and family were invited to join them there for Christmas 1955, when the house, warmed by a huge fire in the Great Hall, was decorated with green swagging for the pillars (recommended by the fashionable Constance Spry), garlands of greenery, sprigs of holly and 'a wonderful evergreen bell hanging from the chandelier', her niece Sally Ashburton remembers.

One of the few occasions when Clarissa aroused comment in the press concerned an incident there over a washing line in January 1956. In one of the farm workers' cottages about 400 yards from the main house lived Maud Butt, who hung her washing out in her back garden, and sometimes beyond that across a path, Lime Walk. Clarissa recalls: 'When we had foreign visitors, we used to take them walking around, and that was one of the places we walked. And then one day there was suddenly this washing line across. I said, I thought very nicely, would she mind the washing not being there?' Maud Butt was adamant that she would not change her practices at the instigation of the Prime Minister's wife, and sold her story to the *Daily Mirror*. Chequers was immediately besieged by reporters. Clarissa was embarrassed at the furore, and full of remorse at the possible damage to Anthony. Her friend Ann Fleming reported to Evelyn Waugh: '[Clarissa] is abed with a cold and maintains that Mrs Botts' [sic] washing line was hung across a lime avenue where the Edens walk on Sundays, far beyond the precincts of Mrs Botts' garden. Apparently [Clarissa's] request was humbly put but altered by the minion who delivered the message.'[37] Anthony was so incensed that he consulted Sir Hartley Shawcross on whether to take legal action against the *Daily Mirror*, but was advised against it. The press were annoyed to find, when they asked other tenants, that there was no further evidence of Clarissa's alleged imperious ways.

This adverse publicity coincided exactly with a rising chorus of attack on Eden's leadership from within and outside the Party. Expectations of a buoyant economy were faltering as wages and the cost of living went up, fuelling fears of inflation. Industrial troubles multiplied. In January 1956 the normally supportive *Daily Telegraph* attacked Eden, accusing him of indecisiveness and calling for 'the smack of firm government'.[38] The *Daily Mirror* under the headline EDEN IS A FLOP reported widespread discontent and an 'Eden Must Go' movement among backbenchers. When Eden unwisely replied to rumours of his impending resignation with an unprecedented public denial, he only fed doubts about his judgement and his perilous over-sensitivity to press criticism. His personal approval rating slumped dramatically in three months – from 70 per cent in autumn 1955 to 40 per cent by spring 1956, though it recovered shortly afterwards.[39] Clarissa was angry on his behalf, believing the attacks to be both unjustified and unfair; according to Eden's Press Secretary, William Clark, 'She never interfered "downstairs" at No. 10, but she resented criticism of Eden as being absolutely intolerable.'[40]

In foreign affairs Eden was on surer ground. The Four Power summit meeting in Geneva in July 1955 achieved some easing of Cold War tensions, and Eden met the new Soviet leaders, Nikita Khrushchev and Marshal Bulganin, who expressed a willingness to visit Britain in the near future. Clarissa hosted events at Le Reposoir, socialised with the leaders and their wives and joined Dorothy Macmillan, wife of the Foreign Secretary, on morning swims from a nearby jetty, despite warnings that the lake was 'very unhygienic'.

President Khrushchev's ten-day visit to Britain in April 1956 was the first ever by a Soviet leader and included a weekend at Chequers where the Edens made every attempt to 'bring something of family life into the stay'. Eden's surviving son, Nicholas, drove Khrushchev's son, Sergei to the country: 'Each spoke a few words of the other's language and they talked together of motor cars, the traffic jams impressing the Russian,' Eden wrote. Clarissa thought Bulganin 'a civilised chap. You could talk to him about this and that and any old thing. Khrushchev you couldn't talk to at all.' She recalls one evening when Khrushchev, who was noted for being outspoken, 'was shouting at [Foreign Secretary] Selwyn Lloyd, boasting about something [to do with] his submarines. And Selwyn Lloyd was absolutely gobsmacked. He said afterwards, "we've been trying to find out about that submarine for *ages*." And there he was – drunk or something – just blurting it out across the table!' Eden 'found their characters, especially Mr Khrushchev's, deeply intriguing'.[41]

By early summer, Clarissa was planning a holiday after a difficult fifteen months in office. They had not been away since Anthony's convalescent trip in 1953: 'My wife and I had firm hopes of three weeks' rest in August. We both longed above all things for hot sunshine and sea in which to bathe . . . We began to count the days.'[42]

As it turned out, the countdown was not to a holiday but to the most dramatic crisis of Eden's premiership. On 26 July, Egyptian President Nasser nationalised the Suez Canal Company. Eden saw Nasser's 'grab' of the Canal – 'a thumb on our windpipe' – as a clear threat to Britain's interests; the Canal held symbolic significance as the lifeline to Empire, and 80 per cent of Britain's oil came from the Middle East; Nasser's nationalism was destabilising Britain's influence in the Arab world and his acceptance of Soviet arms and aid opened the prospect of the Soviets gaining a foothold in the Middle East. Mindful of recent criticism of his 'indecisiveness', Eden was determined to respond firmly to the threat.

He immediately sought international support to force Nasser to 'disgorge' the Canal and return it to international control, and meanwhile ordered the Chiefs of Staff to prepare plans and a timetable for military action if it proved necessary. There followed three months of intense negotiations and the eventual decision to land British troops on Egyptian soil. Though condemnation of Nasser's action was near unanimous at the outset, the crisis precipitated the most damaging divisions in the nation and eventually in the Atlantic alliance in post-war history.

August and September saw intense diplomatic negotiations involving the Americans, French and eighteen interested nations. A constant flow of representatives and leaders from America, the Commonwealth and Europe passed through No. 10 Downing Street. 'It was a non-stop crisis, day after day, week after week, and you got used to the fact that you were in a different dimension really,' Clarissa recalls. 'It wasn't like real life at all. I suppose you could say it was like a nightmare in the sense that it wasn't real. It was so stressful that one wasn't even conscious of it being stressful, the atmosphere was so charged.'

Memorably Clarissa later summed up the experience in a speech to Conservative women at Gateshead: 'For the past three months I have felt as if the Suez Canal was flowing through my drawing room',[43] about which she now says: 'I didn't know what to say to them and I made this silly joke – silly, really idiotic. Awful to be remembered just for that.' Throughout the crisis, she followed events closely: 'you didn't really want to get away from it. You didn't really want to suddenly read a book about something quite different.' As his wife and confidante, she learned from him details of discussions in Cabinet meetings and the daily progress of the crisis, which she recorded in her diary: 'Alec (Home) is warning that Rab is wobbling to the point of lobbying, as a result of which he has found seven members of the Cabinet who agree with him,' she noted during a tense period in August.[44] 'Anthony talked about the troubles in Cabinet, that sort of thing,' she recalls. 'He didn't say "This is what we're going to do and what do you think?" He'd just say what he thought.'

Her role as Prime Minister's wife, she decided, was to 'bolster him up'. She felt protective towards him, but she didn't intervene to try to lessen his load or demand that he rested. She endorsed his actions but, she says, 'I didn't feel I knew enough about what was going on to try and interfere in any way.' To keep abreast of events, she read the newspapers every morning – from the communist *Daily Worker* to the Tory *Daily Telegraph*: 'I used to go through them all and see if there was anything I thought Anthony ought to know – some little fact, what someone was saying, anything that I thought he'd *better* know.'

But at a time of intense political discord she found herself in the firing line. Eden's Press Secretary, William Clark, who found his chief's irascibility difficult to handle, thought she tended to 'stir [Eden] up by drawing attention to press attacks on him'.[45] There was gossip that she was playing a larger part in Anthony's decision-making: 'It seems Clarissa is often present at private lunches and drinks and dinners, where important business has to be discussed with Anthony, and that she gives her opinion and advice,' Cynthia Gladwyn, wife of Britain's Ambassador to France, Gladwyn Jebb, wrote in her diary. 'Worse still, Ivone [Kirpatrick, Permanent Under-Secretary at the Foreign Office] has complained that she rings up Anthony at the last moment, tells him not to weaken, and interferes with whatever line has been agreed on. How dangerous all this sounds. Is it really a case of "Infirm of purpose, give me the dagger"?'[46] Not according to Clarissa. She is aware that she was 'accused of encouraging him to go on – that I was too gung-ho about Suez and kept on egging him on, but I think that's a misunderstanding of my just bolstering him up – without having any political motive'.

By October, there was no diplomatic solution in sight and the use of force seemed increasingly likely. A secret agreement with the Israelis and French which involved the Israelis making a pre-emptive attack on

Egypt gave Eden the pretext to intervene militarily 'to separate the combats'. An Anglo-French invasion force set sail from Malta on 29 October, bound for Egypt. As the crisis neared its denouement, opposition to Eden's actions, led by the Labour Party, reached a crescendo, while up and down the country families and friends were fiercely divided over the issue. Passions ran so high that on the eve of the invasion, with crowds massing outside, a House of Commons debate had to be suspended. Clarissa watched from the Gallery beside Dora Gaitskell, wife of the Labour leader Hugh Gaitskell who was leading the opposition. 'Can you stand it?' Clarissa asked Dora. 'What I can't stand is the mounted police charging the crowds outside,' she replied.[47] Clarissa was present as Eden broadcast to the nation appealing for support for him as 'a man of peace, working for peace, striving for peace, negotiating for peace' who was 'utterly convinced that the action we have taken is right'.

On 4 November, as the invasion force neared Port Said, a massive demonstration in Trafalgar Square against intervention under the slogan LAW NOT WAR attracted the largest crowds in twentieth-century postwar history. The Cabinet ministers who met in emergency session at No. 10 to consider whether to go ahead with the invasion, despite a United Nations resolution calling for a halt to all operations, heard 'a steady hum of noise and then every few minutes a crescendo and an outburst of howling or booing'.[48] Clarissa also heard the hum and decided, amazingly, to go along to assess the mood herself: 'I heard [Nye Bevan] was having this great rally up there so I thought "Oh well, I'll stroll up, that'll be all right, I can just see what's going on". I was interested. I wanted to hear what he was saying, and what the mood was.' As she stood on the fringe of the crowd, a few people began to recognise her. 'Obviously the people who felt strongly were at the front [of the crowd] but people [at the edge] came up, saying to me "Good on you", and "Keep going". And I thought, "Well, I'd better go away" so I came back again.' The messages of support convinced her that Eden still had popular backing. (Polls showed that his personal approval rating then was 52 per cent, to Gaitskell's 44 per cent.)[49]

Eden and the Cabinet agreed that the invasion would proceed at dawn next day. But even as the troops were achieving their objective on 6 November, news came through of a United Nations Security

Council resolution backed by America which threatened economic sanctions on Britain and France if they did not agree to an immediate ceasefire. Eden had not expected the United States, who had been equivocal throughout, to support the use of force, but he hoped for their benevolent neutrality. He did not anticipate outright hostility, or that their principal ally would 'pull the plug' on the whole operation. As Chancellor Harold Macmillan warned of a serious run on the pound, the Americans announced that unless a ceasefire was called by midnight their support for an International Monetary Fund loan to prop up the pound would not be forthcoming. Under such pressure, Eden caved in and called a ceasefire for 5 p.m.

Eden's actions during the Suez crisis have been the focus of intense speculation ever since. For the man who all his life had excelled at diplomacy to reach his nemesis in this manner seemed not only tragic but inexplicable. One answer was that illness affected his judgement, but Clarissa refutes this. Eden was tired and under strain and had suffered a fever in early October which may have weakened him but, according to Clarissa, he was not ill 'until the last three weeks' before his resignation in January: 'I was with him all the time, and it seemed to me . . . he wasn't in any way behaving eccentrically because he was ill. His judgement wasn't vitiated. If it was a monumental mistake, it was his mistake. It wasn't because he was ill,' she says.

There were rumours that Eden behaved erratically due to his alleged dependence on a cocktail of medications, which Clarissa, backed by recently published medical evidence, also refutes, and colourful stories were circulated by William Clark about his fits of temper, including hurling waste-paper baskets and inkwells at various officials. Clarissa says, 'I can't believe he threw an inkpot, can you? Surely not. Think of the mess!' Eden could certainly be short-tempered with the private officials, the more so under extreme stress. But others agreed that he was firm and steady, especially during the critical final days. Even Clark observed on 30 October: 'Both Selwyn & the PM seem curiously euphoric today. The big decisions are over & they seem calm and detached.'[50] Elizabeth Home, whose husband, Commonwealth Secretary Lord Home, was at the centre of decision-making, noted on 31 October: 'Much impressed by how well the PM & everyone in the Govt look & can't understand it.'[51]

After the collapse of the invasion Eden struggled on. Anger at going in was now matched by fury at his pulling out as the debate raged up and down the country. By then his health *was* deteriorating. On 19 November, on doctor's orders, he cancelled all his engagements and on the 23rd the Edens left for a holiday in Jamaica, staying at Goldeneye, the home of Clarissa's friends Ann and Ian Fleming. Clarissa's influence was decisive: 'I thought if we didn't go to Jamaica, he was going to drop down dead, literally. Everyone says it was a bad mistake, he should have gone to Berkshire or somewhere instead. But it wouldn't have worked.' Goldeneye, situated on a remote part of the island, provided peace and isolation. Later Ann Fleming found that security men had carved on some of the trees in the garden 'God Bless Sir Anthony'.[52]

Though there was sympathy for his predicament, there was also resentment at his departure to Jamaica at such a stage in the Suez aftermath. Cynthia Gladwyn noted from Paris: 'As far as I can make out, everyone, whatever their views, deplores the choice of Jamaica, and thinks that Anthony cannot return to be PM. I bet he will: Clarissa won't let him not.'[53] She was wrong there, for Clarissa, greatly concerned for his health, was already keen that he should go. The *Daily Mirror* ran a competition for the best solution to the Suez crisis, offering first prize of a holiday for two in Jamaica.[54]

Eden fully expected to return refreshed to take up the reins, but it was soon clear that, though his popularity remained high in the country, his authority was undermined in the Party and moves were afoot to unseat him. Clarissa noted in her diary on 14 December: 'Returned to find everyone looking at us with thoughtful eyes.'[55] They spent Christmas quietly at Chequers with Eden's son Nicholas, and selected Cabinet colleagues. But the sleepless nights and abdominal pains returned. Three separate doctors reached the same verdict: the fevers were very likely to recur, which would make it impossible for Eden to carry on work. 'Then we knew he couldn't go on,' Clarissa recalls.

On 8 January 1957 Clarissa drove with Anthony to Sandringham to tender his resignation to the Queen. Eden's Cabinet colleague Lord Salisbury, who met them on their return to Downing Street, noticed that Clarissa 'looked very white, but did not dissent from the decisions, for which indeed I believe she had been pressing'.[56] Harold Macmillan

was chosen as his successor over Rab Butler. Clarissa wrote sympathetically to Butler – at Anthony's request: 'Dear Rab, Just a line to say
what a beastly profession I think politics are – and how greatly I admire
your dignity and good humour. Yours ever, Clarissa.'[57]

Anthony Eden was 59 when they left No. 10. Clarissa was only 36.
Many felt the poignancy of Eden's departure. To Violet Bonham-Carter
it was 'a Greek tragedy': 'To be P.M. was his life's one aim,' she wrote
in her diary. 'He waits – loyally but impatiently for W[inston] to go
("those hungry eyes" as W used to say to me). At last the cup is handed
to him . . . Now he faces a complete vacuum. Politics have always been
his be-all and his end-all. He cares for nothing else.'[58]

The Edens set off on a five-week journey to New Zealand, where
they were greeted by the Prime Minister, a red carpet, brass bands and
enthusiastic crowds. Clarissa wrote of the beneficial effects of the scenery
and climate on her 'sick and heartbroken man' but confided to a friend:
'I feel very sad about everything. The most dismal part personally is
that I seem to have lost some of my very few friends in the process.
Though I love Ann [Fleming] for herself, I cannot understand why she
cannot understand why I may not want to meet Osbert Lancaster or
James [Pope-Hennessy] at dinner.' Anthony continued to suffer 'these
vile high fevers that come suddenly . . . & which pull [him] down
terribly'.[59] In April they flew to Boston for another operation, only one
of many he would undergo during the rest of his life. Clarissa, who
nursed him throughout, now looks back with wonder at how he survived
it all. 'He must have been tough as anything . . . We knew everything
that was wrong with him and I don't think we ever discussed it, we
just sort of soldiered on.'

When they returned to Britain in June a new life opened up. Clarissa
was relieved at their departure from politics: 'I was indeed! Absolutely,
yes. I hadn't enjoyed political life very much.' Their future was uncertain, with worries about finances and no house other than Rose Bower,
but for the first time she had Anthony to herself. She calls it 'our time':
'I was so happy when we retired. And we were looking for a house and
we had to spend about eighteen months at my cottage, where I did all
the cooking and the woman who lived next door came and cleaned for
us. That was absolute heaven. Wonderful!' Though Eden may have
harboured some thoughts of a return to politics, according to Clarissa

'there was no question of him ever thinking for one minute he'd come back. He knew he couldn't do it, physically, there was no question about it.'

After eighteen months they moved to Fyfield in Wiltshire but Clarissa's calm was broken when Anthony started writing his memoirs. Their home became an office, with 'young men bringing the papers up and down from London and having their meals with us all the time'. *Full Circle*, for which *The Times* paid £160,000 for serial rights, was begun in 1958 and published in 1960 and was followed by *Facing the Dictators* (1962), *The Reckoning* (1965), and then his successful personal memories of his early life, *Another World* (1976). By October 1960, *Full Circle* had sold 77,000 copies and Eden was relieved of financial worries for the first time in his life.

In 1961 Eden finally accepted the earldom he had earlier refused and Clarissa became the Countess of Avon. Their lives outside politics were busy. Every year they visited Paris, went round galleries and studios, bought paintings and paid calls on General de Gaulle, Eden's wartime colleague. At home, Clarissa transformed the garden, read and kept up her cultural interests, while Anthony took up breeding pedigree Hereford cattle and remained in touch with his political colleagues. Part of each winter was spent in the West Indies. At home, they entertained friends. Cynthia Gladwyn visited and found Clarissa 'good-tempered; charming; intelligent as always, but most civilly so . . . Clarissa has made the house very pretty and comfortable. Everything was carefully thought out, and great trouble was taken. The food was delicious, yet keeping within Anthony's special diet. We walked in their grounds and in their romantic wood, lay in comfortable chairs, and various people came to dinner.'[60] On Anthony's seventieth birthday in June 1967 at Alvediston Manor in Wiltshire, to which they had recently moved, Cecil Beaton recorded 'A quite extraordinary atmosphere of joy and celebration in the pretty Georgian house . . . Despite his plastic duct and continuous fever, Anthony had reached seventy.'[61]

Eden survived another ten years. Though he had periods of energetic activity, by 1976 ill health was 'gradually robbing him of his zest for life', Clarissa wrote to Mrs Thatcher. Anthony Eden died on 14 January 1977 just short of his 80th birthday with Clarissa and his son, Nicholas at his side. Tributes flowed in from all over the world. Rab Butler praised Clarissa: 'You have been simply wonderful in looking after him during so many years when his health was so often bad . . . When I spoke to Horace Evans [Eden's doctor] in the drawing room of No. 10 he said that the length of Anthony's life would depend largely on personal care and it was your care that brought him to a ripe age.'[62]

Clarissa was 56. For several months she lived in a daze, then gradually she took up her life. George Weidenfeld invited her to his regular parties in London, and she resumed contact with some of her friends from the time before Anthony, including Cyril Connolly, Lucian Freud and other artists and literary figures, and went often to the opera and theatre escorted by Arnold Goodman. Always a keen traveller, she preferred places which were unspoilt and remote – Ethiopia, Burma, the Pacific Islands – and she took up scuba diving. Now in her eighties, she still travels regularly. After selling Alvediston she moved to a flat in London, where she is surrounded by mementoes of their life together. She sees herself as the keeper of Anthony's flame, and would wish that his career and reputation be seen by history not solely through the prism of Suez, which occupied so much of their time at No. 10, but in the longer perspective of his achievements as a skilled statesman over four decades of change.

Clarissa shared just four years of Anthony's political life, and eighteen months as Prime Minister's spouse. She took on her duties with style, even though politics was not her natural habitat. She remained her own person – individual, discriminating, direct and honest – as she adapted to the unfamiliar and demanding environment of No. 10 during one of the periods of greatest crisis for any prime minister in the last century.

Chapter Two

Dorothy Macmillan

1957–63

On 29 June 1963 a helicopter containing United States President J.F. Kennedy hovered over Birch Grove, the Sussex estate of Harold Macmillan and his wife, Lady Dorothy. Kennedy and his entourage were there to discuss Western defence issues and a nuclear test ban treaty. Dorothy Macmillan had a more immediate concern: as the helicopter swooped round, it 'got frightfully close to bits of the garden', her grandson, Adam Macmillan, recalls. 'I remember seeing her *rushing* from the top terrace towards where the helicopter was going to land, doing a certain amount of damning and blasting, because the wash had knocked over quite a lot of her plants. I think Kennedy thought she was terribly enthusiastic and he saw her rushing out and he thought she was waving. I don't think anyone had the nerve to tell him that the real reason was that she was simply furious.'

It was a sign of the rapport between the two leaders that Kennedy chose to stay at the Macmillans' private home, but for Dorothy it meant a major reorganisation of her household. America's First Lady, Jacqueline Kennedy, had written to her, concerned that 'these visits can get so out of hand – and really burdensome to the hostess . . . I came upon our French chef last night happily writing out menus for Jack's stay in Birch Grove. He was writing FRENCH BREAD in large letters after each course – which I thought a bit much.' She reassured Dorothy: '*Please* think of Jack as someone David Gore [British Ambassador to Washington] is bringing down for lunch – and just do whatever you would do in your own house – his tastes are distressingly normal – plain food – children's food – good food – he likes anything.'[1]

However, a visit from the US President is never that simple. For 24 hours, the area was invaded and hotels as far away as Brighton were commandeered to house the 110-strong presidential retinue. Kennedy, his valet and security man and leading figures in the US Administration completely took over Birch Grove, as well as nearby Pooks, the house of Macmillan's son, Maurice, which was used as a forward communications post. 'There seemed to be a perpetual flow of diplomats and politicians and their staffs . . . The Security men (in hundreds); the Communications men (with their vast apparatus); British Police (in hundreds) made the whole place a sort of armed camp,' Macmillan recorded. Outside, among the crowds were a hundred CND protesters in silent vigil holding banners calling for the abolition of nuclear tests. 'Since it was the main purpose of our meeting,' Macmillan wrote, 'the demonstration seemed hardly necessary.'[2]

Relations between the Kennedys and the Macmillans were strengthened by personal ties. In 1944, Jack's sister, Kathleen, had married Dorothy's nephew, Billy Hartington, the heir to the Devonshire line. The young Kennedy siblings had played tennis and golf and socialised with the Cavendishes from 1938 to 1940 when their father, Joe Kennedy, had been US Ambassador to Britain. Had Billy not been killed in action over Belgium shortly afterwards, Kathleen would have been Duchess of Devonshire. Then in 1948, she too was killed in a plane crash.

Arriving in 1963 from his triumphant reception in West Berlin, Kennedy had stopped off at Chatsworth, the Devonshire family's country seat, to visit his younger sister's grave. Andrew Devonshire remembers Kennedy's 'empathy with Harold. He always called him Uncle Harold.' From Macmillan's first visit to Washington and Bermuda with Dorothy in April 1961 – when Jack Kennedy had declared in passing to the bemused and monogamous Prime Minister, 'I don't know how it is with you, Harold? If I don't have a woman for three days, I get a terrible headache'[3] – they felt easy in each other's company, sharing a sardonic sense of humour and an interest in history and literature. Macmillan also struck up a friendship with Jacqueline Kennedy, with whom he corresponded for the rest of his life, sending her a letter on each 22 November, the anniversary of her husband's death.

At Birch Grove, according to Macmillan, Kennedy was 'in the highest spirits'. He 'was particularly charming to Dorothy and the children and gave us lavish presents',[4] including, for Dorothy, a golden dressing-table set with her initials on it: 'She was very touched by it,' Jackie Kennedy reported, 'and said "oh, I never had one!"'[5] There followed twelve hours of intensive talks, mostly between the two leaders alone, with Kennedy seated in a rocking chair hurriedly purchased for £3 when Macmillan saw the pain he was suffering from his back. But, recalled Macmillan's Press Secretary, Harold Evans, Dorothy still had time to 'seek my aid in taking two orange coloured posters about Birch Grove open day' to display on noticeboards at the Metropole and Grand Hotels in Brighton. The very morning of the President's arrival, as excitement was growing all around her, she was doing 'a little quiet shopping at the tiny Post Office stores, speaking to the sub-postman Mr Porter and his wife' about the coming Open Day in aid of the East Sussex Nursing Association.[6] It was planned for the very next weekend, which explains why Dorothy, whose pride and joy was the garden, became so furious when the helicopter flattened the plants. Dorothy had the gift of keeping politics in perspective, something which should be in the job description for the spouse of any politician.

The Birch Grove visit was the last time the Macmillans saw Jack Kennedy. Within five months, neither Dorothy's husband nor Jackie's was leader of their country. In October, ill health forced Macmillan to retire from the premiership. In November, Kennedy was assassinated.

For Dorothy, Harold's retirement marked the end of the long involvement in politics which had begun shortly after she married her father's handsome young aide in 1921. Her father, the Duke of Devonshire, was appointed Governor-General of Canada in 1916 and Harold Macmillan, aged 25, arrived as his new young aide-de-camp in March 1919, an appointment engineered by his determined American mother Nellie, who petitioned the Duke's mother on his behalf. He was just out of the Grenadier Guards after service in the First World War and had been wounded several times, in the pelvis and in the leg, at the Battle of the Somme, which left him with a painful and recurrent limp and shuffle. His forebears were Scottish crofters who had moved up through education and grit to become, by the time of Maurice Macmillan, Harold's father, owners of the flourishing Macmillan publishing house. In Ottawa, the erudite Harold earned the Duke's liking and respect for his interest in politics and literature – although his seriousness could occasionally make him seem comic: 'He gave the impression of being very pompous; so he needed pin-pricking all the time,' says Debo Devonshire. With little previous experience of women he soon found himself deeply attracted to his boss's 19-year-old daughter, Dorothy.

Born on 28 July 1900, Dorothy had spent the first eight years of her life at Holker Hall in Lancashire, a modest mansion by Devonshire standards, surrounded by magnificent gardens. Until he suffered a stroke later in life, her father, Victor Devonshire, was an easygoing, dignified and considerate man, with a walrus moustache and florid complexion, a shrewd financial manager who adored his children and missed them sorely when he was away. Her mother, Evie, daughter of the Marquess of Lansdowne, was a more distant figure who, though she liked small children, was later often critical of her daughters.

Dorothy's family was steeped in politics. For the girls, politics was part of the invisible fabric of life rather than a dominating influence, though Dorothy was 'innately very, very political, and very good at it', her grandson Adam Macmillan believes. 'She was very interested in politics, because, you see, all her family were,' says her daughter-in-law, Katharine Macmillan. Before succeeding to the dukedom in 1908, Victor was MP for West Derbyshire (from 1891 to 1908) in what was virtually a Devonshire seat, and served in government as Financial Secretary to the Treasury and Civil Lord of the Admiralty. Dorothy's brother, Eddie Hartington, took over the same seat from 1925 to 1935 before he became Duke; her maternal grandfather, Lord Lansdowne, had been in Gladstone's 1880s administration and was an eminent former Foreign Secretary. Two of her sisters later married politicians.

Much of their early childhood was spent outdoors at Lismore, another Cavendish estate, in Ireland, where they could run wild over the countryside – 'ponies, and scrambling over peat bogs and going fishing in the Blackwater', according to grandson Alexander Stockton. When Victor inherited the dukedom on the death of his uncle, the family moved to Hardwick Hall in Derbyshire while the drains were modernised and electricity installed at nearby Chatsworth, the vast, imposing family seat. The seven children – two sons and five daughters – were brought up, 'pretty harshly – in extreme cold, which life was in those big houses then – and they were sent to practise the piano at seven in the morning, in the freezing cold in winter', relates Dorothy's niece, Debo. Water for washing was never more than tepid, and candles or small lamps provided light.

Their houses may have lacked heating, but the lifestyle was sumptuous. Each year the entire family moved between Chatsworth, Lismore Castle and Devonshire House in London, with stays at Hardwick Hall for partridge-shooting and Bolton Abbey for the grouse season, taking with them a retinue of nannies, nursery maids, grooms and governesses.

While the boys went away to school, their sisters were taught by governesses: Dorothy 'spoke French and German quite well – French with a slightly German accent which was very bizarre', Alexander Stockton says. Never an intellectual, she was 'naturally sharp and quick'; she was a 'doer', according to Debo Devonshire. By the time the Duke reached Ottawa in 1916, Dorothy was thoroughly familiar with the rhythms of life in the wealthy upper strata of English society. She was at ease with servants and at home with the incidentals of running a country estate. Like her father, she was devoid of snobbery: 'They were all very un-grand,' says her nephew, Andrew Devonshire.

She was outgoing and friendly and had no interest in clothes – a trait unchanged throughout her life. 'She was absolutely unaware of appearances. I don't know if she'd heard of silk stockings but hers were certainly always lisle. She was absolutely *physically* unaware. But she had such *joie de vivre*, she enjoyed life so much that you felt better,' her niece Anne Tree recalls. Her charm and her shrewdness would later prove great strengths in political life. 'She was clever, because she picked up from people. She sort of caught on to what people were and what they said,' Debo Devonshire says.

The Devonshire family's life in the Governor-General's residence in Ottawa was a constant round of receptions, parties, travel and sporting activities including golf, at which Dorothy excelled. In these felicitous surroundings Macmillan conducted his courtship of Dorothy: 'Obviously they had a great time, playing tennis, swimming, fishing, canoeing, all that sort of thing. She was a very outdoorsy kind of girl, and striking and rather wayward,' grandson Alexander says. Her vitality impressed everyone, including Harold. 'She wasn't pretty, she wasn't beautiful, she wasn't smart, but she had an indefinable charm and this extraordinary zest for life,' Debo Devonshire recalls. Writing to her from his various trips, Harold's letters became steadily more intimate. She liked his dry wit, his gallant past and his old-fashioned courteousness. 'She was probably very flattered,' Anne Tree says. 'He was very good company and very courtly, and Uncle Harold, quoting Plato and so on, must have been frightfully impressive. Probably Aunt Dorothy was very impressed by him being so educated, as uneducated people are always very impressed by the educated.'

Even so, Dorothy was slow to make up her mind about the thoughtful, monocled young man with the military moustache and bookish interests. When the Prince of Wales stayed during a trip to Canada, he and Dorothy were seen so often together that rumours circulated about a possible courtship, though this was promptly dismissed by the Duke, her father.

For the young ADC with budding political ambitions, marrying the Duke's daughter had distinct advantages; it would give him an entrée into the highest echelons of Britain's still rigidly hierarchical social and political life. Harold was dazzled by the family's history and eminence, but he was also genuinely smitten. On Boxing Day 1919 he proposed and Dorothy accepted. 'I am so wonderfully happy – nobody can know how much – at being engaged to Harold,' she wrote excitedly to his mother. 'I didn't think there could be anyone like he is in the world, and I do love him – I wish that I felt that I could make a better wife for him. I'm a perfectly useless person. We shall be a pretty comic couple, but I am sure that you will help sometimes . . . I dread to think what will happen if he goes on spoiling me a quarter as much as he does now!' Harold reported to his mother, 'She is very young and very modest and so a little bit frightened of married life. She thinks she will never be able to keep house and look after me and that she will cry when the cook gives notice . . . She is superbly beautiful, too – at least I think so. She is more different to look at than anyone I have ever seen.'[7]

Her parents accepted the match, though Evie had harboured plans for her to marry a duke (the future Duke of Buccleuch was in her sights) and her father quipped, referring to her sister's marriage into a brewing family, 'God, trade again. But I suppose books are better than beer.' Dorothy returned to England in January 1921 with the wedding set for 19 April. The night before, Harold wrote to her: 'My darling, I must write the last letter which I shall write before you become my wife. But not, dearest Dorothy, the last love letter you will get from me. For, Dorothy, I shall always be your lover . . . Perhaps there will be storms of wind and rain and high waves may threaten us sometimes, but we'll always sail on together bravely, won't we? . . . Your devoted Harold.'[8]

The wedding at St Margaret's, Westminster, was accompanied by all the pomp and grandeur of such aristocratic occasions. Dorothy was resplendent in a simple gown with a veil garlanded with orange blossoms and sprigs of myrtle. The service was packed with royalty and the country's aristocracy – the Devonshires, Cecils, Lansdownes – all related to Dorothy; and, on the other side, distinguished literary figures published by Macmillans, Thomas Hardy included. The reception at Lansdowne House was equally splendid, as were the presents, which included a number of diamond brooches, one from King George V and Queen Mary, diamond and gold trinket boxes, furniture, antique candlesticks, a golden candelabra and a portrait of Dorothy by Philip de László depicting her as direct, charming and unexpectedly sensuous.

The honeymoon was spent in spartan Yorkshire, and then in Italy, before they returned to their modest house at 14 Chester Square. Nine months later their first child, Maurice, was born. Harold now became a junior partner in the Macmillan family firm. 'We were young; we were happy; everything smiled on us,' Harold wrote.[9] Dorothy employed 'Nanny West', who would be the mainstay of the household as more children arrived – Carol in 1923, Catherine in 1926 and Sarah in 1930 – and stayed with her for forty years. Dorothy's domestic skills were minimal. 'She couldn't boil an egg,' her grandson Alexander cheerfully recalls, though, as Debo Devonshire reminds us, 'Nobody cooked in those days. They didn't have to. She had an excellent professional cook.'

Harold turned to politics. In the 1923 general election he stood for the Tories at the 'hopeless' seat of Stockton-on-Tees in the then depressed, mostly working-class industrial area of County Durham. His first experience of practical politics – the 'rough and tumble of the market place', in the constituency which he was to serve over a period of twenty-one years – was a revelation to him as well as to his wife. Dorothy, pregnant with their second child Carol, threw herself into electioneering with an enthusiasm and skill which Harold could not match, and he later praised 'my dear wife, who was so much more responsible than I for winning the hearts, if not the votes, of Stockton'. On election posters she appeared in her cloche hat with the slogan: 'May I appeal to YOU to VOTE for my Husband. I know that he will serve YOU faithfully and carry out all he has promised to do.'[10] Where Harold was halting in his speeches and diffident in his manner, Dorothy's outgoing friendliness made its mark: 'She was a wizard canvasser, both thorough and quick. She had a very good political sense, and in elections she was marvellous,' her daughter-in-law Katharine says. 'She was a devil for a cup of tea. She adored meeting people,' Anne Tree remembers. Macmillan lost by only 73 votes. The minority Labour Government under Ramsay MacDonald lasted less than a year, and when another election was called in October 1924, Macmillan won the seat by over a majority of over 3,000.

Dorothy embarked on a new life as the wife of a Conservative back-bench MP. The experience of social conditions in Stockton-on-Tees during the depressed 1920s and '30s – the slum housing, unemployment estimated at 25–30 per cent, and the absence of social support – shifted Macmillan permanently to the radical wing of the Party. On Dorothy, too, it made a deep impression. She developed an affection for the North, had an instinctive sympathy with its people and carried out her constituency duties assiduously. 'She was very much loved. There was really no one like her. I would say she was the greater part of his success here,' one constituent remembers. Her background and training were assets, Harold thought: 'She treated the people at Stockton rather as she did the tenants at Chatsworth, talking to them completely naturally – because she was a child of nature – and people are very quick to see what is genuine or fake.'[11]

She was politically adept and 'had this gift of being *exactly* the same to whoever – there was absolutely no side to her at all. That was the secret to her charm,' her nephew, Andrew, says. Pamela Egremont, wife of Macmillan's private secretary, found her 'totally genuine. She loved talking shop to people, and she had a very good memory for people and faces, and for funny little incidents.' She would stand behind Harold when people came up, and whisper to him (for example), 'he was the Mayor five years ago', and Harold would greet them with confidence.

According to Alexander, when canvassing, 'she always turned up at the back door – front doors were for weddings and funerals only – and the wife would answer the door and Granny would say, "I've come round on behalf of my husband," and she'd say, "Nay, nay we don't vote your way," but she'd be nodding her head at the same time. Which meant, "I do, he doesn't." And come polling day, she'd go and drive her in. And then when the husband came back from work, he'd say, "Right, mother, shouldn't we go and vote?" and she'd say, "It doesn't make any difference. It's raining and I've made your favourite tea." Once every four years – a blow for freedom!'

Dorothy encouraged women to get involved in politics. 'Women's gatherings, inspired by Lady Dorothy Macmillan, are a feature of the Conservative campaign,' the *Stockton and Tees-side Herald* reported in 1923.[12] The enfranchisement of women in 1918, extended in 1928, gave them a new importance in the political landscape: they were now an electoral asset to be wooed to the cause. Dorothy came from a long line of aristocratic women who played the role of political hostess and back-up for their husbands, and she needed no persuading of the importance of women's voluntary work in mobilising support through social and fundraising activities at local level; these activities would form the crucial backbone of the Conservative Party organisation through the century. She also believed, says Alexander 'that men were absolutely *useless* at running things like councils – "no practical ability at all. A woman knows how to run a house, so she knows how to run the council," she said. And she was very determined on that. She liked people who *did* things.'

As well as nursing the constituency, she had her own growing family to bring up, aided by Nanny West. Carol Faber, her eldest daughter, remembers her as a 'hands on' mother, who was, by most accounts, always interested in children when they were young, less so as they got older. After 1926, Dorothy's life was divided between London, Stockton and Birch Grove, which they shared with the formidable Nellie, her American mother-in-law. Dorothy got on with her 'in a way', though there were tensions: Carol remembers once coming across her mother sticking pins into an effigy of her mother-in-law which she kept in her dressing-table drawer. Christmases were spent at Chatsworth, where the whole Cavendish clan and their nursemaids, valets and maids gathered, amounting to around sixty people, not including guests, after which the women and their numerous children stayed on for another two weeks of family holiday.

Their routine changed when, in the 1929 general election, Harold lost his Stockton seat. And it was in the same year that Dorothy fell for Harold's political colleague and ally on the left wing of the Party, the raffish Robert Boothby. 'She was desperately in love with him. *Desperately*,' says Debo Devonshire. Boothby was witty, extrovert, flamboyant and attractive to both sexes. He drove a Bentley, listened to jazz, and presented a striking contrast to her more diffident, taciturn husband, who always had difficulty with expressing emotional intimacy. Boothby seems to have brought out the impetuous and passionate side of Dorothy's nature. He reported her once saying to him: 'Why did you ever wake me? I never want to see any of my family again. And, without you, life for me is going to be nothing but one big hurt.'[13] To Boothby, Dorothy was 'a very powerful woman . . . She never suffered a pang of remorse, or she never showed it, anyway – absolutely none about me or Harold . . . But we were absolutely fixed on each other.'[14]

Dorothy appears to have thrown herself into the affair with little concern for the consequences or the effect on other people; several commentators have accused her of selfishness. Letters were carelessly left lying around at home and her phone calls to Boothby were overheard by others in the household. Any attempt by her family to intervene would have been fruitless, according to Debo: 'She wouldn't have taken the slightest notice if anyone tried to dissuade her. [She was] wilful.'

The liaison was widely discussed within society – 'It was an open secret in their circle,' says Andrew Devonshire – but not a word got out to the wider public. Newspaper proprietor Lord Rothermere, a close friend of Boothby's, must have known but newspapers then were discreet about private affairs. When he heard of it King George V is alleged to have directed, 'Keep it quiet.'[15] Illicit affairs were not unusual in society, and nor were illegitimate children. 'It was more common then. It was a leftover from the Edwardian period, so many people had *ménages à trois* of a most discreet kind,' says Anne Tree.

Dorothy and Boothby were in daily contact, and they visited Europe together, chaperoned by a compliant friend. After a holiday in Portugal in 1932 Boothby wrote to their mutual confidante, Cynthia Mosley: 'It was a new world for her . . . It was like taking a thrilled child to play for the first time. She brushed her hair back behind her ears, & actually put lipstick on, & got more radiant every day.' But it was an agonising situation for everyone. Dorothy told a number of people at this time: 'I am faithful to Bob.' Divorce was discussed; Harold refused to accept it. 'We seem to be in a hopeless impasse,' Dorothy wrote to their confidante the same year: 'I wish to God I knew what was the best thing to do . . . The future looks pretty grim.' Boothby meanwhile reflected: 'It has become unendurable . . . Work to hell. Nerves to hell. No-one can ever persuade me that a "liaison" is anything but misery (with glorious, but oh so transitory, reprieves) if you care.'[16]

Boothby did not in the end want Dorothy to divorce, because of the irrevocable damage it would do to his political career: 'It would have scuppered him completely,' says Debo Devonshire. 'It's bloody,' Boothby wrote to a friend. Dorothy was, he believed, 'the most formidable thing in the world – a possessive, single-track woman . . . But if I take her, it's goodbye to everything else . . .'[17] Since Dorothy's love letters to Robert Boothby were destroyed, first by Boothby and later, when more turned up, by Macmillan (who burnt them in the garden incinerator at Birch Grove), there are only glimpses of her side of the story. Clearly she would not give him up. When Boothby married Dorothy's cousin, Diana Cavendish, in 1935, it was an almost immediate disaster. The marriage lasted two years and ended in the divorce he so dreaded and a good deal of added hostility from the Cavendish family and others for behaving like a complete cad. 'Boothby has much capacity,' Churchill, his old mentor, said, 'but no virtue.'[18]

Despite her *grande passion*, Dorothy remained with Harold. When her fourth child, Sarah, was born in 1930, it was widely assumed, but never certain, that Boothby was the father (Boothby was not convinced, believing she had the Macmillan eyes – a feature also pointed out by her brother Maurice to Alistair Horne). Harold's relationship with Sarah was always touchingly affectionate. Their eldest daughter, Carol, doesn't recall being shocked when an older cousin told her about the affair because 'I think I probably knew – children do.' Since uncertain parentage was not uncommon at that time and in that class, if anyone said anything rude to her about her sister Sarah, 'I was quite capable of saying, "Well, what about you?"'

Harold suffered. 'You could see even as a young teenage boy that Uncle Harold was an unhappy man,' Andrew Devonshire recalls. Later, in a rare and painful allusion to his marriage, Harold told Alistair Horne, his biographer, 'I never loved anyone but her – never had a woman friend, or even knew anyone. On her side, there were transient things – unimportant. What counts are the fundamentals . . . I had everything from her, owed everything to her . . . She filled my life; I thought in everything I did of her . . . she was devoted to me . . . We were very close; I told her I'd never let her go – it would have been disastrous . . . a hopeless fellow . . . But what's physical passion compared to things you share, interests, children? . . . But it took a lot out of me, physically.'[19] In 1931 Harold suffered a recurrence of trouble from his war wounds, which was actually a form of nervous collapse. Unsure of Dorothy's movements, Nellie sent him to stay for several months at a sanatorium near Munich. The doctor found '*no* organic disease, only nervous prostration,' Harold reported to her; he had 'only just avoided a complete breakdown . . . I think if I can have this cure and get properly rested I can face my other troubles.'[20]

In her public role as MP's wife Dorothy never let him down. It may be contradictory, Andrew Devonshire says, 'but in spite of this great romance, politically Aunt Dorothy was a very good wife'. Harold was still abroad when a general election seemed imminent in 1931. She stepped into the breach at Stockton and 'wrote continually [to Harold] with all the news she could collect'. Harold, though weak and walking with sticks, returned to find that she had been hard at work, getting the campaign organisation into shape.[21] She was again canvassing energetically on his behalf. Macmillan won Stockton with a larger than expected majority (11,000 rather than the predicted 3,000) and threw himself back into political life. Though Harold was 'by nature a very politically ambitious man', Anne Tree says, several family members believe that the Boothby trouble may have been the 'grit in the oyster' that drove his political ambition: 'all this personal trouble then did strengthen my character', Harold said later.[22]

When Harold's mother Nellie died in 1937, he and Dorothy moved out of Chester Square into Birch Grove, and the marriage, despite the duality of Dorothy's affections, settled down to a steadier companionship. Dorothy took to country life with enthusiasm. 'She was passionately interested in whatever she was doing,' Debo says, and her enjoyment was infectious. In the tradition of Tory women of her class, she played an active part in local charities. She organised open days and fêtes for the East Sussex Nursing Association, supported the nearby Chailey Heritage for disabled children and was an energetic member of the Central Executive Committee of the NSPCC.

She also virtually ran the Birch Grove estate, according to her grandson Alexander. 'She was the estate manager, so to speak. It was quite a big operation and would have employed about sixty people – and she ran it.' 'She knew *everybody* on the estate,' Adam Macmillan says. 'When she came out shooting – she always came out to lunch in horrific sort of gumboots, quite often not a pair, and dreadful old short mackintoshes. She looked a complete mess in a thick tweed skirt and great big thick ribbed socks, she'd have a scarf pulled over her head and walking stick – and she knew everybody there, all the beaters, the keepers, the woodmen. And she was endlessly talking to them, the whole time. So quite often there was a scene with my grandfather saying to her, "For God's sake, Dorothy, let them do their job!"'

Gardening was Dorothy's lifelong passion. Not just overseeing and planning as would happen at Chatsworth in her youth: 'Dorothy *did* it, with her own hands. She'd take the spade and she'd dig and plant the bulbs herself,' Andrew Devonshire says. 'There was a balcony outside her bedroom, and she'd have a camp-bed put up on the balcony so she could feel whether it was going to be frosty or not,' Adam remembers. 'And she would be rushing out in the middle of the night or early morning to go and put fleece or straw or hay round the feet of various plants which weren't going to make it unless they were looked after.' For this and other nocturnal operations, she had 'a hot water bottle tied to each knee [to stop her knees getting damp] and a miner's helmet with a lamp on her head, which Alf Robens [later chairman of the National Coal Board] had given her. She said to him, "I've always wanted a miner's lamp, because then you've got both hands free,"' Alexander adds.

She collected and carefully nurtured plants from far and wide. 'She was very, very good at making things grow,' says her daughter-in-law, Katharine. 'She would only have the one that was most difficult to grow, because that was the challenge, you see.' President Nehru gave her some delicate dwarf rhododendrons, which flourished in her care. Once she asked the young Adam, he remembers, '"Darling, will you pull the weeds out?" And I promptly pulled up a hundred and fifty wallflowers that she'd just planted. There was no great furore or anything, she just said, "No, darling, I think they're not weeds. Shall we put them back?" So then she solemnly planted them all again.' The house was filled with flowers, which 'would appear in what we called the flower room – which was actually the "other" hall, and that was her territory. It smelt of mackintoshes, wet boots, flowers and dampness, all the time. And every single bit of furniture had flowers on it.'

The Second World War turned out to be Harold's political opportunity. When Churchill took over from Neville Chamberlain in 1940, he was at last promoted, after sixteen years without ministerial responsibility, to be Parliamentary Secretary in the Ministry of Supply, and then, in 1942, Under-Secretary at the Colonial Office (a move, he remarked, which 'felt like leaving a madhouse in order to enter a mausoleum'). Birch Grove was given over to an evacuee scheme for forty children from a school in Balham, London, along with a group of Czech refugees, mainly Jews who had fled Nazi Germany. With Harold away in London most of the time, Dorothy moved into Pooks, a smaller cottage on the estate. As well as supervising the evacuees, she was County Commissioner in charge of the East Sussex branch of the Women's Land Army with ten district commissioners reporting to her, each with around 100 to 150 land girls on the various farms. 'She was a bit of a tyrant with farmers,' her daughter Carol remembers. 'If a girl rang up or wrote and said the farmer was doing something wrong, she'd go there fighting. She was very good with the land girls, and with the helpers at the school.' Everyone 'made do' in the face of wartime shortages and Dorothy, who found the absence of cooks and petrol particularly irritating, was no exception. 'It's true that her underclothes were made out of flags. Flags weren't rationed – "There was some material, so why not use it?" It was entirely practical and completely unselfconscious. I think they were made by Nanny West,' Anne Tree remembers.

Macmillan's steady political ascent began in 1942 when Churchill appointed him Minister Resident in Algiers. Within weeks, he was in attendance as adviser at the Casablanca Summit conference where

Churchill and President Roosevelt were planning the next stage of the war. In long, almost daily letters he kept Dorothy in touch with events. Dorothy sent weekly news from the home front about family and domestic life – 'Blake is anxious lest the pheasants start laying too soon. He says the partridges are pairing now. He is also nervous lest we have not left sufficient cocks' – with encouraging comments about Harold's progress. On his 49th birthday she sent greetings: 'I should think your last visit from the PM must have been great fun. I am told that he is delighted with you and thinks you are doing amazingly well . . . all of which is very satisfactory.'[23]

The strain of separation sometimes told on Harold. In February 1944, her description of spring in Chatsworth stirred him to a touching nostalgia: 'I read and re-read your letter and could see Dorothy Cavendish – first a little girl I never knew with pigtails – then Canada – and then the young woman and always that love of trees and woods and streams which I (poor fool) dared to imprison in the stucco and railings of Chester Square. Dear, dear Dorothy – please forgive me . . .'[24]

When Dorothy decided to join him in Algiers for a four-month visit in April 1944, Harold was delighted: 'Hurrah, hurrah! It is splendid and we are all very much excited. It will be such fun.'[25] In this, her first experience of being a statesman's wife, she met General Eisenhower and General de Gaulle (nicknamed 'Ramrod' – 'a man who was alleged to have all the rigidity of a poker without its occasional warmth'), attended numerous lunches, dinners and picnics, and was popular with all Harold's colleagues. He took her on expeditions to his favourite spot, the Roman ruins at Tipasa, and 'my own private rocky cove' where, he had written to her in advance, 'only a few stray fishermen come, and you can bathe naked. You can lie on the blazing rocks, till your body can bear it no more; and then roll over into the healing water. This you can alternate as long as you like – a sort of perpetual rhythm of pleasure.'[26] As the Allies advanced into Italy, they moved their base to Naples and Caserta, where they led a lively social life among the British, Italian and Yugoslav diplomatic and military personnel who were gathered there.

On Harold's return to Britain in May 1945, the unknown back-bencher of 1939 was now among the most respected of the inner Tory political circle, with a Cabinet post (as Secretary of State for Air) in the caretaker government. The 1945 election was a bitter disappoint-ment. Macmillan lost his Stockton seat, but at a by-election in November he was returned with a comfortable majority in the safe seat of Bromley. Though Dorothy was sad to give up Stockton, where she 'knew and was known in almost every house',[27] she soon adapted. Much of the constituency work fell to her while Harold was consolidating his place on the political ladder as the Tory Party reinvented itself in opposition.

At Birch Grove they settled back into a more domestic routine. Harold appreciated Dorothy's straightforward earthiness, while she admired his well-stocked mind, lightness of touch in conversation and wit. 'She didn't share it, but she did see it as rather marvellous. It amused her,' Pamela Egremont thinks. They respected each other's differences, and teased one another a lot.

Harold relied increasingly on Dorothy. He depended on her vitality: Birch Grove 'never seems anything but empty and forlorn when she is away', he wrote, and he trusted her good sense and judgement. She was a shrewd observer and 'had absolutely unerring judgement about people, instinctively. In conversation Dorothy would suddenly come up with an amazing insight, which was very, very acute about the person we were talking about. He'd learned from experience that she was practically always right about that kind of thing,' Pamela Egremont recalls.

Dorothy was interested in furthering his career, and acted as his ears and eyes at all the major political events, reporting back on how his appearances had been received: at the 1950 Party Conference, after a major speech: 'Dorothy received good accounts from all sides and I feel much more confident of my position in the party,'[28] Harold wrote. When he was writing his speeches, he always asked her what she thought, and Dorothy was invariably direct: 'She'd say, "that's too complicated, Harold. Make it simpler. I couldn't understand a word you were saying." She was a bit of a touchstone. Not the man on the Clapham Omnibus so much as the woman in the wellies,' says Alexander.

Harold consulted her over major decisions. After the Conservative victory in the 1951 election, Churchill asked Macmillan, at a meeting at Chartwell, to be Minister of Housing: 'He asked me to "build the houses for the people". What an assignment! I know nothing whatever about these matters.'[29] Harold hesitated, then asked Dorothy, who was walking in the garden with Clementine Churchill, for advice. She reminded him that the appointment to Algiers had 'for the first time earned me real status in the political world. She also reminded me of my experience at the Ministry of Supply and the many friends with whom I had kept up from those days. Surely we could build the houses in the same way that we built the tanks and the guns.'[30] Strengthened by her boldness, Harold accepted. Even so, he felt sidelined, shunted into a backwater – he had wanted Minister of Defence, which Churchill kept for himself.

As it turned out, his period at Housing brought him to new public prominence. By achieving his goal of building 300,000 dwellings a year he was identified with the vanguard of renewal as Britain struggled out of a period of shortage and economic uncertainty into a more settled period of growing prosperity.

Dorothy accompanied Harold to all the major events, including the Festival of Britain in 1951, George VI's funeral in 1952, and the Queen's Coronation in 1953. Invariably she drove him round the country and to and from Birch Grove. One of the first generation of women to take to the wheel, 'she was a very good driver, but fast', Alexander recalls. 'She had a great friend who once went in the Monte Carlo rally and she said she ought to do that, and my grandfather said, "No, please not."' Her son, Maurice, borrowed the car one day and turned it over 'and people rushed out and said, "Lady Dorothy, we knew you'd do that one day", and were very surprised it wasn't her,' Katharine Macmillan recalls. She had a Ford 8 which had no heating, so she wore large ATS knickers to keep her warm, and was once caught changing out of them on the way to a meeting.

Later when Harold was Prime Minister, she was stopped for speeding in Croydon. 'The policeman said, "Can I see your licence?" and she said, "I haven't got it with me, it's at home." And he said "Name?" and she said "Lady Dorothy Macmillan" and "Address?", "Number 10 Downing Street." And he said, "I'll have you know, Madam, it's an offence to impersonate someone." With a bit of loss of temper on both sides, she was dragged off to Croydon police station and the penny then dropped and she was released after the inspector had been rung from Number 10,' Alexander recalls. 'I was going down with her that weekend and she drove me to Croydon police station. She said, "Come along, I need a witness." So she stomped in and was met by a policeman horrified about seeing her again. She said, "Where's the charge?" So he said, "What do you mean, Lady Dorothy?" And she said "Well, I want to be charged. I was speeding." He said, "Under the circumstances . . ." And she said, "Circumstances be buggered. Who do you think I am – Mrs Attlee?" Because Clem's wife had got off a speeding charge not long before. She said, "If it gets out that I've been speeding and haven't been charged, Harold will have hell to pay. Now, come on. I want this charge. Don't waste time."'

With Harold busy building homes for the people, Dorothy concentrated on the family. Maurice had in 1942 married Katharine Ormsby-Gore (who was related to Dorothy) and their first grandchild, Alexander, was born during Harold's absence abroad in 1943. Carol married Julian Faber from the Lloyds banking family in 1944 and soon gave birth to another grandchild. Catherine married MP Julian Amery, son of Macmillan's political colleague Leo Amery, in 1950. Maurice became the first victim of the 'Cavendish disease' – alcoholism – in the late 1940s and spent years struggling to recover. In turn, each of their family members would succumb, though it bypassed Dorothy. Sarah went through a difficult period connected to an abortion (arranged not, as is often alleged, by Dorothy, who was away at the time, but by another intimate) and later, when she decided to adopt, Anne Tree recalls, 'I got the feeling that Aunt Dorothy and Sarah were very, very close indeed . . . there certainly was a terrific impression of intimacy.' Tragically, Sarah descended into alcoholism and died in 1970.

Dorothy was now in her fifties – tall, imposing and rather stout – and she took immense pleasure in being a grandmother. 'She liked children enormously and she got on with them *frightfully* well,' her first grandson Alexander recalls. As they got older: 'She'd organise them – cricket matches and playing tennis. And she'd organise treasure hunts and help the little ones so they could keep up, and she always had an egg hunt at Easter,' says Katharine Macmillan. Grandson Adam remembers another side: 'She was an incredibly good listener. One of my fantasies was that I was going to send Granny to the moon. And she spent many hours with me sitting on the grass beside her while she was gardening, telling her exactly how I was going to do it, and she absolutely adored it.'

On the other hand, they all knew when she disapproved. She could display a fiery temper and 'she did have a reputation for being quite foul-mouthed at times, though not really with the children', Adam says. 'My mother used to always ask Nanny – "how was it down at the big house?" and she'd say things like "Oh her Ladyship was damning and blasting again," usually because something had gone wrong with the garden, or she hadn't been told that twenty people were coming for the weekend – my grandfather was a bit vague about things like that.' She was meticulous about some things and could explode: 'The only time she clocked me one,' says Adam, 'was when I said something about the maintenance man, and I think I called him "Stephenson", and I was given a firm clip around the ear and told, "You've no right to call him that until you run this place. You call him *Mr* Stephenson."' Adam believes Dorothy thought that it was better to get it out – 'You explode, and literally five minutes later, it's gone. It's in effect being incredibly spoiled to be able to lose your temper like that and get away with it.' Her daughter Carol often said to her mother, 'You mustn't lose your temper like that. It upsets people. And she said, "Well, I always feel much better."'

When Anthony Eden became Prime Minister on Churchill's resignation in April 1955 Macmillan was offered the job of Foreign Secretary. In the election which followed immediately, Dorothy was in Bromley, 'always the first out on the street, stomping away fast – like a galleon under full sail'. Encumbered by high office, Harold 'left the conduct of the campaign in Bromley almost entirely in the practised hands of my wife'.[31]

She was also enlisted to support Maurice, who was standing for Halifax. At one meeting, Dorothy went to sleep on the platform when Harold was speaking, 'and someone shouted from the audience "Does the speaker know his wife's gone to sleep?" She said, "My father's a politician, my brother's a politician, my husband's a politician, my son's a politician, and my son-in-law's a politician – I've heard it all before. So if you don't mind, I'm going back to sleep." It got a sort of roar.' When Maurice won, Dorothy was on the point of tears. Harold won Bromley with an increased majority, and was soon off with Dorothy to the Geneva summit, where she attended receptions, met the Soviet leaders and swam with Clarissa Eden in Lake Geneva, though, as so often happens with politicians' wives, they were otherwise not close friends. They moved into the Foreign Secretary's official residence at 1 Carlton Gardens, where Dorothy hosted diplomatic receptions.

After only six months, Macmillan was offered the post of Chancellor of the Exchequer, but hesitated. Dorothy urged him to stay on as Foreign Secretary until the end of the year, cautioning that if he were to leave after only a few months, 'it would both be and seem to be a strange and inexplicable proceeding.' When he finally agreed to move, she remained 'extremely unhappy . . . instinctively – for she had an inborn and inherited shrewdness about public affairs – she felt that the change was a mistake'.[32]

They moved into the Chancellor's residence at No. 11 Downing Street in February 1956. With a Cabinet crisis looming, she instructed the workmen to 'stop putting up pictures etc. in No. 11, because she thought we would be moving out again soon!'[33] When Macmillan introduced Premium Bonds in the Budget, Dorothy was brisk in her dismissal of those critics who thought he was leading the country down the road to gambling ruin, notably the Archbishop of Canterbury, Fisher: 'I always thought that man was a fool, now I'm convinced. Pay absolutely no attention to him,' she told Harold.

The Suez Crisis took over their lives from July 1956. As Chancellor, Macmillan was charged with the task, after the Anglo–French invasion of Egypt in November, of delivering to Eden the Americans' verdict that they would not support an IMF loan if the British and French did not at once declare a ceasefire. After Eden resigned on grounds of illness in January 1957, it was soon clear that the choice of his successor lay between Macmillan and Rab Butler. While the Party was being sounded out, Dorothy showed her political acumen when she warned Harold against going next door to No. 10 to 'talk to my old friend [Eden] about his future', since, she pointed out, it would be noticed by messengers and the Private Office, and might be construed as canvassing for support.

Next morning Harold passed the time waiting for the result by reading *Pride and Prejudice*. When he heard that he had been chosen for the leadership, he did not immediately tell Dorothy but sent a message asking for lunch at one o'clock sharp. 'When I appeared in a tail coat, this unusual costume, combined with the insistence on punctuality, led her to an accurate deduction.'[34] When she saw the tail coat,

'Aunt Dorothy said, "Harold, why on earth are you dressed up like that?" "I've been summoned to the Palace." And she took a longish time to take it in,' Andrew Devonshire says.

Harold and Dorothy Macmillan moved into No. 10 in January 1957. Dorothy was 56, twenty-two years older than Clarissa Eden had been when she crossed the same threshold. Almost immediately Harold told a Party meeting how he viewed Dorothy's role: 'She serves to remind me of the realities of life . . . If I show signs of becoming remote from those everyday problems that perplex people in their homes . . . then my wife brings me back to fundamentals.'[35] According to Alexander Stockton her task was 'to keep my grandfather sane' in the often feverish atmosphere of No. 10. When he became Prime Minister she gave him a framed photograph of the front page of the local paper, the *Mid-Sussex Times*, which he always kept on his desk: the lead story was that Gatwick was going to be London's second airport, after that the news that Brighton and Hove Albion had made it into the third round of the Cup, and below that under the headline EXTRAORDINARY HONOUR FOR SUSSEX MAN was the announcement that he had become Prime Minister. Dorothy said, 'Just to remind you, you're not as important as Brighton and Hove Albion and Gatwick,' Alexander recalls.

Dorothy adjusted to living at No. 10, though she 'fled to Sussex whenever duty allowed'. She did her best to make Downing Street as much like a family home as possible and she soon got to know the staff, which contributed 'a certain warmth and geniality to the new regime'. The family stayed regularly, filling the front hall with bicycles, tricycles, scooters and an occasional perambulator. Dorothy imposed few restrictions though she was alleged to have put up a notice forbidding roller-skating in the corridors on Cabinet days, and Harold told his grandsons that if they wanted to play draughts with the policemen, they should not obstruct the arrival of ambassadors or Cabinet ministers.[36] Adam remembers another instruction: 'If we were going to play dominoes with the policemen, would we kindly do it in the cubbyhole on the left, not in the hall, because sometimes people thought it was odd to see us gambling with the police.' One grandson brought his hamster, which escaped through the drains and was eventually found in the Treasury. Staff at No. 10 found all this bustle and happy informality endearing, and the Duke's daughter was, as usual, completely at home dealing with a large house and staff.

Every Monday she brought up a supply of flowers and vegetables from Birch Grove in her car: 'The old Vauxhall shooting brake was *stuffed* with flowers. And she stomped around in the grubby wellies, looking like a flower lady, heaving them into the hall downstairs, amid consternation from the staff because there were buckets everywhere and water all over the highly polished marble floor,' Adam remembers. Harold tactfully intervened: 'Since she generally appeared about the time when the flow of ministers and other notables was beginning, some confusion ensued. I had to try to persuade her to time her arrival and unloading to a more appropriate hour.'[37]

The accommodation at the No. 10 flat was small, Alexander thought 'poky', and she made a 'boudoir' for herself – a working sitting room upstairs. They ate in the flat when there were just a few family members, and otherwise used some of the downstairs rooms. Dorothy was not entitled to any secretarial help, and only later used Harold's own secretary for her correspondence. During the week, her staff at Birch Grove – Nanny West, Mrs Bell, her cook, 'who ruled with a rod of iron, and my grandmother supported her completely' and Edith Baker, her housekeeper and maid, along with a butler – came up to No. 10: 'She couldn't have done it like she did if it hadn't been for [them]. Because nothing fazed them; suddenly someone coming to dinner – that didn't worry them,' Carol says. On Friday she left, often with Harold, for the Bromley constituency, on the way back to Birch Grove.

Dorothy never much liked Chequers, so she went there only as necessary – when Harold went, and when there were visitors, 'but she didn't *use* it', her daughter says. For one thing, she couldn't garden there: 'She always said they would never let her plant anything. I remember her saying furiously to me, "They want me to plant pansies", and she didn't like pansies,' says Katharine. Macmillan was none too keen on Chequers either – having described on an earlier visit: 'the sham panelling, the fake decoration, the "antique" furniture and the over-painted and over-varnished pictures'. Though 'it is wonderful to see masses of servants – all WAAFs or WRENS or whatever they are – like a chorus of excellent parlour-maids and house-maids'.[38]

Since the war Chequers had been staffed by service personnel, whose efficiency sometimes upset Dorothy, as Katharine Macmillan recalls: 'She was very funny about how she rushed out to fill her bath and then forgot something and went back – to get a towel or something – and the Air Force people had let the water out and were cleaning the bath.' Carol remembers an occasion when 'I saw my mother putting jerseys under the bed, and I said, "What are you doing, Mother?" "Oh, I don't want the Wren to wash my jerseys because Edith does them so much better." And this woman came to me and said, "Do you know why your mother puts all her washing under her bed?" And I had to tell the truth.'

Despite being in the public spotlight, Dorothy remained oblivious to fashion. 'She wasn't in the *least* bit interested. Her clothes were what her cousin described as "coverings". She could look like a sort of tramp. She was always in the garden, you see, so that doesn't make for great cleanliness or high-heeled shoes,' Debo Devonshire says. Legend had it that she had only two smart dresses, though, according to Alexander, this is an exaggeration. 'She had three. There was a blue one and a blue-grey one, and a silver-grey one – all pretty much of a muchness. She wore sensible tweed skirts and that sort of thing.' To one newspaper, she admitted: 'Once in a while I may go to town in a grand evening dress from one of the couturiers, but it is very rare.'[39]

Her maid, Edith, who had been an officer in the WAAF and played bowls for Sussex, took her in hand: 'She did *everything* for my mother,' Carol recalls. 'She'd say "You need some new petticoats, I'd better go and buy them." Or "I'm going to buy you some stockings."' When it came to an event, 'You'd hear my mother saying to Edith, "I'd better put that bloody blue thing on, I suppose," and she'd put it on and some jewellery and look marvellous. Come back and hurl the jewellery off and go and undress.' Hats and gloves were obligatory in the 1950s: 'She didn't like a brim. She liked something that was off her face, so it would tend to be a round thing – furry in winter and flowery in summer,' Alexander recalls. 'She had all these terrible hats', about thirty in all, her daughter remembers. 'My sister and I decided to sell them for charity after she died. We made a fortune for the village hall.'

Newspaper coverage of Dorothy in the 'goldfish bowl' of No. 10 was minimal compared with later. Dorothy was quite canny about photographers. Once she turned up to a French television studio interview in a white silk blouse, Cavendish necklace and an old tweed skirt. The British Ambassador's wife who accompanied her was taken aback by the skirt: 'Oh, my dear, I know these TV people,' Dorothy declared, 'they only want to photograph me from the waist up!'[40] She accompanied Harold when he recorded the television broadcasts which were rapidly becoming an essential part of a politician's repertoire of skills, and always kept a beady eye on the process.

Press intrusions could make her furious: 'She minded terribly about whether things were truthful or not. She used to get in a terrible rage about that and say "it's absolutely intolerable,"' says Katharine Macmillan. Hounding of the family enraged her. Once a reporter followed one of her grandchildren, who was on his bicycle, down the drive at Birch Grove 'to try and get him to talk'. The boy tried to evade him by riding on to the tennis court – 'he never thought the man would come on to the tennis court not in proper shoes – and he was cornered'. When Dorothy met Jackie Kennedy in 1961, they discussed the children's privacy: 'Mrs Kennedy was complaining about the children not being able to get out of view, and of course my mother knew exactly what hedge to plant that would grow very quickly, where they could have their sand heap behind it,' Carol remembers.

Dorothy embraced her busier schedule. She looked forward to the Trooping of the Colour, with the bagpipes and bands, and organised huge teas for children, cousins and relations, and old friends who she thought would be pleased to visit Downing Street. She also enjoyed the annual visit with Harold to Balmoral: 'not merely the intimacy of the royal circle but the experience of seeing what is really a museum piece of Victorian decoration',[41] and staying in the prime ministerial suite decorated with maple furniture, Stuart tartan curtains, brass inkstands and Winterhalter prints. The drawback was that she had to be on her best behaviour but it had the advantage of being only a short distance from many of the regular haunts for her favourite activities of fishing, swimming and golf.

When hosting events at No. 10, Dorothy 'made it seem like a family gathering in a country house with guests continually coming and going,'[42] Harold wrote. Though Dorothy 'hadn't got a terrific lot of self-confidence', according to Pamela Egremont, she went into events thinking 'she was jolly well going to do her best. She was never anything except absolutely herself. She was incapable of trimming with any wind, simply didn't know how to do it. People found her warmth and naturalness very endearing.'

Government Hospitality paid for and organised the official receptions. Dorothy always liked to involve the family, but rules were strict: 'Government is incredibly parsimonious,' says Alexander Stockton. 'Granny used to invite us or my parents to help circulate. And she'd say, "The Nigerian High Commissioner's on his own, go and talk to him." And they used to bill us for our drinks, because we weren't official guests.' Similar rules applied to the use of official cars. Dorothy was only entitled to an official car if Harold was in it with her, even when travelling to official functions. 'If Granny went in the car with Grandpapa, and he went to the House of Commons and then the car took her on to the Army and Navy Store, they used to collate this and say, "Three-tenths of a mile times six equals, say, one pound fourteen shillings", and write out who was in the car alone and when' – and they had to pay.

Just as in the constituency, Dorothy encouraged the work of women Party members who by the 1950s were a formidable element in the Party's organisation, working for the cause at the grass roots through networks of social and fundraising activities. It was where Conservative women interested in politics found a voice. She spoke at the annual Conservative women's conferences; in 1960, after a debate about women's responsibilities in the age of affluent consumerism, she welcomed the rise in wealth and prosperity during the Tory years and exhorted her audience: 'Let us make sure that everyone can see we are a human and kindly party, a friendly party and a happy one.'[43] She organised tea parties at Downing Street and at Birch Grove for Conservative MPs' wives and Party workers from all over the country, and toured the constituencies attending luncheons for Conservative ladies' clubs as well as opening hospitals, fêtes, bazaars and Christmas fairs, and launching several ships.

On a series of 'meet the people' tours around the regions, she met Party workers and, in the West Midlands, visited a carpet factory, where she and Harold ate in the works canteen – Dorothy went for the 1s. 6d. lunch of braised liver, onions, baked beans and apple and black-berry tart; then on to porcelain and chain works factories, old people's bungalows, and a hospital, and they dropped in for tea with a couple on a housing estate. On a North-East tour in January 1959 they made a sentimental return to Stockton and were welcomed with cheers for 'Good old Dorothy' and placards saying 'Mac's back'.[44] In this formerly depressed area, they visited thriving local factories – ICI at Billingham, the iron and steel works at Thornaby, the fish market and heavy industrial plants in Hartlepool (all since closed down), and the newly opened Tyne Tees Television studio in Newcastle. Dorothy joined the local Darlington WVS at the canteen kitchen to pack and then deliver meals on wheels to old people, and visited one bedridden woman of 65 in a 'sparsely furnished room' where there was no running water, or fire in the grate, and 'a single gas lamp hung from one wall'. Dorothy assured her she would see about getting a new wick for the small oil stove on which she cooked.[45]

By April 1959, when they toured to the North-West, they were in the run-up to a general election. They visited the still flourishing cotton mills in Bury, Oldham and Rochdale, and at a Bury and Radcliffe Women's Unionist Association tea Dorothy exhorted the women to 'work just as hard in the future – in fact a little harder', and added cheerily: 'I seem to spend all my life encouraging people to work a little harder!'[46]

When the election came in October 1959 the Conservatives, under Macmillan, won with a 100 seat majority on a platform of the Tory record on progress, prosperity and rising standards of living which was summed up in the slogan 'You've Never Had it so Good'. Or, as Dorothy put it in another speech, 'The Socialists have tried very hard to . . . show us as a party of wealth and privilege that cares nothing for ordinary people. But it doesn't carry much conviction . . . We have had pensions increased, better opportunities for all, more hospitals and a much higher standard of living for ordinary wage-earning people.'[47]

Despite the 'One Nation' image which Macmillan cultivated, when it came to government appointments, Dorothy's family connections occasionally caused trouble. When Dorothy's nephew, Andrew, then 11th Duke of Devonshire, was made Under-Secretary at the Commonwealth Office in 1960, Macmillan was widely accused of nepotism. He later justified his action with the throwaway remark: 'Andrew is awfully good with the natives. The Devonshires have always been good with the natives',[48] though Alexander regarded this as a show of his power – 'Handing out patronage – his revenge on the Cavendish clan!' He also made his son-in-law, Julian Amery, Secretary of State for Air, and David Ormsby-Gore, brother to his daughter-in-law, was made Ambassador to America in 1961.

Having established her presence as Prime Minister's wife at home, in 1958 Dorothy had faced a further challenge as a statesman's wife on the world stage, when they embarked on a six-week Commonwealth tour, visiting India, Pakistan, Ceylon, Singapore, New Zealand and Australia. All agreed, as Harold was fond of quoting, that 'whatever Macmillan may have done for the Commonwealth, the Commonwealth has certainly done something for Macmillan'. The trip was a success. As well as boosting his image, it seems to have brought the couple closer, and Dorothy's confidence was strengthened by her 'first experience of an almost royal progress'. Harold observed that: 'it seemed to bring to the surface some of the hidden qualities of her deeply sympathetic character.' 'The remarkable powers which she had of making herself understood and loved had hitherto only been exercised on a restricted scale; now they had found their opportunity. She had at once conquered the hearts of the people by her own special gifts . . . the unexpectedly enthusiastic welcome which she was given seemed to have affected her deeply', he wrote. 'She returned happy, and, for all her modesty, conscious of having succeeded.'[49]

In January 1960 they set out on an even more gruelling six-week tour, this time of Africa. In Cape Town Macmillan made his celebrated 'Wind of Change' speech, acknowledging that Britain, in the face of rising nationalism on the continent, could no longer sustain its imperial role. On this trip, however, there were fewer friendly welcomes, and more difficult political problems. Dorothy was noted for her good humour throughout, despite needing treatment for toothache in Ghana: 'One of my last three teeth, on which everything else hangs,' she warned Press Secretary Harold Evans; gashing her leg in Kariba: 'She came into the aircraft dripping blood all over the carpet and swearing hard (with apologies). Cause of the trouble – the aircraft steps', and being plagued by stomach upsets. 'Lady Dorothy is engagingly her cheerful self,' Evans noted on the return boat trip. 'She took a lively interest in boat drill . . . being much struck by the piratical appearance of the crew,' enjoyed the gossip, and chatted about Harold: 'she bought him a new toilet case to bring on the tour but he said it was much too good to use and put it away. Nor will he have anything that is in any way different from what he has always had.'[50]

Back in England, after Dorothy expressed concern that Harold was overdoing things, they managed a week's rest in Yorkshire in August followed by a few days' golfing at Gleneagles in Perthshire. It was interrupted by the sudden rise in Cold War tension when, on 12 August, the East Germans began building the concrete wall that would divide East from West Berlin. The press invaded their holiday, being 'very tiresome, pestering us all the time. At every tee some new ones came up and asked for my views', and Macmillan: 'rather lost my temper with them . . . undoubtedly a "gaffe.".'[51]

Dorothy's carefully managed family atmosphere at No. 10 was disrupted when, in July 1960, they were moved out of Downing Street to nearby Admiralty House while repairs and partial rebuilding of Nos 10, 11 and 12 Downing Street went ahead. Subsidence in the houses built originally in the 1730s on a marsh had become acute. Long-term structural faults had been exacerbated by blast from wartime bombing, and piecemeal repairs over the years had only added to the problems. The buildings were clearly 'on the move', and a carpenter was employed almost full-time on easing the doors and windows. Floors were weak, in some cases rotten, and the brick in places had rotted away. Alexander remembers: 'The kitchen of the flat was on a slope, it had blocks under two legs of the kitchen table to stop the rolling pin falling off. When Granny gave a party for us here, we were limited by the Office of Works to eighty – because they were worried the floor would collapse.' The wall of No. 11 leaned in at the back and lunged at the front, and panelling often covered brickwork which had turned to rubble. Extensive underpinning of the whole front wall was needed, while the roof and attic space had to be overhauled and new dormer windows put in.[52]

Dorothy adjusted to the move to Admiralty House. She brightly told a meeting of the NSPCC which was offering a house as a prize in a competition: 'I have just been evicted from one house and have been generously provided with another, but I feel it would be very wise to try to win this one because, in my husband's job, one never knows quite when one will need one.'[53] The refurbishment and restoration took three years and cost considerably more than originally estimated, eventually topping £1 million. Dorothy had little say in the designs of the architect, Raymond Erith, but was later involved in furnishings and decoration; a member of the team remembers going with her to various stores to choose kitchen and sanitary fittings and wallpaper. She had definite ideas which did not always coincide with those of the architect or the Ministry of Works, and relations were sometimes strained, with Erith once walking out of the room for fear of 'losing his rag' during a disagreement over patterned carpets. When she was seen coming across Horse Guards' Parade, people tended to disappear. Adam Macmillan remembers: 'She decided that, in the White Drawing Room, she wanted to keep the curtains, because she thought they'd faded to quite a nice colour and they weren't in holes, so she chose a whole lot of furniture and cushions to go with the faded curtains. Unfortunately a gentleman from the Ministry of Works had unpicked the bottom of the curtains and matched everything to the unpicked bit, which hadn't faded. And she threw a complete wobbly and there was a lot of damning and blasting about "Whoever told you to unpick it, I *specifically* wanted it matching up to the fadedness."'

There were larger preoccupations on the political front. With the Cold War at its height, visits by foreign leaders were a regular part of Dorothy's schedule. The recently elected President Kennedy paid a short official visit to London in June 1961 with his wife, on his way back from his first bruising encounter with Soviet President Khrushchev at the Vienna summit. Dorothy entertained Jackie with stories of canvassing, a political ritual unknown in America. 'They don't do door-to-door canvassing. She was absolutely fascinated,' Alexander remembers. 'She told Jackie the story of my father in Halifax going to a house and there was black crêpe round the downstairs window, and when a lady came to the door, he said, "I'm sorry to see there's been a death in the house." And the woman said, "Aye, that's right, Mr Macmillan, Granny passed on t' other evening. Would you like to come up and see her?" So – corpse stretched out and [he said], "Doesn't she look peaceful?" "Well, to be quite frank with you Mr Macmillan, first time that bitch has been peaceful in twenty-five years. But don't you worry – Granny had lucid moments. Just before she went God put X in right place on postal vote – a vote from the other side, you might say."

Granny told that story and Jackie couldn't believe it – you went *in* to a house to collect votes for your husband and you saw a corpse!'

When the French President, General de Gaulle, an old wartime colleague, requested an invitation to stay at Birch Grove in autumn 1961, Dorothy was less than patient about his arrangements. In the middle of the Algerian war of independence, de Gaulle insisted on carrying with him supplies of his own blood – which had to be kept refrigerated – in case of assassination attempts. Dorothy went to Harold, he reported, 'in a state of uneasy concern and even anger. "I have been rung up," she declared, "by a young man from the Foreign Office with a short black coat and fancy pants." "How on earth can you tell what he wore?" I asked. "Oh," she said, "he spoke like it." "Well, what did he say?" My wife explained that what he said in a high plaintive voice was this: "Lady Dorothy, what are we going to do about the General's blood?" Faced with this unexpected problem, I said, "I think you had better tell him we will ring him back" – always a safe argumentative position'. Mrs Bell absolutely refused to have the blood in the family fridge ('It's not frightfully sanitary,' she said). So, according to her grandson Adam, Dorothy 'thought the only thing to do is to get hold of one of those terrible young men at No. 10 and tell them they'd got to bloody well get hold of another fridge. This was Friday evening. I think some poor man in East Grinstead was woken up and told to go and open the store and produce a fridge and deliver it.' De Gaulle brought a team of surgeons and nurses who also had to be housed, adding to the security problems. To make matters worse, the gamekeeper, Mr Blake, was indignant that with the police Alsatians roaming in all the woods and into the coverts, there wouldn't be a bird left for the shoot that coming Monday: 'This has got to stop, sir,' he announced, undeterred by Macmillan's plea that 'this is a great international occasion'.[54]

Dorothy was more sympathetic during the 'Night of the Long Knives' in July 1962, when Macmillan responded to a downturn in the economy and bad showings at by-elections by simultaneously sacking the Chancellor of the Exchequer, Selwyn Lloyd, and one third of his Cabinet – an act which he later viewed as a misjudgement – Dorothy was 'very robust' and advised him that he should immediately write personal letters to those purged. She was at his side when he confessed to being left 'exhausted, almost shattered by the events of the last two days' (which later prompted Jeremy Thorpe's witticism, 'Greater love hath no man than this, that a man lie down his friends for his life'). But at a fête a few days later, when the wife of a Shadow Cabinet minister suggested to Dorothy that 'it must be a nerve-racking time for you', Dorothy replied: 'Terrible . . . I can't keep my mind off those four grandchildren in the swimming pool.'

Dorothy always felt that 'she was the representative of reality in this totally unreal existence', Alexander believes. Whenever she saw that Harold was under strain, she would intervene with the Private Office, and say, '"Don't give him anything you don't *absolutely* have to." And they accepted it. They saw he operated better when he was allowed to stand back a bit.' Once asked by a journalist how she provided 'the constant reassurance required by a man under intolerable pressure', she answered, 'I listen.'[55]

During the Cuban missile crisis in October 1962, when nuclear war threatened as Russia and America confronted each other over the Russian build-up of missiles in Cuba, Dorothy 'was very conscious of the situation. He was up half the night, telephoning Jack [Kennedy], and Elizabeth Home [wife of Lord Home, Foreign Secretary] used to come round and the two of them would sit. And I remember Granny saying to me once, "I think that meeting should be coming to an end. Just go out and bring him in, and bring Alec too,"' Alexander recalls. 'And she would try and get them away from the officials and get them to sit down and not think about it, or not talk about it, and say, "Have you got your shooting arranged, Alec, for this year?" and that kind of thing. Try and get some normality into this hysterical situation.'

Khrushchev backed down over Cuba, but the terrifying confrontation which had taken the world to the brink of disaster led to renewed calls for a test ban treaty. Macmillan was among the foremost advocates of the de-escalation of the arms race, but for years he had been the target of demonstrations by anti-nuclear protesters; one tactic they used was to lie down in front of the car. 'My wife had a robust contempt for such antics,' Harold noted, 'and when she was driving me accidents were with difficulty avoided. However in the contest of wills she was generally successful.'[56] At a Conservative fête in Bromley, CND protesters sat down in the road as Dorothy was attempting to leave. When she put the car into reverse, more protesters flung themselves behind the rear wheel. Dorothy 'was very calm and nobody was hurt', according to Harold, though he noted 'that the police were lost in admiration of the idiomatic language with which she rebuked these genteel protesters'.[57]

The Test Ban Treaty, the main topic of discussion during Kennedy's visit to Birch Grove, was eventually signed, to Macmillan's relief, in August 1963. When the President told him of the agreement, 'I had to go out of the room. I went to tell D. and burst into tears. I had prayed hard for this, night after night.'[58]

Before then, in late 1962, Macmillan had been feeling the strain of leadership. The economy was faltering, a succession of by-election defeats was demoralising the Party which was trailing around 12 points behind Labour, his personal popularity was plummeting (by mid-March 1963 a *Sunday Telegraph* poll showed 62 per cent felt he should resign),[59] and a 'Macmillan Must Go' group was forming in the Party ranks. Now approaching 69, he was portrayed as old and out of touch in the emerging youthful and satirical culture of 'swinging' Britain. As criticism mounted, rumours of his imminent resignation led to a press siege in December 1962 while he and Dorothy were staying with the Homes at Castlemains in Scotland. The weekend was wrecked as the entire Home family was roped into answering calls from the press.

Macmillan was not ready to resign, though he had weighed up the prospect for some months. The sudden death of Labour leader Hugh Gaitskell in January 1963 and his replacement by Harold Wilson did not influence his deliberations. But Macmillan was appalled at the press coverage: 'He mused over the Gaitskell tragedy,' to Harold Evans: 'It was terrible how the newspapers had given every detail of the progress of the illness. "Don't let them behave like this when I die, will you, Harold." A man should be allowed to die alone and in peace. "Dorothy will keep them away."'[60]

From March 1963, the unfolding Profumo scandal, a heady mix of sex and spies, further destabilised Macmillan's government. Shortly after a series of espionage trials had induced a jittery nervousness about the security services, spy mania took a new twist. Speculation became public that the Minister for War, John Profumo, had had an affair with a 19-year-old call-girl, Christine Keeler, who was at the same time allegedly involved with the Soviet air attaché, Captain Ivanov. In the

House of Commons, Profumo denied any impropriety, though he admitted that he had met Keeler, and announced that he would sue for libel and slander if scandalous allegations were repeated outside the House. Backed up by Dorothy, who firmly declared, 'He must be OK, he wouldn't perjure himself in Court',[61] Macmillan was reassured: Profumo's 'categorical statement in my eyes settled the matter', he wrote.[62]

Despite warnings from several sources over the next months that Profumo had lied, the unflappable Macmillan departed with Dorothy for a week's holiday in Scotland with instructions that 'I am to get only the minimum of telegrams and papers. It should be a real rest.' While there, he was told that Profumo 'had admitted that he lied to me, to the House and to the courts', but he remained sanguine and they completed the holiday at Iona and Gleneagles, even as a major storm was brewing in London. He returned in June to 'a serious and at times dangerous crisis which seemed likely to involve the fall of the government as well as my resignation'.[63]

The press was swept up in the daily revelations of scandal in high places: 'More than half of the Cabinet were being accused of perversion, homosexuality and the like,' Macmillan observed. 'Day after day the attacks developed, chiefly on me – old, incompetent, worn out.'[64] Polls showed that his personal popularity had dipped to its lowest ever: 35 per cent compared with Harold Wilson's 54 per cent.

Dorothy came to her husband's defence by revealing her own thoughts on 'the grave and anxious situation' in a speech at a Conservative fête at Holker Hall, which was widely reported. Reminding the gathered faithful of their Conservative ideals, she warned: 'We must not let our vision be clouded by false sentiment, hypocrisy or cheap cynicism. Neither must we allow any human weaknesses to detract from the nobility of these ideals or destroy their truth.' Her husband had carried 'a very heavy burden of responsibility' – few realised just how heavy, but he had always 'tried to do his best for the country as a whole', and would continue to do so.

In the debate that followed in the House of Commons on 17 June, Macmillan spoke frankly of shortcomings in handling the crisis ('I do not live much among young people myself,' he said), and afterwards looked 'bowed and dispirited'. Harold Evans recalls Macmillan admitting that 'it had been touch and go: only the support of his dear wife and his staff at No. 10 had seen him through it: but he had then decided that even if there had been a majority of only five in the Profumo debate he would have carried on. "I wasn't going to have the British Government pulled down by the antics of a whore.""65

The crisis wounded Macmillan politically, and perhaps struck deep at the heart of his personal vulnerability. Home remembered the debate as 'the only time he had been worsted – he so fundamentally hated the whole thing'. Macmillan noted in his diary, 'I do not remember ever having been under such a sense of personal strain. Even Suez was "clean" – about war and politics. This was all "dirt"' – the language he used suggesting profound disgust. He was not puritanical, but the scandal deeply offended his sense of propriety: 'In the old days, you could be absolutely sure that you could go to a restaurant with your wife and not see a man that you knew having lunch with a tart. It was all kept separate but this does not seem to happen these days . . . Profumo was incapable of keeping the two sides of his life separate.'66 And perhaps at some level he had ignored the warnings because it struck at the deep wounds he had felt over Dorothy's betrayal with Boothby, when he had learned painfully that private anguish must be sealed off from the public part of his own life.

One bright spot lit the gloom. The crisis was at its height when President Kennedy paid his visit to Birch Grove. It is unlikely that Jack Kennedy chose to meet there to avoid the seething scandal of London (his own peccadilloes were kept a close secret in the more discreet American press of the time), but Jackie Kennedy recalled that her husband was 'very depressed, at the prospect of what he considered to be a great hero brought down; so Jack wanted to do something really nice and give him a nice present, and to hell with the State Department budget' – so he presented Dorothy with the golden dressing table set.67 In the circumstances, Macmillan was as much diverted as delighted by the visit.

While on holiday later with Dorothy grouse-shooting in Yorkshire, Macmillan began seriously considering the timing of his resignation. As speculation on the subject mounted Dorothy gave a rare interview to *Daily Sketch* journalist Godfrey Winn, who had interrupted her as she weeded Michaelmas daisies wearing 'a rather shapeless grey woolly jumper and a simple plaid skirt' that reminded Winn 'irresistibly' of actress Margaret Rutherford. She was both loyal and shrewd. 'Of course the people who want him to go are busy making him out so old and senile, as though he had one foot in the grave,' she declared robustly. 'But actually he amazes me by his resilience. I think his whole attitude to life is now bearing fruit.' When her husband makes up his mind, 'he *will* tell me first', she said.[68]

On their return to London the couple moved back into the newly refurbished No. 10 Downing Street. Harold made the decision on 7 October to delay his resignation until after the next general election, and to inform the Party Conference the following week. Dorothy, who 'had been doubtful of my physical strength (perhaps she had watched this strange apathy coming on me) . . . now seemed relieved at my new determination'.[69] But that night, he was overcome with spasms of pain. Dorothy called the doctor, who diagnosed inflammation of the prostate gland. Harold managed to conduct Cabinet next morning, 8 October, and briefly attended an early evening 'back to No. 10' house-warming party for the staff. Harold Evans met him on the stairs: 'He had a good colour and his manner was brisk and cheerful. It was all a stroke of Providence, he said. It gained time. He could pull out with honour if the doctor's verdict went that way – no-one would be able to say that he ran away.'[70] The doctor's verdict was that an immediate operation was necessary. He went into hospital that evening.

Over the next few days, Dorothy visited him regularly as Macmillan conducted the business of government from his hospital bed. It was clear that he would not have the strength to fight the next general election and arrangements for the leadership succession went ahead swiftly. Alec Home emerged as the new Party leader and Prime Minister. In Macmillan's farewell speech, read to the Party Conference by Home, he spoke of the Party's achievements in his political lifetime: 'the silent, the Conservative revolution', 'that pragmatic and sensible compromise between the extremes of collectivism and individualism' which he had personally worked for since the 1930s.

On 18 October Harold and Dorothy left No. 10 to begin what he called his 'life after (political) death' and Dorothy the countrywoman now came into her own at Birch Grove. She had never disguised her dislike of London; Harold Evans recorded how after being in the news for getting a parking ticket from 'one of the new traffic wardens', she had 'looked tired and wearily enduring. Oh, how she hated London, was (cheerfully) her theme. I suggested that she would at any rate be escaping to Scarborough next week, at which she threw up her hands and exclaimed, "With all those Conservatives!"'[71] At Birch Grove, she gave her full attention to her garden, her charities, shooting, hunting and golf, and the family. Harold read books incessantly through his convalescence, and he and Dorothy were often found at separate ends of the house, each getting on with their own business. They were content, the family agree, and devoted to each other. 'It was a very comfortable relationship. They had great mutual pleasure in each other's company,' Pamela Egremont remembers. 'I think she was pleased to have him at home', says Anne Tree. 'On the other hand he was a fearful hypochondriac – every cold for Uncle Harold was flu. And Aunt Dorothy I don't think had many illnesses other than falling down dead. I think she wasn't sympathetic to that at all. There was a touch of, "pull yourself together."'

In 1964 Dorothy was awarded the DBE for her charitable and political work. The new wing of the Chailey Heritage home for disabled children, to which she had devoted so much of her life, was named 'Dorothy Hall' after her and opened by the Queen Mother. Dorothy and Harold travelled together to Ireland, played golf and fished on their annual holiday, and went on occasional trips abroad.

Macmillan refused the offer of an earldom and turned up only rarely at the House of Commons, though he retained the chairmanship of the Macmillan publishing house which he visited twice a week – it 'kept him in touch with people'.[72] In August 1964 he began writing his memoirs and, as with the Edens, the house was filled with researchers and typists who stayed in the cottage behind the house. At a cocktail party given by one of the 'Garden Girls' (the women who worked in the secretarial pool in the basement rooms overlooking the garden at No. 10) he told Harold Evans that 'it was very nice down there at Birch Grove, being so well looked after by Dorothy, but he got a little fed up being surrounded by women'.[73]

In spring 1966, Harold and Dorothy went on a trip to Arran in Scotland. One of those working at Birch Grove noticed 'a new serenity and kindness and gentleness' in Dorothy, though Carol remembered that her mother was worried about Harold. 'On 21 March she opened the garden for all the Sussex churches. She got out all these tables with prickings and bits of gentian and so on that she and anybody else wanted to sell. That night I went down to my mother and she said, "Come on, we must put the tables away." And I said, "Oh Mother, do let's wait for the morning because you'll have three gardeners to help you." "No, no, I've got to do it tonight."' Next morning she was making arrangements for Sunday lunch: 'She rang me up and said, "Did Anne want to come to supper or lunch on Sunday?" And Tufton Beamish was coming to lunch, so I said, "I think she'd rather come to supper." And that was the last thing I said to her.' Katharine Macmillan, with Dorothy's daughter, Catherine, and their children were just about to set off to a point-to-point with Dorothy, when Dorothy rushed back into the house to get something. 'And she didn't come out, so I went in and I saw her at the bottom of the stairs and I knew she was dead.' At 65, she had suffered a massive heart attack.

Dorothy was buried in the church at Horsted Keynes under a gravestone of Scottish granite. A packed memorial service at St Margaret's, Westminster, was attended by representatives of the royal family, the various aristocratic families to whom she was related, her cook, housekeeper, nanny and the staff of Birch Grove, former land girls, representatives from the Conservative Party and the two constituencies and from the many charities she had supported.

Without her, Harold was bereft: 'She filled my life . . . I thought in everything I did of her,' he told his biographer, Alistair Horne. 'She was devoted to me . . . I had my reward . . . in doing what was difficult, I had my reward in the end.' Everyone felt the loss. 'When she was around, you felt the house was full,' Jane Parsons, one of the No. 10 Garden Girls, recalled; 'when she died, Birch Grove suddenly seemed very quiet.'[74] He missed her very much, Anne Tree remembers: 'he missed her *joie de vivre*, and the fact that she was uninhibited, and I think he missed her naturalness and the fact that he could ask her anything.' Carol says that he often went to visit a relation, Hugh Cavendish, at Holker Hall, where Dorothy had spent her childhood: 'My father was always fond of it, and he used to say "I wish your mother could see the garden now".'

Harold, who was to live another twenty years, gradually came to terms with Dorothy's absence. Publishing, public commitments like the

Oxford chancellorship and his memoirs kept him occupied, and he frequently visited his many London clubs. 'He had a sort of renaissance. Went round every hostess and bowled on to the train at half-past four and had an absolutely smashing time,' says Anne Tree. He enjoyed playing the role of elder statesman. 'He was a marvellous conversationalist. People were like alcohol in a way. He responded tremendously to company,' says Andrew Devonshire.

At Birch Grove in the quietness of old age Harold lived mostly in a small, spartan room in the attic, overlooking the back door. 'He said it had no view and didn't face south, but he said, "You've no idea how amusing it is, you see the grocer's van arrive, you see the coal man arrive. It's wonderful. Something happening all the time,"' Debo Devonshire recalls. He kept up the open days which had given Dorothy such delight, and according to her daughter, the only things he changed were the plastic lampshades in the sitting room, 'which she still had from the war'.

Their marriage had survived, despite the Boothby affair, because of the strength of their personal and political union. A headstrong and passionate woman in her youth, she had an earthy charm, a forceful presence and an intuitive understanding of politics on which Harold relied unfailingly throughout their life together. No. 10 was not a challenge to Dorothy, who was accustomed to overseeing large houses and had long experience of the demands of a ministerial wife at the hub of political life. She treated it as a town residence and imposed her family life on the official routine, while escaping as often as possible to pursue her own interests, as the countrywoman she had been since her days as the Duke's daughter at Chatsworth.

Chapter Three

Elizabeth Home

1963–64

On 22 November 1990, almost 1,500 people gathered in Westminster Abbey to pay tribute to the Countess of Home. It was an appropriate turn-out for a woman who, throughout her eighty years, seems to have captured the hearts of all who met her. The Home family had booked St Margaret's Hall, Westminster, for the memorial service, but it was soon apparent that it was too small to accommodate the numbers who wished to attend.

For the Cabinet ministers and political colleagues present, there was an added *frisson*: that very morning Margaret Thatcher had announced her resignation as Prime Minister. The Conservative Cabinet members who listened to the celebration of Elizabeth Home's life of service in a political partnership which spanned over half a century knew that even in this moment of reflection the manoeuvrings for Mrs Thatcher's successor had begun. A new chapter was opening in Conservative fortunes.

Elizabeth's widower, Lord Home, at 87 the Party's respected elder statesman, had been determined to be present at the memorial service in spite of two turns he had suffered before leaving his Scottish estate. Three days later he suffered a minor stroke. He returned to his beloved Scotland and never came south again.

It was Harold Macmillan's dramatic resignation through illness in October 1963 that had launched the 14th Earl of Home to the premiership. Few, least of all Home or his wife, had predicted this. Neither was ambitious for power; both saw politics as primarily a matter of public service: 'Pa's politics from the very beginning were, "I must try and help the country",' their daughter Caroline Douglas-Home says.

Her mother's view was 'If it's really what you feel you should do, then do it.' She backed him completely.

With Macmillan confined to his hospital bed, Home was dispatched to Blackpool to read out the resignation speech to the shocked delegates at the annual conference. Home assumed he had placed himself outside the leadership contest, but it was soon apparent that none of the possible successors – Macmillan's initial favourite, Lord Hailsham, Reginald Maudling or Rab Butler, who had been a candidate alongside Macmillan in 1957 (when Lord Salisbury memorably asked the Cabinet, 'Well, will it be Wab or Hawold?') – could command decisive support. Within hours, colleagues were arriving in Home's hotel room pressing him to stand as the only candidate with enough support to restore Party unity.

Home consulted Elizabeth, who was with him at Blackpool, at every stage. 'It was all so quick . . . absolute pandemonium,' her son, David Home, recalls. 'She didn't really have time to think it through. So she was very much thinking on her feet as it went along.' One of her main concerns was Alec's health, which had not been robust in the past. When his doctor assured him he was fit to take on the task, Home sighed, 'the escape route was closed'. At 61, leadership was 'the last thing which I had anticipated, and the last thing which I sought. My succession to Macmillan had simply not crossed my mind.' He foresaw 'a convulsion in my life for which I was not prepared'. He would have to renounce his peerage dating back hundreds of years, become a commoner and acquire a constituency; he was reluctant to 're-submit myself to the rough and tumble of electioneering and the House of Commons'; and it meant 'assuming the most testing and responsible of all the political offices in Britain, with all the physical strains which go with the occupancy of No. 10'.[1]

Rab Butler, his main rival for the leadership, reported that Elizabeth was encouraging him, and got the impression that '[Alec] was person-ally not keen to stand himself but could be persuaded'.[2] When the Queen's private secretary, Michael Adeane, rang to ask Elizabeth in confidence whether she thought he would accept the premiership, she replied that if the situation demanded it he would.[3]

Not all Cabinet members agreed with the choice. A dramatic last-minute revolt took place at a midnight meeting of Rab Butler's supporters who declared that a peer was unlikely to win an election and would spoil the image of modernisation which the Tories had been cultivating. Home hesitated. Instead of unifying the Party, he was in danger of further dividing it. Macmillan kept in close touch with events, and held firm to his support of Home, a man he described as an 'urbane but resolute character – iron painted to look like wood'.[4] On 17 October Home agreed to stand as leader and the next morning he set off for the Palace where the Queen, unusually, invited him, not to form a government, but to attempt to form one. With all the furore, Home had not had time to tell Elizabeth of the final decision. When she heard on the wireless that he had left for the Palace she exclaimed: 'Heavens! In that suit!' 'I thought he would at least have come home and changed,' she later said.[5]

That afternoon Elizabeth and Alec moved into No. 10 Downing Street. The revolt fizzled out next day when Rab Butler (destined to be 'always the bridesmaid and never the blushing bride') accepted the post of Foreign Secretary and only two of the five rebels – Enoch Powell and Iain Macleod – refused to serve in the Cabinet. Home's first broadcast promised no stunts – 'merely plain, straight talking'. Elizabeth sportingly agreed to be interviewed by selected women journalists.

Their partnership had been cemented on 3 October 1936 when 26-year-old Elizabeth Alington – tall and poised, with soft brown wavy hair, and an open smile – married the young Unionist MP for Lanark, Alec, then Lord Dunglass. The bride's family was not, at first glance, so closely linked to the circles of power as those of Clarissa Eden or Dorothy Macmillan – the Churchills and the Devonshires. But Elizabeth was used to living among people who knew the Establishment from the inside. Her father, Dr Cyril Alington, was headmaster of Shrewsbury School and then Eton, and later Dean of Durham Cathedral. He was a writer, thinker and classicist with 'a fine presence – tall, with classic features and a head of white hair', and at Eton was remembered for his intellectual influence over the boys, his powerful sermons delivered in a scarlet cassock and his dry wit.[6] Once asked by a small boy if there was a difference between God and the headmaster, he replied, 'Yes, but it is not a difference that will concern you for the next five years.' When the Senior Chaplain of Eton who was about to preach to the royal family at Sandringham asked for advice, Alington replied: 'Quite simple, treat it as though one was preaching to the junior boys in Lower Chapel, but with all the difficult bits left out.'[7]

Elizabeth's mother, the vivid, round-faced, red-haired Margaret Hester, was the youngest of fifteen children of the 4th Baron Lyttelton. In this family, too, links with Party politics, Empire and state stretched back to Georgian times, through their relatives the Lytteltons, the Clives and the Talbots. Elizabeth's maternal uncles included a bishop, a general, a powerful colonial administrator and another Eton headmaster. Hester was, Alec recalled, 'a truly remarkable person', a hostess of 'impetuous hospitality and endless fund of humour', with a unique way of expressing herself: of a woman who was a known liar she commented, 'She has a somewhat open mind as to fact.'[8] Alec's less reverent brother, William, said she 'reminded me of the Duchess in *Alice*,' though she was 'a lady with a heart as big as herself and a warmth of personality' which set even nervous boys at their ease.[9] She was loved for her wide sympathies and her cheery sense of the ludicrous, which she passed on to her daughter.

Born on 6 November 1909, Elizabeth spent her childhood from the age of seven living 'above the shop' at Eton, where Hester presided over the growing family of four daughters and two sons. Christianity was at the centre of her life, and she made sure she passed it on to her brood, although she wore it lightly. Elizabeth's announcement during 'Holy Reading' at the age of four that 'Adam was expelled from Paradise for taking all the apples shows,' her mother noted, 'that she has at least imbibed sound ideas about the rights of property'.[10] Elizabeth inherited her mother's liberal instincts, a strong social conscience and a Christian spirit. Her religion was 'very real, very strong, but unostentatious. She was just full of loving kindness the whole time . . . caring without sentimentality,' a later colleague, Oliver Wright, believes.

Known as 'Tiny Wee', Elizabeth gained an early reputation for storminess: her 'desire to do and say what is not expected of her is likely to give those in charge of her plenty of occupation,'[11] Hester wrote. Family life was a rich social and cultural mix. A number of dignitaries visited: Mahatma Gandhi once stayed at Eton and brought with him a devoted follower, Miss Slade, who never left his side and told Hester that she *must* sleep on the doormat outside Gandhi's room: 'No my dear,' Hester declared, 'not while I am a member of the Mothers'

Union.' Her husband was a staunch Conservative but she usually voted Socialist – 'without much conviction', Alec believed, though she was immune to his later attempts at conversion.[12] Later she viewed her eldest daughter Kathleen's Conservative proclivities 'with undisguised concern'.

Hester was committed to numerous philanthropic causes, and was sympathetic to women's equality. With the birth of their first son, Giles, in 1914, she noted: 'The fact that he, unlike his sisters, got his [name] inside page 6 of *The Times*, is likely to lead to trouble when they are old enough to realise the implication.'[13] Both parents believed in the value of education, including for the girls, who were taught at home by governesses. Their schooling was rigorous. Elizabeth's timetable for 1915, when she was six, began at 8.40 a.m. and finished at 4.40 p.m., Monday to Saturday. It included Naturework, Music, Knitting, Number, History/Story, Phonetics, Poetry, Geography, French, Expression Work, Composition, Dictation, Copy, Reading and Handwork – most subjects studied at least twice a week.[14] The following year, Elizabeth was learning Drill and Deportment from a Miss Dempster, and French from a Mme Jacquet. She was intelligent rather than scholarly: Antony Acland, later Alec's Private Secretary, thinks she had 'a very sharp mind, and was more genuinely intellectual [than Alec] – quick at crossword puzzles, games, problems. And a good conversationalist, quick and amusing.'

Unusually for the time, she and her sisters were expected to continue their education and take up an occupation. Elizabeth enrolled on a course at St James Secretarial College; by the end, 'she had to be put in a separate room on a typing course, she was so fast she put everyone else on the course off', says her daughter Caroline. 'Her secretarial work was very much organising who she was working for and putting the systems into place' – skills which she would later deploy in every sphere of her life. Her younger sisters, Lavinia and Joan, were more academic: both went to Oxford where Lavinia gained a double first, the prelude to a distinguished career in leukaemia research.

After her presentation at court in 1928, Elizabeth entered the social round of parties and balls. Her first job was a three month stint as social secretary to the wife of the American Secretary of State, Henry Stimson, during the 1930 Conference on Naval Disarmament. She worked from an office in the Ritz Hotel, where her connections and knowledge of social proprieties would have been valued as much as her efficiency, and she bought herself a second-hand Morris Oxford car. Employment was intermittent, however. In 1932, she was secretary of the committee organising the 'New Homes for Old' exhibition at Olympia, and she also undertook voluntary work for the Personal Services League which distributed clothes to unemployed mining families in County Durham. In her spare time she visited country houses, and went to regattas, the races, theatre and art exhibitions.

Her first contact with the Home family was through her friendship with Alec's sister Rachel, whom she met when their brother, William, was putting on a play at Eton. In 1932 she stayed with Rachel at Douglas, the Home estate in Scotland, followed by a week at the Hirsel, their other estate on the Borders in Berwickshire, where a motley group of young Homes – five sons and two daughters – lounged around, picnicked, walked and went shooting or fishing. It was Elizabeth's introduction to the regular rhythms of country life on these estates, over which she would later preside. The family was among the oldest Border aristocratic landowners, though not the wealthiest: their houses were comfortable rather than ostentatious. At regular house parties guests included Field Marshal Douglas Haig, Lord Robert Cecil and the Bowes-Lyons family.

Alec's banker father, Charles (who had inherited the title in 1918) was 'a small, red-haired man with a friendly smile and a very loud voice', who, according to Alec's later colleague Jock Colville was 'as near to being a saint as any uncanonised human being'.[15] So great was his reverence for his family and forebears, authority and royalty, that he required the entire family to stand whenever the wireless played 'God Save the King', though his independent-minded wife Lilian continued to knit on her feet.

Lilian, the daughter of the 4th Earl of Durham, gave Alec and the other children weekly religious instruction after their Sunday visits to church. Under her influence, living was frugal: Elizabeth noticed after they married that Alec never took a second helping: 'The simple reason,' Alec explained, 'was that in our family, unless you took what you wanted on the first round, there was nothing left to take.' Pocket money was for saving, not spending, and the butler Collingwood – one of a large household and estate staff which then included thirty gardeners – earned the youngsters' gratitude by tipping them for doing odd jobs when they were short of money.[16]

Elizabeth's and Alec's paths had crossed at Eton, which Alec attended from 1917, though she paid scant attention to the reticent young scholar with an impish sense of humour who dined at the headmaster's table when she was only 13. Neither remembered this early encounter. When Elizabeth visited Douglas in 1932, Alec, the eldest son and heir to the earldom, was 29, tall, with deep-set blue eyes and a fair moustache, and dressed invariably in ill-shaped tweeds. His outward diffidence masked an inner assurance and a calm integrity: he was noted for 'his absolute trustworthiness, his complete lack of side and pomposity, his charming manners and his sense of humour'.[17] He had an encyclopaedic knowledge of nature, with a particular affection for butterflies, and a love of country sports – fishing in the nearby River Tweed and shooting on the moors at Douglas – as well as a keen interest in cricket and horse-racing. Later, one of his hobbies was flower-arranging.

It was some time before their friendship turned into romance. Elizabeth shared with Alec a mischievous sense of humour and an appreciation of life's absurdities. She had a quick wit and a warm sensitivity to other people, and was, according to her daughter Meriel Darby, 'a very passionate person', who 'did feel things very strongly. She was big in her moods,' which could be 'stormy'; Alec was 'reasonable, tolerant and calm – the steady one'. Elizabeth appreciated Alec's straightforwardness – 'I cannot ever imagine him trying to put on an act,' she later said; he was 'very kind and extremely good-tempered. He has excellent judgement.'[18] Both were well-informed wordsmiths who set and solved crossword puzzles – one of their joint compositions was accepted by *The Times* in 1933, which earned them a prize of £5. Her organising abilities and good sense would have been apparent to Alec, who paid very selective attention to practical details. Each had a strong sense of public duty. Elizabeth expressed hers in her care for people's welfare; Alec channelled his into his political career. In 1931 he had been elected as Unionist MP for Lanark constituency.

In June 1936, Alec took Elizabeth to the Oaks at Epsom races, backed the winner and won the Tote Double. They went on to the gardens at Dropmore where, with the rhododendrons and azaleas in full bloom, he proposed. Their engagement was welcomed by both families and was announced in all the fashionable society newspapers and magazines. The wedding was set for 3 October 1936 in the great Norman cathedral at Durham where Cyril Alington officiated. Elizabeth wore a gown of gold brocade with long tight-fitting sleeves, a tulle veil held in place by a wreath of orange blossom and she carried a bouquet of lilies. She was attended by pageboys, with seven young and seven adult bridesmaids wearing green velvet dresses and carrying sprays of flame-coloured gladioli. Alec gave Elizabeth a garnet necklace and ear-rings. Elizabeth, ever practical, gave Alec field-glasses. At Douglas, a fifty-foot bonfire was lit by the oldest employee to celebrate the heir's union.

For their honeymoon, they motored through Europe sightseeing and picnicking. They returned to live at Springhill, on the Hirsel estate, which his parents had given them as a wedding present; in London they set up home in fashionable Chester Square. Elizabeth found herself at the centre of London political life, and joined Alec on his engagements in the constituency and with the Boys' Brigade in Scotland and the Junior Imperial League, of which he was chairman. With Alec she attended the coronation of George VI in May 1937. Alec had moved rapidly through the ranks and was already Parliamentary Private Secretary to Neville Chamberlain, who was then Chancellor of the Exchequer, and he remained in the post when Chamberlain became Prime Minister later that year.

In the Homes' long political partnership, Elizabeth was happiest in the background. She 'never forgot a face and could always match it to the name',[19] Alec wrote. In the constituency she canvassed, handed out prizes, opened fêtes and, as her daughter Caroline remembers 'drew endless raffles when she invariably drew out her own name – it became a sort of joke. It was incredible how often she drew her own ticket.' She always 'viewed the give and take of politics with amusement', according to Alec's brother, William, and would firmly draw the line on taking part. At one village hall meeting, she sat outside in the car knitting while Alec spoke because 'she had already heard the speech two or three times that evening'. When she overheard a passing miner declare that he wasn't going to Alec's meeting because 'I've been a Tory now for forty years or mair and I'm just thinking that long-haired young fellow in there might put me off!' Elizabeth went on knitting and smiled.[20]

She put up with, rather than enjoyed, constituency work, but she loathed making speeches. 'I'm a hopeless speaker and Alec is not in favour of me making speeches,' she explained later. 'It made her physically ill to think of it,' says Caroline. 'She'd agonise for hours as to what to say for two minutes,' David recalls. 'Quite often my father would write the two-minute speech, but then she'd disappear and learn it for hours before she said it . . . Even opening the local flower show, which a member of my family has done for the last hundred and thirty years, was bad enough. You can say what you like, nobody listens anyway so it doesn't matter. But she didn't like it.'

In October 1937 she gave birth to their first child, Caroline. Alec was increasingly swept up in political crises as the European situation deteriorated after Hitler's annexation of Austria in March 1938. He stood unobtrusively by his leader's side (in a silk shirt hastily borrowed from his brother, William) when Chamberlain went to meet Hitler at Munich that September. He was present, too, when Chamberlain returned waving the piece of paper signed by Hitler, proclaiming 'Peace for our time'. Elizabeth went to Heston airport with Anne Chamberlain to greet them on their return from what, to Chamberlain's supporters at the time – including Elizabeth – appeared a triumphant act of diplomacy. In addition to a general exhaustion after the encounter with what Alec described as 'this little, very grey, dull and dour man' and Chamberlain thought 'the nastiest piece of work he had ever had to deal with',[21] the entire team had not eaten all the way home, because Chamberlain refused to open the hamper packed by a German hotel. In Whitehall, among cheering crowds, she bought a silk handkerchief embroidered 'Souvenir in Commemoration of the Great Peace Without Bloodshed', which she saved, apparently without irony, in her scrapbook.

The initial euphoria over the Munich agreement did not last. In the House of Commons debate on 6 October thirty Conservative MPs including Churchill and Eden abstained; the First Lord of the Admiralty, Duff Cooper, had already resigned in protest against the appeasement of dictators. Alec, sensing that the Prime Minister was so exhausted that he was near to nervous breakdown, invited the Chamberlains to stay with them at the Hirsel.

Chamberlain was among the first of Alec's political colleagues to experience the Homes' legendary hospitality. He greatly appreciated the way the Home family treated him 'as one of yourselves and that was just how I felt and still feel about you'.[22] Over the years, friends and colleagues of every rank were always made to feel at home. 'One almost became a member of the family,' Antony Acland remembers. Oliver Wright recalls, 'wherever [Elizabeth] was there was bustle and laughter and a good time was had by all. She made an enormous impact on people.' 'You were just welcomed in,' says Shelagh Collingwood, a junior Foreign Office secretary, who recalls 'the friendliness and the incredible politeness and the sheer fun we had, there was so much laughter and giggles.' Everyone found them unaffected and 'un-pompous' – generous, natural and inclusive.

At their regular house-parties Elizabeth rarely joined the men when they went shooting: 'She enjoyed more the social side of it,' says Caroline. The women stayed at home, writing letters, sewing, knitting or doing the inevitable crossword. Then Elizabeth would 'bring out the most wonderful picnic lunches, but she wouldn't actually stay on after lunch. She would go home and take the ladies and go for a walk or sit around . . . Or [go to] the Edinburgh Festival.' It was a social life that remained almost unchanged throughout their lives.

As war loomed closer after the Germans marched into Prague in March 1939, Alec was often working eighteen hours a day. With Elizabeth expecting their second child, they managed to get to Scotland for shooting in August. On 3 September, the day Chamberlain announced the declaration of war, Home took solace in nature. He rang his brother Henry (the BBC's 'Birdman') to suggest they drive out of London to the South Downs to look for Chalk Blue butterflies. When he returned to Downing Street, a thunderstorm broke. As he stood on the steps with a colleague, he remembered, 'almost simultaneously the words came to us that this was the gods weeping for the folly of man'.[23]

Elizabeth retreated to Scotland, where she remained throughout the war. In common with many owners of great estates, the Homes gave most of the Hirsel over to evacuees – in their case sick and crippled children from the Margaret Rose Hospital in Edinburgh – and Elizabeth helped organise their welfare. Meriel, their second child, was born in November. At No. 10, though 'the charming, inoffensive and extremely sensible Alec'[24] enlivened the Private Office, he looked drawn and suffered increasing fatigue.

It was the onset of an illness which would alter their lives. After Chamberlain resigned in May 1940 and Churchill took over as Prime Minister, Alec applied to enlist in the Army, but to his surprise he was turned down and told he was exhausted and needed to rest. When he reapplied after three months, the doctors recommended an urgent examination which revealed tuberculosis of the spine. The foremost surgeon in Scotland, Sir John Fraser, urged that without an immediate and highly risky operation, the outlook was grim: 'It was: "you have the operation and you may never walk again, or you don't have it and you're dead within six months,"' says Caroline. Alec opted instantly for the operation and Elizabeth, when consulted, agreed. It took six hours, and when he emerged his entire frame was encased in plaster. Later he joked to the surgeon: 'You have achieved the impossible; you have put backbone into a politician.'[25]

Elizabeth, pregnant with their third child, made the 120-mile round trip each day to visit him. He could move almost none of his body without pain. After three weeks, he insisted on being discharged. Diana was born eight weeks after his return home. He was to be imprisoned in his plaster cast for two years, cared for by Elizabeth and a nurse, when one was available. 'It must have been living hell for her, and for him, a lot of it,' says their son David. 'They were both rather reluctant to talk about that time . . . probably there were a lot of pressures . . . It was obviously very difficult to get nursing help at that time, so she had to do a lot herself. So she was wife, nurse and mother all at one moment.' It is almost impossible to imagine how Elizabeth coped with an invalid husband, a newborn baby and two children under four. She was told she could keep her nanny provided that she did some charity work, so she ran the WVS (Women's Voluntary Service) car scheme for Berwickshire, transporting people to hospital and doctors' clinics. She read to Alec, fed him, and wrote or typed his letters, keeping him in touch with friends and Westminster events as he lay immobile in his cast.

An elaborate pulley system with a ramp was rigged up with Elizabeth's help to wheel him outside to breathe fresh air and watch the passage of nature and the changing aspect of the Cheviot Hills as the children played around him. At night in the stillness they could hear the drone of German bombers heading for Glasgow's shipyards. Gradually Alec was able to embark on his own extensive reading programme, including works on communism, political biographies, detective stories, and the classics. Elizabeth's encouragement sustained his sometimes flagging spirit. His mother introduced him to needlework and embroidery and he was proud to show off the eight diningroom chairs he worked in *petit point*. Though he could not chase butterflies, he observed them through binoculars, and Elizabeth typed his side of a lively correspondence in the *Scotsman* about sightings of rare specimens. When a colleague, Walter Elliot, suffered the similar misfortune of being encased in plaster, Alec wrote brightly to his wife, 'Give Walter my love and tell him there are compensations about bed which he will discover, especially the feeling of power when one's wife has to do up one's shoes.'[26]

After more than a year, Home's plaster was cut away only to be replaced by another, with instructions from the doctors that he must not move. Elizabeth later told Antony Acland: 'For a moment I thought I'd lost him. His eyes flickered and he thought that they'd come every year and say, "You're getting on all right but you've got to be on your back for another year."' But the plasters became shorter, and after a time a spinal brace was applied while he gradually learned to move his limbs again. By May 1943 he was well enough to go on holiday with the girls and Elizabeth, who was now pregnant again. The son and heir, David, was born in November: 'There was an enormous celebration when he appeared,' Meriel says; 'though they adored all of us, it was very special for Dad to have a son.'

Alec's illness deepened their already close relationship. Their ability to see the humorous edge to things must have helped them through the darker times. As well as the practical ordering of his life, Elizabeth had for two years sustained him in his every need. 'From the moment they married – and certainly from the time when he was ill – she really almost totally devoted her life to him and never did anything much outside,' David Home says, adding: 'She was very much in love with him all her life.' Eventually Alec became fit, even tough – 'If he had the air of Scotland in his lungs and the turf of Scotland under his feet, he'd walk a man half his age off their feet in a day,' Antony Acland says. But even then Alec always remained her first priority, and the children knew they came second: 'It was her role to look after him. She would lie awake at night anticipating everything he could possibly need. She just knew he needed her around,' Meriel remembers.

Alec returned to Parliament in 1944, and was appointed Under-Secretary at the Foreign Office in the 1945 caretaker government. But with the Labour victory in the 1945 election he lost his seat at Lanark, despite the 'deferential' vote – much of Lanark was Douglas land, owned by the Home family. As the Conservative Party reorganised in defeat, the Homes stayed mainly in Scotland, managing the estate and nursing the Lanark constituency. But when he regained his seat in the 1950 general election, his return to the House of Commons was short-lived. In July 1951 his father died suddenly and Alec and Elizabeth rushed to Scotland. Called out of the Chamber of the House of Commons to receive the news, he left some notes on the bench. He returned to get them and learned later that he had been reported for breaching the rules: already he had become a member of 'Another Place', the House of Lords.

Alec succeeded to the earldom and Elizabeth's title changed from Lady Dunglass to the Countess of Home. Eventually she gained a place in the *Guinness Book of Records* for having five names while being married to the same man. 'Considering the number of different names I have had in my life,' Elizabeth commented, 'it is surprising how infrequently I've been married.'[27] With the Conservatives' return to power under Churchill in 1951, Alec was made Minister of State in the Scottish Office. 'Home, sweet Home it shall be,' Churchill said as he agreed to the appointment.[28]

Elizabeth organised Alec's and the family's lives. With her restless energy, she always had something on the go. 'She made lists,' her son recalls, 'and she had lists of which lists she had – endless lists for everything.' She did her own cooking with only occasional help on busy holidays. 'They had a cook who came in from the village and one of the foresters on the estate buttled while they were there; he didn't wear a butler's uniform, he wore jacket and trousers, just like he did on the moors,' Oliver Wright says. Nanny Coulson helped out and the girls had a governess and were educated at home, though David was sent away to school.

All her life Elizabeth kept scrapbooks. Whenever she had any spare time she would set up a card table and cut out and paste in newspaper articles about Alec, herself and the family along with her own photographs – 'The great thing of my life is my scrapbooks. It's the way I keep a diary,'[29] she said later. She loved doing it – it was an assertion of herself, and 'where she put a lot of her creativity. If there was anything that tickled her fancy, it had to be recorded as quickly as possible.' Eventually the scrapbooks ran to over a hundred volumes. In a black-lined exercise book called the Joke Book, she helped Alec collect jokes and anecdotes for use in his speeches. Her other creative hobby was embroidery, including samplers, tapestries and a Beatrix Potter bedspread – 'absolutely beautiful – each little square had an appliquéd figure in it, and it had a certain light-hearted humour and joyfulness to it', Meriel recalls. She 'knitted all my father's shooting stockings . . . on the plane, in the car and on the train – pullovers and socks,' Caroline adds.

Few ever saw Elizabeth being anything but cheerful, though she could be temperamental, according to Meriel: 'if she was cross she was very cross, so we certainly behaved ourselves . . . She was quite moody. If something was on her mind she would be miserable, or if she was happy she was very happy.' Even so, says David, 'she would never shout, ever. If she was angry, if anything her voice would go quieter, not louder. It was a danger sign.' She could be critical and disapproved if people were nasty about others, but was good at hiding it in public if she disliked people. She had 'quite high standards, not necessarily moral standards but just about the way people behaved. She was very keen on good manners. People who didn't have good manners used to go a long way down in her estimation,' David remembers. She had strong opinions, and made clear her disapproval in private: 'There was just an atmosphere for a bit,' Caroline recalls. 'It would be very, very clear that she wasn't amused.'

Elizabeth's formidable organising skills – and her often self-deprecating humour – were invaluable as Alec's political career progressed. From early on, Elizabeth did all Alec's typing, thumping away very fast on an ancient machine, and, except when he was in office, she acted as his secretary, sometimes signing herself 'L. Green' if she thought it better not to identify herself as his wife. In addition to the family, she could be responsible from then on for running or overseeing up to five houses, including official residences. 'He was very dependent on her,' their son, David, says. 'She was the one who made sure he had a passport when he was going somewhere, or had some money . . . She always took spare things of everything on tour in case he did leave them behind.' In one of her first notes to the Foreign Office staff later, she enclosed 'spare spectacles of my husband's. He usually loses *about* one pair a fortnight.'[30]

She bought all his shirts and ties and suits, though 'he was never the best dressed man in town,' according to David. Always thrifty, Elizabeth would occasionally have an economy drive: 'Alec was walking across St James's Park one day with Oliver and he said, "I do wish Elizabeth would stop making me wear David's [his son's] old shoes",' Oliver Wright's wife, Marjory, recalls. Since they moved so often between their different houses, it was a great advantage later that he was the same size as his Private Secretary, Antony Acland: 'He used to borrow all my clothes. In spite of Elizabeth's heroic efforts, he didn't always have them in the right place at the right time. He had a rather grand government chauffeur who used to come to our little house and say to my wife, "I'm afraid we haven't" – he always used the royal "we" – "We haven't got our evening shoes. We haven't got our stiff shirt. We're going to Buckingham Palace tonight. Can Mr Acland lend his Lordship his stiff shirt, his cuff-links, his white tie, his dinner jacket?"'

Elizabeth cared little about clothes for herself: 'She always looked tidy, but she was never going to set the fashion,' her son says. Her reputation was for discreet good taste – sensible well-cut tweeds in the country and tailored suits, dresses with elegant accessories, and evening dresses as the occasion required. Meriel recalls, 'She wanted to be appropriate, but she wasn't interested. She would sit down at the mirror for about forty seconds, if that, and whack a comb through her hair, which was naturally curly, and slap on some lipstick and a quick dab of powder, and off. She didn't approve of vanity at all. I had to hide my early face powders and things in a toothbrush box.'

In 1955, when Eden succeeded Churchill as Prime Minister, Alec was appointed Secretary of State for Commonwealth Relations. When he travelled abroad on official tours, Elizabeth insisted that she accompany him on journeys that could then take weeks, even months. She told a reporter later, 'I said to Harold Macmillan, "Can I go along?" and he said, "Wives don't travel." ~~Every three days I'd ask him again,~~ and he got fed up with this and in the end agreed.'[31]

In October 1955 she joined Alec on the return leg of a Commonwealth tour. It was her baptism as a ministerial wife abroad, and Alec's first real step on to the global stage. For much of the trip through Ceylon, India and Pakistan, she had a separate agenda from Alec – visits to a settlement, a welfare extension project, a cottage industries emporium and a buffalo farm, where she asked 'ceaseless and intelligent questions'. She had luncheons and teas with the wives of officials and with groups of women, including, in India, with President Nehru's daughter, Indira Gandhi, who was 'charming and very friendly' and had 'a wreath of stephanotis round her head which smelt quite heavenly'; at a gathering of the All India Women's Conference she sat next to Meena Bundaram, an activist who was 'passionately interested in the "exploitation of women" and was much disappointed to find that it wasn't also my pet subject'.[32]

At the official dinner with Indian President Nehru, the conversation, given the rising tension in Britain over Egypt, suddenly became sensitive: 'He said to me, "I've just had a nice present of mangoes from my friend Colonel Nasser in Egypt." I felt mad to be talking to Nehru about Nasser,' she reported. When Alec's conversation with Nehru went beyond the allotted time, Elizabeth, seeing the restlessness of the officials present, eventually advanced on them when they were still talking at 10.45 p.m. She could sometimes see the irony in her overriding concern for Alec: 'Someone told Alec he would get "hook-worm" if he walks about barefoot for an instant – the result is that I scuttle around ceaselessly risking the full disease looking for his slippers.' She noted the pressure on him: 'Alec endlessly reads brief and telegrams from the CRO [Commonwealth Relations Office] in every aeroplane, or else writes speeches or broadcasts for the next country to be visited. He really has no let-up at all. We fondly think after Calcutta it will be less hectic.'[33] It was not. During the entire month-long trip the weather had been relentlessly hot. As she set off for home, she found herself 'very excited at the prospect of wearing a vest again'.[34]

Abroad and at home Elizabeth 'inspired enormous devotion', Meriel says. 'She was a very supportive, attentive person and a very attractive personality. We all loved her,' Alec's Private Secretary, Tom Bridges, confirms. She made lists of everyone they met, with details about their personal circumstances, and followed up meetings with correspondence, at the same time keeping in regular touch with family, friends and political colleagues. Antony Acland recalls trips abroad, when 'she would have this capacious, huge bag out of which would come her correspondence. And she might write fifty, sixty, seventy letters in longhand on the plane, and when she'd finished that she would do her tapestry.'

At the Commonwealth Office in 1955 she set up an organisation, CROWS, the Commonwealth Relations Office Wives' Society, to help diplomatic wives negotiate their way through the protocol and practicalities of service in London and abroad. Elizabeth herself was closely involved. 'She would jot down that somebody's third son was having a problem over something, or somebody's daughter was quite happy flying but didn't like going by train,' Caroline remembers, 'or somebody would say to her, "I can't get something or other" in wherever they happened to be, and she'd say "Oh, I'll send you some", find whatever it was and it would probably go out in the diplomatic bag.'

Elizabeth soon grew accustomed to a more demanding political pace. During the 1956 Suez crisis, Home sat on the inner decision-making committee. He was at the state banquet in Downing Street for King Feisal of Iraq when the dramatic news of President Nasser's nationalisation of the Suez Canal Company came through on 26 July: 'He telephoned back at 11 p.m. to say he had gone to a meeting & hoped he would not be very long.' When he wasn't back by 2 a.m., 'I was beginning to agitate & at 2.30 he came in flinging off his very incongruous looking white tie and tails & said, "That idiot Nasser has seized the Canal." And that was the end of all peace – world peace or domestic peace.'[35] There was no quiet grouse-shooting in Scotland that August. Caroline Douglas-Home remembers the teleprinter hammering away and the telephone endlessly ringing and her father being helicptered off the lawn at the Hirsel to be sped down to London – 'but there was never any flap', she says. On 1 November, the day after the Anglo-French bombing attack on Egyptian airfields, Elizabeth, as she did so often, went to hear Alec speak in the House of Lords debate on Suez. They watched Eden's ministerial broadcast on television which both thought 'extremely good. He looked and sounded surprisingly well & robust. A. back to meetings at 10.30 and returned ultimately at 1. am.'³⁶

After the ceasefire and withdrawal of troops, the crisis began to take its toll. Illness forced Eden to depart in November for a holiday. Home was also struck down, feeling 'very tired indeed & low about the whole situation', Elizabeth recorded.³⁷ On Eden's resignation in January 1957, Elizabeth sent her sympathies to Clarissa Eden: 'I feel I *must* let you know how dreadfully sad this news has made us. Of course the only thing that matters is that he should get quickly and completely well again but meantime we shall all miss you both more than bears thinking about. Yours ever, Elizabeth Home.'³⁸ As Macmillan formed his administration, Home remained at the Commonwealth Office quietly consolidating his authority in the inner circles of government.

His reward came when, in July 1960, Harold Macmillan unexpectedly made him Secretary of State for Foreign Affairs. Alec had discussed the offer with Elizabeth and she 'pushed him a bit to be Foreign Secretary because she thought he was up to it', their son believes. 'He'd made a success of the Commonwealth [Office] . . . He was partly worried being in the House of Lords. It was the first time there'd been a Foreign Secretary in the House of Lords for some time and he wondered whether that was going to work. So I think she tried to reassure him on that point.' The appointment caused an outcry. There was stupefaction in the Party. A backbench revolt threatened at the idea of an 'insufficiently distinguished' and 'faceless earl' in one of the senior offices of state. The *Daily Mirror* screamed that it was 'the most reckless political appointment since the Roman Emperor Caligula made his favourite horse a consul',³⁹ but Macmillan stood by his decision. Elizabeth came to Alec's defence: 'Of course my husband has no qualms about this new job. As far as I am concerned he is able enough for any post in the Government, even Prime Minister',⁴⁰ though a placard proclaiming HOME DISASTER tickled her sense of humour and she asked the newspaper seller if she could have it.

The Homes moved into the Foreign Secretary's residence at Carlton Gardens, and Elizabeth soon strengthened her reputation as a hostess at official and diplomatic functions. She was informal with the political and secretarial staff, and paid almost daily visits to the office for chats. Always ready to help with any personal problems, she remembered birthdays, and was a great giver of presents. When the Pakistan Foreign Minister sent her a large box of mangoes, her first thought was to divide it up among the Private Office staff.

As Elizabeth's confidence grew, so did Alec's political stature. An air of calm efficiency pervaded the Foreign Office under their stewardship. 'We're not the worrying kind,' Elizabeth later said. 'I never worry. My husband is even more a non-worrier than I am. I mean, after he's done his best, he just stops worrying.'[41] She organised their homes and domestic life so that he could 'devote himself a hundred per cent to work when he had to work and a hundred per cent to the family when he had time for family and leisure,' says Oliver Wright. Alec could work even with the family around him. David remembers 'Mother sitting at the desk doing whatever she was doing and he would be writing speeches with all the family and our friends screaming and shouting, playing racing demon or whatever. He never got used to actually sitting at a desk writing, he always used to sit on a sofa and just scribble away.'

The Homes had the use of Dorneywood, the country house near Burnham Beeches in Buckinghamshire, which was given as a gift to the government by the Courtauld family in 1947 with a generous endowment for its upkeep. Originally a Tudor house, it had been restored after a fire in 1912, had a pleasant garden, and held romantic associations for the Homes because of its proximity to Dropmore Gardens, where Alec had proposed. Unable to get so often to Scotland, they used it regularly during their tenure both at the Commonwealth Office and the Foreign Office. The whole family liked Dorneywood, even though Elizabeth was not always entirely at ease: 'You were hardly allowed to move an ashtray in the house. The Dorneywood Trust was very, very strict and they had a manager who would appear and, literally, if he saw an ashtray wasn't where it usually was he would query it,' Caroline Douglas-Home recalls. The staff 'weren't cosy, and she loved to be cosy with her staff. She hated to be grand,' Meriel says. Sometimes they entertained heads of government, including Australian Prime Minister Bob Menzies, and Alec was delighted when the Australian Cricket Eleven came for lunch and played cricket on the lawn with David and his Eton pals.

On visits to Scotland, Foreign Office business usually intervened: 'There's apt to be so much business on the line & *either* President

Kennedy can't get on because Meriel is talking to her chums *or* the cook can't order the roast because some of you are fixing the world,'[42] Elizabeth wrote to Antony Acland, pleading for an additional scrambler telephone.

In 1958 the Homes had moved from Springhill into the Hirsel, and Elizabeth was gradually opening up the rooms and refurbishing the house. A young Foreign Office secretary, 18-year-old Shelagh Collingwood, who often took up the ministerial red boxes, remembers Elizabeth's embracing hospitality. After only a day she recorded in her diary, 'very difficult to remember one's not a member of the family'. There were walks and picnics on the banks of the Tweed or 'in some cold, windswept shepherd's hut somewhere' with sandwiches and boiled eggs and cherry brandy and lots of laughter and teasing. Sometimes Shelagh joined the men who were shooting on the moors, and Elizabeth manned the phone in her place. More often she helped Elizabeth as she sorted photographs, lined shelves, hung portraits. Elizabeth was 'incredibly funny' and always 'put a light side on to things'. Once when there was a possibility of Shelagh driving with Caroline to Berwick, Shelagh pretended she couldn't drive round corners, and Elizabeth teasingly complained that an accident was bound to happen and then she'd have to organise a double funeral. If really serious things happened, her view was that 'you dealt with it, got it out of the way, and went on. You didn't let yourself sink into self-pity.'

Foreign trips were enjoyable when Elizabeth was on board, and the staff were included in games and solving crosswords as Elizabeth knitted or sewed her way through plane journeys. She took care of details. On arrival at a destination, she is alleged to have whispered, 'Peking, Alec, Peking, Peking,' as he walked down the plane steps 'to prevent his saying to his host, as he stood before the microphone, "I'm very happy to be back in Montreal."'[43] On a trip to New York, the team noticed at breakfast that she had laid out presents. 'She said to him, "Alec, darling, I know you will have forgotten about this, but this is my present to you."' It was a Mexican silver grouse. 'And he said, "But it's not my birthday, is it? Oh," he said, "could it be our wedding anniversary?" And she said, "Yes, and this is your present to me." And it was the opposite article,' Tom Bridges remembers.

The Foreign Office schedule was heavy: they made eleven trips in the first six months, starting with a state visit to Nepal with the Queen and Duke of Edinburgh which included a tiger shoot with 327 elephants and an army of servants, though it was marred for Elizabeth when her elephant ran off at speed, out of control. On an official visit to Japan they had three days of sightseeing, to be followed by talks. Oliver Wright recalls 'Elizabeth coming up to me once during a visit to a Buddhist shrine and saying "Oliver, we've got to do something about this. Alec's *had* Buddha."' There was the ritual of present-giving at every occasion: 'We had an absolute trunk-load of presents that we had to give out, and we always had a pow-wow with Elizabeth as to whether this guy merited a watch or that guy merited a fountain pen. And I remember Elizabeth saying to me once, "Oliver, are we in disgrace? We've been sitting here half an hour and we haven't had any presents."'

Her comments about the job in public were unfailingly optimistic: 'I love it all. I love eating foreign food, Japanese food was marvellous. I can eat anything. I only wish we could stay longer in all the different places.' When it seemed possible that they would go to meet Soviet Premier Khrushchev at a Black Sea resort, she declared breezily: 'it sounds enormous fun. I shall certainly pack a swimsuit for myself. My husband is not very keen on swimming actually, but I think we can put a hand on a costume for him somewhere.'[44]

Home presided over the Foreign Office in the period when Britain, in the words of former American Secretary of State, Dean Acheson, had lost an empire but not yet found a role. Though it still had overseas commitments, foreign policy was dominated by the tensions of the Cold War, when Britain was invariably the junior partner to America – in negotiations over Berlin, the Far East and the Test Ban Treaty. At the time of the Cuban missile crisis in 1962, Elizabeth, with Dorothy Macmillan, did her best to foster an atmosphere of calm during the period of hectic telephone consultations between Prime Minister Harold Macmillan and President Kennedy, at which Home was present, often through the night. His ability 'to switch off, even for three or four minutes at a time and think about something else' helped, Caroline thought.

By 1963, Conservative dominance was looking unsteady after the Party's thirteen years in power. The economy was faltering, Macmillan's authority was being questioned as the Party fell badly behind in the polls, and a run of by-election defeats was causing concern. A series of spy scandals which culminated in the Profumo affair damaged public confidence, tarred the leadership with what would now be called 'sleaze' and opened up divisions within Conservative ranks about Macmillan's fitness as leader. There were few bright spots in Home's field of foreign affairs. De Gaulle's rejection of Britain's application to join the Common Market in January was a serious blow to the government's European policy and dispiriting to the leadership. President Kennedy's visit to Birch Grove in June, at which Home was present, helped dispel the gloom, and the signing of the Test Ban Treaty in August, in which Home played a key part, was seen as the major achievement of the later days of Macmillan's administration.

The political debate sharpened when Harold Wilson took over the Labour leadership after Hugh Gaitskell's death in January 1963. He focused the agenda on modernisation harnessed to the 'white heat of technology', the establishment of a 'classless' and 'meritocratic' opportunity state, and attacked Britain's reliance on leaders (such as Home) in public life 'whose only claim is their aristocratic connection or the power of inherited wealth or speculative finance . . . We are content to remain a nation of Gentlemen in a world of Players.'[45] This emphasis on change and renewal chimed with a gathering mood of irreverent scepticism targeted at the 'Establishment' with its 'entrenched interests' and 'worn-out principles', which found expression in television's *That Was the Week That Was*, launched in 1962, and the satirical magazine *Private Eye*, in which Home was portrayed as the diminutive laird 'Baillie Vass'. Both were treated with light-hearted humour by the Homes; at least the younger family members are reported to have watched *TW3*. Alec found the personal attacks 'tiresome': if the exposed politician 'reveals he is affected he is an even more tempting target, so the alternative is to present the hide of a rhinoceros, which is singularly unattractive'.[46]

Macmillan had vacillated throughout the summer of 1963 about whether to resign, causing speculation about the succession. Home was not then a serious candidate; Macmillan had consulted him during his deliberations precisely because, as a peer and loyal supporter, he stood above the fray. When Macmillan was struck down by prostate illness and resigned, Elizabeth 'didn't push him at all to be Prime Minister,' says David Home. 'The only thing she pushed him on was to see that his health was up to it.' Even so, Oliver Wright believes, she gave him the courage to go forward and 'persuaded Alec to persevere' when some Cabinet members expressed opposition to his leadership.

For Home, the appeal to duty had characteristically been the deciding factor: 'Throughout my political career I have done what I have been asked to do when I thought it was my duty,' he declared.[47] Elizabeth is said to have felt that, whatever happened, it would be worth while to have been Prime Minister of England, and she was proud of Alec's success. She was by now quite canny about dealing with the press, and set a precedent by agreeing to talk to a group of women journalists, who were 'totally disarmed by her', according to her secretary, Lorne Roper-Caldbeck. Elizabeth came over as a surprisingly un-grand down-to-earth 'devoted family woman', who shared the concerns of ordinary wives and mothers and had a 'gift of witty, nonchalant, lively conversation'.[48] As so often, she came publicly to Alec's support: 'Anyone who underestimates him does so at their peril. He doesn't look nearly so tough as he really is – he can really lash out. I don't flinch at the thought of Mr Wilson cutting him up.' He was, she claimed, perfectly capable of taking the sort of criticism likely to come his way: 'He never gets very wound up about criticism or any toodleoo. He's just frightfully good-tempered. The only time he gets annoyed is in traffic jams.'[49]

Before moving into No. 10 Downing Street, Alec had to renounce his title and get elected to the House of Commons. It had been an anxious few weeks for Elizabeth. Her sister Lavinia ('Vin') visited Carlton Gardens and found Elizabeth 'cooking in a pinny and no colour at all in her face and very funny saying, "Oh, what has hit us?" . . . Her life is tiring and distressing and sleepless, apart from Alec's job, which might be said to be the main thing,' she wrote.[50] After a brief consultation, the family all agreed to give up their titles: David ceased to be Lord Dunglass, and Alec jokingly referred to the girls as the 'near-misses', each having lost her prefix of 'Lady'. Alec now become known as Sir Alec Douglas-Home (having been made a Knight of the Thistle the previous year) and Elizabeth acquired her fourth name, Lady Douglas-Home.

Home stood in the by-election at the Kinross and West Perthshire constituency after the candidate, George Younger, stood down in his favour, and won by a comfortable majority. Elizabeth, who hadn't fought an election for over a decade, took notes of everyone Alec met and of all the questions asked, but worried about the outcome. 'It's the counting – just standing there waiting – that makes me nervous . . . It's amazing there aren't more heart attacks while the counts are taking place.'[51] On his first appearance in the House of Commons, on 11 November, Home confessed that he was 'shaking at the knees' under the 'sheer impact of the noise after the quiet and civilised proceedings of the House of Lords'.[52] Up in the gallery Elizabeth, with David at her side, watched with pride as he received a standing ovation.

Elizabeth was 54 when she moved into No. 10 in November 1963, having sent presents and warm letters of appreciation to all the Foreign Office staff who were 'very gloomy' at their departure. Of the décor, which had been completely renovated under the Macmillans, she said, 'It's all delightful. I shall make no changes at all',[53] though her sister thought the flat 'rather recklessly carpeted and wildly designed' and Meriel decided 'it was exactly like a hotel', with its green carpet, off-white striped wallpaper and floral chintz curtains throughout. Elizabeth did make it 'more homely' – it was later described as a 'cosily untidy sitting room, bowls of flowers and knitting strewn around'[54] – but it didn't occur to her to re-do anything, because 'she was economical and that would have been a great waste,' Caroline says. They used the small dining room in the state rooms for meals as there was no suitable dining room in the flat and 'the kitchen was so small, it was like a ship's galley', Lorne Roper-Caldbeck remembers.

Her role did not change substantially. No. 10 had 'made no alteration in my life, except that it is more hectic', she told reporters. 'One has rather less time for domestic chores.' When staff didn't want to worry Sir Alec with a problem, it was reported, they'd say, 'let's ask Lady Douglas-Home. She'll know.'[55] Her life was busier, she found it impossible to keep their private life separate from politics – 'an evening to ourselves is a treat', she said – and there were more official functions to oversee, 'which she wasn't used to. So I think she probably found it pretty hard work. But she was very stoical, she never showed she was tired, she'd never show she was worried. But she always knew when my father was worried because he used to hum. And that would begin to concern her a bit,' David Home recalls.

For the first time, Elizabeth had a secretary, albeit reluctantly, since she was used to doing it all herself. Sister 'Vin' on her first visit found her 'knee-deep in letters, many from lunatics'. Lorne Roper-Caldbeck, just out of secretarial college, was employed to deal with correspondence and organise her schedule; one third of Lorne's salary was paid by Elizabeth and two-thirds by the Cabinet Office. Elizabeth was astonished to receive letters from Scotsmen protesting that Alec put sugar, instead of salt, on his porridge; from small shopkeepers complaining that she shopped at a supermarket; from people asking for her old sofa covers and old hats.[56] While Government Hospitality organised the official functions, Elizabeth employed a regular cook for the first time, a housemaid and two dailies.

Shortly after Home took over, news flashed through on 22 November 1963 of the assassination of President Kennedy in Dallas. After a moving tribute by Alec, who felt the tragedy as 'a personal shock and loss', he and Elizabeth rushed off to attend the funeral in Washington. When it was discovered that the Duke of Edinburgh had not been allocated a seat for the service at St Matthew's Cathedral, Elizabeth saved the day by giving up hers, 'which was emphatically not the right position for the Consort of the Queen', Home noted.[57] For another funeral, that of India's President Nehru in May 1964, the press found out that Alec couldn't locate a change of shirt, which Elizabeth, at her homespun best, explained was because: 'He doesn't have a great many shirts, so normally we're in such chaos – you know, one on, one off, and one in the wash.'[58]

Elizabeth had no problems with arrangements for the state visits, formal dinners, and other occasions in the prime ministerial calendar. She had a large party book in which she kept details of everyone invited and the menu – a habit of most hostesses at the time. She took on her duties with her usual wit, which could puncture pomposity at a stroke. 'She was killingly funny,' says Marjory Wright. At a formal state occasion at Covent Garden where some of the guests wore not one, but two tiaras, Elizabeth whispered to Marjory as she passed, 'They light up well, don't they!?' Of her own tiaras she announced, 'Oh, they're not mine, they're family. I just happen to be around to wear them now. They go on, you know.'

Though Elizabeth often had her own agenda, she preferred to be ~~with Alec. One of her main concerns~~ had been that she would see much less of her husband because he would be so busy. 'They would always be looking out for each other, at a cocktail party or some huge [event],' says David. 'My father would say, "Oh I must go and find Elizabeth", and then people would say, "Why, is Elizabeth lost or is she all right?" They would ask other people about each other. Or it would be "OK, well that's my programme, what's Elizabeth going to be doing?"' Meriel recalls, 'He was incredibly happy and relaxed if she was around. They were absolutely devoted to each other – to the point of being symbiotic.'

Elizabeth continued Dorothy Macmillan's practice of giving teas at No. 10 for the wives of Conservative MPs, officers and key Party workers and, with her strong religious background, was an active member of a group of Christian wives of MPs whom she called the 'Holy Hens'. She also attended the annual Women's Conservative Conference, where in 1964 she overcame her nerves to make her début political speech, described in the press as 'one minute of home-spun cheerfulness' in which she rallied the audience for the challenge of a coming election: 'If we are sufficiently convinced that we are going to win – as we are – we shall start an epidemic of optimism that will sweep all over the country,' she declared, having already told reporters: 'My husband is an incurable optimist. There is nothing so infectious as optimism.'[59]

Elizabeth took an interest in politics as it affected Alec, and viewed it through his eyes. She never tried to influence him, but had 'a passionate interest in his work, and of course, the telephone is always ringing and people coming and going. It would be impossible not to take an interest,' she told a reporter. Though he 'talks over his problems and worries with me',[60] and she had her own views in private, she never expressed a view on political issues in any public forum: 'In any interview she gave to the press or anything like that, she simply wouldn't be drawn. She simply said, "That's my husband's job, you've got to ask him,"' says David Home.

During the whole of the Homes' period at No. 10, the knowledge that an election was due within a year dominated the agenda. Alec's task from the outset had been to restore confidence in the Party and to build his authority in the country. Dubbed in the press the 'Unexpected Prime Minister', the Party's concern was that, as one MP put it, 'If he can't get across we've had it.'⁶¹ Labour's new leader, Harold Wilson, was a testing opponent, never passing up the opportunity to jibe at 'the 14th Earl of Home' for his lofty connections, though Home believed he had countered what he saw as inverted snobbery with a reference to 'the 14th Mr Wilson'. To heighten his public profile, he and Elizabeth embarked on a series of whistle-stop tours round the country. Part of the aim, with 'man-of-the-people' Harold Wilson waiting in the wings, was to present Alec as less the aristocrat, more the man who understood the nation's concerns – or, as Elizabeth helpfully said: 'there is nothing of the proud aristocrat about my husband. He is a warm and sympathetic person. I think he is very much like the average Englishman – or Briton.'⁶²

During the first five months, Elizabeth accompanied him as he made over sixty speeches and attended numerous meet-the-people events, where, according to Oliver Wright, 'the moment anybody came in contact with him, they were completely bowled over by his naturalness; he talked to everybody exactly the same'. Not having had to go on the stump for so long, Elizabeth was worried about the pace and all the 'charging around'. 'If it's been your life, then you just go up a gear, but in this case he had to go up six gears,' David Home says. They visited every major city, toured factories, visited local Party workers and attended rallies.

At a time when image was assuming a key place in the political process, Elizabeth, who was always candid with journalists, fitted the expected role of prime ministerial spouse as 'essentially a wife and mother and grandmother' who had 'great charm and vivacity', was kind and extremely efficient, and whose job was to listen.⁶³ Alec's image was a source of constant frustration, and Elizabeth was concerned on his behalf. He became a measured and effective speaker, but not one who inspired excitement. He was ill at ease with television, and it showed: 'I fear I could not conceal my distaste for the conception that the political leader had also to be an actor on the screen,' he wrote, and recalled an 'unpromising start' when a make-up woman was preparing him for a performance:

Q. Can you not make me look better than I do on television?
A. No.
Q. Why not?
A. Because you have a head like a skull.
Q. Does not everyone have a head like a skull?
A. No.[64]

Elizabeth 'minded very much' that 'he looked so gaunt and cold, which he certainly was not', Meriel says. She resented the new pressures, David recalls: 'Everybody said he had to smile, or not have half-moon spectacles or have round spectacles instead of square ones . . . and everybody gets at you, and she finally said, "Why can't you just leave him alone and [let him] be himself?".'

At No. 10, Elizabeth was keen to retain the usual informal family atmosphere as the children, now young adults, came and went. David, who was at Oxford, kept a low profile and Caroline was then lady-in-waiting to Queen Elizabeth, the Queen Mother so could visit only occasionally. Twenty-four-year-old Meriel, who wore fashionable black plastic macs and high boots, and had recently graduated from art school, was working in a bookshop; she 'used to change in a phone box on the way home' – out of her black jeans and 'paint' and into her twinset and pearls for Downing Street. When she married economics don Adrian Darby at Coldstream in March 1964, Elizabeth organised the wedding with charts and timetables and lists of everyone's duties. Alec was responsible for arranging all the flowers in the church. They were besieged by the press, to their surprise: 'It never crossed our minds that anybody would go up to cold Scotland in March,' Meriel remembers, and the whole family spent their time fending off enquiries until Britt Ekland got engaged to Peter Sellers 'and pushed us off the front page, thank God. We had a pretty awful time of it. It was quite interesting to see how inaccurate the papers could be. It was an eye-opener.'

Their youngest daughter, Diana, had married distillery manager James Wolfe Murray in June 1962 and Elizabeth had arranged the wedding. With the birth of Diana's daughter, Fiona, in April 1964, Elizabeth became a grandmother. She 'was mad keen on grandchildren' and was delighted that mother and child stayed at No. 10 for three months. She regularly took Fiona on her visits to the secretaries in the Garden Room for chats, catch-ups on their personal lives, and cups of tea, and wheeled Fiona unobtrusively in her pram through St James's Park. Sometimes after a formal dinner at No. 10, she brought Fiona down and put her on the rug, 'and everyone would break down and chat', Marjory Wright remembers.

For a couple so devoted to the countryside, the prime ministerial residence at Chequers was a godsend. Alec appreciated 'the rolling countryside clothed with beech woods' and the gardens to the south and front of the house 'filled with a wide variety of species roses by Lady Eden'.[65] Elizabeth liked Chequers, and got on, as always, with the staff, but, as at Dorneywood, she 'felt a bit restricted'. While it was convenient if there was a large lunch or dinner party because, Caroline says, 'she didn't have to worry, she didn't actually have to *do* it . . . on the other hand, she was always worried that it wasn't going to be done quite as she would have liked it' because she 'wasn't the boss – not in a "bossy" sense – but it wasn't their house'. Home particularly relished a personal family connection with one of the treasures of Chequers – a ring kept in the Long Gallery which had been given immediately after Queen Elizabeth I's death to the first Lord Home by James I, as a mark of his esteem and a reward for his services.

There were frequent visits from dignitaries and foreign statesmen, including Robert Kennedy, and during the Commonwealth Heads of Government Conference in 1964 most of the leaders went there to dine and stay the night. When at 10.30 in the evening one of them suddenly announced that he had to return to London on urgent business, transport was hurriedly arranged – after which four or five other prime ministers decided that they, too, must get back. Dr Hastings Banda, the President of Malawi, stayed on 'but could scarcely conceal his merriment . . . He said that the curtained Elizabethan four-poster beds had so scared them that they were afraid to sleep in them.'[66]

After the general election was announced for 15 October 1964, Elizabeth launched into the campaign, travelling alongside Alec during their nationwide tours. The Conservatives had made up the large gap of 12 points behind Labour when Home took over in 1963: by September 1964 polls showed the Conservatives 2.9 per cent ahead of Labour, which would give them a win by 80 seats, though Wilson was well ahead of Home in personal popularity.[67] By 7 October the overall Tory lead had dropped to below 1 per cent and the situation was tense.[68] Home often faced noisy barracking at meetings; on one occasion in Birmingham, he was completely drowned out by steady chanting from Labour supporters. On another, it was reported, Elizabeth had to be saved from the crowd, prompting journalist George Gale to write in admiration of her 'stoic calm and craggy dignity, and determination never to let the side down . . . If I wore a cap,' he declared, 'I would be doffing it to Lady Douglas-Home.' She had endured 'with the utmost aplomb the slings and arrows of outrageous opposition, innumerable uncomfortable seats on lorries, cars, flower-decked platforms and in the backs of cars, aircraft and helicopters'.[69]

By election day, the parties were running neck and neck: 'It isn't the end of the world if we lose,' said Elizabeth sanely.[70] News that China had exploded an atomic bomb, and that Soviet Premier Khrushchev had been ousted from power was announced that evening, but was eclipsed by the election drama. As the results came through, gloom descended on the family gathered at Downing Street. Alec got up at 2 a.m. 'and went grinning off to bed, saying it would be a dead heat as far as he could see', Elizabeth's sister Vin reported. Lorne Roper-Caldbeck 'kept thinking it feels a bit like a wake'. The unexpected loss of Brighton Kemptown to Labour by only seven votes after seven recounts (the Conservative candidate had allegedly been in Scotland trying to find the Loch Ness monster during part of the campaign, while the entire Women's Conservative Association had decided to go ahead with their pre-booked shopping trip to Calais on the day) was the final straw. The name of Kemptown would be to him as that of Calais was to Mary Tudor, Home was later reported to have said.[71] Labour won with an overall majority of only four seats. Elizabeth's dismay was greater than she had anticipated: 'She was deeply disappointed,' Oliver Wright recalls, 'but both of them had the strength of character to know it wasn't the end of the world, [and] they didn't mope'.

The Homes had been in Downing Street for only eleven months. On 16 October, within hours of tendering his resignation to the Queen (when protocol dictated that an official car took the retiring Prime Minister to the Palace, but he had to provide his own transport back), the Homes were packed up and ready to make the hurried and undignified exit from their home which is the fate of all Britain's prime ministers and their spouses. After tea in the drawing room in the flat, where Elizabeth fielded phone calls from well-wishers (including Alec's brother William who, assuming life went on, rang with a hot tip for the 3.30 race that day), they said goodbye to the assembled staff. Many were in tears. All the secretaries from the Garden Room, who had felt so included in the family and were devoted to Elizabeth, came to the office wearing blue: 'I'm afraid they were very naughty . . . and it was announced in the press that this had happened and it was not a good start,' Oliver Wright remembers.

The couple left by the garden gate carrying a few possessions and a rolled-up umbrella, with photographers milling around to record their departure and the sounds of cheering in the background as the Wilsons arrived at the front door. Home left a hurried note addressed to 'the Prime Minister' in an envelope containing the key to his dispatch box. As was the custom, they spent the weekend at Chequers, before returning to clear up the flat the following Monday. In the absence of a London residence, the chairman of the Savoy hotel group, Hugh Wontner, offered them a penthouse suite at Claridges until they found a small flat in Victoria.

With their departure from No. 10 the Homes felt some relief that the pressures were now reduced. Alec agreed to stay on as Conservative leader, despite his reservations; he had been brought in to restore confidence in the Party but had ultimately presided over its electoral defeat. After so long in power, the Tories were unfamiliar with their new role: 'None of us were accustomed to Opposition – we didn't know quite how to handle it,' Home commented later.[72] Though he sparkled in debate with Wilson in the House, there was murmuring among a minority of younger MPs that he was not forceful enough, and from January 1965 moves were afoot to seek a new leader.

When, in July 1965, he decided to resign it was the only occasion on which Elizabeth strongly disagreed with him: 'He thought it was right and I think she had doubts,' says Antony Acland. 'She thought he should have stayed on. Because in a way, resigning could have been taken as an admission of failure. I mean, he so nearly won the election, didn't he? Against all the odds . . . And I think she thought he'd actually done rather well to have got as near to winning as he did and therefore there was no particular need to hand over.' His colleague Selwyn

Lloyd recalled a dinner shortly afterwards: 'Elizabeth was very angry that he had done it. She didn't think it at all necessary. I agreed with her. Alec was quite unmoved.'[73] Elizabeth accepted the decision. In Alec's farewell speech to the Party, he expressed his appreciation for the trust and confidence they had shown in him, and in his wife, 'who has been my constant ally. I'm not sure she shouldn't have been leader of the Party.'[74]

Their life in politics continued; when Edward Heath became leader in 1965, he appointed Alec as Shadow Foreign Secretary. When the Conservatives were returned to power in June 1970, Alec again became Foreign Secretary. That October, Elizabeth was appointed the first-ever Lady Fellow of Eton College, which she considered a great and unexpected honour. They spent another four years at the Foreign Office. For Elizabeth it was a return to the familiar beat of diplomatic entertaining and overseas trips, and working again with old friends in the Private Office. She had lost none of her earlier enthusiasm, and at 61, with several grandchildren, she was still tireless in her care for people and her attention to the details of everyday official and domestic life. Her quick wit could still lift the most dour or formal occasions.

Their schedule was again demanding. In 1972 they made the first trip to China by a British Foreign Secretary since the 1949 Revolution, following US President's Nixon's historic visit six months earlier. At the final fourteen-course banquet in the Great Hall of the People's Republic in Peking, the Foreign Office team were astonished when the Chinese played the Eton Boating Song and Scottish bagpipe tunes from the Borders, and Elizabeth and Alec walked together up the full length of the hall to thank the band.

As the Conservatives were facing defeat in the February 1974 election, Home considered his future. Aged 70, it was time to go: 'I'm afraid it's the end of the road,' he said to Antony Acland on a walk in Richmond Park, 'but it's been great fun.' He resigned his parliamentary seat on 10 March and departed the House of Commons. In November 1974 he was offered a life peerage and returned to the House of Lords as a respected elder statesman; he spoke in debates, usually watched by Elizabeth, and was often consulted, including by the new leader, Margaret Thatcher, for his wisdom and judgement of the issues of the day.

Elizabeth now acquired her final title, Lady Home of the Hirsel. Their son David had married Jane Williams-Wynne at St Margaret's, Westminster, in October 1972. Soon more grandchildren arrived, which added to Elizabeth's enormous pleasure in their expanding family. They lived in a series of small flats in Victoria, with Elizabeth doing the housekeeping, organising, typing, keeping up with their friends, family and former political colleagues, and filling her scrapbooks with photos of the children, grandchildren and one great-grandchild. Her energy was undiminished – a hip operation slowed her down only a little – and they continued to travel between London and Scotland. But Caroline remembers that in July 1990, when Elizabeth was 80, 'they both came back from London saying "we've *had* London" – I think they were both getting very tired'.

In August they went to Douglas for the annual family shooting holiday. When Meriel saw her, 'she was in a very happy mood, really very happy'. On 3 September she had breakfast and chatted to Alec before he went out on the moors. Then Elizabeth went up to her room and had a massive heart attack. She died within eight hours.

Tributes followed from all over the world. Mrs Thatcher praised 'the goodness and kindness' which 'radiated from Elizabeth to all the people she came in contact with'. At her memorial service in Westminster Abbey, Lord Charteris paid moving tribute to Elizabeth's profound belief in God, her 'commanding intelligence', her 'all-embracing heart' and the 'shrewd political insight built on realism and an understanding of people' which had made her the perfect political partner to Alec for fifty-five years.

After the memorial service, Alec went to stay with his brother William, and while there he suffered another small stroke, but returned to Scotland before Christmas. He never recovered from Elizabeth's death. 'I used to go and see him,' says Antony Acland. 'He had the sparkle, but I think he was lost without her.' He died at the Hirsel on 9 October 1995. His memorial service, held at St Giles Cathedral, had been organised entirely by Elizabeth before her death. It was the final act of her devotion to a man with whom she shared complete trust, whom she adored and with whom she had lived a lifetime's partnership of rare understanding. In death as in life, she smoothed his path. She was, as *The Times* noted, 'an outstanding example of how a wife can share her husband's statesmanship'. Harold Macmillan gave her the intriguing and perhaps the best accolade: 'Elizabeth I would have made PM, if I could!'[75]

Chapter Four

Mary Wilson

1964–70, 1974–76

The Labour victory in 1964 marked a huge change in the direction, and style, of British political life. Harold Wilson arrived with a sense of mission, determined that socialism should make its mark after thirteen years of Tory rule, that his government should be one of technological and social modernisation. And it was not just the policies that changed, but the people too. In contrast to the aristocratic allegiances of the Edens, Macmillans and Homes, the Labour leader who came to power, and his wife Mary, came from a class that had made its voice heard loudly in British politics since the mid-nineteenth century, the powerful working-class and bourgeois tradition of provincial Nonconformism, which had provided a host of educationalists, reformers, trade union leaders and fighting politicians. The Wilsons' background, attitudes – and approach to No. 10 – could not have been more different from their predecessors'.

In Liverpool, on 14 October 1964, the day before the general election, Harold Wilson made his most forceful speech of the campaign. Mary was with him on the platform, as was the aged Lord Attlee, Labour's leader in the 1945 victory. 'We are engaged in a crusade,' Wilson declared. As they returned to the Adelphi Hotel, they were jostled and cheered by the crowds. 'It was very exciting,' Mary remembers. 'Harold was borne away by people. I remember going down the steps of the Town Hall in Liverpool and my feet didn't touch the ground because I was hemmed in. And then we went to the Adelphi Hotel and they opened the windows, and all the crowds [were] down below.' Two thousand people were chanting 'Wilson' and, echoing the Beatles, 'We love him. Yeah, Yeah, Yeah'.[1]

The campaign had been exhilarating but gruelling, and the outcome was still uncertain, even though most polls predicted a small Labour lead. As Mary and Harold toured his Huyton constituency on election day there was a feeling of optimism: 'a sense of something new happening – the "time for a change" mood enveloped everything', Marcia Williams (later Marcia Falkender), Wilson's Political Secretary, recalls. But there was caution among the inner team who watched the results on television later that evening. The election was turning into a cliffhanger. When Wilson returned to Huyton for the count and heard that he had trebled his majority, he jubilantly kissed Mary twice – the second time for the cameras – but then lost her in milling crowds, and shouted 'Is my wife there?'[2] Despite his personal victory, Wilson's early evening prediction of a 20-seat majority was steadily downgraded as more results came through. After a few hours' sleep, they caught the early train to London. While the Wilsons dozed, the Labour team crouched anxiously over a transistor radio. By the time they reached Nuneaton, Wilson was gloomily predicting that Labour had lost by one seat. 'I was very much afraid that Harold would step into the train ahead and step out at Euston with Labour well behind,' wrote Marcia.[3]

That afternoon, as the Wilsons waited at Labour Party headquarters at Transport House the result came in giving Labour an overall majority of four. As Sir Alec Douglas-Home emerged from No. 10 announcing, 'I'm going to see the Queen', his two private detectives discreetly detached themselves from him and made their way to Transport House to join his successor. Summoned by the Queen to form a government, Wilson, with Mary and their eldest son Robin, drove to the Palace wearing, not the traditional morning coat, but a black jacket and striped trousers. Following behind in a second car, and again breaking precedent, was his family – Harold's father, Herbert, and sister, Marjorie. While Harold was with the Queen, Palace staff chatted to Mary and the family in the Equerry's room.

When they arrived at Downing Street they found it packed with cheering supporters. The noise outside contrasted with the silence in the hall of No. 10. Members of the Private Office staff swept Wilson off to the Cabinet Room to begin the business of government. Nobody was there to greet Mary; everyone had disappeared: 'I felt really unwelcomed. It all went quiet and we went in and there was nobody there. And Grandpa said, "I'd like to see this place," so we said, "Would somebody show us around?" And one of the messengers showed us around.'

There was a certain amount of tension at the start of the new regime. The Labour government's small majority generated a feeling of impermanence, a sense that this could be a mere interruption to rule by the Conservatives, who were, by many, considered the 'natural party of government': 'The atmosphere at No. 10 was ice cold and very restrained. We were treated as ships passing in the night,' Marcia Williams decided.[4] The Principal Private Secretary, Derek Mitchell, recalls the 'utter gloom' of election night, 'with a large number of the supporting staff, I mean the garden girls and typists and so on actually in tears' at the departure of the Homes. To the civil service staff, after so many years of Conservative rule the Labour successors were as yet an unknown quantity.

For Mary Wilson, the move to No. 10 was a major upheaval in an ordered life. Up till then, she had kept her family life largely separate from the hurly-burly of politics. Delighted as she was with her husband's success, the prospect of leaving her secure home in Hampstead Garden Suburb to enter the unfamiliar portals of power was not appealing. On the Monday after the election, she went to No. 10 and encountered Elizabeth Douglas-Home who was doing the final clearing of their possessions. In the bathroom, Elizabeth's secretary, Lorne Roper-Caldbeck, recalls, 'We were giggling away, and there was a knock on the door and one of the messengers appeared and said, "Oh, Lady Home, excuse me, but I have Mrs Wilson here." And Mrs Wilson, she looked more nervous than we did, she was sweet, she said, "I'm so sorry to intrude", and they sat down and had a chat.' Elizabeth Douglas-Home, Mary remembers, 'was lovely . . . and she showed me round everything, was really very sweet . . . and Alec was lovely – a real gentleman, as they say, and was very, very helpful'.

For the first few weeks, Harold commuted from Hampstead Garden Suburb to Downing Street as Mary arranged for their furniture and belongings to be stored before their house was let to a tenant. At half-term in November she moved to what she would resolutely call, not a home, but 'a flat in a very big office building'. No. 10 is no ordinary flat, surrounded as it is by an organisation geared entirely to the needs of the office of the Prime Minister. Here, Mary found, the family's interests often get overlooked by those concentrating on the affairs of state. The spotlight shone into their private lives from the start. Banks of press photographers recorded the arrival at the front door of Robin's harmonium, Mary's furniture and the cat, Nemo, in its basket. Downing Street 'put her on her mettle' from the moment of her unpromising welcome.

Gladys Mary Baldwin was born on 12 January 1916, the second child and only daughter of Daniel Baldwin, a Lancashire-born Congregational minister who worked in Dugdale's cotton mill in Burnley from the age of 12 to help support his family. He achieved his ambition of becoming a minister only by studying in his spare time, with his books propped up against the loom. He was 29 before he went to college. Mary's mother, Sarah Bentley, a fair-haired, merry woman, also worked at the mill, running four looms. 'They were both very strict, puritanical, but they were devoted parents,' says Mary.

Religion was at the core of her upbringing. When Gladys, as she was then known, was born, her parents were living at Diss in Norfolk. As a small child, she attended chapel up to five times on Sunday and listened to her father who 'used to preach a rousing sermon', which gave her a lasting appreciation of a good speech. The discipline of religion ensured that, as well as learning much of the Bible by heart, she developed a strong social conscience and learned the virtues of reticence and humility: 'I had been brought up in a tradition in which showing-off was frowned upon, and in which the Bible was taken literally.'[5] Even speaking-out had rules: 'Time to a man is more than cash,' she remembered her father quoting, 'so waste it not in talking trash. But in few words say all you require, and then without delay retire.'[6]

The itinerant nature of her father's life as a minister meant that Mary never had a settled home. When she was five, the family moved to the small village of Fulbourn in Cambridgeshire, where the congregation consisted of mainly poor rural labourers. She and her brother Clifford, two years older than her, were invited to the local manor house where, on Empire Day, they would 'have a free tea and tug-of-war and tilting-the-buckets. We all dressed up in red, white and blue.' A streak of rebellion emerged when, aged seven, she founded a club called 'the Rebels' – 'I've always been a bit of a rebel,' she says, yet in her memory of this period, under the big East Anglian skies, 'it was always summer'.

Mary went to the village school, but it was at home in the pale brick Victorian manse, where there was no electricity, water came from a pump and they lived frugally on the minister's small income, that she developed an interest in reading. By the time she was eleven she had read all the classics. Since the age of six she had been writing her own verse, inspired 'by the splendid imagery of the Bible' and the hymns she sang in the small white chapel. Later she wrote of Fulbourn and her family in a poem, 'The Old Manse' – her mother baking bread, hens clucking at her feet, her brother riding his bicycle, and her father reading the Bible.

She was wrenched from this rural life at the age of 10 when her father's job took him to Hucknall, a mining town in Nottinghamshire – 'where Byron's buried, although his heart's out in Greece', she points out. Here, 'everything was covered with soot, black from the pits . . . There was a pall of smoke all over the town the whole time, and the miners used to come up black from the pits and all you could see were their gleaming teeth and their eyes.' Mary grew to love the congrega-- tion of miners, and later enjoyed above all other events the splendour of the Durham Miners' Gala with the parade, the silk banners, the drums and the marching bands. But being uprooted from the countryside had a disastrous effect. Within a short time she fell seriously ill. Nobody knew what was wrong with her but she withdrew to her bed and stopped eating: 'I was convinced I was going to die.' She got into the habit of reading, and writing poetry. It was a year before her health improved. Then, at 12, she was awarded a bursary for the daughters of ministers to a Congregational school, Milton Mount College, in Sussex. Here, living among fellow students, many from backgrounds similar to her own, she 'gained a stone the first term', she recalls. 'It was the country air and getting away from the mining town.'

At school she had a good general education in a romantic setting – a country mansion 'with silk on the walls and great big heavy mahogany doors with gold handles – it was a beautiful place to go to school'. It was also high-minded, dedicated to training the girls to be 'wives, mothers, teachers and missionaries', and to 'love unselfish work and Christian usefulness'.[7] Her education included drama and music and she was a compulsive reader. Emily Brontë was her favourite – *Wuthering Heights* the book she later chose to take with her on *Desert Island Discs*.

From very early on, she says, 'I always wanted to write.' She had won prizes for her Empire Day essays, had written short stories (though she thought they were terrible) and was determined to write novels. There was never any question of her going to university, which she later regretted, although at the time she accepted the prevalent belief that university was for the sons of the family, especially when income was short. 'I got my School Certificate and that was it,' she says, though her brother, Clifford, won a scholarship to Cambridge to study Electrical Engineering and went on to become a professor.

She left school at 16 and took a course in shorthand, typing and bookkeeping at the Gregg School in Carlisle, travelling each day from her parents' home, then in Penrith, by train – 'with frost on the windows, oh it was cold'. Despite a good qualification there was no work to be had in Penrith so she 'went sadly' south, found digs with a family on the Wirral in Cheshire and, at 18, took a job as shorthand typist at 24 shillings a week with Lever Brothers at Port Sunlight. Her romantic view of the world now 'took a few hard knocks'. In the mid-1930s, with unemployment high in the North – she had seen the hunger marchers pass through Penrith – she says, 'you were expected to feel very grateful for having a job at all'.

Mary joined the company tennis club, and it was here that she met the young Harold Wilson. Two months her junior, he was still a schoolboy at the Wirral Grammar School working for his Higher School Certificate exams. Harold had taken time off from revising to go and watch his father, Herbert, do one of his renowned mental arithmetic tricks (he could work out the square root of telephone numbers, people said). On the way he passed the tennis court and caught sight of the extremely pretty, fair-haired, slightly-built Gladys Mary Baldwin. 'It suddenly became blindingly clear to me that life was not designed for cramming the words of long dead poets, but that there was another world,' he wrote.[8] 'He came up and he caught my eye,' Mary recalls. 'I saw him looking at me, that was all.' Harold later admitted it was love at first sight – 'It really was, you know. She looked lovely in white'[9] – but Gladys was not as readily smitten. The following weekend, Harold 'invested fifteen shillings in a tennis racquet and another pound in membership of the club. A week later we both laid up our racquets and began "walking out" together.'[10]

Within three weeks, Harold had made up his mind that he was going to marry her. Mary was not so sure, but Harold 'of course had it all worked out. He was going to go to Oxford, and then he was going to become a don, and then when he was 30 he would stand for parliament.' Mary took little notice – 30 seemed such a long way off. She knew little about politics, apart from the old-fashioned Nonconformist Liberalism of her parents: 'I think they thought the Labour Party wasn't quite respectable' – it was 'a bit revolutionary'.

Harold and Mary shared a Congregationalist upbringing, with chapel a punctuation point in their week. Though neither was by then a fervent believer, religion underlay their shared moral values. Mary was attracted to the earnest young scholar who was compared later to 'a lively fox terrier' with his quick wit, his tendency to boast, his inveterate talking and his fondness for jokes. They both liked music – Gilbert and Sullivan was Harold's particular favourite; he enjoyed quoting later from *Iolanthe* – 'the House of Peers, throughout the war / Did nothing in particular, and did it very well.' But there were differences. The Boy Scouts was for Harold a central part of family life and probably a formative influence: 'He was a King's Scout, of course – he *would* be, wouldn't he? With all the badges. I got one badge, that's all,' says Mary. But she respected him, all the same.

When Harold left for Jesus College, Oxford, in 1934 to study History, they wrote to each other regularly and she visited with his parents, Ethel and Herbert. Mary loved 'this beautiful mellow city with the wonderful towers and the lovely colleges and quads – oh, it was so beautiful'. They saw each other in the long vacations, and when they were 22, in summer 1938, Harold formally asked her father for her hand in marriage. He took her down to Oxford, and during a romantic punt ride on the river, he proposed. Mary moved into digs in Oxford and got a clerical job at the Potato Marketing Board.

Having graduated with a first-class degree, Harold was set on an academic career: 'When Harold told me he wanted to teach at Oxford I thought it was wonderful. My idea of heaven,' Mary later said. 'There's nothing I would have liked so much as being a don's wife . . . Very old buildings and very young people. There is everything anyone could want, music, theatre, congenial friends, all in a beautiful setting and within a fourpenny bus ride. It symbolised so much for me.'[11] He became a junior don at New College, then a Research Fellow at University College and was research assistant to the awesome and often irascible Sir William Beveridge (later the founding figure of the Welfare State), who reinforced Harold's already developed taste for long hours of intensive work. He also joined the University Labour Party – the first step in his political career.

The wedding took place on 1 January 1940 – the beginning of a week, the beginning of a year, and the beginning of an era, Mary says. As snow fell outside the chapel of Mansfield College, Mary, wearing a full-length white wedding dress of crêpe de Chine, a tulle veil and carrying a large bouquet of fern and carnations, promised, not to obey, but to cherish Harold. The college's Nonconformist Principal Dr Nathaniel Micklem, 'the only saint I've ever met', says Mary, presided over the ceremony, in which her father took part. Their organist friend John Webster played the academic march *Gaudeamus Igitur*, and in the congregation was Giles Alington, younger brother of Elizabeth Home and Harold's close friend from undergraduate days, who later became Dean of University College and after whom they would name their second son. The reception of a buffet and fruit cup was in keeping with the couple's modest tastes and Nonconformist tradition. Mary had taken the pledge at the age of eight and didn't have a drink until she was 20.

Their planned honeymoon in the Scilly Isles proved impossible in wartime, so they travelled through heavy snow in a car laden with books to stay at Minster Lovell, near Oxford. But the honeymoon was interrupted after five days when, Mary recalls, 'Beveridge telephoned and said, "A week's long enough for a honeymoon. Come back and get on with your work." So of course he did.' She hid her disappointment as they trudged back to their flat in Oxford, not yet registering that this was a foretaste of a married life in which her husband would frequently let his work take precedence over his private life.

Wartime Oxford teemed with a swollen population of students, civil servants, people engaged in 'work of national importance' and all the RAF men who came in from Abingdon in the evening to the pubs in Oxford: 'We had a wonderful time during the phoney war,' says Mary, echoing Clarissa Churchill's friends in the same town. But their stay was short-lived. Eager to play a role, Harold accepted a post in London as a research statistician, and they embarked on a new life in the un-familiar capital.

From their small flat in Twickenham, Harold travelled by train each day to work long hours in Whitehall, while Mary, a full-time house-wife, volunteered as an air raid warden during the heavy bombing raids. Even now, the sound of ice being swept up off the road 'reminds me of the next morning – all the glass windows had fallen out on the pave-ment – and people brushing up the glass. It still makes me shiver to hear it.' When the bombing got too much, she escaped to her in-laws in Cornwall, and then to Oxford, where Harold visited as often as he could, and later to her parents in Duxford, Cambridgeshire. Their elder son, Robin, was born in December 1943. Mary returned to London 'just in time for the buzz-bombs', she recalls. 'I used to climb on top of Robin in the cot in case the ceiling came down.'

In 1944 Harold was selected as the Labour candidate in the Ormskirk constituency. Meanwhile he returned with Mary to take up a fellow-ship at University College Oxford. Soon Mary had her first experience of electioneering in Ormskirk: 'When I went to my very first meeting, it was quiet and orderly and I said to Harold, wasn't it nice and quiet. He didn't think it was nice. It was too quiet and dull. The next meeting was terrible, I thought. A lot of shouting and anger and at the end of it, I found I was actually trembling. But he was delighted. That was a lesson to me. I stopped minding. Why should I mind if he didn't?'[12]

It was the start of a long life as a politician's wife. At the 1945 general election, Harold was returned with a comfortable majority, and within a week he was offered the post of Parliamentary Secretary to the Minister of Works. Mary stayed in Oxford and Harold came down when he could. As for many young couples after the war, it took time to get back to a settled life. Mary adjusted to the routine life of an MP's wife, who may see her husband rarely during the week if she remains in the family home rather than moving to London.

In September 1947, the Wilsons' holiday in Cornwall was interrupted by a phone call from Chequers, where Prime Minister Clem Attlee offered Harold the Cabinet post of President of the Board of Trade. 'The Lad from Huddersfield – Britain's White Hope – at 31', the *Daily Mirror* proclaimed of this 'bluff and tough' prodigy who had 'a genius for figures'.[13] He was the youngest Cabinet minister since 1806, and

Mary the youngest wife. The increased salary of £5,000 at last made a more settled life possible. With Mary now expecting their second child, they bought a three-bedroomed house in Hampstead Garden Suburb, where they lived for the next sixteen years. On their eighth wedding anniversary, 1 January 1948, they left Oxford after giving a small party centred on a tin of caviare which Harold had brought back from a Board of Trade trip to Russia.

After a childhood without a permanent home followed by constant disruption during and after the war, the house at No. 10 Southway was for Mary a haven, and became a fortress. In May 1948 she gave birth to their second son, Giles. Clem Attlee and his wife Violet were the godparents at his christening in the crypt of the House of Commons. The romantic Mary got on well with the austere Attlee. He once asked her, 'Who are the people that you most admire in history?' and I said, 'Charles II, Bonnie Prince Charlie, Rupert of the Rhine, Lord Byron.' And there was a pause, and he said, 'Bad history. Wrong people.'

While Mary embedded herself in the orderly life of Hampstead Garden Suburb, building friendships with neighbours, attending the Free Church and caring for her small children, Harold came home each evening bearing his ministerial red box. A friend from that time, Marjorie Kay, recalled Mary as 'small and slim. Her blue eyes, fair hair and fine skin made a first impression of extreme femininity . . . I discovered that Mary had a quick sense of humour, mischievous yet compassionate, a complete lack of any pretension and a set of values which were able to resist any kind of seduction . . . It was quite surprising to find so much strength of will existing beneath an outward appearance of feminine charm . . . A high regard for politeness made her a good listener to well-meant advice, but she was equally polite in disregarding it.'[14]

After a while she employed an au pair so that she could go with Harold to the constituency, which she always enjoyed, to the Labour Party annual conferences, and to the House of Commons to listen to his speeches. She campaigned with him during the 1950 general election when he was elected to represent the constituency of Huyton, near Liverpool (boundary changes had altered the Ormskirk constituency). With a tiny majority and the government in constant danger of sudden defeat, unlike the radical changes enacted during the first parliament much of the legislation was uncontroversial. But when Nye Bevan, Labour's former Minister of Health, then Minister of Labour, resigned over Cabinet proposals to introduce charges for false teeth and spectacles, Wilson, after some anguish, followed suit: 'Mary remembers how I agonised about my own resignation, walking up and down the bedroom floor all night trying to make up my mind,' Wilson wrote.[15] 'I went to him and said, "Harold, I think you ought to resign,"' Mary recalled.[16] Next day she watched from the Gallery as he made his resignation speech and discovered that 'nobody loves you when you resign and your own Party treats you as if you're invisible, so it was a bit sad'.

That evening Churchill's aide, Brendan Bracken, sought Wilson out, 'charged, he said, "by the greatest living statesman, for that is what Mr Churchill is", to give me a message to convey to my wife', Wilson wrote: 'His concern was with my wife, an innocent party in these affairs, who would undoubtedly suffer in consequence. He recalled the number of occasions his wife had suffered as a result of his own political decisions. Would I therefore convey to Mary his personal sympathy and understanding? Thanking Bracken, I went home. It was about 1 a.m. I repeated the message to Mary, which was greeted with gratitude and tears. I was enjoined to express her personal thanks.' Next day, when he found Winston 'in the Smoke Room on his favourite settee', he expressed Mary's thanks. 'Immediately . . . tears flooded down his face, as he expatiated on the way that wives had to suffer for their husbands' political actions, going on to recall a number of instances over a long life.' When Wilson got home at 2 a.m., Mary was still awake, and he recounted the exchange. She again burst into tears, and Harold 'was moved to say that whereas two days earlier I had been a minister of the Crown, red box and all, now I was reduced to the position of a messenger between her and Winston Churchill, each of whom burst into tears at the receipt of a message from the other'.[17]

After Labour's defeat in the 1951 general election, a steadier domestic life became possible. Theirs was, and remained, a tightly knit family group. 'There was always lots and lots of laughter and lots and lots of jokes . . . We were always making jokes,' their son, Robin, remembers. ('[Harold] had a wicked sense of humour for puns,' his wife, Joy Crispin Wilson adds.) 'And there was a lot of singing when we were growing up.' Mary joined Robin in the School Choral Society and each Sunday evening they 'listened to *Sunday Half Hour* followed by *Your Hundred Best Tunes*,' on the wireless, usually singing along with the band. The whole family was fond of light classical music. Robin, who later wrote books about Gilbert and Sullivan, recalls: 'They took me to the *Mikado* when I was eight. I quite enjoyed that. And then they took me when I was 12 to *Yeomen of the Guard*, because the Golders Green Hippodrome was just walking distance from where we lived.' Robin remembers how his parents kept politics at a distance: 'They encouraged us to come to our own conclusions on things, they never shoved it down our throats.' Though Mary was outwardly calm, she could be passionate in defence of her family: 'If anybody attacked the family, I'd be out after them like mad,' she says. When she had time, she wrote poems about her feelings, her children and her sharp observations of the natural world – 'whatever happens to be my mood at the moment'.

As the Labour Party engaged in virtual civil war during the 1950s, Harold and Mary stood aloof. Neither was interested in social entertaining, and Harold did not have any political friends as such, he said: 'Politically I've been very much on my own.'[18] Mary participated in politics to the extent of her interest, and in so far as she could help Harold. Marcia Williams remembers that, then and later, Harold discussed politics as well as the family with Mary, and he respected her views. 'He took all his affairs home and used to chatter about them . . . He didn't want to go against anything that she believed in . . . He would say, "Mary's right", and we all used to say, "Oh yes, quite right." . . . And he placed such an emphasis on it that anybody who got into her bad books got into his bad books – because I know! . . . Yes, he was a little frightened of her.' Mary believed that 'every wife has a right, a duty, to influence her husband, especially if he has any power'. But she says lightly, 'I used to say whatever I thought to Harold. But he wasn't listening half the time anyway so it didn't make any difference' – an experience shared by many of his advisers.[19]

At party conferences Mary met Harold's political colleagues. Nye Bevan and Jennie Lee they counted as friends, along with Barbara Castle and Richard Crossman: 'We always sat together and plotted away! Barbara was a great plotter! . . . We had a lot of fun,' Mary says, though she tended to observe rather than participate: 'I sat in. I didn't open my mouth. I was considered to be "the wise old owl who sat in the oak, and the more she heard the less she spoke",' but to some she gave the impression of being unhappy or shy. 'I'm not shy at all,' she later insisted. 'I'm reserved. Harold likes a lot of people around. I'm a loner . . . I'm very happy alone.'[20] She went regularly with him to the constituency and visited the Labour clubs there – 'which was terrific'. A Labour official, Ron Hayward, recalled her at regional events: 'She never pushed herself forward, but she was very popular, one of his greatest assets, first class. The women would take to her. She could talk children, she could talk anything.'[21]

Marcia Williams first met Mary at a political dinner in 1956: 'She was amazingly good-looking . . . I was taken by her because you are, very much so. She was very pretty, very small – small and very dainty. Mary danced with my husband . . . [She was] an amazingly good dancer. You just sat there and were riveted by it.' Marcia Williams, as she then was, had recently become Wilson's private secretary after working at Labour headquarters at Transport House. A 24-year-old recent graduate in history from Queen Mary College, London, married to a fellow undergraduate Ed Williams, she had chosen to work for Wilson because she admired his energy and modernising zeal and saw him as a rising star in the Party. With a keen political brain but no ambition to be a politician herself, she later became his political adviser, admired by many of Wilson's colleagues for her acute judgement and political acumen, though some found her abrasive nature difficult to handle. She became a mainstay in the Wilsons' life as she organised Harold's diary, ran his office, liaised between office and home, and helped Mary find her way: 'She knew more about the Civil Service and people like that than I did . . . [and] she made it very important that when I went around with Harold, I was given my place,' Mary says.

Mary kept in touch with the issues of the day, but she disliked the political skulduggery. 'I was interested in ideas, but not in the manoeuvring for position that goes on,' she explains. Never happy with confrontation, she was often appalled at the cut and thrust of House of Commons debate which she watched from the Gallery: 'I used to get very upset – not only for Harold but for any of them,' she said later. During the Profumo debate in 1963, she watched Harold Macmillan at the dispatch box 'looking so wan and frail, and he made that famous remark about,

"I don't see many young people these days", something like that, and the howling that broke out was terrible. And I thought, "if that was me, I'd just about totter out of the Chamber and go home and collapse." Ten minutes later, as I was going home, I caught sight of Mr Macmillan just behind the Speaker's chair, laughing and joking with somebody or other, and I thought I'd rarely seen him looking so well. Well I thought, "If *they* don't mind, why should I?"'[22]

Mary rarely expressed her views in public, even though she felt strongly on some issues. 'Politics makes me unhappy from time to time,' she said later. 'Your heart tells you to do something and your head tells you not to – it's a terrible tug-of-war really.'[23] She once described herself as 'a natural radical'. Over the H-bomb and unilateral nuclear disarmament, which dramatically divided the Party and the country in the late 1950s, she supported the Campaign for Nuclear Disarmament. Harold, then Shadow Chancellor of the Exchequer, did not. In the volatile atmosphere in the Labour Party at the time she never spoke out: 'I wanted to go on the first CND march. It was Easter [1958] . . . the first one, they walked out to Aldermaston with Canon Collins and Michael Foot and Barbara Castle, and I remember saying, "I ought to be with them, I ought to be with them!" But my mother was staying and I had the children – and I couldn't . . . I never went. I just wore the badge. I've still got my CND badge. It was just in my head. You see, I wasn't a joiner, I'm afraid.' Instead she expressed her feelings in a poem, 'After the Bomb':

> After the Bomb had fallen,
> After the last sad cry
> When the Earth was a burnt-out cinder
> Drifting across the sky,
>
> Came Lucifer, Son of the Morning,
> With his fallen-angel band,
> Silent and swift as a vulture
> On the mountain-top to stand.
>
> And he looked, as he stood on the mountain
> With his scarlet wings unfurled,
> At the charnel-house of London
> And the cities of the world.

And he laughed . . .

And as that mocking laughter
Across the heavens ran,
He cried 'Look!' to the fallen angels –
'This is the work of *Man*
Who was made in the image of God!'[24]

Her views about the place of women were also clear. 'Women aren't having a square deal, I still think it's a man's world and that women don't get a fair chance of making themselves economically independent. Wives in particular don't get a square deal. I got on a plane to the United States eighteen months ago. The plane was full of men having a good lunch and drinking champagne, and I said to myself, yes, and I wonder what expense accounts you allow your wives back home, washing the clothes, stoking the boiler and keeping the children amused,' she told an interviewer in 1965. She was 'all for women having careers' but 'if they want to be married, whether they have careers or not, they must be *wives* as well . . . so long as they are wives they must not compete with their husbands, they must help them . . . There are ways in which women can show love and affection and concern which men can't.'[25]

When Harold later promoted women to his Cabinet, Mary – who had no doubt that 'women make very good politicians' – was delighted. Marcia Falkender believes it was due to Mary's influence that Harold had such respect for women's abilities, enjoyed their company and was noted for treating them with consideration and kindness: 'He loved women,' Barbara Castle said. 'He loved their company, believed in them',[26] and was a natural egalitarian.

In public, Mary's identity was defined by Harold's life. Her refuge was in her family and in poetry. Then another channel opened up for her after 1952, when she and Harold for the first time visited the Scilly Isles, which they loved, and returned to each holiday. When the Duchy of Cornwall offered some land for sale, Harold bought a plot and built a three-bedroomed bungalow which they completed in 1959 and called Lowenva – Cornish for 'House of Happiness'. For Mary, it carried strong symbolic significance. Bought in her name, it gave her a sense of independence: 'It was always my bungalow.' Away from the pressures of London and politics, she could be herself. The family enjoyed the place, where they spent uninterrupted time together, eventually three times a year. They felt part of the small mixed community, made staunch friends, 'and no one asks you political questions', Mary said.

For Mary it felt like home: 'You know everybody, and you can't be grand or self-important in Scilly. And it was the sort of society that I was used to when my father was a minister in the village . . . the sort of society that I'm happy in.' Surrounded by the sea and a sensuous natural beauty, she felt renewed. The air, as you walk off the helicopter, smells like wine, she says. She remembers going one morning early on a boat to Tresco: 'the sand was fresh and damp and white as far as you could see, and everything was very still and peaceful, but alive, very alive at the same time. Life without conflict. It was like the beginning of the world.'[27]

When Harold was elected Party leader after the death of Hugh Gaitskell in January 1963, Mary found her life again transformed. She was proud of him: 'I did what he wanted, and if that was what he wanted I did everything I could to help him. But what I wanted didn't so much come into it. It was wonderful for *him*.' Now, as he struggled to unite the Party and to establish his public profile as a man of simple tastes who could connect with the ordinary voter, Mary was even more careful not to put a foot wrong, or say anything that would rock the boat. She found it difficult 'not to say what I really thought . . . It's so easy to say the wrong thing.' With opinion polls showing Labour around 12 points ahead of Douglas-Home's Conservatives in spring 1964,[28] Wilson had the air of a prime minister in waiting – a leader from a different mould: a man from a modest provincial background, and the first graduate from a grammar school to reach that position.

By the early 1960s the old hierarchical order was beginning to crack as new 'meritocrats' came of age. Wilson appealed to a nation seeking solutions to the problems of a rapidly changing Britain. A brilliant showman, he translated socialism into the rhetoric of modernisation, which would harness under-used talent to the task of regeneration. It was the technocrat and specialist, not the amateur, in every field of national life who, he believed, would mobilise the opportunities which science and technology, allied with rising affluence, had opened up. The message chimed with the growing sense of optimism and a willingness to embrace the 'new', to break down old barriers, instil purpose into politics, be rid of deference in the pursuit of egalitarianism and – among the young – to march and dance to a different, more vibrant tune offered by rock and roll, the Beatles, and the singer Bob Dylan, for whom 'the times they are a-changing'.

During the 1964 general election campaign Mary was excited and involved as she toured the country with Harold and his team, facing the crowds and the cameras, though she confessed: 'As we walk to the platform I have a curious feeling. I always have it. I feel like the invisible woman. I feel their eyes sliding across me as if I wasn't there, straight across to him. They want to see him, not me. Sometimes they call to me, things like, "Take care of him, look after him, we need him." It's marvellous and heartening. But I don't really need to take care of him. Only to be there.'[29] When the Labour Party won, she welcomed the victory and was proud for Harold: 'Obviously for his sake she wanted it all to work out OK,' but 'she was as nervous as, of course, we all were, because her life was going to change completely,' her son, Robin, recalls.

Moving into No. 10 was not an easy transition. Unlike her predecessors, she had no experience of high ministerial office, and no familiarity with the workings of the Civil Service machine or of living in an official government residence. But she was determined to do the job well, guided by a powerful sense of duty: 'If you're going to do it, you must jolly well do it to the best of your ability, or you're a bit of a wimp,' she told an interviewer. 'Of course, in the beginning, *everything* seemed strange . . . I got thrown in at the deep end.'[30] 'It was tougher at first than I thought it would be. I remember the first few days when I was physically sick every morning with the nervous tension involved. But slowly one gets used to it. When you're Prime Minister's wife you're very much on your mettle.'[31] She was 'inclined to flap a little' if she felt she was not doing the job properly – 'I make a mistake and then I wake up about three in the morning and start to think about it . . . I wish I were more like Harold. If Harold woke up at three in the morning, he'd say, "Good Lord. It's three o'clock in the morning. What am I doing awake?" And he'd turn over and go back to sleep at once.'[32]

It was a wrench to abandon her home. As Mary fitted into the larger

No. 10 machine, she felt control of her private life slipping from her: 'It's difficult, because you're translated from being a wife, mother, gardener, cook in your own little kingdom and plonked in that flat up there – you can't even hang a picture on the wall without asking permission of the Ministry of Works. And it is a big thing. And proud as you are of your husband and think it's absolutely wonderful, you yourself have to do it and it isn't easy.'

There was no one there to guide her through the maze. Like all prime ministers' spouses, Mary had to find her own way around. Nobody showed her the ropes. She invariably had to ask. The atmosphere was not unwelcoming, she says, 'except that I couldn't get to know anything'. She was upset that she didn't get her own letters – 'they used to go down to the office down below, and they said, "Well, Mrs Attlee always let her letters go down below", and I said, "Well, I want my own letters." So consequently I got all the death threats and everything, but I did have my own letters to go through for myself. They used to send pictures of graves.' At their first Christmas, the Wilsons were told that they personally had to pay for all Christmas cards and stamps; only after probing did they discover the previous custom – that the official machine paid for all cards except those to their political and personal friends.[33]

At first Mary was never included in the Prime Minister's official diary. 'They did send me the diary, but they didn't tell me when I was supposed to be there and what I was supposed to do. In the end I said, "Look, you must tell me if I'm supposed to be going," so they put "and Mrs Wilson" for anything I had to go to', though it took some time to put in place. Once she was included in the diary, she was not always briefed. After a trip with Harold in December 1964, when she arrived in Canada, and was taken alone to the Governor-General's residence with no idea of who he was or what was expected of her, she insisted that the Private Secretary who did Wilson's diary sat with her and told her anything that she wanted to know.

After these setbacks, Mary's style became quietly assertive. According to Marcia Falkender, she 'didn't change anything dramatically, she changed it little by little . . . and by assessing the staff. She looked at them all, and she knew which ones she could get really angry with, and which ones would try and do their best. In the end her will predominated, she would get what she wanted. She was very strong.'

Mary did little to alter the No. 10 flat. It had recently been renovated under Dorothy Macmillan and she did not wish to invite press criticism by incurring further expense. It was not a 'home', but she adapted to it, despite some inconvenient features. 'We had the little [kitchen] at the back of the flat, and of course there were several steps, and if you had to take a tea trolley through to the drawing room, you had to lift it up the steps.' She brought in her modern Swedish-design furniture and hung some of Harold's favourite L.S. Lowry paintings on the wall, but left everything else as it was.

Meanwhile she tried to rebuild family life. If Wilson's engagements allowed, he had lunch in the flat with her and, unless he was at the House of Commons, supper in the evening before settling into an armchair with his dispatch boxes, radio music humming quietly in the background. Robin stayed during his university vacations, when the sound of his harmonium would drift through the building. Giles, now 16, lived with them, and each morning Mary put on a headscarf and took him to the tube on his way to school. Anxious to protect the privacy of her younger son, who entered No. 10 through the front door and daily risked running the gauntlet of press photographers, Mary asked that he have a key to the rear garden gate. It was refused at first. So frustrated was she that 'she burst out crying when she was given the news [at a state occasion] that at last the security officer had handed her the key', Marcia recalls. (The garden gate is now closed for security reasons.)

By this time prime ministers only rarely, if ever, used the State Rooms downstairs for private occasions. Though she felt she had no influence here, she managed to effect some alterations. The pictures of former prime ministers had originally lined the staircase, but had been moved to a corridor. 'When I got here, Dame Megan Lloyd George wanted to come, and the MacDonald daughters – so they came and saw it. And Megan said, "Why are the prime ministers put in that corridor and why is my father behind the door?" I said, "More power to my elbow!"' Mary had been trying to get the Ministry of Works to put them back on the stairs, but they 'stalled and stalled . . . And in the end a man came to me and said, "Well, they just look like a lot of postage stamps, but if you wish, I'll put them back on the stairs." So I said, "Thank you very much, put them back. And everyone loved it.'" She also arranged for the official presents from dignitaries and heads of state – enamel drinking glasses from the Russians, porcelain horses from President Nixon, mother-of-pearl rosaries from the Pope – to be put in glass cases on public view downstairs, so that other people could enjoy them, but her suggestion that people be allowed to come in and tour the building was turned down on security grounds.

As all prime ministers' spouses discover, the privacy of the No. 10 flat is constantly invaded by officials coming in on business – 'Oh, in the middle of the night sometimes. I remember waking up and seeing a secretary standing by Harold's bed taking notes at three o'clock in the morning!' Mary says. Marcia Falkender wrote: 'Whenever Harold was there the messengers were coming in and out, the telephone was ringing, the files and the red boxes were being delivered. It was a place in which you couldn't even enjoy a good family row because if you did the whole building would soon know.'³⁴ When Michael Palliser, Wilson's Private Secretary, went up with papers, Mary was 'always very friendly, very welcoming, slightly – not exactly distant, but a bit reserved'. The pressure on Harold's time, as on all prime ministers, was relentless: 'Do you know I used to have to go down to his secretary and say, "Please give me half an hour of the Prime Minister's time. I must talk to him on one or two things".'

It is perhaps not surprising that some civil servants and functionaries found her aloof and concluded she did not like being at No. 10. They were there to serve the Prime Minister; to them Mary, who was both reticent and proud, could seem almost invisible. Gradually she asserted her will. She now says ambiguously, 'I enjoyed it very much, really – most of it.'

As Mary's commitments increased, Marcia found them a young Irish housekeeper, Mary Wright, whom the Wilsons paid for themselves. She stayed until she married, when Marcia, through a contact in Northampton, found Mrs Pollard, who remained from then on. Wilson had consistently projected his image as the 'ordinary' family man. Much had been made in the press of the Wilsons' 'simple' and 'unaf-fected' lifestyle, in particular their liking for plain food – for instance, Harold's favourite HP sauce: 'Oh, Harold kept on about HP sauce . . . Of course he liked it. It used to have the Houses of Parliament on it, do you remember?' Mary says firmly: 'We lived the lives we'd always lived,' which was a far cry from the country house image that clung to previous Conservative prime ministers.

When their 'ordinariness' gave rise to dismissive comments from some Labour colleagues, she fought back in her own way. Richard Crossman had once offended Mary by complaining that there was only Nescafé in the Wilson household. According to Crossman, one evening at an unscheduled Cabinet gathering at No. 10, Mary said to him: "'I remember the only time you came to see us at our home in Hampstead, I offered you Nescafé and you said you'd rather not and we went out to a restaurant and there you got some ordinary coffee. So I suppose you don't like tinned salmon but that's all we've got tonight apart from a bit of cold ham" . . . "But I like tinned salmon," I said to Mary, "especially in fish cakes." "Oh, you do like it in fish cakes?" she replied. "So do I." And somehow part of a terrible barrier had been broken down between us. I'd been made to realise how snobbish the Wilsons regard the Crossmans' attitude to tinned salmon and Nescafé and a thousand other things.'[35]

Though she sometimes felt uneasy at No. 10, Mary immediately took to Chequers. The Wilsons went as often as possible at weekends and Harold was the first prime minister to use it for work, holding Cabinet and other meetings there during the week. Chequers was 'old, it was interesting and it was peaceful, and you could go down there and relax and just have lovely meals and . . . be looked after', she says. Bred in the country, she loved the rural surroundings and walks. At weekends: 'If we didn't get out to Chequers it was awful, because everyone around us used to go back to their homes, and I'd lost mine.' She wrote poetry, usually in the White Parlour, a favourite room with all the women who have lived in No. 10.

Each year they went to Chequers for Christmas with the family; people from the estate were invited for drinks on Christmas Eve, and they held a reception on Boxing Day as well as a party for disabled children from the nearby Stoke Mandeville Hospital before travelling to the Scilly Isles for New Year. During the rest of the year they entertained friends and political colleagues as well as hosting official functions. Mary particularly enjoyed the Commonwealth Heads of Government meetings when the leaders stayed at Chequers for three successive nights. For her first conference, in 1965, she remembers that she was 'determined to get it right. I had a sheaf of photographs of all the Prime Ministers, and my secretary would shuffle the photographs, then draw out one for me to identify the name and country, until I was 100% accurate.'[36]

Mary enjoyed taking visitors on tours: 'She was very good at that, because she liked all the minutiae,' Joy says. And she was more relaxed as hostess. 'I remember Tom Driberg. He was a terrific snob. We had a [Labour Party] National Executive down there, and they put on soup and then a cold dish and then pudding or something adequate for sixty people . . . And afterwards he wrote to me saying thank you for entertaining us at Chequers – "I know of several good restaurants in the district if you would like to know about them." And I thought, "Well, you . . .!" – outrageous! He was wonderful,' she laughs.

There were some drawbacks. Though Chequers is put at prime ministers' disposal for official entertaining and rest and relaxation, they have to pay for all private entertaining, including the laundering of napkins and tablecloths and bed linen. Mary at first had the impression that if the Prime Minister was called away, 'there was no encouragement for her to stay' – an impression reinforced when the blinds were drawn, rugs rolled up and the furniture covered in dustsheets the minute Wilson left.[37] Even today, things are put away as soon as the Prime Minister leaves, though they don't go as far as the dustsheets. But when the rules of the Chequers Trust were studied, it turned out that Mary was, after all, allowed to arrive before the Prime Minister, and could stay overnight alone if he was summoned back to London on urgent business. 'Everything had to be discovered by accident or by probing, nothing was volunteered in those early years,' wrote Marcia, who did much of the probing.[38]

As Prime Minister's wife, Mary saw her role as 'supporting Harold as far as I could, in every way I could, if I could. But it wasn't defined. Everybody has to make up their own minds what to do.' She went to the House of Commons every Tuesday and Thursday to watch Harold from the Ladies Only Speaker's Gallery at Prime Minister's Question Time and was there during major debates. At meetings and party conferences, her function was 'to be there. To be with him. On the platform. In the background. I don't think of my function as a positive one,' she told a reporter. It was the role of a prime minister's wife 'to be unobtrusive at times of crisis, to be as wise as a serpent, harmless as a dove'.[39]

She had no wish to take an active part in his everyday political life. 'Harold's work was Harold's work, and it didn't involve me in that sense,' she says. 'There are plenty of people around to advise him and discuss important things with him,' she told a reporter. 'Sometimes I ask him questions . . . At the end of the day he is sparkling and stimulating. He likes me to ask him questions because he positively enjoys telling me the answers.'[40] Attacks on Harold upset her, whether from the press or members of his own party, and she could be fiercely partisan, refusing to speak to people who had undermined him, even though she had concluded early on that, unlike her, he loved a row: 'Harold is aggressive, you see. He's never more himself than when he's hitting out. He likes a good stand-up fight. After a first class fracas, he comes in looking as if he's had a day off on the golf course.'[41]

They understood each other well: 'They actually thought the same things about people and used to have a laugh with the same jokes about the person concerned. She was a perfect foil for him,' Marcia says. One Labour Party official, Tom McNally, found her serene – 'a very quiet and self-effacing but substantial presence in his life'. A later aide, Bernard Donoughue, thought she provided a 'total respectability, total sense of decency. All those Nonconformist values which he was brought up with, she demonstrated.' Harold recognised her contribution, once suggesting to his press adviser, Trevor Lloyd-Hughes, that they should let the press know that 'Mary is my secret weapon', an idea eventually turned down but nevertheless keenly felt by Wilson. It was his way of saying that he appreciated what she did behind the scenes. Though not effusive about Mary in public, Harold was fiercely loyal: he wanted to say to the press, 'Watch out, lads . . . if you attack Mary, you're attacking me,' Lloyd-Hughes recalls.

Mary did not make political speeches: 'because I thought, in the first place, I wasn't responsible to any constituency, and in the second place, I didn't want to criticise, throw a spanner in the works in any way, so I kept quiet. I don't mean to say I didn't think.' She did not always support the policies, and was against Britain's entry into the Common Market, for instance, but never publicly disagreed with Harold: 'I thought, well, his job's hard enough as it is. He doesn't want me saying things . . . I thought, no, just don't be there, just abstain. For good-ness sake, don't make it harder for him.'

This did not mean that she toed the Party line in her friendships, and she made friends across the political spectrum. When MP John Stonehouse was in disgrace pending charges of fraud (having contrived his own disappearance on pretence of drowning) Mary, who consid-ered him a friend, warmly shook his hand when they met in public: 'It was so funny, because I said to Joe Haines [Wilson's Press Secretary] and Harold, "Oh I've been photographed shaking hands with John Stonehouse. I never thought." And you could see the wheels going round in their heads – "How is this for publicity, is this good? Is this bad?" I never thought about it . . . Because it's so rotten thinking oh, better not, just in case, better not to speak to him although he hasn't been sentenced yet. Well, that's why I've got so many friends who go to prison, it seems,' she laughs. 'I like rogues, you see. That's my trouble.' Regardless of party affiliation, she admired good speakers, including Churchill, Nye Bevan and Michael Foot. Northern Ireland MP, Ian Paisley, though a 'terrible man', preached 'a fiery sermon – just the sort of sermon my father used to preach'. Conservative MP Enoch Powell would 'bring the sentence round and finish it nicely – beautiful'. Mary liked whom she liked, and she stuck by them.

Going to official events with Harold could be hazardous; sometimes his sense of humour got the better of him and he would 'drop me in it terribly': 'We were both great punsters and we used to laugh a lot,' she says. 'At the Queen's supper party after the diplomatic reception . . . Horace King [Speaker of the House of Commons] was there dressed up in his knee-breeches and his tailcoat, standing there, and Harold said to me, "God, look at Horace. He looks like a bloody great crow." And I burst out laughing. He kept a straight face, and was looking round the room and Lord Plunket came across to me and said "Is some-thing amusing you?" I think he thought I was laughing at Her Majesty, you see.'

On visits to Balmoral, Mary was enchanted. The Queen and the Duke of Edinburgh met them at the castle, dressed in kilts and surrounded by corgis. She recalls little touches such as a bowl of gentians placed in her room and 'books they thought we'd like' on the table. On one occasion, the Queen suggested they go over and have lunch with the Queen Mother at Glamis: '"You don't need your detective," the Queen said, "let me drive you over." She rather enjoyed getting away from her bodyguards,' Harold wrote, 'but of course they always followed in close attendance.' In September 1975, the Queen drove them over herself to a lodge in the grounds for tea. She put the kettle on, Mary helped her make drop scones and laid the table, and 'after a most agreeable tea, the Queen passed an apron to Mary, put one on herself and they both proceeded to wash up the crockery'.[42]

Mary also had her own separate schedule of engagements. She employed a part-time secretary, Brenda Dew, who was paid for half by the Wilsons and half by the Labour Party – not by the government, even though much of her job related to Mary's role as Prime Minister's wife. Brenda organised the diary, helped with her letters and accompanied her on visits, overseen by Marcia Williams: 'She [Marcia] taught me such a lot about how to go on and what to do, and letters and how to deal with all that,' Mary says. Teas at No. 10 with the Party Women's Officer and fifty or sixty Labour MPs' wives became a regular event. Later, she toured the country giving her popular talk about 'Life at Number Ten' to Labour Party women's groups. She soon attuned herself to public speaking: 'Once you've got used to sitting on a platform and being stared at, that's half the battle, because then you don't so much mind standing up.'

As well as opening fêtes, hospitals and schools, she supported charities, including the *Woman's Own* Children of Courage awards for which she presented the citation at Westminster Abbey. She focused on the elderly, and in her first year she visited the London County Council's old people's homes in London, and asked to see senior citizens' homes in Rome and Paris. There were regular invitations to open exhibitions and art shows. She became Vice-President of the Women of the Year awards, and was an active supporter of War on Want, a charity initiated by Harold. For the 1965 autumn fayre of the Civic Trust of Penrith, a town where her parents had lived, she wrote a poem which appeared in the programme. But when a magazine offered her £33 to publish one of her poems, the Cabinet Secretary, Burke Trend, told her she 'couldn't accept because he'd only published it because I was married to the Prime Minister. I had to give the money to charity. It would have been nice, too – £33,' she says.

In 1965 she was asked to launch a Warspite submarine, for which, by custom, she was given a diamond brooch. At first she said, 'I can't launch a nuclear submarine', but Harold said it was already agreed, and anyway it was only nuclear-powered. It was launched at Barrow, and Mary quoted Masefield – 'I must go down to the sea again.' When she showed Harold a photo of the submarine, he said, 'That's ugly.' Mary was very cross: 'Don't talk about my submarine like that,' she retorted. From then on she remained closely involved with Warspite and finally was invited to the decommissioning ceremony, where she was presented with the submarine's pennant.

As hostess at No. 10, she oversaw arrangements for the official events. Once a week there was a dinner or reception which gathered in guests from all walks of life who were welcomed in a receiving line up the stairs. There were tea parties for charities and disabled children from the London boroughs who had to be carried upstairs by the policemen, garden parties in summer, and dinners for visiting heads of state followed by a reception of around a hundred people.

The guest list for entertaining at No. 10 changed radically under Wilson, who decided to prune out the Establishment figures because 'they don't actually sum up the business of Number 10 under a Labour Government – it had to be wider', Marcia says. Guests who represented British culture, like the sculptor Henry Moore, singer Janet Baker and conductor Colin Davis were chosen, as well as the 'new aristocracy' of 'swinging' Britain, who added a glitter to the regime and made Downing Street seem more accessible: leading figures in popular entertainment, design and fashion, footballers, cricketers, pop stars, actors and comedians – including Wilson impersonator Mike Yarwood – painters and singers, who had not formerly crossed the threshold of No. 10. Laurence Olivier impressed Mary when he came to dinner – 'he had such charisma, you could feel it' – and she was delighted when the first US astronauts to land on the moon arrived bearing a piece of moon rock, which remains on display at No. 10 to this day. They held a party which included a group of comprehensive schoolchildren and Labour MP Eric Moonman, and Mary wrote a poem 'The Lunarnaut' to commemorate the event.

Conscientiously, Mary carried out her duties, even though she sometimes found them tiresome. 'She was very much a person in her own

CLARISSA EDEN

1. Clarissa Churchill outside No. 10 Downing Street after her engagement to Anthony Eden, 12 August 1952. It felt 'like being in the path of a typhoon.'

2. Clarissa and Anthony at their wedding reception at No. 10 given by her uncle Winston and aunt Clementine Churchill, 14 August 1952.

3. Clarissa at the Comedie Francaise in early 1955 with Cynthia Jebb (*right*).

4. On the election trail, April 1955: 'All I had to do was keep smiling.'

5. At the Geneva Conference July 1955, with (*l to r*) Mrs Eisenhower, Lady Dorothy Macmillan, Clarissa and Madame Faure.

6. Greeted by the Queen and the Duke of Edinburgh
at Balmoral, October 1955.

7. Attending a
film exhibition,
summer 1956.

DOROTHY MACMILLAN

8. Dorothy Cavendish, aged 20, shortly after she met Harold Macmillan.

9. Dorothy marries Harold Macmillan at St Margaret's Hall, Westminster, 19 April 1921.

10. Election poster, Stockton-on-Tees, 1923 general election.

May I appeal to **YOU** to VOTE for my Husband.

I know that he will serve **YOU** faithfully and carry out all he has promised to do.

DOROTHY MACMILLAN.

11. Dorothy and Harold at No. 10, January 1957.

12. The Macmillans at Birch Grove in 1956 with nine of their grandchildren. 'She liked children enormously and got on with them frightfully well.'

13. Dorothy Macmillan at Birch Grove. 'She wasn't beautiful, she wasn't smart, but she had an indefinable charm and this extraordinary zest for life.'

14. In Ghana during their Africa tour, 1960. 'She loved talking to people.'

15. With President Charles de Gaulle and his wife at Birch Grove, November 1961. 'Lady Dorothy, what are we going to do about the General's blood?'

ELIZABETH HOME

16. Elizabeth and her sister Lavinia (*right*) with Alec's sister Rachel,
on a visit to the Hirsel, c.1935.

17. Elizabeth Alington marries Alec Dunglass at Durham Cathedral, 3 October 1936.

18. With Alec and the children Caroline, Diana, Meriel and David in 1945,
after Alec was released from his plaster.

19. With her scrapbooks.

20. Elizabeth and Foreign Secretary Alec greet President Senghor of Senegal at a Covent Garden Gala opera performance.

21. With Alec on the terrace at No. 10.

22. At Meriel's wedding, which Elizabeth organised, in 1964.

right,' Gerald Kaufman, Wilson's Press Officer, recalls. 'Everybody liked her. People enjoyed talking to her . . . She had interesting things to say . . . She was popular because she was a nice person with interests of her own who did not pretend to be anything she wasn't.' But she did not always find it easy. In one poem, 'The House at the Edge of the Wood', she wrote of the tension between public life and her private longing:

> Sometimes, as I struggle through crowded rooms
> Thick with tobacco and whisky fumes,
> And vapid voices shrilling high
> In one continuous parrot cry –
>
> Suddenly I can see it there!
> I can see the bluebells, can smell the air,
> And the evening sunlight slants in lines
> Across my house at the edge of the pines.[43]

Whenever things got on top of her, Mary would travel incognito on the tube to see her friends in Hampstead Garden Suburb, bearing a half-bottle of champagne: 'She had various friends who were totally non-political and totally trustworthy. And she would go there and get out of this hothouse,' says her daughter-in-law, Joy, who, as family, 'was on the receiving end of quite a lot of moaning'. Once, exasperated by the whole thing and believing nobody was interested in her anyway, she 'asked Michael Halls, one of the private secretaries up to the flat: and he said, "Yes, what is it Mrs Wilson?", and I said, "I suggest you get a dummy and put a nice hat and dress on it and a bunch of flowers in its hand and put it in a cupboard, and when you need it, you pull it out and there it is, and when you don't need it you push it back again." And he said, "What's the matter, Mrs Wilson?" He was very sympathetic.'

After the 1966 election, which Labour won with an increased majority of 97, the sense that they were temporary occupants of No. 10 evaporated. It was a comfortable result, and a vote of confidence in Wilson's government and leadership. Mary was popular – 'the priceless woman at No. 10,' journalist Marjorie Proops called her – 'a reflective, sensitive, self-analytical woman. Romantic. Dreamy. Poetic.' She was 'a passionately devoted mother . . . passionate about injustice . . . warm

and human and amused and sometimes funny and always endearing'
who had 'a soft pretty face and sexy legs'.[44] She had been with Wilson
throughout the campaign, interested, but, according to Gerald
Kaufman, 'vulnerable': 'She said to me, "Gerald, there's so many
hostile people". And I said to her, "Look, ten million people are going
to vote against the Labour Party. Some of them have got to feel hostile
towards you." She hated it. She didn't like antagonism. She didn't like
confrontation.' Sometimes during the rush and noise on the trail, 'I
had to keep at bay the longing, as if for a drug, for solitude and utter
silence,' she confessed.[45]

Wilson now had the mandate he needed. On their arrival at No. 10
this time, the Private Office and staff lined the entrance hall and clapped
him as he walked along the red-carpeted hall to the Cabinet Office.
Assured of their place in Downing Street, the Wilsons sold the house
in Hampstead Garden Suburb, a decision they later bitterly regretted.

Mary's self-confidence grew. Richard Crossman described her at No.
10 'coming downstairs looking elegant and *soignée* . . . She had become
totally different from the woman I remember when Harold was leader
and she sat in No. 9 Vincent Square [his home] feeling embittered and
unhappy and not wanting to go to No. 10. Now she is one of the great
successes of the Government and she's created her own completely
independent personal image.'[46]

Dealing with the press was a minefield. In the early days, Wilson
made a point of establishing friendly relations with the Westminster
lobby journalists. Mary gave interviews because, she says modestly, 'I
thought it would help – say something nice and be noncommittal and
be a bit stupid. . . . It's very useful to act stupid.' She came over as a
warm personality – straightforward and candid: 'Increasingly she
became a political asset in publicity terms, and extra thought had to
be given to her projection, though she asked for little help,' Marcia
Falkender wrote.[47] But she was unhappy about press intrusions on
her privacy, and that of her children. One newspaper reporter upset her
by 'snooping around our dustbins at seven o'clock in the morning,
looking for champagne bottles after one party . . . another newspaper
had been trying to find something to suggest we're living on the fat of
the land'. They seemed only to 'want to find things out to harm us.
Our predecessors never had that,' she said tartly.[48]

After 1966, Wilson's early honeymoon with the press turned sour. Criticism of the government intensified as the economy took a downturn, culminating in the 1967 devaluation of sterling, which forced the virtual abandonment of much of the strategy for planned economic growth. Divisions opened up in Labour's ranks over incomes policy, resulting in widespread trade union strikes. There were massive demonstrations against the Vietnam War, and Wilson's tacit support for President Johnson – though he resisted sending British troops to Vietnam – further divided the Party and the country. Backbench revolts were frequent, and the political infighting distressed Mary.

From an unusually relaxed rapport with journalists, the relationship turned to outright hostility on both sides, exacerbated by a row over the handling of sensitive defence (D-notice) information. Mary was upset, sometimes to the point of tears, by attacks on Harold: 'Of course when you are in politics you learn to expect hostility and criticism, and some of it can be very bitter. But often the attacks on Harold went beyond this – they were personal, cruel, unfair. I was hurt by them, and I know he was, though he tried not to show his feelings.'[49]

Even now she feels bitter about misrepresentations of herself: 'I used to get angry. And one thing I used to get angry about was when they got it wrong.' In the end she wearily despaired of ever correcting the many distortions – 'The thing with the press is to accept that you can't win' – and concluded it was better to see the newspapers as tomorrow's fish and chip wrapping. For years Mary was saddled with the dismissive tag that she had flying ducks on her wall. 'I made a mistake. When the press came,' she says, 'I thought they were kind. And they came to interview me *en masse*, and Trevor [Lloyd Hughes] said, "Do you think you can manage this?" and I said, "Oh yes."' Mary showed them round the flat, 'and Giles, then sixteen, had a mobile of flying storks in his bedroom. Cyril Aynsley [of the *Daily Express*], a friend of mine, said that I had flying ducks on the wall. I never got rid of those bloody flying ducks. They came with me everywhere!' Much later, when the ducks reappeared, she wrote to the *Daily Express* editor telling him how it happened 'and they published it in the paper and that was the end of it. After twenty or thirty years!'

'Mrs Wilson's Diary', a regular column penned by John Wells in the satirical magazine *Private Eye*, caused her some anguish until she decided that it was light-hearted rather than malicious, and that she, too, could laugh at it: 'I used to read Mrs Wilson's Diary and I used to get so angry, and then I used to roar with laughter because if they only knew what went on inside No. 10, it was much funnier than that.' She once burst out, 'If I ever meet the man, I shall bite him', to which John Wells, who claimed he was a little in love with her, responded, 'Well, nothing I'd like better than to be bitten by Mrs Wilson.' 'And finally I met him, and I frightened him to death. I put on a rather regal air and entertained him in the flat, and we got on like a house on fire. He was a lovely man, you know.'

For the first time, attention focused on her clothes, a topic largely unmentioned during her predecessors' time. Mary always dressed stylishly. She used a young designer, Bill Pashley, who designed the dress she wore when the Queen came to dinner at No. 10, and the couturier Digby Morton, who made her an outfit for a visit by Madame Pompidou, wife of the French President: 'Of course they were all dressed by the French houses, and Jean Rook [*Daily Express* columnist], who was a very acid writer, said I had a little dress run up by a little dressmaker round the corner.' Mary was furious. Digby Morton wrote an enraged letter to the journalist, but Mary told him, 'Digby, it's no good. You have to remember it's all forgotten next day.' But it still rankles. Eventually, from being cautious, Mary became 'frightened – it's so easy to get it wrong'.

There were more insidious pressures. The close working relationship between Wilson and Marcia Williams was interpreted at intervals by journalists and politicians as an affair. Rumours to this effect had first been aired during the leadership campaign in 1963 and were given a small boost when Quintin Hogg intemperately called on the opposition front bench during the 1964 election to examine whether any of its members could be accused of adultery. He was rounded on by both sides of the House. But the rumours persisted, and regained currency in the post-1967 climate of hostility to Wilson. Marcia and her husband had separated in 1959 and divorced in 1961. In 1967 she began an affair with journalist Walter Terry, by whom she had two children before he decided that he could not, after all, leave his wife, though this was not made public until much later. Mary and Harold were godparents to Marcia's two boys.

Marcia played a key role in Wilson's inner circle as his Political Secretary and link with the Labour Party, an unusually powerful position for a woman at that time. She was outspoken in her manner and admired by most of his colleagues for her political shrewdness, though a few found her directness and volatility hard to manage. Almost no one in the inner circle believed the rumours. The innuendo irritated both Mary and Marcia. 'Well, it was awful, really . . . it was very, very difficult,' Mary says. 'The press just built it up, quite honestly.' Mary couldn't see the point of answering back: 'What is the good? . . . I said "It'll disappear." And it made me ill, if I answered back. Even now if I answer back I feel quite ill. And I just let it roll over me, if I could.' When she was approached by a sympathetic friend, she said adamantly, 'It's nonsense, you don't have to respond.' Marcia points out: 'They never asked the question, ever – not one paper, not one journalist, nobody said "Do you get on with Mrs Wilson or don't you get on with her?" No. You were assumed to be part of the act that they had given you to play, and if you didn't play it the way that they wanted you to play it, then hard luck – "I shall just not write at all about them." That's the attitude they took.'

It did not affect the mutual support that the two women had built up over the years, and it did not, Marcia says, 'cause any awkwardness or any rows' between them. Marcia had fierce rows in the office with Wilson and with colleagues, but never with Mary: 'I never heard in all the time I was around one cross word between them. *Absolutely never*,' Gerald Kaufman recalls. They played separate roles and respected each other for what they did. Marcia respected Mary's place. She knew that Mary was the emotional anchor of Harold's life, and Mary, says Marcia, 'knew why I was there, she knew how I worked, she knew she couldn't possibly do the role I did because she didn't know how'.

Mary deeply appreciated the help Marcia gave her, especially during their time at No. 10 when she showed her the ropes, and was always on her side – 'She was great at fighting in one's defence.' She showed her support for Marcia. On one occasion, when rumours were again in the air, Mary and Harold were receiving guests at a reception in Downing Street. There was a hush when Marcia arrived and approached Mary. Mary held out her arms, and the two women embraced. Later, Mary again came publicly to Marcia's defence in a

1977 letter to *The Times*: 'I was like a rather unwilling recruit to a group of professional soldiers when I first went to Number 10, and Lady Falkender's help and advice were invaluable to me in all the work I tried to do there. Of course there were tears and tension, particularly at election times – there must be clashes of temperament in all large organisations – but there was plenty of laughter and enjoyment too. And I should like to add that Lady Falkender's family were also extremely helpful to me over the years. Her kindness to so many people in the Labour Party and Number 10 is, or should be, well-known. Nobody was refused help if it lay in her power to aid them.'[50]

The Wilsons' solicitor, Arnold Goodman, who did not believe the rumours, succeeded in keeping them out of the press by threatening litigation. When a pop group implied a liaison on its record sleeve, the company responsible was successfully sued.[51] Damages – all the royalties from the record – were paid into a charitable trust, which now sponsors various causes including the British Screen Advisory Council and a scheme for helping students pay tuition fees. 'The record's still selling, apparently,' Mary says. 'It's been very useful because I can help more than I would normally be able to do.'

Both women have been through much since then. Now they regularly lunch together at the House of Lords and appear at other public occasions. Marcia says, 'she's someone who you can always rely on, you could go and say, "I've got a problem", and you could always get the right answer – and that's been from then until now. I've built it up and she's built it up. We've built it up and it became so we knew each other without even having to acknowledge that we knew each other. It sort of grew, the relationship, and now she *is* my oldest friend.'

As Mary consolidated her position at No. 10, she extended her own interests. In her poetry she could express her unmasked self, and celebrate what interested her – the Comet Kahoutek, the Durham Miners' Gala, the opening of Parliament, the splendid agapanthus hedge in her garden on the Isles of Scilly. In 1966 she met the Poet Laureate, John Betjeman, at an opera evening at Covent Garden. He wrote to her afterwards, and she sent him a poem she'd written about Westminster Abbey. Soon they got into the habit of meeting and reciting poetry to each other, either at his flat or at No. 10: 'He'd say, "What shall we read today, darling,"' she recalls. Their friendship gave her lasting pleasure, and his confidence in her was inspiring. 'I believe in you and so does your family and so do thousands of people,' he wrote.[52] In 1968 they went together on a nostalgic visit to Diss, where Mary had been born and lived in her youth. Each wrote a poem about the experience:

> Dear Mary
> Yes it will be bliss
> To go with you by train to Diss,
> Your walking shoes upon your feet;
> We'll meet, my sweet, at Liverpool Street.
> That levellers we may be reckoned
> Perhaps we'd better travel second.

Mary replied,

> Dear John,
> Yes, it is perfect bliss
> To go with you by train to Diss!
> Beneath a soft East Anglian rain
> We chug across the ripening plain
> Where daisies stand among the hay;
> We come to Diss on Market Day,
> And cloth-capped farmers sit around,
> Their booted feet firm on the ground.[53]

When they got to the actual house, Mary found that she didn't have the nerve to knock on the door and ask if she could see inside: 'I didn't know who they were and wouldn't knock on a stranger's door,' confessed the Prime Minister's wife.

Mary's real solace was their family holidays in the Isles of Scilly – in summer, at Easter and New Year. The press came for one day only for interviews and photographs and then left them in peace, a convention which sadly is no longer respected on prime ministers' holidays. The Customs House was converted into a communications post, Garden Room girls came down bearing boxes by ferry or helicopter and detectives patrolled the immediate vicinity. Most people respected their privacy: some would come up and ask for Harold's autograph, but more often they'd say, 'Excuse me, Prime Minister, do you know the cricket scores?' – because the detectives had walkie-talkies.

Mary took part in local activities, especially the Women's Lifeboat

Guild of the RNLI in Scilly, of which she was President for many years and for which she raised funds and was awarded a silver badge for her work. 'Whenever we needed help, she was always there,' says fellow member Shirley Taylor. Mary cut short a trip to the Commonwealth Heads of Government meeting in Bermuda with Harold to attend a ceremony in 1975 to commemorate the victims of the *Schiller*, a liner sunk off the islands a century before. She has named a lifeboat, attends the annual Lifeboat Service held at dusk in the Methodist chapel, and shares the islanders' concern and respect for the lifeboat crews who face the hazards of the sea. She and Harold attended services and events at the local church and Methodist chapel and Mary still does poetry recitals, where 'huge numbers of people turn out to support her. She is much loved on these islands,' says the Reverend Julian Ould. In this close community, where she could be herself, there was time with Harold for swimming, walks and family picnics; at shops they stood in the queue like everyone else. She had space to write poems which touch on the people, historical events and beauty of these islands surrounded by sea under the wide sky.

On foreign trips, Mary usually had a different agenda from Harold and his Foreign Office team and secretaries; so busy were the team with the Prime Minister, and so separate was her agenda, that few officials could remember that Mary was even there. She met Lady Bird Johnson with President Lyndon Johnson on a visit to their ranch in 1965: 'She always deferred to Lyndon – "See what Lyndon thinks about this", and so on. And she had everybody throwing flower seeds on the road – she made all the roads blossom,' Mary recalls. She also met President Richard Nixon. Mary has a group photograph taken at the White House showing Pat Nixon holding a big bunch of red, white and blue flowers with ribbons. She had suddenly turned to Mary 'and she said, "My Gaad, I'm supposed to have given you these flowers!" So I said, "Just pass them to me and nobody will notice." So she passed them to me and in the other pictures, there I am holding the flowers. Shows something can go wrong at every ceremony,' she adds cheerfully.

When they visited the Pope, Mary, a born and bred Congregationalist, 'felt my back turn cold, I really did'. On a tour of Israel, she thought of her minister father who 'would have given anything' to go there: 'It was so exciting to see the Holy Places. I felt as though I was seeing it for him as well. I went with Harold's sister and we arrived at the point where the River Jordan meets the Sea of Galilee and there was a fisherman mending his net. I turned and looked and, like me, she had tears rolling down her face. It was the Bible come to life, a marvellous experience that renewed my faith.'[54] From elsewhere she carried a kaleidoscope of memories: 'Moscow under snow, the river frozen and silent, the birch trees heavy and silent . . . and the exquisite grace of the dedicated young dancers at the Bolshoi Ballet School'; Washington in the spring, 'cherry blossom by the Potomac', and President Kennedy's grave 'where it was not yet made up with the marble, but covered in flowers, his uniform caps, lying in the grass, wet with dew'.[55]

The Labour Party defeat in the 1970 general election came as a devastating shock. The Conservatives under Edward Heath had gained a lead in the polls after 1968 as Wilson steered his way through economic doldrums and Party divisions over trade union reform, as well as war in Nigeria, unrest in Northern Ireland and radical opposition to the Vietnam War. But by 1970, the Labour Party was again ahead. Wilson appeared confidently with Mary on the new-style walkabouts, though there was much heckling and booing as well as applause; on one occasion Mary had to retreat to the hotel after an egg was thrown at her by young Conservatives. The sun shone brilliantly on the June polling day. But as the results came in, the mood turned from expectation to gloom when the first Guildford result showed a 5.3 per cent swing to the Conservatives. 'He caught my eye and gave a slight grimace,' Marcia Falkender recalled of Wilson.[56] After only the third result, she telephoned the women in the political office at No. 10 and told them to pack up their papers and belongings. As they travelled down by car to London, with Harold occasionally dozing on Mary's shoulder, they planned their departure. The Conservatives won with an overall majority of 30.

At Downing Street, the political staff met them with a subdued cheer. One of the 'girls' handed Mary a bouquet of flowers. The business of hurried packing-up began. 'That was dreadful,' says Marcia Falkender. 'Mary was in tears, and all sorts of people were. And I thought, well, one thing you can't do, you must not cry a tear. And I said to Harold, "You're not going to cry, are you?" And he said, "No,

I'm not." And I think he and I were the only two who didn't. But oh, it was terrible. It was really dreadful.' Harold remained impressively calm. A few hours later, as the exhausted team departed, they heard the cheers as the crowds outside and staff inside welcomed Edward Heath into Downing Street – the same experience Elizabeth Douglas-Home had had when the Wilsons first arrived.

Mary knew how deeply upset Harold was by the defeat, one of the few major setbacks of his career. She was also outraged: 'The manner in which the Prime Minister leaves No. 10 is barbarous,' she later declared: '. . . the exposed front door like a public stage, the crowd in the street, one Prime Minister out, another in within two hours, to a chorus of boos, cheers and gloating. Furniture hustled out of the back gate. It's just like having the bailiffs in . . . The whole affair seems so undignified.'[57] With nowhere to live as they prepared for opposition, following tradition they spent the weekend at Chequers, while Marcia and her staff found a house in Vincent Square. They rented this for a few months until they took out a 20-year lease on an elegant Georgian house at 5, Lord North Street, close to the Houses of Parliament. It was the twenty-second house Mary had occupied in her life.

They left Downing Street in debt. As Mary settled into Lord North Street, Wilson took the same course as Anthony Eden and immediately began writing his record of his time in office,[58] for which he had been offered serialisation rights of £224,000 by the *Sunday Times*.[59] Along with lecture tours in America this enabled him to keep on his core staff of Marcia Williams and Joe Haines and pay off his overdraft. A trust fund was set up by wealthy supporters to keep the office going as Wilson planned for the next election. He finished the 800-page book in a year, a prodigious effort. In 1971 they were able to buy Grange Farm, an oak-beamed farmhouse at Great Missenden in Buckinghamshire, where they spent their weekends.

John Betjeman had always encouraged Mary to publish her poems. Robert Lusty of Heinemann had shown interest in her work, but she hesitated, concerned that it would be thought that she was published only because she was the Prime Minister's wife. Lusty persevered and her first volume, *Selected Poems*, came out in 1970, shortly after Labour lost the election. When she held the book in her hands it 'was thrilling', she says. And then 'I said the most terrible thing. I said "This is the most exciting thing that has happened to me in the last" – I thought about my children being born – "in the last twenty years." I thought – oops! I shouldn't have said that.' At a book signing in Oxford Street, at which Harold dropped in to show support, the queue stretched over 200 yards down the road. She was even more delighted when the volume sold 75,000 copies, confirming that people 'appreciated the poems for themselves'. As well as gaining a new identity as a poet, with the royalties she paid off the mortgage on her Isles of Scilly home, a joyous assertion of ownership and independence: 'The building society . . . said it would be much more sensible for me to keep the mortgage. I said, "I want to hold the title deeds in my hand." Which I did. It was lovely to feel it was *my* bungalow.'

A new life opened up – of book signings and recitals, including one at the Albert Hall to a crowd of thousands. Mary was no longer the invisible woman on the platform but the centre of attention, and people came up to express their appreciation of her work. She made new acquaintances on the literary circuit and continued to enjoy her times with John Betjeman. Though her schedule was less busy, there were still official functions to attend, and she kept up her steady support of charities. She had more time for her family. Giles had left school and Robin had married and was teaching at Oxford and at the Open University. Although life was no longer interrupted at all hours by private secretaries clamouring for Harold's attention, there was still a constant stream of visitors to the house going about the business of opposition.

They were out of power for only four years. With the country virtually paralysed by a state of emergency precipitated by a miners' strike, Heath called a general election in February 1974 on the slogan 'Who Governs Britain?' Labour won, but with a knife-edge majority of four seats over the Conservatives, and no overall majority in the House of Commons. As the Wilsons waited while Heath decided whether to concede or try to form a coalition with the Liberals, their son Giles came up the stairs in Lord North Street and announced: 'Dad, there's a grand lady with a headscarf on outside. She says she's called Mrs Elizabeth Windsor. She'd like to have a word.' It was a prescient joke, since, next day, Wilson was for the third time on his way to Buckingham

Palace to kiss hands with the Queen. 'He very much wanted to get back, understandably, which he did. And which was good. And I was delighted for him,' Mary recalls.

Significantly, they did not return to live at Downing Street. Mary decided to remain in Lord North Street, thus setting a precedent by being the first prime ministerial wife that century to refuse to live at No. 10. It suited Harold, who adopted a much less aggressive style as premier – he would be a 'sweeper' in defence, not a 'striker' in attack, there would be no repeat of the 'first 100' days of change, and ministers would be left to run their own departments. Harold and she went each day the short distance to the 'office' at No. 10, where she dealt with her large correspondence and engagements, but home was separate. The arrangement worked well. Mary took up her schedule of official engagements helped by a new half-time secretary, Marcia Falkender's sister, Peggy Field.

Wilson's swift settlement with the miners heralded a return to stability, but another election was inevitable. In October 1974, Labour was returned with an overall majority of three, much less than they had hoped for, but enough to govern and to confirm Wilson's authority. There were continuing divisions over Britain remaining in Europe (which Mary opposed, but not in public) – decided by a referendum in 1975; over the proposed Social Contract with the unions – culminating in the imposition of a statutory incomes policy, and over public expenditure cuts in the face of a gathering financial crisis. With a vociferous women's movement organising for change, the government passed legislation advancing women's position: the Equal Pay Act, passed in 1970, came into force in 1975, provisions were set up for statutory maternity leave, and the Sex Discrimination Act, 1975, outlawed discrimination against women.

The Wilsons continued to enjoy Chequers. Under Heath's premiership, the dark oak panelling had been stripped to a lighter tone, giving it less of a feeling of a gentleman's club. The American ambassador to Britain, Walter Annenberg, had donated an indoor swimming pool, which was much appreciated by subsequent residents, even though the Wilsons hardly ever used it because the oil-fired heating was so expensive to run.

In 1975 the Wilsons' twin grandchildren, Catherine and Jennifer, were christened in the Long Gallery at Chequers. When she heard of their birth, Mary, who normally respected that Cabinet meetings at No. 10 could not be interrupted, remembers going up to the Private Secretary guarding the door and saying, '"Would you get the Prime Minister out of Cabinet, please?" And he just looked at me and said "Yes" . . . It was a great moment – the power to get him out of Cabinet, it was really something.' As Grange Farm was nearby, Mary went to Chequers only when she was needed for official or informal functions, or to relax when she felt like it. When diplomat Nicko Henderson visited in June 1974, he found Wilson a changed man from the leader of 1964: 'He was less prickly, less on the defensive . . . "They keep me here," he told me, "not because they love me but because there is no-one else who can keep the party together."'[60]

Throughout his second premiership, only a few people in the very inner circle knew that Harold Wilson would resign after two years in power. He had told Mary in 1974 of his intention to go at 60, and she had later marked it with a large 'D-Day' in her diary for 11 March 1976: 'It was a family secret before it was generally known,' says his daughter-in-law, Joy. According to Robin, it was because 'he'd promised my mother, but also he'd led the Party for thirteen years and he'd been PM for eight years and he said, well, the same problems were coming round, because of course they come in cycles'.

Marcia Falkender was told during a conversation on a long walk with Harold and Mary in the Isles of Scilly in summer 1974, and tried to dissuade him. She and the family had known even during his first administration that if he won in 1970 he intended to only stay on for two years. After the 1970 defeat, the question was left open. But on his return to power in 1974, he reiterated to his closest aides that he would resign. At Balmoral in September 1975, he told the Queen informally of his intention; by early December he had notified her of the expected date of his departure. Even so, Mary remembers saying to him, '"Well, look, why don't we stay on for another year?" Because I thought it would be nice for him to have the Queen's Jubilee. "No," he said, "I don't want to. I'll go." He finally went when he decided to go. So it wasn't I who persuaded him to go – although I'm not going to say I was sorry, but he had the choice and he went.'

On 16 March 1976, Wilson went to the Palace to hand in his

resignation, and returned to deliver the bombshell to the shocked Cabinet members. Almost no one knew in advance. He gave as his reasons his length of service – thirty-one years in Parliament – his desire to give a new leader time to prepare for the next general election, and his fear of becoming stale. Among the farewell events was a dinner at Downing Street on 5 April attended by the Queen and the Duke of Edinburgh – only the second time this had happened, the first being for Winston Churchill's resignation.

After they left Downing Street to make way for Jim Callaghan and his wife, Audrey, Mary had time to reflect on her life at No. 10: 'Of course I shall miss part of it,' she said in an interview captioned 'At Last I'll Be Free to Be Me': 'I've met some fascinating people. But on the whole, yes, I'm relieved. I'm a little tired of being pushed and shoved. It will be wonderful to be free of the pressures, not to have to travel so much, to have time to myself. And naturally I'm pleased for Harold. Nobody has any idea of the strain of being a modern Prime Minister.'[61] Tony Benn saw her shortly after the resignation. 'I have done my best,' she said, 'but I now just want to slip back into obscurity again.'[62]

In retrospect, she concluded that a prime minister's wife did not, as so many people thought, have any position of authority: 'She is a private person with no real power.' The fickle business of politics was never really to her taste; 'It's here today and gone tomorrow,' she says. 'I remember Joy was helping me when we lost the election in 1970, and she came to me and said, "I'm terribly sorry, I've just sworn at the press, because they were trying to get into the removal van. I swore at them. I'm awfully sorry." And I said, "Look, Joy, you could walk down Whitehall now naked and nobody would give a damn." Because that's it – you're out. Disappear.'

In 1977 the Wilsons gave up the Lord North Street house and moved to an elegant flat in Ashley Gardens, overlooking Westminster Cathedral, where Mary still lives. Harold was appointed Knight of the Garter in 1976 – a source of particular pride to them both. They attended parties, dinners and lunches, and Mary continued to write. *New Poems* was published in 1979; she was commissioned to write a poem for the Silver Jubilee in 1977 and has carried out occasional commissions since then. The press was now interested in her as a poet, and discussed her work:

'The hardest thing to learn is to discard. The best lines, as John Betjeman says, "come kindly provided by the management,"' she told Gillian Reynolds.[63] 'A poem always insists on being written,' she said, 'and I can write anywhere, even walking down Victoria Street. I find I'm mumbling to myself, and I get out a little scrap of paper and a pencil that I carry with me, and write down the odd line, and finish it later.'[64] In 1983 she published *Poems I Like*, an anthology of her favourite poets.

In the same year, Wilson gave up his parliamentary seat and took his place in the House of Lords as Baron Wilson of Rievaulx. 'He loved the Lords,' Mary says – and so did she. As his health deteriorated after an operation for stomach cancer in 1980 and his memory began to fade, she would go to the front of the Ladies' Gallery where he could see her: 'Arthur Bottomley used to take him in and sit him down, and when Jim [Callaghan] was there and Harold came in, Jim moved up and they all moved up, and he sat there just below the gangway. And then when we were ready to go out, I'd stand up and catch his eye and we'd meet outside . . . and then go and have tea in the Tea Room and go home.'

Gradually, from 1986, Harold retired from public life. When journalist John Torode interviewed him on the publication of his memoirs, *The Making of a Prime Minister 1916–1964*, he observed that Mary 'plants herself firmly at Lord Wilson's feet. She is ready to help him over any lapses of memory and to stop things dead if the going gets rough.'[65] Mary cared for him steadfastly through those final painful years. Few people came to see him apart from Marcia Falkender and her sister, Peggy Field. Of Wilson's political colleagues, Mary points out, only Roy Jenkins, who had often been at odds with him in the past, was a regular visitor, even though by the end Harold had difficulty recognising him.

Harold and Mary went more often to the Isles of Scilly, where they felt at ease among their protective and kindly neighbours. On 23 May 1995, Harold Wilson died. After the funeral service at St Mary's church on Scilly, three groups of six bearers – the lifeboatmen, the gig teams and firemen – carried his coffin in perfect relay, followed by a long procession of mourners all the way to Old Town Church, which faces the sea on a bracken-covered hillside, where Harold was buried. Mary wept when she learned that some of the bearers had bought black shoes specially for the occasion. It was 'one of those blissfully sunny days, when it couldn't have looked better, it was – I suppose it was wonderful', Robin remembers.

Mary continues to take a lively and wry interest in current events. By special dispensation of Black Rod, she goes regularly to the House of Lords, where she has lunch with Lady Falkender and entertains guests, though she rarely goes into the Chamber, having 'heard enough speeches in my life'.

A proud, self-effacing and very private woman, Mary Wilson was determined to carry out her role in No. 10 in her own way and not according to the expectations of the system. She was not always at ease in the political world where attention focused on her husband and her domestic life revolved around the demands of the office. Sometimes she felt invisible and often she wanted to retreat into privacy. Her survival mechanisms included a strong sense of duty, a wicked sense of humour and an ability to escape from the pressures of Downing Street whether to friends, her beloved Isles of Scilly or, in the second term, her own homes in London and Great Missenden. Trained from youth not to push herself forward, Mary had felt the role of prime minister's spouse deeply uncomfortable at times. But she found her way through the maze of political life at No. 10, and carved out a role for herself, as all prime ministerial spouses must, with dignity and with a native wit that she carried with her from those early days as a minister's daughter in the Manse.

Chapter Five

Audrey Callaghan

1976–79

Where the Wilsons had brought a different style of politics to No. 10, Audrey Callaghan introduced another new element. She was the first prime minister's wife to have an independent career and she was a forceful public figure in her own right before she entered No. 10, even if her work was unpaid. She was one of a generation of Labour women of strong political convictions who felt a duty to participate, if not yet to aspire to political office, during a transition period when women were emerging from the political shadows and making their presence felt.

When Harold Wilson shocked his Cabinet with his dramatic resignation in March 1976, James Callaghan, his Foreign Secretary, was one of the few people warned in advance. Three months earlier, a close Wilson aide, Harold Lever, had tipped him off that the decision was irreversible and that Callaghan 'must make ready', but Callaghan had refused to believe it, and did almost nothing about it.[1]

On 11 March, Harold Wilson's 60th birthday, Callaghan and his wife Audrey attended a small celebratory dinner at the home of Wilson's publisher, George Weidenfeld. At around ten o'clock, Callaghan left with Wilson to vote at the House of Commons. As they travelled along the Embankment, Wilson told him in confidence that on 16 March he would announce his resignation. So stunned was Callaghan that, 'in a bemused state' when they arrived at the House, he almost failed to grasp that the government was in the throes of a crisis. Amidst angry scenes, thirty-seven Labour MPs abstained on a motion approving public expenditure cuts, bringing a humiliating defeat for the leadership. It was a signal of continuing troubles ahead for whoever would take Wilson's place in an administration surviving on a majority of only one. When Callaghan told Audrey later that night, she 'took the news in her accustomed calm, competent manner' and made it clear that she would expect him to stand for the leadership.

At 64, Callaghan had been anticipating retirement rather than the premiership. Both he and Audrey had long experience of the routines of office. Since 1964, when Callaghan was made Chancellor of the Exchequer in Wilson's first government, he had served in all the major offices of state. Though the responsibility of leadership was daunting, it would not be a major upheaval. Audrey recognised her husband's political ambitions and shared and respected his goals. Over thirty-seven years of marriage, they had developed a close partnership, with Audrey the calm ballast to his more volatile personality.

Like the Wilsons, the Callaghans came from provincial, Non-conformist backgrounds. When they first met at the Maidstone Knightrider Street Baptist church in 1929, Audrey Moulton was a 16-year-old sixth-former at the local grammar school, 'a bookworm, ready to curl up on the garden seat or on a sofa with her head in a book, yet always in an instant jumping up to do whatever was necessary', Jim says. Then called by his first name, Leonard, the 17-year-old tax clerk had just been transferred from his home town, Portsmouth. He was a working-class lad, who had been brought up alone by his mother in considerable poverty, after his father, who had served in the Navy for twenty-six years, including the First World War, had died in 1921 when Jim was nine.

On his second visit to the Baptist church, Audrey came up to him 'and said to me the immortal words, which I've never forgotten, "Mrs Boorman would like you to come to tea today."' Mrs Boorman was the widow of the owner of the local *Kent Messenger*. 'I looked at Audrey, and I'd not seen anyone quite like that before. It struck me straight away that there's a presence about her, a slight air of withdrawal and grace. The word I'd use is grace,' Jim recalls. He was immediately intrigued by her.

Audrey was born in Maidstone on 28 July 1913. Her father, Frank Moulton, the director of a metal firm, the Lead Wool Company which employed a couple of hundred people, was teetotal and a pillar of the local Baptist church. They were sufficiently well-off for her mother, Clara, who came from a family of ten children, to afford a full-time, live-in maid. Audrey's youth was ordered and secure, and she made steady progress through school and went on family holidays to coastal towns in Britain and trips to France to improve her French. At home, she enjoyed walks, read voraciously, and played tennis, where, Jim says, 'her steadiness was renowned – she always returned the most demon services and shots, and always seemed cool and not under pressure'. Middle-class 'lace-curtain proper' respectability and Nonconformist religion guided the family's routine. Each week she attended the Baptist church, where she taught in Sunday School.

Jim took up tennis in order to join her, and they began to meet outside church activities, to go on walks in the country, through the woods and along the Pilgrims' Way. Together, they embarked on the political road. When Jim 'discovered' socialism at Maidstone, Audrey shared his enthusiasm. After a senior in the Tax Office gave him some books, both became avid readers of G.B. Shaw, H.G. Wells, H.N. Brailsford, G.D.H. Cole, Harold Laski and others, which gave Jim 'a sense of exhilaration' that his 'boyhood sympathies were backed by a convincing criticism of the shortcomings of society as well as by a well-argued philosophy of the alternative'. Fired with purpose, he joined the Maidstone Labour Party and attended Workers' Educational Association classes in social history and economics. He gave the impression of being 'an impatient and unreasonable young man in a hurry',[2] not least to Audrey's parents, who were old-fashioned Liberals. 'I was a bit of a nuisance in the family when they used to invite me to formal lunch on Sundays because I would argue with her father.'

On long walks together Jim and Audrey discussed the issues preoccupying the left – unemployment and the Depression, poverty and social injustice and the need to restructure society along more equitable lines: 'She was always more left-wing than I was,' Jim reflects. 'She was more idealistic . . . She wasn't so much of the practical politician.' As Jim became active in his local branch of the tax officers' union, the AOT (Association of Officers of Taxes), Audrey continued her school education. Even then, Jim readily acknowledges, she had a 'tremendous . . . strongly felt, but indirect somehow, influence' on him: 'I was a very rough, uncouth youth at 17, brought up in a working-class family and she smoothed out a lot of edges.' With her family Jim felt at ease, gradually seeing in her father something of what he had missed through his own father's early death, and enjoying the stability of Audrey's background: 'She made me much more considerate of other people . . . to think about other people and to think what their views were and what their needs were . . . She made me kinder.' She was, he admits, 'much higher in the social scale than I was' and she gave him middle-class respectability.

At 18, having successfully passed her Higher School Certificate but without a clear idea of what she wanted to do, Audrey enrolled at Battersea College of Domestic Science. 'She was quite ready to do Domestic Science, but I think what she would really have liked would have been to have got a degree in the Arts. That's what she ought to have done, and gone to university,' Jim says. He often travelled up to visit her at her student hostel until he was moved to London and found lodgings close by. Audrey then found a job teaching Domestic Science at Eltham, but she soon signed up for a four-year evening course in Economics at Eltham Hill School organised by the Royal Arsenal Co-operative Society. One of her tutors was the young Hugh Gaitskell, later the Labour Party leader, who became a friend. She specialised in the causes of children's malnutrition and its remedies – a preparation for her lifelong commitment to children's welfare – and became involved in local politics in Lewisham through her friendship with Freda Corbett, a well-known activist on the London County Council.

As the threat of Fascism loomed over Europe during the 1930s, their involvement in left-wing politics deepened. They attended Fabian Society lectures and were avid readers of the Left Book Club publications. When the Spanish Civil War broke out in 1936, they joined in the demonstrations against Franco and campaigned to raise funds, through Jim's union, for medical aid for the Republicans. Watching events unfold, Jim, like many young people on the left, was overcome by 'a feeling of political hopelessness'[3] as war came steadily closer.

Their political concerns did not, however, prevent them having fun. They bought a not very reliable 1921 Wolseley coupé and visited Audrey's parents, played tennis, watched cricket, picnicked in Brishing Wood and holidayed in Cornwall and Devon and at Whitby and Llandudno. In London they had season tickets for the Promenade Concerts conducted by Henry Wood, Thomas Beecham, Adrian Boult and Toscanini; from high in 'the gods' they watched Sybil Thorndike in *Saint Joan*, and Audrey was particularly fond of ballet at Sadler's Wells.

On Audrey's 25th birthday, 28 July 1938, they were married at the Knightrider Street Baptist church in Maidstone. It was a traditional white wedding, with the men in morning dress, the bridesmaids in ice blue silk crêpe, and Audrey wearing a white slipper-satin gown with a train and veil and carrying a sheaf of white lilies. After signing the register to the accompaniment of Dvořák's Humoreske, they went on to a nearby restaurant for champagne and a sit-down tea. But the fundamentalist Baptist beliefs on which both were reared had faded; now the Nonconformist values etched into their personalities found expression in socialist philosophy.

They spent their honeymoon in Paris and Chamonix before returning to a rented semi-detached house in Norwood – a new experience for Jim, 'since I had lived in other people's homes for most of my life.'[4] With his promotion to an official post in the Inland Revenue Staff Federation, they were comfortable but not well off. Within three months, the Allies capitulated to Hitler at Munich and Hitler moved one stage closer to war when he occupied the Sudetenland region of Czechoslovakia. Jim and Audrey contacted an organisation for refugees from the Nazis. German Social Democrat journalist and author, Bernhard Menne, later editor of *Die Welt am Sonntag*, who was on the point of arrest, came to live with them until his wife escaped from Prague.

The Callaghans' first child, Margaret, was born in November 1939. Jim continued his job in a reserved occupation and joined the Home Guard. Audrey was evacuated to Llandudno in North Wales, where she spent most of the war living above the evacuated offices of Jim's tax union, from which she had a view over the bay and could see the glow of Liverpool burning. Their second child, Julia, was born in October 1942, just before Jim was released to enlist in the Navy. Audrey and Jim formed a branch of the Fabian Society, which she then ran in his absence and invited along prominent speakers including Harold Laski and John Parker. She was known in Llandudno as a sensible, kind and generous woman, who always made sure, despite rationing, that her babysitters had a meal when she left the children.[5]

With Jim away in the Navy, and Audrey unable to visit her parents because Kent was designated part of the war zone, she did not come south again until early 1945, when her mother found her accommodation in Maidstone. Jim had been selected in 1943 as Labour candidate for the Cardiff South constituency, even though, in common with other candidates, he was still on active service – at sea in the Far East. As the 1945 general election approached he flew back to fight the campaign. In his absence Audrey established her presence, speaking at a May Day rally in Cardiff, and she joined him during the election campaign, bringing Margaret and Julia with her. Now pregnant with their son, Michael, born in September 1945, she attended all the evening meetings. 'Audrey placed the care of the children first, but, as always throughout our political life, she somehow managed to combine that without me ever feeling that she didn't support me fully,' Jim says. A later aide, Tom McNally, observes: 'one got the impression that in the early launching of his career, Audrey had been a great source of strength and confidence.'

Callaghan won the Cardiff seat with a majority of 5,944 over the candidate who had held the seat, almost uninterrupted, for over twenty years. The Labour Party's victory seemed like a new dawn for the Labour parliamentarians, many from humble backgrounds, who, Jim believed, 'brought hope and understanding to millions of workers who asked only of society that it should give them and their children a fair deal in life, a chance to live decently, to bridge the gap between great riches and harsh poverty, and to ensure dignity in their old age'.[6] The new government's mandate to restructure the nation on more equitable lines was popular: the taxi driver taking Jim to the first meeting of the Parliamentary Labour Party refused to accept a fare.

Audrey was an assiduous constituency wife, travelling regularly to Cardiff, where, according to Jim, she 'was always liked very much by the women members of the Party . . . She came to the "surgeries", waiting in the outer office with the public, chatting to them and to the councillors, and then would slip away to go shopping in Queen Street and St Mary Street before we returned to London.' She was a very good MP's wife, Colleen Merlyn-Rees, wife of later fellow parliamentarian Merlyn Rees says, 'because she was interested and concerned and she would make everybody feel welcome, and she would remember about their children and what they did'.

As Jim's career progressed from backbencher to a junior minister at the Department of Transport from 1947, and then to Parliamentary Secretary at the Admiralty in 1950, Audrey went as often as possible to Cardiff, joining him at meetings and in canvassing as he was returned at successive elections in 1950, and in 1951, when the Labour Party lost to the Conservatives.

Though much of her time was absorbed with being a wife and the mother of their three growing children, she chose not to give up her own interests. She was not 'a housewife in any sort of traditional sense', her son Michael says, because 'she was always going out and doing something else'. She became chairman of the Maidstone Labour Party, and also ran the local Fabian Society. Their daughter Margaret Jay recalls, 'She was the one who was the political activist in our lives because it was in our house that all these people appeared. I was much more aware of *her* Labour Party, of local politics rather than Parliament, flowing through the house.' From an early age, the children were taken to the Fabian Society Easter School, where Michael remembers playing ping-pong in the games room of Beatrice Webb House while weighty discussions went on elsewhere. As they grew older, they helped out in the Cardiff constituency, or Audrey left them in the care of 'Auntie May', Jim's old landlady.

When in 1953 they moved to Maze Hill in Greenwich, Audrey built up close friendships with neighbours, often strengthened by their shared activities as mothers of school-age children. They mixed at family events where politics was little discussed. Audrey liked their company, and talked about art and books, and family concerns. At home, Audrey was the steady presence: 'She was always there when we were children,' her daughter, Julia Hubbard, recalls. 'She must have had everything in separate compartments. She would whiz off and do her work, and then come home and it would be the family time, and [she'd ask] "what have you done?"' With Jim often away late in the evenings, the only family meals were at weekends. Sunday lunch was a ritual: 'It would always appear, it would always be delicious – a wonderful roast, pudding and all the rest of it, and yet somehow she'd been out in the garden and she'd also been on the settee reading the newspaper.' She was 'completely unflappable', her friend from that time, the architect Ursula Bowyer, recalls. 'No situation would faze her. She would just get on with it, she'd do what was necessary.'

Their home was comfortable: 'She wasn't obsessively neat and tidy and she would pop things behind the sofa in a sort of glory hole,' Julia remembers, but she was organised as she juggled the various elements of her life. Each year they went on a fortnight's holiday to the coast, and after Audrey inherited some money from a relative, she bought a small cottage on the Isle of Wight, furnishing it from sale-room auctions.

At a time when there was not much money to go round, Audrey took a dressmaking course at the local adult education institute: 'We were very dowdy in those days – I'm not sure if we still had clothing coupons, but certainly there wasn't much in the way of fashion around to buy unless you had a lot of money. And she used to make clothes from the patterns in *Vogue* at this class. She always used to say, "I'm not a needlewoman", but she made her own clothes and they were always very elegant.' With a friend, Marja Kinsella, she progressed to a hat-making course.

At the same time, her interest was turning towards social work, and particularly work with children. Her teaching job had ended when she got married, for, as in a number of professions, women had to resign on marriage (a practice continued in the Civil Service until the 1970s). Using her training in nutrition, she took a part-time job as a dietician in the local hospital, advising pregnant mothers. Margaret was roped in to help: 'we all made charts, drawing green vegetables and carrots and so on, which she would hand out to them.'

She became involved with the management of several children's homes nearby, including the Hollies in Sidcup, which could later accommodate 320 children aged between one and a half and 16 in either cottages or houses, and had a swimming pool and gymnasium. Margaret remembers going to the Hollies for carol services: 'She was very much engaged with it. All the difficult things would be referred to her, like the children who'd run away and the ones they couldn't foster. She was pretty hands-on.' Julia adds: 'She was very *concerned* for children. She was very good with them, but not a great hugger and kisser of children. She was *socially* aware that children should be looked after and protected and given the care and love that they needed to develop.'

Guided by a powerful social conscience rooted as much in her Christian upbringing as in her political principles, Audrey felt strongly that she should 'be doing something for society, however small or large – making a contribution', Julia says. Her sympathy for people showed in all aspects of her personal life: 'Audrey was always on the side of kindness . . . she was a very caring woman. She would always be helpful and supportive when there were problems,' architect friend Gordon Bowyer recalls. Helen Denniss, the daughter of family friends, remembers her as 'an earth mother', who provided a 'sense of security and confidence' because 'she gave us respect and space'.

As Jim's political career progressed, he spent long hours at the House of Commons, and in 1956 he was appointed by Labour leader Hugh Gaitskell as Shadow Colonial and Commonwealth Affairs Secretary. Jim respected Audrey's need for her own vocation: 'Being separate as we were, in the sense that I was in the House, she was able to develop her own side, irrespective of me. She did what she thought was appropriate, I certainly didn't discourage her.' Later, Audrey offered some sage advice to all politicians' wives: 'We politicians' wives are grass widows a great deal of the time. And it's easy to become discontented and unhappy. If you're sensible you avoid a clash between your own interests and his.'[7]

By temperament Audrey was a tactful conciliator: 'She could be quite forceful, but she would try and find a way round things rather than head at them straight on,' her son says. Though she rarely spoke about herself, and could appear emotionally detached, she made her feelings known. 'She had a way of expressing herself – you knew what she was thinking. You knew particularly if she was very pleased or if she was very unhappy. She didn't need to tell you – you knew,' Jim says. She did push him, he confesses, but 'in an indirect way, so that I wasn't aware of what she was doing until it was all done in a nice way, and I would find she'd done it'.

She deployed her conciliation skills effectively in all areas of her life. 'If my father was cross with you, the family knew all about it, but my mother poured the oil on the troubled waters all the time. She saw that as her role,' Michael recalls. When anything went wrong, 'she was stoical', Jim says, and although she had a temper, she rarely showed it: 'If she felt like blowing up, her usual response would be to go into the garden and furiously dig the weeds out until she felt calm enough to return.' Julia remembers only one occasion 'when Mummy said

"Damn!" And Daddy looked so shocked. "Audrey!" he said. I think that must have been a very trying day.'

In 1958 they moved into their own house, designed and built by Gordon and Ursula Bowyer, on the edge of Blackheath. Audrey took an interest in the whole process and went with Ursula to choose colours, materials and fittings which, though not avant-garde, reflected the latest in modern design. On Sundays during the planning stages, Ursula and Gordon would drop by: 'We used to have a laugh,' they remember. 'It was all very modest in those days . . . We always had the most gorgeous quiches . . . and a bottle of Maltese white wine between the four of us.' Audrey 'always sees the funny side of things', Ursula says, but often she 'had a job to keep her eyes open. She was obviously exhausted at the end of the day, but she was always a quiet person.'

Audrey had meanwhile begun her own political career. In April 1958 she stood for election to the London County Council to represent her local Lewisham North ward: 'When the count was being declared in the Lewisham Town Hall, Audrey and I were at home having our supper when the phone rang, and the nice woman agent said, "Audrey, I think you're going to win." So we rushed off to the poll and when we got there Audrey was declared the winner. The *Daily Express* came along to get down the details, because it was unusual for a woman to become a councillor. They saw me and they said, "Tell me, Mr Callaghan, what do you do?"' Jim says, proudly. He was Shadow Colonial Secretary at the time. Soon Audrey was appointed chairman of the LCC Children's Committee, which had been set up after 1948 to oversee child welfare. The aim was to modernise child care, with a shift away from institutionalised care towards fostering and adoption, the acquisition of smaller, modern homes able to meet the emotional needs of children in care, and preventive work with families carried out by trained child-care workers. By 1961, the Children's Committee was responsible for 9,000 children in care, and the figure continued to rise.[8]

Audrey was at the heart of these reforms. She was 'immensely companionable, with an extraordinarily keen and good administrative mind', according to her colleague Peggy Jay. With her charm, quietness and humour, 'she could see though a mound of papers [and say] – a,b,c, this is what needs to be done. She was a very good committee chairman and everyone would play their part. She wouldn't stand any nonsense. She didn't want any guffing about. She wasn't raw and clumsy, she was graceful and tactful, and so she got her way.' A fellow member of the committee, later an MP, Christopher Chataway, recalled her as: 'One of the few people you always listened to with respect and care. She made no Party speeches. She was outspoken and actually tough, forthright. You knew she was sincere.'[9]

At the LCC, Audrey was one of a group of Labour women who had great influence in local government and later in the 1964 Labour government. Even before being elected, Audrey had made contact, partly through her work with children and partly through Jim's activities, with women working in the same field. Margaret recalls: 'They had a kind of gang. And it was a half-term treat to go and visit them in County Hall and have lunch.' The group included Peggy Jay, wife of Labour MP, Douglas Jay, Bea Serota who was Chief Whip at the LCC and Minister of State at the Department of Health in the 1964–70 Labour government, and Pat Llewellyn Davies, among others.

All were married women of prodigious energy and social conviction. None had been brought up to expect to earn a living *after* they married, and each, including Audrey, saw voluntary work as their contribution to improving society. 'We were a powerful group, growing in self-consciousness and effectiveness,' Peggy Jay says. Most were also bringing up children, constantly dashing home on the tube to arrive before the children came home from school. Peggy Jay wryly recalls arriving at the front door slightly late to hear one of her daughters on the phone saying, 'No, Mummy's not at home. She's giving a lecture about the importance of mothers being at home when their children get home from school.'

They were not 'career women', as they would have been in the next generation, even though their work amounted to a career. But during her time at the LCC, Audrey gained first-hand experience and understanding of politics and the political process, as well as taking on responsibility for running committees and organisations. She 'was a transition wife', Margaret Jay says, 'because, although in public perception she was very much a background, conventional, fifties and sixties wife, because of her own career in local government and her own interest in the various things she had as her particular causes . . . she did have her own identity'. When she lost her seat on the LCC in 1961, she continued as a co-opted member of the Children's Committee. In 1964 she became an alderman, and continued her work as chairman of the South Eastern district Children's Committee.

During the 1964 general election, Audrey campaigned with Jim in Cardiff. When Labour won, she was 'excited, oh, she was excited, as I was, although she wouldn't have shown it much', Jim says. Wilson appointed him Chancellor of the Exchequer, and they had their first experience of living in a government official residence, No. 11 Downing Street. As they were moving their personal belongings, a *Daily Express* photographer appeared 'and tried to get into the [Co-op removal] van and take photographs in the van. Audrey rang me up because I was over in the Treasury, and she said, "This man —" she was really upset that her private belongings were [being pried into]. So I rang up the editor of the *Daily Express* and said, "I think it's monstrous, absolutely disgraceful doing this sort of thing." And do you know, they didn't print the photograph!' According to their daughter Margaret, within minutes a huge bouquet of flowers arrived to greet Audrey at No. 11 Downing Street – with an apology from the editor.

From the outset, when Callaghan discovered that they had inherited from the Conservatives the highest ever balance of payments deficit, estimated at £800 million, the Wilson government's focus was on the economy. Callaghan recalled the amiable outgoing Chancellor, Reginald Maudling, who dropped into the office, carrying a pile of suits over his arm on his way out of No. 11, and said to Jim, sitting at his desk reading his briefs: 'Sorry, old cock, to leave it in this shape. I suggested to Alec [Douglas-Home] this morning that perhaps we should put up the bank rate but he thought he ought to leave it all to you. Good luck.' And with that he ambled off.[10] With only a small majority, the task ahead was huge.

While Audrey was adapting to being Chancellor's wife, in 1965 she became a grandmother to Margaret's daughter, Tamsin. Margaret had married Peter Jay, son of Audrey's LCC colleague Peggy and Jim's fellow parliamentarian, Douglas. Audrey was concerned to maintain a family atmosphere. The flat at No. 11, rebuilt in the early 1960s by architect, Raymond Erith, is really a purpose-built and spacious self-contained house, with none of the makeshift feel of the No. 10 flat. Though they did not entertain regularly, friends visited. 'Audrey was so easy and she would just get on and do things. She'd just rustle up a toad-in-the-hole or something for everybody to eat, and she laughed a lot. She could always see the funny side of things,' Colleen Merlyn-Rees remembers. A key element in their family life was still the ritual Sunday lunch: 'She'd ring up on Sunday morning and say, "I'm just starting to think about how many potatoes we need,"' Margaret remembers. Her brother Michael, then at Cardiff University, had a room at No. 11 and, he says, 'just bowled up in my Mini and parked at the end of the road'. His 21st birthday party was held there. Julia lived upstairs, in 'this rather nice Central London flat, perched up in the attic rooms. It was incredibly relaxed. There was so little security in comparison to today.' With a regular secretarial job Julia was also doing social work at the Blackfriars Settlement across the river. In 1967 she married ophthalmic surgeon Ian Hubbard from No. 11, where the hall with its elegant staircase and adjoining reception rooms provided ample space for the wedding reception.

During the 1966 general election, with Jim preoccupied with affairs of state, Audrey took over from him in Cardiff. As she canvassed door to door in a floppy brown artist's beret and a checked rust-coloured suit, she gave a local reporter 'an impression of tremendous inner strength'. Most constituents knew her as she stood at the doorstep listening to their problems. 'Generally I am welcomed when I knock at the front door,' she said, unless something has gone wrong and the children are around their feet, when 'they very likely think that I would be greater help washing the dishes than chatting on the doorstep'. She enjoyed going to pensioners' meetings, and found talking to people stimulating: 'She understands the housewife's problems,' one constituent said. 'Talking to her woman to woman is more reassuring than talking to a man. You get the feeling that nothing, however small, is trivial in her eyes.'[11]

The 1966 election delivered a comfortable majority for Labour, but almost immediately the government faced another fiscal crisis, as sterling reserves drained away, the trade deficit worsened, and the emotive solution of devaluation was canvassed. Inevitably these important political events had an impact on the whole family living at the centre of them. Jim opposed devaluation. His son-in-law Peter Jay, then economics editor at *The Times*, supported it. In private, though normally there was little discussion of politics, Audrey listened to the opposing arguments put by Peter and by their son, Michael, who was now studying at Manchester Business School and followed his father's line. 'She wrestled with it a lot,' Michael recalls. 'She would go through the arguments with you – "Well, what about . . .?" "Well, why don't we . . .?" It was the worry of "What do you do? Are you going to have to resign?" – and [he'd say] "I've given guarantees to various foreign governments about what we're going to do, and I said we wouldn't devalue and now we're going to have to."' Michael found it 'quite traumatic. I'm sure she did as well. And you feel exposed even though you're not able to do anything about it. I think she absorbed all that pressure.' When an old friend, Marja Kinsella, visited her during the crisis, it was the only time she'd ever seen Audrey upset: '[Jim] got brutally attacked and she was very distressed about that. I think she needed the comfort of an old friend.'

The devaluation on 19 November 1967 was seen in the press as a national defeat. It damaged the government's standing and Wilson's personal prestige after he made the evasive claim that it did not mean that 'the pound in your pocket or purse or in your bank has been devalued'. Callaghan was accused of being a traitor. Talk of his imminent resignation was in the air when Susan Crosland, wife of Jim's potential successor, Tony Crosland, met Audrey at an official lunch: 'Her husband's career in ruins, she was dignified as ever, discussing with Mrs Mulley something sensible like dry rot.' When Susan Crosland asked: 'How can you get through a week like this?' the normally calm Audrey replied, 'I can't sleep. I wake up and I can't make my brain stop. I would never advise Jim on politics, but I can't make my brain stop.'[12] Jim reflects that he was not surprised that she had sleepless nights – 'but she wouldn't have told me'. Although, he remembers, 'She moved out of the double bed into a single bed. I think that was to help me because I had dispatch boxes all around me.'

Though Callaghan offered his resignation, he was instead transferred to the Home Office, where he faced a period of gathering unrest. Almost immediately conflict erupted in Northern Ireland when the emergence of the Civil Rights movement in 1968 opened up deep sectarian wounds. British troops were moved into the province to establish order and separate the hostile factions in August 1969. When Audrey visited Northern

Ireland with Jim, she told an interviewer: 'what shocked me most was the strength of feeling of young children and old ladies, the hatred, the way they shouted at us'.[13] Opposition to the Vietnam War and Wilson's failure to dissociate from US President Johnson's policies fed growing dissent among Labour backbenchers and galvanised the radical left into protest on the streets. A massive anti-Vietnam War demonstration in London in March 1968 ended in violence, but Callaghan refused to bow to pressure to ban a second, which went off peacefully in October; 'Sunny Jim' strolled into Grosvenor Square at the end to mingle with police and the rump of the protesters.

In one area of his responsibility as Home Secretary, Audrey had a part to play. During the passage of the Children and Young Persons Act 1969, her knowledge and experience influenced him in discussions over the long-overdue reforms to the child welfare system 'to make it more flexible and responsive to the varied needs of individual children'.[14] Audrey was also a helpful ally to MP Leo Abse in his campaign to change the adoption laws, an area where she had considerable experience. Though she did not force her case, she was, according to Jim, 'very strong in her opinions . . . She would say clearly what she thought ought to be done, without making life difficult for me.'

Because of the pressures of being Chancellor's wife Audrey had resigned from the Children's Committee in October 1967. But in 1969 she was appointed by her former GLC colleague Bea Serota, now Minister of Health in the Labour government, as chairman of the Board of Governors of Great Ormond Street Children's Hospital, a post she held through many years of turbulent changes in hospital administration. She was immediately faced with the merger and reorganisation of several hospitals into a new group, including Tadworth and the Queen Elizabeth Hospital in Hackney. 'There were major difficulties trying to ensure cohesion and co-operation,' fellow board member, Caroline Bond, testified.

As she visited the hospitals and met the staff, her 'courtesy, common sense and ability were recognised'; particularly her ability to listen which, according to Caroline Bond, 'stood her in good stead when difficult decisions had to be made', and, as her colleague at Great Ormond Street Sir Anthony Tippet testifies, her 'quiet, imperturbable gentleness, her absolute sincerity, her uprightness and lack of self-regard' were greatly appreciated.[15] 'You couldn't but love Audrey because she's such a very gentle, caring, understanding person,' her colleague on the board, Ann Riches, says. 'She was the boss of the whole shooting match. She always seemed rather cool, calm and collected, and got on with things', and though she was never a tough chairman she was an effective one who could command the loyalty of staff: 'She was always around, she was seen in the hospital. She had a lovely sense of humour. Things very easily made her laugh, and she'd always be smiling. She's got the most *wonderful* smile. She was always very well prepared at every board meeting. Obviously if she was doubtful about something she would have gone and talked to somebody about it.' Though she was not keen on personal publicity she was always available to open new hospital units, conduct tours of wards and facilities for visiting dignitaries and donors, give out prizes to nurses and attend other ceremonies associated with the hospital. When Cherie attended the 100th birthday celebrations for Great Ormond Street in 2001, Audrey was still remembered with great affection.

Shortly after their departure from No. 11 Downing Street in 1967, the Callaghans decided to fulfil a plan they had been harbouring for some years, to buy a farm in partnership with an old friend in Sussex, Gordon Denniss. Upper Clay Hill Farm was a part-Elizabethan, part-Georgian farmhouse with 138 acres amidst rolling countryside in Sussex, and Audrey took great delight in its refurbishment. For both it was an escape from politics, and an ideal place for the expanding family of grandchildren. Meanwhile they found a small flat in Kennington, conveniently close to the House of Commons, as their London base.

Audrey converted the farm's old stables in order to rear pigs, an interest she shared with the Archbishop of Canterbury, Robert Runcie – 'whenever they met, they talked pigs', Jim recalls. Each time she went down, 'one of the first things – open up, cup of tea, down to the pigs . . . feed, check them, water them. All the scraps from the kitchen – take them down to the pigs . . . they were her project,' Brenda Shepherd, their housekeeper, says. Though she didn't do the mucking-out, she handled the business side herself, dealing with vets, ordering supplies, and buying and selling. 'I think they grew very quickly and could be eaten rather quickly, to be honest,' says Julia, 'that was their role in life . . . to turn themselves into pork chops or bacon or whatever.' Audrey was not sentimental when it was time for market about either the pigs or the eight bullocks which she also reared.

The vegetable garden was another passion. With the help of Bill Puttocks, who had been the stableman 'in the old horse and plough days', she erected a huge wire cage which produced an ample supply of raspberries, blackcurrants, redcurrants and gooseberries, alongside the fruit trees and blackberries and the sweet peas which grew in rows between the crops. She redesigned the whole garden, but when her life became busier later, as well as having to give up the cattle, she replanted it with the help of landscape gardener, Rhys Nowell, to introduce more bushes and shrubs for all year round colour. Meanwhile Jim read *Farmers Weekly* on the train, cultivated wheat and discussed farm management on long walks around his land with his partner, Gordon Denniss.

During the 1970 general election, Audrey was philosophical: 'I'm optimistic about the outcome,' she said initially, 'but if it goes wrong, there'll be no good moaning and groaning about it.' With Michael and Julia both married, she was now grandmother to three children – 'Being a grandmother is my great joy at the moment. I can't see my grandchildren now for three weeks,' she told a reporter.[16] After Labour lost, Audrey found more time to build up her interests on the farm. In 1970 she gave up her position as alderman at the renamed GLC (Greater London Council) and focused on Great Ormond Street Hospital. So settled was she that when Jim, at 60, allowed his name to be put forward as a candidate for Managing Director of the International Monetary Fund in Washington, Audrey made clear that she wanted to remain in Britain close to her children and grandchildren. Jim was thus 'relieved' when his candidature went no further after it was boycotted by the French.

On the Labour government's return to power in 1974, Jim was appointed Foreign Secretary and Audrey faced the prospect of moving into the official residence at Carlton Gardens. But the departing Elizabeth Douglas-Home had warned Audrey that the building's drawbacks included a roof leaking so badly that she had had to put a bucket in the bedroom to catch the drips when it rained, the house was infested with dry rot and some of the external stone parapets were dangerous. Audrey never moved in, though she oversaw the repairs which took up the whole of Jim's time as Foreign Secretary. Dorneywood was made available, but they used it only for official entertainment. Their daughter Julia remembers visiting once: 'Rather fierce sort of people looked after it, so you hardly dared go in, really. We were allowed in under sufferance for about an hour and then maybe we could leave, was the impression you got. It wasn't welcoming at all.' This impression was conveyed to most Foreign Secretaries' wives. Colleen Merlyn-Rees thought 'Dorneywood was lovely. The butler and his wife were very helpful. The cook had cooked for Churchill and she did it under great sufferance . . . You got the message.'

As well as her work for Great Ormond Street, Audrey's time was now taken up with the more demanding schedule of official entertaining and trips abroad. Once again, the experience as Foreign Secretary's wife proved a valuable apprenticeship for life at No. 10. Audrey continued Elizabeth Home's work of playing hostess to diplomatic wives and taking care of the practical and family problems associated with new arrivals. On foreign trips, she was well briefed: 'I always did my homework,' she told an interviewer. 'It is much more fun if you know something about the country before you visit it.'[17] Though much of Callaghan's time was taken up with renegotiating the terms for Britain to remain in the EEC in a climate of fierce Party division (a referendum in 1975 decided in favour of staying in), Audrey travelled with him on a twelve-day trip to the Gulf States and Africa in January 1974. This included Malawi, where she recalled a great enthusiastic African banquet with women down one side and men down the other, Victoria Falls – 'a rainbow of splashing water' – and 'horrific traffic jams' in Nigeria. On her own separate schedule, she took a professional interest in the hospitals and schools she visited. Often she had to remind herself to leave behind her carrier bags full of books and odds and ends as she walked down the plane's steps to face the waiting photographers and dignitaries.

On several trips to America Audrey and Jim forged a lasting friendship with President Gerald Ford and his wife Betty. Long after each had left office, they holidayed together at the Fords' home in Colorado. Audrey also got on with Russian Foreign Minister, Andrei Gromyko. 'She liked Gromyko. She and Gromyko got on well together. Extraordinary!' Jim remembers. In London in March 1976, Audrey took him and his wife, Lydia, to the Tate Gallery. 'They both liked pictures.

She arranged for him to go and visit galleries . . . He always asked about her, and when we went over he always made a point of seeing her. That was rather nice of Gromyko, but he was a rough old boy.' Jim delighted in Audrey's successes. At a German Embassy dinner, he sat next to a woman who wanted to know about each of the other guests: 'We went round the table, we got to Audrey, and she said, "Who is that lady with the lovely smile?" I said, "That's my wife!"'

When they returned from Harold Wilson's 60th birthday party in March 1976 and Jim told her of the Prime Minister's impending resignation, Audrey did not hesitate to back him as the candidate to succeed Wilson. At nearly 63, with experience as the wife of the holder of three major offices of state – Chancellor of the Exchequer, Foreign Office and Home Office – she had lived in government residences, presided over official entertainments and was familiar with the way Civil Service routine impinged on private life.

She found the three-week process of selecting the new leader trying, but not tense, since Callaghan led in each of the three ballots. With a well organised campaign team he took a rather detached attitude to publicising himself, declining to take part in press or television interviews: 'our fellow Members . . . were unlikely to be impressed by pictures of me on their TV screens dressed in a striped apron and pretending to wash up in the kitchen, as had happened during the Tory leadership election,'[18] he chuckled, referring to Willie Whitelaw's campaign the previous year. When Jim won, Audrey accompanied him to Buckingham Palace and waited in an ante-room while the Queen invited him to form a government.

Callaghan's emergence as a leader by a decisive margin was greeted with qualified approval by the Party and in the press. THE NATION IS BEHIND HIM, *The Times* headline announced. But with no overall majority, and inflation and unemployment still rising, Callaghan was in no doubt about the difficulties that lay ahead. 'We are not in a position to make easy promises,' he warned. 'There are no soft options facing Britain.'

Audrey was perceived as a powerful factor in his success. His 'remarkable resilience and the atmosphere of fulfilled contentment which he so often and reassuringly exudes', *The Times* declared, was due to his wife, who 'gives him a sense of stability, of reassurance and security as well as a wonderful home'.[19] Audrey was variously described as 'the unflappable first lady of Downing Street'[20] and 'The Quiet Woman Moving into No. 10' who 'kept out of her husband's limelight', and whose apparent shyness hid an 'iron determination and stamina and the passion for causes of the dedicated committee woman'.[21] By the time Audrey got to No. 10, she 'was very confident, there was nobody that fazed her', Tom McNally, Jim's later political adviser, concluded.

The Callaghans moved into No. 10 in May. At first, following the Wilsons' precedent, the Callaghans chose to remain in their Kennington flat because Jim preferred to get away from No. 10's hothouse atmosphere. But Audrey took the decision to move in: 'One day she said, "I'm not doing this any more, dear. I'm coming up to No. 10." Just like that. She wasn't seeing enough of me.' Audrey thought it an advantage to be in touch with everybody, but she disliked being recognised – 'I'd like to be an anonymous face. I'm afraid it will become more and more difficult,' she told a reporter.[22] She generally used the back gate 'to escape prying eyes' and made clear 'that what she called "the goldfish bowl existence" of No. 10 was not particularly to her taste', Jim says. Invariably she travelled by bus: 'She could come and go. Mummy kept a sense of what the real world is like, getting a bus and going to the shops and doing it on her own, unnoticed. She always seemed to be able to fade into the background,' her daughter Julia says.

Jim and Audrey Callaghan, like those before and after them, found the No. 10 flat a bit poky. The dining room and kitchen were both small and inadequate and she wished the flat would catch up with modern technology, but Audrey was happy to live with décor which had been 'beautifully done up by Colefax and Fowler'[23] during Edward Heath's tenure. Both she and Jim liked the view over Horse Guards'. Parade and St James's Park. With her interest in art, she took her friend, Ursula Bowyer, to choose pictures from the Government Art Collection: 'It was very much part of her principle to support living artists and living architects [and] to go along with the current style,' Ursula recalls. A Hugh Casson watercolour of Downing Street, the original of which now hangs in their farm, is still used on the menu cards for official functions at No. 10.

Though Audrey would have liked to change more, she was cautious, not knowing how long they would remain there in the precarious political climate: 'I'd never really expected to go on for three years . . . and Audrey never really settled down in No. 10 because of that,' Jim says. With no majority in the Commons, and the constant possibility of defeat, they kept on the Kennington flat; Jim felt 'he might be out of here by Friday and he didn't want to have to go looking for something, like the Wilsons did in 1970. Everyone was conscious about that,' says Policy Unit adviser, Bernard Donoughue.

Callaghan's government faced a series of crises from the moment he took over. With inflation at over 20 per cent and sterling under severe pressure, in November 1976 the government was forced to negotiate an International Monetary Fund Loan to prop up the pound and restore confidence in the economy. The price of the loan was massive public expenditure cuts and the continuation of a pay freeze, which Callaghan secured in co-operation with the trade union leaders. But Cabinet divisions and backbench dissent threatened to undermine their hold on power. With no majority, the government was dependent on the support of the minority parties to survive. A pact negotiated with the Liberals in March 1977 eased their difficulties for a time.

Audrey had concluded that 'there was no defined role for the PM's spouse except to be a hostess and helpmate', Jim says. She took official entertaining in her stride and, though she was 'fundamentally a fairly shy woman', 'she took a grip of it and did it, and did her bit. She was very good at introducing one to other people,' Gordon Bowyer recalls. At formal state occasions she was warm and welcoming, though later, Jim remembers, she was 'sorry that it was not always possible to savour the occasions when visiting prime ministers and others were entertained by her. She always liked to linger longer – she never cared to be hurried.'

Believing that she could use her influence at No. 10 for the good, Audrey was keen to make herself, and Downing Street, more accessible. She told Colleen Merlyn-Rees, '"Because I'm Prime Minister's wife now, I've got extra clout, so I will use it." She was always writing begging letters to people, which wasn't what she liked doing, but if it was a good cause she would do it.' As well as holding regular teas at No. 10 for the wives of MPs and inviting in people from the constituency, she opened it up to receptions for charities, and held one of the first No. 10 charity lunches on behalf of Great Ormond Street Hospital. People from other charities – the Chailey Heritage, National Children's Bureau and the Pestalozzi Villages – were invited to social events, and she hosted the Variety Club children's parties, and parties for children from the London boroughs, as well as presenting the *Woman's Own* Children of Courage awards.

Audrey told Jim that she had decided to continue with her own interests while at No. 10, chief among them Great Ormond Street Hospital. Within months of her arrival, she launched a £1 million appeal for research into child health and children's diseases at London University's Institute of Child Health.[24] As chairman of the Board of Governors of Great Ormond Street, Audrey attended their regular meetings, fitting them around her other engagements: 'She left No. 10, usually on foot, walking down Downing Street. There was usually a handful of photographers but . . . she deliberately used to regulate her pace to avoid being caught inappropriately, turned into Whitehall and caught the bus at the nearby stop to go to the hospital,' Jim says.

With her experience of work in her own right, Audrey was more confident than her predecessors about making speeches, although she made as few as she could. She worried over them and often asked Jim's advice: 'I might alter it a little, but rarely . . . Because when she made a speech, and she'd written it out and she made it, it was splendid. Because it was *her*. It was *her* speech and it came across as her speech, and something she wanted to say, and she said it.'

Despite a busy official schedule, Audrey's only secretarial help was Ruth Sharpe, a former wartime SOE (Special Operations Executive) operative and a stalwart who had been with Jim as constituency and then Private Secretary for over twenty years. Ruth Sharpe was 'one of those old-fashioned, absolutely dedicated secretary/personal assistant types – and very much a prop, who came a lot to the house', Margaret recalls. In the flat, Audrey had the help of two cleaners, with whom she kept in touch for years afterwards, and she did most of the cooking herself, except for official functions which were organised by Government Hospitality and co-ordinated by the Social Secretary, Sue Goodchild, who remained at No. 10 until 1998.

Though Audrey cared much more about people than about appearance, she was aware that, as Prime Minister's wife, she needed 'to have nicer, better things than she might have done buying them at department stores beforehand,' Margaret Jay recalls. Early on Audrey told a reporter: 'the wife of a Prime Minister doesn't get a clothes allowance, although some mayoresses do, I believe . . . Jim would get a shock if he knew the extra clothes I've bought.'[25] An old friend, Violet Denniss, who was well-off and always extremely elegant and fashion conscious – 'a profess-ional shopper', her daughter, Helen Denniss, says – introduced her to a designer, Ian Thomas. She wore conventional clothes with some nicely cut suits, but 'it was a bit of a worry, because you have to have so many', Julia says. With her public profile as an older woman and grandmother who concerned herself with charities and outside activi-ties, comment in the press about her fashion sense was relatively scarce, though, Jim recalls, 'all the snobs used to say she wasn't well dressed and the fashion people in the *Daily Mail* and so on would write her down. Not that it would have bothered her in the slightest. It would have gone totally over her head, even if she'd known about it.'

In 1977, the year of the Queen's Silver Jubilee, the nation celebrated with festivities, carnivals, bonfires and fireworks. Street parties were held up and down the country, and Union Jacks sprouted on every street corner, as well as on the clothes of anti-monarchy punk rock groups. Audrey's schedule became busier. She was decked out in a feathered and spangled hat and cloak to launch the Pearly Bus Appeal in Covent Garden on behalf of the cockney pearly kings and queens of London in January: WE'RE AFTER YOUR BEES AND HONEY read the slogan on the bus which gave her a lift back to Downing Street. She appeared for the first time on television presenting the Nurse of the Year Award in Birmingham.

When the Ministry of Defence invited her to launch a frigate in April, Tom McNally hesitated; since it was called HMS *Battleaxe*, he warned, 'the press will have a field day if she does it'. But 'the next time I saw her, she said, "That ship – of *course* I'll do it. It will be great fun!"' The only press comment was that she might have waited for the launch of HMS *Brilliant* – not due until the next year – 'by which time it is unlikely . . . that the Callaghans will still be tenants of 10 Downing Street'.[26] Audrey kept in touch with the ship's crew and 'It was always made clear to me that whenever Audrey was aboard, she was regarded as the principal guest by the ship's company, not me.' When it was finally paid off and sold to the Brazilian Navy, nine of the captains who had served as commanding officers gave her a grand farewell dinner aboard HMS *Belfast*.

The Jubilee festivities in June coincided with the Commonwealth Heads of Government Conference. Delayed by one of their meetings at Lancaster House on 9 June, Audrey and Jim narrowly avoided being late for lunch with the Queen and Prince Philip on the royal yacht, *Britannia* after an 80 mile an hour dash with a police escort to Tower Bridge. 'Of course, you can't keep royalty waiting. I thought we would never make it,' she told an interviewer.[27] In the evening, Audrey hosted a formal dinner at No. 10 followed by a visit to the Shell Building on the South Bank to watch the fireworks. The following day, there was a Chequers lunch for Commonwealth delegates' wives, and she received the heads of delegations and their wives at No. 10 before the Queen's birthday parade and Trooping the Colour. Shortly afterwards, they were off to Scotland to stay at Gleneagles for formal meetings, more entertaining and receptions, and Audrey led coach tours for the wives to sites of interest.

Whatever the occasion, Audrey tended to keep a low profile and get on with what needed to be done with the minimum of fuss. She was never 'in awe of anybody above her, or looked down on anybody below her', says Tom McNally. On their visits to the Queen at Balmoral, Callaghan, like Wilson before him, was delighted. Audrey was more circumspect: 'She was always very sensible about that. She would take it in her stride. She was never overwhelmed by it,' Jim says. She told an interviewer, Diana Farr, that it was 'one of the nicest things we did. The high tea and all the people gathered round reminded me of home on the farm.'[28] Jim 'liked the walks and I liked driving round with the Duke of Edinburgh in the Land Rover' where, according to Margaret, they used to 'sing loud, rollicking hymns'.

The Callaghans used Chequers for private rest as well as official entertainment, which Audrey enjoyed, 'especially as she didn't have to do the work, and she took great pleasure in taking guests round and explaining the history of the house and its contents'. Callaghan occasionally held Cabinet meetings there 'because they liked the fresh air and to have a look around the garden and be free of prying cameras', explains one of the staff who worked under the housekeeper, Vera Thomas. Audrey oversaw the menus and 'was meticulous in watching that problems with diet and religious taboos did not arise'. Once she had to use all her skill and tact to prevent the housekeeper marching out shortly before a lunch for a visiting prime minister because of the dietary demands made by his staff.

When she was the hostess, the atmosphere was welcoming and usually informal enough to feel like home. The diplomat Nicko Henderson met her during the visit of French President Giscard d'Estaing in 1977: 'Mrs Callaghan . . . is a warm-hearted, apparently uncomplicated person who does not feel inhibited from enjoying the pleasures and comforts Chequers offers to the wife of the Prime Minister.' Talking with him over tea, 'she seemed at a loss to know what to do, exactly like the rest of us, cast aside by our political masters as they indulge in private talks'. While the leaders dined alone, though it was suggested that she have dinner upstairs on a tray, she asked if she might join the officials as 'it would amuse her more to be with us'; she 'gave every appearance of enjoying herself enormously' and their two French colleagues were 'intrigued by the lack of pomp about the whole affair'.[29]

As always, Christmas at Chequers was 'a real delight, absolutely wonderful', says their son, Michael. Audrey was pleased because the children and their ten grandchildren could be together in one place. One staff member recalls: 'We used to have to get high chairs in. It did change, but in a nice way. Chopping and changing the sheets with chocolate on them!' Staff put up an enormous 20-foot tree in the Great Hall, and one in an ante-room on the first floor, and decorated them with 'different scenes. We used to make little deers and things like that,' the staff member says; and they created a near life-size snow-covered cardboard reindeer and sledge outside the grandchildren's bedrooms.

On trips abroad, Audrey was 'very good, very confident'. She frequently had a separate agenda, and usually asked to see hospitals and children's facilities. On a trip to China, Jim's doctor, Montague Levine, who always travelled with him, went with her to visit centres of medical interest and she kept in touch for years afterwards with women she met in many different countries. In America, with President

Carter's wife, Rosalynn, she visited cancer wards for children aged from one to early teenage years. Because on that trip she planned to join her daughter Margaret and son-in-law Peter Jay, Britain's ambassador in Washington, to celebrate Jim's 66th birthday, Audrey was meticulous about paying her own fare.

She read her briefings carefully and took an interest in social and cultural events. On a visit to the Taj Mahal, a member of the accompanying press corps, Anthony Holden, recalls Audrey correcting Callaghan on the Indian dynasties, and quoting some lines of Indian poetry: 'She knew it all. She's a very bright, intelligent lady,' he decided. Later she enjoyed watching Southern Indian classical dance to the tune of sitar, tabla and harmonium in Fatehpur, before visiting a bird sanctuary.

Audrey was always interested in the detail of politics. Though she could give the impression of being self-effacing, she held firm opinions on some policy issues about which she knew a great deal and felt strongly: 'I don't think she ever offered me advice, but she would always give me an opinion if I asked for it . . . She didn't tell me what to say, or what she thought I ought to be doing . . . She'd give me her honest opinion about what she thought, but she would temper it to my known prejudices!' Jim explains.

Almost no one heard them debate policy, but Tom McNally observed how 'she would make quiet comments and observations . . . she would often say something quietly, but with a "darling" at the end of it, which would make him pause and think . . . If you were talking about benefits or something, and if the conversation was moving in terms of – "we can't have them scrounging", or whatever, she would say, "Well, you know, it is extremely hard if you're in those circumstances."' Jim listened to her 'very carefully when she brought things from the shop floor, when she would say, "In practice this is what happens. In theory it might be wonderful, but actually on the ground this is what works,"' their daughter, Julia, says.

Jim respected her opinions: 'He certainly viewed her as an expert in the health service, local government and so forth,' Bernard Donoughue noted. When cuts in public expenditure following the IMF loan in 1976 were being discussed, she had a direct influence on him. The Cabinet had agreed massive cuts, including in the Health Service, Donoughue recalls, 'and Jim came in on perhaps Monday morning, and he said to me: "Audrey says that you can't do that. It won't do. You can't cut that much, it will do damage." And so he said, "We're going to recover some of that. I'm going to speak to Denis [Healey, Chancellor of the Exchequer]."' When Callaghan achieved agreement to restore £50 million from the proposed cuts, he 'wrote to the Secretary of State, David Ennals, saying, "There's fifty million coming. I want it to go for the care of patients",' an objective which was achieved despite protest from health union workers concerned about their low-paid status.

Audrey also exercised her influence in other areas. When a seven months' pregnant British woman, Mrs Susan Rabkin, was detained in solitary confinement by South African police in July 1976, Audrey, in her capacity as chairman of the Great Ormond Street Hospital, sent a letter to the South African Ambassador expressing deep concern about her treatment; Mrs Rabkin was released on bail. Audrey was 'always writing little notes for other people', says Roshan Horobin, a Pakistani probation officer who had mentioned to Audrey a delay in a Home Office report; Audrey brought it to the attention of the relevant department, which had an immediate effect.[30]

On a personal level, colleagues at No. 10 observed her consideration for Callaghan's staff and civil servants. Jim 'wasn't the easiest person . . . He could be very severe and grumpy. But if Audrey was around, that was very helpful,' Bernard Donoughue says. When Jim was under pressure, Tom McNally remembers, 'she would just quietly remind Jim of things which he sometimes needed reminding to do – a "thank you" or an appreciation that staff had actually been up since 6 a.m. to get all this ready – just little things, just tweaks'.

Callaghan constantly referred to her in conversation. 'Often he'd say, "oh yes, Audrey was saying that,"' Bernard Donoughue says. When she was involved in an accident as she drove out of Downing Street in February 1977 and needed hospital treatment, he was so anxious he left an important Cabinet meeting to make sure she was all right. Her calmness steadied him: 'He had this permanent problem that when he had to give a speech – and Jim wrote quite a lot of his speeches – he would always feel he'd got nothing to say, and he would panic the day before and he'd say to Audrey, "I don't know what to say. I've got nothing to say." And she would say to him, "Don't worry. Calm down.

Yes you do. What about this? What do you think about that?" And she would get him moving and then before he knew where he was, he'd written a speech.'

Jim also showed consideration for Audrey's concerns. Their daughter, Margaret Jay, vividly remembers one evening when she was in the flat at No. 10 'watching the news with my mother. There was a political drama going on which was reported as a major crisis. You would have thought, watching it, that my father wouldn't be able to think or talk about anything else. But when he came in, the first thing he wanted her to tell him about was how some crucial meeting had gone at Great Ormond Street that afternoon. That was the first thing they talked about, and that wasn't unusual.'

By mid-1978, although the government had succeeded in bringing inflation down to 8 per cent another crisis was looming. The deal struck with the unions to stick to a 5 per cent pay limit was faltering. Callaghan held the line; he had turned down the chance of an election that year because there was no certainty of a sufficient majority, and he believed that the pay policy backed by the TUC leaders would hold. But with no easing of restraints in sight, unemployment still up, and wage claims as high as 30 per cent threatening to breach the guidelines completely, the government's problems multiplied.

In times of crisis, Audrey's presence was reassuring. 'Every day there was a problem during that government, but you knew when it was really serious, because going over to the House at Question Time, when we'd normally sit in the car, Jim would suddenly say, "Oh, if you don't mind, I'd like Audrey with me today." And then you knew,' Bernard Donoughue recalls. When he was making one of his really important speeches, 'she would sit up in the Gallery. And I used to watch him. He would get up to the dispatch box and he would look up at her, and she was just sitting there looking at him, then he'd look at his feet and then he was off, he was all right. It was as if he needed a reference point that was supportive.'

In the autumn, when the Trades Union and the Labour Party conferences both voted against the continuation of the pay policy, and the government was defeated when left-wing Labour MPs also voted against it, the floodgates opened. Strikes, official and unofficial, spread across the country. During the freezing, snow-bound January of 1979, oil tanker drivers and road haulage drivers, railwaymen, water workers, and 1.5 million low-paid public service employees brought the country to a standstill. After three years of wage restraint, a long list of further pay claims, including by civil servants, was banking up. The appalling weather added to the industrial chaos.

Callaghan's authority was badly undermined when he returned with Audrey in early January 1979 from a Four Power summit with President Carter in Guadeloupe, where they had been photographed relaxing on the beach. At the airport, he ignored the dictum never to speak about domestic subjects when returning from abroad until he had been thoroughly briefed, and he was at his most bluff and avuncular as he assured the country that this crisis could be overcome. But he missed the mood of the moment; the statement was dramatically translated by the *Sun* newspaper into the bold banner headline: CRISIS? WHAT CRISIS?[31] – a phrase that would haunt him. The abiding image of the Winter of Discontent was of streets piled high with black bags of rotting rubbish; of food and supplies unable to get through, railways at a standstill, and people turned away from Merseyside cemeteries, unable to bury their dead, as the trade union leadership lost control.

Callaghan grew visibly more gloomy as he tried to devise a policy to cope with the deteriorating situation. But Audrey, too, had become embroiled in the disputes. She had experienced the growing tensions over the previous months as unofficial lightning strikes by public service union members disrupted operations at the children's hospitals in her charge. The previous October, the opening of a new unit to treat spina bifida and other severely disabled children at the Queen Elizabeth Hospital in Hackney was delayed after action by hospital ancillary workers in a long-running dispute over staffing levels and low pay. Faced with pickets outside the hospital, Audrey was restrained as she expressed her sadness at the action, and her hope that the dispute would be resolved soon, though other voices condemned industrial action 'whose target is the halt and the lame'.[32]

In February, at the height of the strike by the health service unions, NUPE and COHSE, both Queen Elizabeth Hospital and Great Ormond Street Hospital were targeted by 24-hour strikes and stoppages, causing major disruption. Callaghan appealed angrily for a return to work at all hospitals: 'It is not acceptable in any community that sick human beings, whether adult or children, should have their food denied them and proper attention forbidden to them.'[33] At a Cabinet meeting on 1 February, according to Joel Barnett, Chief Secretary to the Treasury, he addressed his dissenting colleague Tony Benn with the question 'What do you say about the thuggish act of a walk-out, without notice, from a children's hospital?' Tony replied that: 'When decent people become irrational, something else must be wrong if they are driven to such desperate acts.' Jim Callaghan's response was that 'he had never in fifty years been so depressed as a trade unionist'.[34]

Others who felt that Audrey was being targeted because she was the Prime Minister's wife were more forthright. During a Great Ormond Street board meeting chaired by Audrey, her colleague, Ann Riches, exploded in fury when the young union representative started dictating terms about who would be allowed to fill in for the striking porters and domestic staff in order to keep the hospital going. 'I was *furious*. I just hit the roof,' Ann Riches recalled. 'He was saying to a very senior nurse, "Well, you and one of your nurses can clean the wards", and possibly looking at me and the others, "and you can work in the laundry", and telling us what we could do in a not at all pleasant way. I thought it was quite unbearable and rude and I just stood up and said, "Madam Chairman, how can we sit here and let this man talk to us [like this]?" I was feeling angry for Audrey because I knew he was completely taking advantage of the fact that Jim was the Prime Minister and her husband.'

Audrey remained calm, but by March, with the dispute still going on, sick children being turned away, and Great Ormond Street Hospital a continuing target, she spoke out: 'Naturally, I condemn the action of the strikers . . . I would have thought that nine per cent was a reasonable offer. I feel extremely sad and sorry for those children who cannot be admitted to the hospital as a result of the strike. Children are very vulnerable, you know!' When unions protested at the number of volunteers being brought in to replace strikers, she countered: 'If necessary I would have been prepared to get down on my hands and knees and scrub the floors', though the hospital administrator assured her it would not be necessary, and the dispute was settled next day.[35]

The legacy of the Winter of Discontent was a massive drain of support, including among trade unionists, and a steady increase in support for the Conservatives under Margaret Thatcher, their leader since 1975, who was uncompromising in her hostility to union power. Callaghan, a lifelong believer in the values of trade unionism, had suffered a severe setback to his faith. There seemed to be no solution to the impasse as wage claims surged and further strikes were averted by settlements in the region of 20–30 per cent – far above the line the government had tried to maintain, which in turn fuelled inflation. For a couple of weeks, Callaghan withdrew to his study or to the No. 10 flat upstairs, failing to communicate with his advisers, though he continued meetings with Cabinet and civil servants.[36] 'The last couple of months wore me down,' Callaghan reflects. 'I'm afraid I was a bit of a weak link at that stage. I simply didn't know how to handle it. There was nothing much I could do . . . I wanted to take a strong line with the unions over a number of things,' but he didn't have Cabinet support, he says. 'If I couldn't follow the strong path that I wanted to follow, then I didn't know what else to do. That's it, frankly.' Throughout, Audrey 'helped me tremendously. She was always there. She was always consoling.'

The government struggled on in constant danger of instant defeat as its shrinking support base, depleted by defections and deaths, was undermined by dissenting left-wingers. The pact with the Liberals which had brought some calm in 1977 had ended in July 1978. Each vote was a cliffhanger. 'Everybody was tired all the time. There was no respite at all,' Colleen Merlyn-Rees remembers. 'You had to be there. They were bringing people in on stretchers to vote. It was appalling.' Sometimes Audrey expressed irritation with the Party when Jim came in after a bad day, but generally she 'kept her sense of humour, and said, "Well, we just plough on. We go on with it".' If colleagues dropped by at the flat, Audrey was ready with supper, says Colleen Merlyn-Rees: 'That was her role, how she saw herself – to provide the home comforts and be here.'

When the election came, the timing was not of Callaghan's choosing. A vote of confidence was called on 28 March 1979 over the long-running issue of devolution for Scotland and Wales. Up to the last minute, the outcome was uncertain. The government lost by one vote. A general election was called for 3 May. During the long six-week campaign all the polls indicated a Tory victory, and the Labour campaign team had few illusions about the outcome. Audrey 'was there all the time, she was always in the car with him . . . a constant companion', carrying a bag of things that might be needed at any time, says their son, Michael. Before each nightly speech, Callaghan had dinner with Audrey, Michael and the campaign manager, Derek Gladwyn. As Michael recalls, 'We'd sit round at dinner and the tension would start to build, there'd be all the issues that had come up during the day . . . and Derek and I would have to conspire during the day to think of all the good news there'd been that day, so we could ease this difficult conversation over dinner. And I thought of my poor mother sitting there having to deal with all this.'

Callaghan was resigned to defeat. Towards the end of the campaign, as he drove round Parliament Square towards Whitehall with Bernard Donoughue, he said quietly: 'You know there are times, perhaps once every thirty years, when there is a sea-change in politics. It then does not matter what you say or what you do. There is a shift in what the public wants and what it approves of. I suspect there is now such a sea-change – and it is for Mrs Thatcher.'[37] Polls showed the Conservatives 7 per cent ahead on election morning. At three in the afternoon, Callaghan phoned the Private Office from Cardiff to say: 'We have lost', and instructed his staff to be prepared to leave Downing Street by 3.30 p.m. the following day. Mrs Thatcher's Conservatives were returned with an overall majority of 43.

Both of them had expected the result but, Jim thinks, 'Audrey was disappointed for me. Probably more disappointed for me than for herself but I don't think she ever expressed any great feelings about it. That was not her way, to go into paroxysms of despair.' Colleen Merlyn-Rees remembers 'she was very, very upset. I think she would have liked Jim to have won an election. We all felt at the time that it was just about to get better. The clouds were beginning to part.' Inflation was down to 8 per cent, the balance of payments was in surplus, the currency was secure, though fissures had opened up in the social fabric which would widen in the coming years. For Jim, it was a relief: 'As a matter of fact, I didn't mind leaving. Because I'd got to the stage when I thought, "well (a) we can't win, (b) I don't know what to do next anyway." It was a relief to me . . . I didn't want to stay on.'

As soon as Jim and Audrey arrived at No. 10 from Cardiff that morning, Audrey began packing, helped by Ruth Sharpe and the family, while Jim, as he is now 'really rather ashamed to say', retired to bed.

MARY WILSON

23. Mary Wilson in the early 1950s:
'She had a quick sense of humour,
mischievous yet compassionate, and a
complete lack of any pretension.'

24. Gladys Mary Baldwin marries Harold
Wilson in Mansfield College chapel, Oxford,
1 January 1940.

25. During the 1964 general election
campaign. 'My function was to be there,
to be with him. On the platform in the
background.'

26. Mary in the Isles of Scilly, where she
felt at home.

27. Mary and Harold with their sons Robin and Giles on holiday in the Isles of Scilly, 1963.

28. At No. 10 on the way to a Guildhall dinner, September 1965.

29. With the wives of Russian leaders, Mrs Brezhnev (*left*) and Mrs Kosygin, at a reception in Moscow, 1966.

30. Tea at No. 10 for Madame Fonsha, wife of the Vice President of the Cameroons, October 1965.

AUDREY CALLAGHAN

31. Audrey Moulton marries Leonard James Callaghan at Knightrider Street Baptist Church, Maidstone, 28 July 1938.

MESSAGE FROM MRS. CALLAGHAN.

Every woman longs, above all else, for peace and I believe sincerely that a Labour Government will be more active than the present Government in working for peace.

Labour's Programme

PEACE
No more H-Bomb tests.
Review of length of National Service.
Positive Policy to raise the standard of life of Asian and African people.
Urgent disarmament talks.

COST OF LIVING
Price controls where possible.
Control Profits: limit shareholders' rewards.
Long-term agreements to buy from Commonwealth countries.
Cut out waste in distributors' costs.
Curb Big Business cartels.

HOUSING
Leaseholders to have powers to buy their freeholds.
Councils to have powers to buy out landlords and repair rented houses.

HEALTH SERVICE
Dentists' and opticians' charges to go.

OLD AGE & WANT
Annual review of Pensions and Benefits.
National Assistance to be abolished.
Voluntary additional pension schemes.

32. Audrey's statement to the Cardiff South-East electorate for the 1955 general election.

33. Arriving with Jim in Sydney, Australia. She had a separate agenda and always read her briefs carefully on foreign trips.

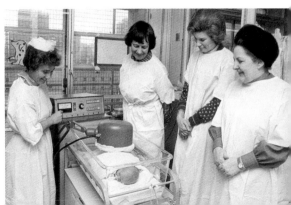

34. At Great Ormond Street Hospital, November 1977.

35. Audrey and Jim with children, Margaret, Julia and Michael and grandchildren, celebrating their ruby wedding at Chequers, 29 July 1978.

36. Leaving No. 10 after the general election defeat, May 1979: 'Audrey was always there…always consoling.'

DENIS THATCHER

37. Denis Thatcher marries Margaret Roberts at Wesley's Chapel, City Road, London, 13 December 1951: 'It was clear to me at once that Denis was an exceptional man… He had a certain style and dash.'

38. With Margaret, Carol and Mark at Dormers, 1959.

39. Outside No. 10 on the day of Margaret's general election victory, 5 May 1979.

40. Denis on duty: 'Better to keep my mouth shut and be thought a fool rather than open it and remove all doubt.'

41. Margaret's greatest supporter. 'He belonged to the Thatcher Party not the Tory Party. As far as he was concerned they were there to serve her interests.'

42. On the golf course. His friends took him away – 'almost anywhere, to get him away from No. 10'.

43. At Chequers during the visit by President and Raisa Gorbachev, December 1984.

44. With President and Nancy Reagan in Washington, November 1988. Denis admired Reagan – 'a super chap and an excellent host… You're not short of a sentence when you're talking to him.'

45. Norma Johnson and John Major marry at St Matthew's Church, Brixton, 3 October 1970. He proposed shortly after they met: 'It's rather strange to discover love and politics at the same time.'

46. Norma at the wheel: 'He was better at talking and I was better at driving.'

47. With Lady Harris and Brian Rix at Chequers, where she introduced charity opera evenings, October 1991.

48. During the 1992 general election campaign: 'She fiercely wanted us to win, and carried with her the cheery aura of someone in no doubt about the result.'

49. Boating with Barbara Bush, Elizabeth and James, at Kennebunkport, August 1991. 'I don't think it does to underestimate Barbara Bush.'

50. Author at Chequers, 1996, on the publication of her second book, a history of Chequers.

51. Norma and John with President and Hillary Clinton on their visit to No. 10.

52. With John, Mary Wilson and Cherie Booth at Harold Wilson's memorial service, 1995.

The Callaghan team had negotiated a few more hours for their departure before the Thatchers' arrival, but the procedure remained rushed and undignified. Margaret, who flew back from Washington to join them, remembers 'putting huge numbers of Audrey's personal things into black sacks, because we couldn't find enough suitcases, and taking them into their own car, which was parked out on Horse Guards' Parade' so that they didn't have to take them out of the front door where the press was gathered. They had time for lunch as they were sealing up the last bags. It was allegedly the same shepherd's pie that was served up to Mrs Thatcher later that evening. As Bernard Donoughue went to collect his car a cavalcade of black limousines sped past him and Mrs Thatcher 'waved regally to me' from the first car. The rear car, he noticed, was driven by Mr Callaghan's former driver.[38]

After the traditional last weekend at Chequers, the Callaghans retreated to the farm in Sussex. Callaghan remained leader of the Party as it went through the tortuous process of tearing itself apart, unable to reconcile the chasm between the militant left wing and the centre leadership. Audrey 'was very hurt by the unpleasantness that was going on in the Labour Party at that time . . . the bawling from the hall against Jim [at] the first conference afterwards . . . and the disloyalty I think she felt some people showed towards Jim,' Colleen Merlyn-Rees says, though she was 'the sort of person who would say, "Well, we pick ourselves up and go on."' Though Callaghan's inclination was to retire from the leadership immediately, he stayed on, despite the 'atmosphere of mistrust and cynicism in which the motives and actions of Party Leaders were continually questioned'.[39] With his eventual resignation in October 1980, he returned to a calmer life on the back benches.

Audrey and Jim now devoted more time to the farm, but continued to live in London during the week. Audrey remained chairman of the Board of Governors of Great Ormond Street Hospital until 1982, when, aged 69, she was appointed chairman of their Special Trustees. She was responsible for overseeing plans to raise a massive £21 million for redevelopment of the wards, and modern premises and equipment – a bold plan which 'required her to inspire and take others through a challenging period of changes in hospital administration.' Audrey made frequent presentations during the fundraising for what became known as the Wishing Well Appeal, and then decided to continue with a further appeal for annual support – 'a tricky period calling for delicate footwork and great sensitivity – both of which Audrey had in sufficiently good measure to carry us through with hardly a hiccup,' Anthony Tippet testifies.[40]

Audrey eventually retired from the hospital's Special Trustees in 1990, after twenty-three years of service. Callaghan, who had been elevated to a peerage in 1987, was instrumental on Audrey's behalf in ensuring, after a debate in the House of Lords devoted largely to the subject of fairies, that the royalties of J.M. Barrie's *Peter Pan* should continue to benefit Great Ormond Street, as Barrie had willed, despite the expiry of copyright.

Audrey turned down the offer of a damehood from Mrs Thatcher. 'She didn't think it was the kind of thing you should do from a philosophical point of view, and she didn't really want it from Mrs Thatcher,' her son Michael Callaghan says. She did her work because she enjoyed it, and because she thought it was right, so she didn't feel that she needed an honour for it. They kept up a social life of receptions and dinners, which Audrey enjoyed even more because she wasn't the centre of attention, and they now had time for art exhibitions and visits to the theatre and opera.

She went abroad with Callaghan to China, India and America, where they still stayed regularly with Gerald and Betty Ford. Each year Callaghan and Ford were joined by ex-President Helmut Schmidt and ex-President Giscard d'Estaing and their wives at Ford's house in the mountain resort of Vail, Colorado, for the annual Vail Interaction Group meetings, where they reflected on past and future problems of government.

At home, Audrey was preoccupied with the farm and her expanding family, which now included several great-grandchildren. Her garden was her great joy, while Jim ran the farm and was proud to receive an award for growing the best field of corn in the district from the local agricultural society. Their mutual devotion and respect were even more apparent. Throughout their lives, Audrey had been 'always there for him . . . He could concentrate on his career whatever was happening, and she'd keep everything running smoothly so that he had no worries,' their housekeeper, Brenda Shepherd says. 'They chatted about different things around the farm or alterations in the house, and she would organise it and he didn't have to . . . She would get everything ready and she made it happen. She was a rock.'

During the 1990s, when Audrey was in her eighties, friends and family began to notice lapses of concentration and slips of memory which steadily worsened. It was the onset of an illness – Alzheimer's disease – which would gradually remove her from the world around her. Though physically robust and often aware of what was going on, slowly her ability to communicate faded. Jim devoted himself to her care. 'He said, "For sixty years she gave up everything for me, and now I'm going to give up everything for her,"' Bernard Donoughue remembers. He was distraught when the family reached the painful decision that only in a nursing home would she get the care she needed. Every day he visited her. In the long years of her illness, Jim reflected on their life together. He was, in a sense, the keeper of *her* flame: 'Her lovely smile continues always to enchant me, and for her generous spirit, her patience and kindness, her wisdom and practical common sense, I love her more than I can say,' he told us.

In March 2005, Audrey died peacefully. Eleven days later, weakened by illness and perhaps unable to bear the burden of his loss, Jim died. He had worried, as he looked back on their life together, that he may have made too many demands on her, that perhaps she sacrificed too much for him. But he acknowledged that she provided the stability on which he could rely in any circumstances.

She was, one colleague noted, 'the launch-pad which allowed him to reach the top'. But throughout their political partnership, Audrey had built an independent life in which she could express her own powerful sense of social duty and where she gained respect in her own right. At No. 10, she did not give up her own interests, but fitted them into her demanding agenda as prime ministerial spouse. Her innate understanding of politics, her long familiarity with the demands of ministerial office and, above all, her humour and strength of personality all saw her proudly through their turbulent time at No. 10.

Chapter Six

Denis Thatcher

1979–90

On the day in February 1975 that Margaret Thatcher became the first woman leader of the Conservative Party, her husband Denis went to work as usual at Burmah Oil Company in Swindon. Nearing 60, he was contemplating retirement after a successful business career, and although he intended to keep on several non-executive directorships, a more relaxed life of golf and dinners at his various clubs beckoned.

Some months before, on 21 November 1974, Margaret had announced her intention to challenge Edward Heath for the Party leadership. Denis Thatcher did not have an intense interest in politics, though he had encouraged his wife since her election as MP for Finchley in 1959. Unlike many men of his generation, he saw nothing out of the ordinary in having a wife with a separate career. He had never doubted her ability and drive, and for years the couple had fitted their parallel careers into their family obligations.

But Margaret's decision to stand as leader had 'shocked' him. 'You must be out of your mind,' he said. 'You haven't got a hope.'[1] According to Alistair McAlpine, the Party Treasurer, his initial response was: '"Margaret, leader of what?" It didn't occur to him that she'd lead the Conservative Party.' He offered his support despite his misgivings. He had 'grave doubts whether it was possible to win, whether she'd be able to get enough of her colleagues to vote for her', he told his daughter, Carol Thatcher.[2] His main concern was that she might damage herself irrevocably if her bid failed: 'Obviously your friends will be disappointed if you don't stand, but you should make sure you're able to make a good showing. If you go down badly then you'll be slaughtered afterwards, that's for sure,' he is reported as saying[3] – a view she endorsed: 'I had no doubt that if I had failed against Ted that would have been the end of me in politics.'[4]

After three election defeats, the last in October 1974, opposition to Ted Heath's leadership had grown within the Conservative Party. Margaret Thatcher, then deputy Treasury spokesman, was one of a band of right-wingers who believed that only a change of policy – 'a return to fundamental Conservative principles' – under a new leader could save the Party. When Keith Joseph, the apostle of radical change, told her he would not stand, she was 'on the edge of despair. We just could not abandon the Party and the country to Ted's brand of politics. I heard myself saying, "Look, Keith, if you're not going to stand, I will, because someone who represents our viewpoint *has* to stand."'[5] After Edward du Cann, chairman of the 1922 Committee, also pulled out, it fell to her to make her bid.

With a new image-maker, Gordon Reece, Margaret Thatcher was presented in the leadership campaign as not only a resolute hand at the tiller, but also, in softer focus, as an ordinary housewife, old-fashioned and home-loving, 'leading a very normal life – seeing that the family have a good breakfast', and enjoying shopping, which 'keeps me in touch'. Denis joined in. On the morning of the first ballot, she was filmed cooking breakfast for him and putting out the milk bottles. 'Mrs Thatcher has all her chores neatly lined up at the weekend . . . And after that she had to tidy up the Tory Party, polish off Ted Heath, and give Britain a good spring cleaning,' the *Daily Mirror* intoned.[6]

To Denis's surprise, Margaret beat Heath in the first ballot. 'In the required second ballot, he 'thought she had a very good chance,' he told Carol. He was in the directors' boardroom at Burmah Oil on 11 February when his secretary brought in a note showing her clear victory – 146 to her nearest rival, William Whitelaw, who got 79 votes. 'She's done it!' he exclaimed, and threw up his arms in the air. After his colleagues had murmured their congratulations and shaken his hand, he got on with the day's business: 'I don't recall shivers sprinting down my spine – not until I really got involved in the damn thing.'[7]

That evening he went to a party held for Margaret at fellow MP Bill Shelton's house. 'It was a life-changing moment. When I walked into Bill's house and heard the whole room erupt with a roar of "Hear! Hear!" I suddenly realised SHE was Leader, and one with an enormous number of friends. Being a non-political person up until then, I suddenly realised that she was enormously important,' he recalled.[8] Margaret was swept off to face the press and photographers and plan her campaign. Norman Tebbit found Denis alone in the House of Commons lobby and took him out to supper. Next morning, when photographers arrived at their Flood Street home, Denis was in his car on the M4 to Swindon.

By the time Denis retired four months later, in June 1975, he was adapting to the role of male spouse to the Party leader – a situation unprecedented in British politics. His business career had not entirely ended, but his wife's career now invaded his life, forcing some adjustments: 'The timing was very important,' says their son, Mark. 'He had financial security. He wasn't pressed by a whole array of other competing time commitments . . . He was able to re-order his life . . . He was very comfortable with himself. He'd achieved everything that he wanted professionally, and was able to take a fresh look at things . . . And he felt that it was his obligation to support her in every way.' At first, Carol noted, 'The thought of playing second fiddle to his wife didn't even occur to him. After all, he was a businessman, not a political consort.'[9]

Although he had always encouraged Margaret in her career, he had remained detached and absorbed in his own work. Now he was thrust into the hub of political activity. Margaret's political staff and secretaries invaded their Chelsea house. When a security man turned up one evening and was chatting to Mark, Denis assumed it was one of his son's friends and went off to get changed for dinner. 'When I came back down this chap was still there and when Margaret arrived we started leaving and, bugger me, if this chap didn't follow us out. No one told me who the hell he was.'

As Mrs Thatcher raised her public profile, he was required to take part in an increasing number of political events, and it was a revelation: 'I realised I was a shy man who had to un-shy myself pretty damn quick,' he told Carol later. 'If anyone had said to me when I was fifty that I would go round roomfuls of complete strangers, start shaking hands and try and talk to them, I would have said, "you've got to be out of your mind".' He was shocked at the pace: 'We had a hell of a day meeting and greeting and lunching. It was non-stop and by early evening we arrived somewhere and the chairman of the local association asked me if I'd like a drink. He poured me a tumbler full of whisky . . . there wasn't any room for the soda. It barely touched the sides and he poured me another. It was sinking in fast, what I had let myself in for.'[10]

Denis had known from their first meeting that Margaret was not going to be a traditional wife. He met Margaret Roberts in February 1949 at a dinner given by Dartford Conservative Party for the 23-year-old Oxford Chemistry graduate who was about to be adopted as their candidate. Denis was the managing director of the paint and chemicals business, Atlas Preservatives, and, at 33, was living a comfortable bachelor existence in a flat in Swan Court, Chelsea. They got on well – she approved of his 'no-nonsense Conservatism' and they both loathed the socialism of Attlee's Labour government. After the dinner, he gave her a lift to London in his Jaguar sports car so she could catch a train to Colchester, where she worked as a research chemist in a plastics firm. 'It was clear to me at once that Denis was an exceptional man. He knew at least as much about politics as I did and a good deal more about economics,' Margaret wrote later. 'He had a certain style and dash . . . and, being ten years older, he simply knew more about the world than I did.'[11]

Denis was born on 10 May 1915 into a middle-class household in Lewisham, South London. His father Jack had come to England from New Zealand to expand the family firm and married red-haired Kathleen Bird, the daughter of a South London horse dealer, an astute businesswoman who had a vivid, outgoing personality and a penchant for gambling. With Denis's younger sister Joy and a nanny, they lived in a large house on an exclusive estate in Lewisham. His father, a quiet and rather serious man, who was interested in Freemasonry and the poetry of Rudyard Kipling, 'laid down the correct standards by which to live your life . . . he was a gentle man and a gentleman. His standards of behaviour and of honour were above reproach,' he told Carol.[12]

After prep school, Denis went on to Mill Hill School in North London, as he later described: 'One moves into one's public school. There, one is received with neither enthusiasm nor welcome – as befits the junior boys in the school and the lowest human beings ever to go there – and for two years is treated as such. This is called character forming. The only instruction given is, "Keep your mouth shut."'[13] This suited the lad who suffered from often debilitating shyness, but he was a conscientious student and enjoyed sport, particularly rugby. He thrived in the atmosphere of the annual Duke of York camps organised by the Industrial Welfare Society, which brought together 400 boys from very different social backgrounds for a week of organised outdoor activities 'in a competitive and friendly spirit', where the only rule was 'Play the Game'.

On leaving school, after taking an industrial training course he joined the family business, and was works manager at their base in Erith, Kent when he went on a company trip to Europe in 1937 and witnessed Hitler and the Brown Shirts on the streets of Germany. Convinced there would be a war, at the age of 23 he joined the Territorial Army. When war was declared in September 1939, he was section commander of an anti-aircraft unit based in Kent, scouring the night sky for German bombers.

Denis thrived on the discipline, order and male comradeship, though he never saw any real action: 'I liked my fellow officers and I liked the troops. I owe such success as I've had to the Army. They taught me to think and they taught me the elements of leadership,' he said.[14] One fellow soldier recalled him as 'a competent young officer with decisive personality, business-like and efficient yet with a pleasant manner and a great deal of character . . . he was never dull and possessed a good sense of humour and fun'.[15]

On 48-hour leave in London in 1941 he was introduced to Margot Kempson, a beautiful young blonde wearing an electric blue silk dress, whose job was driving lorries round the country delivering aircraft parts. Denis fell in love. At their snatched meetings on leave, they usually stayed at the Dorchester Hotel – 'which was lovely. It was *the* place – I mean it was so expensive, £5 a night or something. We used to meet in the little cocktail bar round the side,' she told Carol Thatcher,[16] who met her after discovering for the first time in 1976 that her father had been married before. The wedding was in March 1942, but they never established a settled life; their times together became shorter, and separations lengthened.

In 1943, Denis was posted abroad to take part in the invasion of Sicily. He moved with the Allies through Italy until he was transferred to Marseilles where he was charged with the tasks, first of extraditing Poles from Switzerland to join their fighting units, and then, in February 1945, with the transfer of the whole of the 5th Canadian Division from Italy to north-west Europe in secret, for which he was awarded a military MBE. Billeted in an elegant château, when he and his team discovered that the drink supplies had run out, they made their own gin with alcohol and juniper juice mixed in a bath. It was just drinkable, and when it was mixed with fruit juice from the Americans' rations, guests were offered 'gin and jungle juice' – 'as if it were the most sophisticated cocktail on earth'.[17]

He was demobilised in 1946 to a family business in difficulties and a broken marriage. The strain of separation, as with so many marriages contracted in a rush of romance and the uncertainty of war, had proved too much. He and Margot were divorced in 1948 and Margot married again that year. Denis was 'devastated'. 'He came out [of the Army] as a sort of gallant, elegant major – the breakdown of his marriage shattered him totally and he seemed rudderless,' a former schoolfriend said. Denis never mentioned his first marriage again.

He put his energies into rebuilding Atlas Preservatives as its managing director, and spearheaded an export sales drive which took him on lengthy trips abroad, including to South Africa, which he called 'God's own country'. In his spare time, he played rugby with the Old Millhillians and discovered an enthusiasm for refereeing, which would occupy most of his spare time from then on. In sport he discerned a moral framework for life: 'The desire to win is born in most of us, the will to win is a matter of training, the manner of our winning is a matter of example. If we fail in the latter, we do so at our peril,' he said later.[18] It was when he was consolidating his company that he met Margaret Roberts. She had been brought up in a strict Methodist household where the virtues of self-improvement through hard work and thrift were inculcated by her grocer and lay preacher father, Alfred Roberts, a Liberal councillor who eventually became Mayor of Grantham. Her mother, Beatrice, was a shadowy domestic figure but after her death Margaret acknowledged that she 'had been a great rock of family stability . . . It was from my mother that I inherited the ability to organise and combine so many different duties of an active life.'[19] Even before Margaret gained a place at Somerville College, Oxford, in 1943 to read

Chemistry, her commitment to hard work and her political ambition were apparent. She became chairman of the university's Conservative Association and soon after her graduation she set about finding a constituency.

Their courtship was slow, since both were absorbed in their own activities. To Denis, Margaret was 'beautiful, gay, very kind and thoughtful . . . Who could meet Margaret without being completely slain by her personality and intellectual brilliance?'[20] When Margaret was once asked by an interviewer if it was love at first sight, she replied, 'Certainly not!'[21] but she was 'very flattered by Denis's attentions'.[22] Bill Deedes, who knew Margaret at the time, 'felt that Denis came along at the right moment, when she had got a very long way by herself and felt the need for further support'. At that stage, Deedes suggests, she may have needed not only a supportive male but one who was also financially secure: 'If you had ambitions, as she had, to get forward, Denis would have had an attraction.' Later, she told a biographer: 'Denis's money got me on my way.'[23]

They went out to the theatre and restaurants, and when Margaret fought the 1950 general election, Denis's admiration grew for this forceful young woman, the youngest candidate in the country, who addressed the voters on 'the battle between two ways of life, one which leads to slavery and the other to freedom'. He chauffeured her to meetings and 'was an immense help in the constituency – problems were solved in a trice and all the logistics taken care of',[24] she wrote, though his occasional explosions of impatience and swearing could disconcert her. Denis never overcame his dislike of elections: 'Why we have to go through this carry-on for three bloody weeks is beyond me,' he would say.[25]

Margaret lost, but was readopted as candidate for the 1951 general election. On his return from a trip to France during the campaign, Denis proposed. Margaret 'thought long and hard about it' before accepting. 'I had so much set my heart on politics that I really hadn't figured marriage in my plans . . . But the more I considered, the surer I was.'[26] Their engagement was announced from the platform of Dartford Town Hall on the day of her election defeat: 'She stood for Dartford twice and lost twice and the second time she cried on my shoulder, I married her,' Denis told Carol.[27]

They were married on 13 December 1951 at Wesley's Chapel in City Road, London. Denis wore conventional morning dress with a white carnation in his buttonhole while Margaret was dressed in a long sapphire blue dress, a matching hat with a jaunty ostrich feather and she carried a muff. They honeymooned in Portugal and then Madeira with a few days in Paris, before moving into Denis's rented flat at Swan Court.

Unusually for the 1950s, it never occurred to either of them that Margaret should give up her career. She had decided to study Law and 'she was working from the day we married', Denis told us. 'I don't think it was demanding on me at all. Well, I never had anything else. She was absolutely determined to get on with her Law and even more determined to get into the House of Commons. I mean, that was her *one* determination, from the moment she went to Oxford. And it never occurred to us that she wasn't going to achieve it, sooner or later.'

Denis's routine altered little as he commuted daily to Erith and returned often late in the evening for a supper hastily prepared by Margaret, who took care of all household organisation. For Denis, a wife with a career had advantages: 'It brought me into touch with people who I would never otherwise have met – namely the lawyers, and we had odd dinner parties, attended the Inns of Court receptions, which I would never have got near in my own commercial life . . . One's never short of friends or acquaintances if both of you have your career,' he told us. Living 'in comfortable circumstances' when the country was beginning to recover from 'the petty indignities of post-war austerity', the Thatchers 'went to the theatre, we took holidays in Rome and Paris (albeit in very modest hotels), we gave parties and went to them, we had a wonderful time,' Margaret recalled.[28]

When their twins, Carol and Mark, were born on 15 August 1953, Denis was watching the Test match against Australia at the Oval, and would not in any case have expected to be present at the birth. When he saw them, 'Denis took one look at us and gasped: "My God they look like rabbits. Put them back,"' Carol reported. Later he quipped: 'Typical of Margaret. She produced twins and avoided the necessity of a second pregnancy.'[29]

Four months later she passed her final examination, and was called to the Bar just before Christmas: 'Bar intermediate in May, produced twins in August and Bar Finals in December. I'd like to meet another woman who can equal that record,' Denis said proudly.[30] Denis still left the domestic organisation to Margaret, who employed a full-time nanny. In common with most of his generation, he took little part in parenting and was often away at work or on business trips abroad, though he saw himself as a fairly indulgent parent, who rarely disciplined the children, and apparently failed to notice when they argued: 'Never had any trouble with my two,' he once told a *Spectator* journalist. 'They always got on so well together. I can think of only one occasion when we had a problem.' He paused for a re-fill to his drink. 'On the road to Portsmouth, it was. Carol and Mark started bickering in the back. So I put my foot down. I stopped the car and said: "Right, you three – get out." So they got out of the car. And I said: "Right, Margaret! Deal with them".'[31]

Every Saturday he refereed rugby matches – he was touch judge for the 1956 international between England and France in Paris – until a back injury prevented further participation. In 1957 the family moved into Dormers, a five-bedroomed detached house with a large garden in Farnborough, Kent. They took annual holidays by the sea and went skiing in winter, but 'family holidays didn't appeal to Denis or Margaret', Carol noted. 'We've never been very good holidaymakers. Neither of us is good at lounging around,' Denis said.[32] When Margaret was Prime Minister, the holiday duty was known by their accompanying officials as 'Château Despair'. They often stayed with friends in Switzerland, but the atmosphere was tense, Margaret would never settle, she always wanted to find local dignitaries to visit or looked for an excuse to get home. It was, says one adviser, 'dangerous to be within 50 metres of her on holiday'.

Margaret continued her search for a parliamentary seat, despite several failed attempts during the 1950s. Denis accompanied her to the selection committees, when the question most frequently asked, particularly by Conservative women, was how she could possibly combine her family responsibilities with being an MP. She resented this: 'beneath some of the criticism I detected a feeling that the House of Commons was not really the right place for a woman anyway'. She had declared the reach of her ambition in a *Sunday Graphic* article 'Wake Up Women!' in 1952 as the new Queen ascended the throne: 'Women can – and

MUST – play a leading part in the creation of a glorious Elizabethan era'. Married women could combine careers and family, they should be encouraged to enter politics and use their talents for the benefit of the community: 'Should a woman arise who is equal to the task, I say let her have an equal chance with men for leading Cabinet posts. Why not a woman Chancellor – or a woman Foreign Secretary?'[33] – though later she was notable for doing little to advance the careers of other women; only one woman ever served in her Cabinet over her entire eleven years as Prime Minister.

When she was selected as candidate for Finchley in 1958, Denis was away on a business trip in Africa. Since he rarely got in contact and sent only intermittent postcards while abroad, even on long trips, he only discovered the news when he was changing planes in Nigeria and found a copy of the *Evening Standard* on the seat next to him. During the 1959 general election, fought by Prime Minister Macmillan on the slogan 'You've Never Had it so Good', to the amazement of the family, Denis gave up refereeing for three weeks to join in the campaign. He sat on the platform but never spoke, and he didn't canvass with Margaret as, notably well dressed, she toured the constituency. He 'found meeting a lot of strangers a bit of a strain – I still do, to be honest, but I got a bit more confident', he told us. On polling day, 8 October, he hugged her warmly as she was returned with a comfortable majority of over 16,000. Six-year-old Carol was enthralled when she saw her mother's car festooned with blue streamers and balloons surmounted by a photo of her on what looked like a WANTED poster from a cowboy film.

Being a politician's spouse made little difference to Denis's routine, since he was not required, as are the wives of MPs, to give out prizes or open bazaars, and he selected which events to attend: 'If there were political demands on me that I didn't have time to meet, then they had to take second place. I've always taken the view that my job came first. People often said, "You do so much for Margaret in politics." It's a beautiful theory, but it's not really true. I've had a wife and two kids to keep, and my job came first,' he said.[34] But he went to Finchley when he was available: 'I might have done half a dozen or ten visits in a year. And the annual dinner. Come Christmas time you get award parties and the AGMs and bun fights, etc.,' he said. But sometimes he 'had to psyche himself up between the car park and the entrance with an audible "Thatcher, get your enjoyment shoes on",' Carol noted.

In 1961 Margaret was appointed as government spokesman on pensions and national insurance and later became shadow spokesman on housing and land. Looking back, Denis accepted that 'the work went up as she went up. But by this time you're in the groove. You've served your time, haven't you? And it was just one more job. It was just automatic that she was not always home for dinner and that sort of thing.' Their family life centred on the weekends, though after 1960, when Mark went to prep school before going to Harrow and Carol soon followed to boarding-school, they were together only as a family at half-terms and during the school holidays. Later Carol lived at home when she studied for her A levels at St Paul's Girls' School.

In 1964 the pressures of work began to tell on Denis. He was 49 and working long hours at Atlas, often not leaving until 9.30 p.m. He was worried that the company was undercapitalised, and concerned that he might not be able to fulfil his financial responsibilities for his family and relations. According to Carol, he was 'on the verge of a nervous breakdown'. His doctor told him firmly that he must take time off. Denis sailed for South Africa, terribly depressed, deeply worried about the future and determined to sort himself out.[35] He stayed for three months visiting game parks, taking photographs, and thinking. By the end, he concluded that, in fairness to the family, he would have to sell Atlas.

He was abroad during the 1964 general election when the Labour Party under Harold Wilson won a narrow victory. He returned to find Margaret at a low ebb, concerned about his illness and bitterly disappointed at the Conservative defeat. He sold the company in August 1965 to Castrol Oil without consulting her. Within a year Castrol was taken over by Burmah Oil, and he again feared for his job, but instead he was rewarded with share options, became a highly paid oil executive and was appointed to the board. They moved to a flat in London and bought a second home, The Mount at Lamberhurst near Tunbridge Wells, where Denis learned to play golf with his neighbour, Bill Deedes, and soon established a new network of golfing companions.

When the Conservatives under Ted Heath were returned in 1970, Margaret achieved her first ministerial post as Secretary of State for

Education. She still organised their domestic arrangements and made Denis's breakfast every morning in the Flood Street house which they bought in 1972. Once she surprised civil servants by interrupting a meeting to say, 'I've just got time to pop down to the grocer's on the corner to buy some bacon for Denis.' When it was suggested that the secretary might go, she insisted, 'No, I know just the cut he likes'.[36]

Denis discovered what it means to have your spouse in the public firing line when Margaret, under pressure to find savings in public expenditure, ended the provision of free school milk for children over seven. There was an outcry in the press against 'Margaret Thatcher, Milk Snatcher'. The experience 'shook her. She almost went the colour of shamrock,'[37] her son, Mark, said, though Denis was philosophical: 'It was hurtful but you didn't show it. If you're in public life then you're going to get hammered. I suppose it wasn't bad training. After a bit it just washed over me and I certainly didn't lose any sleep over it.'[38]

By 1973, the Heath government was in crisis, and within a year Labour was back in power. Among the Tories, moves now began for a leadership change. Margaret – then a much more cautious politician than she later turned out to be – emerged as the most prominent challenger. And although Denis had been anxious about her chances, when she beat Heath in the first ballot in February 1975 and a TV reporter asked him if he expected his wife to lead the Conservative Party, he replied: 'I do'. And how did he feel about it? 'Delighted. Terribly proud, naturally. Wouldn't you?'

Denis stayed out of the spotlight as his wife moved centre stage. His main role, he decided, was to back Margaret. 'He came from a generation who had a sense of duty and silence . . . And he felt that this was your duty. You'd signed on for this, you did it and if you didn't like it very much, you didn't grumble, you just got on with it,' Alistair McAlpine observed. When they were on tours or campaigns, 'she would worry about him in case he got trampled on. And you heard, "Where's DT?" at receptions. She would keep an eye on him. She would always, if he was with her, keep a watching eye out for him,' says Harvey Thomas, the Party's Communications Director. In the leader's office, '[Denis] featured in the imagination of her staff as a sort of offshore rock . . . as a point by which she fixed her compass,' an office junior, Matthew Parris, recalled.[39]

Denis soon made his presence felt with her inner team. Before her first keynote speech as leader at the 1975 Party Conference, her speech-writers, as so often, had worked through the night on endless rewrites. At ten past five in the morning, writer Ronald Millar recorded, Denis was sitting silently on the windowsill in his black tie and dinner jacket, listening with the others to the umpteenth 'final' version. "'That's the one," he said softly . . . The Leader looked up sharply. "Do you think so, dear?" He nodded. He had been a rugby referee and knew when to blow the whistle indoors as well as out. There was a pause. "Right. That's it," said the Leader and gave one of those all-time dazzlers that almost made you disappointed not to be starting again from the top. "Well we'd better get some sleep." "Bit late for sleep," yawned DT. "Only make you feel worse."'[40]

In his four years in opposition, Denis grew accustomed to his role as the leader's consort. When James Callaghan called a general elec-tion in May 1979, he anticipated a full part in the campaign. He had watched the dramatic 'No Confidence' debate from the opposition box on the floor of the House of Commons on 28 March, and shouted 'Done it!' when the result was declared, which earned him a swift rebuke from the sergeant-at-arms. The Winter of Discontent had played into Mrs Thatcher's hands, and the Conservatives had real hopes of winning as polls showed a consistent, though narrowing, Tory lead. Denis toured the country with her in the 'Battle Bus'; and took part in photo-shoots, including one in a damp field where Margaret was photographed holding a calf until Denis, standing in the background, was clearly heard to say: 'If you're not careful, you'll have a dead calf on your hands.'

He visited factories, schools, shopping centres, attended dinners and endless receptions, went on walkabouts, usually a few or more steps behind Margaret, and watched back at home as speeches were written and rewritten, occasionally interjecting with 'My God, you're not on another flaming speech. Do you know what time it is?' or 'Good Lord, you're not writing the ruddy Bible, for Christ's sake!'[41] He recalled it as 'a pulverising campaign, but for most of the time it was looking good', and, though he 'hated every minute of campaigns. The days of gin and tonic and sandwiches; the tension, the strain of reading the newspapers and studying the opinion polls next day',[42] he was more involved than ever before.

The Conservatives won the election with an overall majority of 43. Denis went with Margaret to the count, then drove down for celebrations at Conservative Central Office, where he waved and smiled behind a jubilant Margaret. Next afternoon (4 May) at 3 p.m. the family were gathered at Conservative Central Office waiting for the call to Buckingham Palace. 'Margaret sits down once more in the upright chair. Presently she kicks off her shoes and flexes her toes; they play nervously with her high-heeled court footwear. Denis wonders aloud if she has the Palace confused with a Hindu temple. She cuts him short with a look but steps back into her shoes,' Ronnie Millar recorded. When the call came, she 'reappears in her most businesslike manner. "Right. We're off," she says briskly. "Prime Minister," says her son (Mark). "Not yet, dear." "No," from Denis, "the car might break down".'[43] At the Palace, Denis, Carol and Mark waited in an anteroom attended by ladies-in-waiting, while Margaret went though the ceremonial with the Queen.

On their return to Downing Street Denis watched from the No. 10 doorway as Margaret stepped forward to deliver her speech to the waiting microphones. Cameras flashed as they waved then turned inside to be greeted by applause from those assembled in the hall, before Margaret disappeared with her political staff. Carol recalled: 'Denis, Mark and I were suddenly surplus to requirements and no-one quite knew what to do with us. The Callaghans had not yet moved out of the Prime Minister's private flat above Number Ten, and my parents wouldn't move in for another month. "A car will take you back to Flood Street," a messenger told us.' Denis left to stay the weekend at the small flat they had bought instead of The Mount, not far away from Lamberhurst at Scotney Castle, Kent, and that evening he settled down to supper of baked beans on toast.[44]

The Thatchers moved into No. 10 on 4 June. Denis, now 64, took some time to find his way around. 'They don't say so, but you're on your own – you're on your own, mate, if they're busy,' he said. There was no precedent for a male spouse to a prime minister in Britain and very few worldwide (the Queen's consort, Prince Philip, fulfilled an entirely different role), so he was breaking new ground. He valued his independence. With the Downing Street officials' activity centred on his wife, he 'never asked them to do anything for me, ever, ever, ever', he told us. Denis 'had developed a confidence that he would do exactly what he wanted to do, and would not allow any officials to get in his way. He would do it quite nicely, and he might joke at them and he might even say, "Oh, come on, get out of my way, I want to get out of here", but it wouldn't be personal,' Harvey Thomas recalls. He did not expect or want to be taken into account by the Downing Street officials. 'He was very independent, very undemanding, he didn't want to be a nuisance,' Robin Butler, the Cabinet Secretary, says. But Bill Deedes. 'thought they didn't treat him very well, quite honestly. There were occasions when he was treated very much as if he was almost a non-figure while she was here – "the Prime Minister is the Prime Minister and her spouse is nothing to do with us."'

When he wasn't required to be on parade, or he decided he was 'surplus to requirements', Denis got on with his own life. Work still occupied much of his time. His portfolio of non-executive directorships on six companies – including Halfords, Chipman Chemicals and Quinton Hazell – as well as his work as adviser to the chairman of CSX, a railway company in the United States, involved regular board meetings and trips abroad. In his small study in the flat, he organised his work and dealt with his sudden increase in correspondence – about fifty letters a week, all answered in longhand with a fountain pen, helped occasionally by Joy Robilliard, Margaret's constituency secretary, his only secretarial help. 'I worked hard when I was here, plus my businesses,' he says. He also had requests for photos and autographs: 'They used to send out hundreds. What people don't realise – it's jolly costly!' He paid for his own photographs, 'and then you've got the envelopes, then you've got the stamps'.

Denis kept up a busy social life. He had close links with several charities – the Sports Aid Foundation, the Sports Aid Fund, the Army Benevolent Fund and the Lord's Taverners – and as Vice-President of the London Society of Football Referees he took part in awards ceremonies, trophy presentations and dinners. When he hosted events alone at No. 10 it was because of their link with sports or achievements such as the conquest of Everest by Chris Bonington and his team in 1985. With his Army background and continuing interest in military affairs, he was invited to regimental dinners, where he sometimes made a speech.

He ate regularly at his own clubs and others, including a dining club of which the ousted leader Ted Heath was a member: 'We always got on perfectly well together. He was always invited to come, and that gave me an opportunity of making a crack or two [about Mrs Thatcher], which he always applauded loudly and rather enjoyed. He was very good value,' Heath says. Denis was regularly seen disappearing over Horse Guards' Parade to dinner – 'out of the front door and into the night, wearing his black cloak and cane, a sort of Dracula figure', Charles Powell, Mrs Thatcher's adviser and later Private Secretary, remembers. He insisted on walking everywhere or he travelled by tube or bus on his senior citizen's pass. Few people stopped him on public transport, though when he was accosted in a bar in Berkeley Square by a drunken man who announced, 'You're Denis Thatcher,' he said, '"I'm absolutely bloody sick of this! I know I look like him, but I'm sick to death of people mistaking me for him. Go away!" So it ended up that this chap kept bringing people up to us to say, "I'd like you to meet this man who's not Denis Thatcher",' Tim Bell, Mrs Thatcher's publicity and advertising consultant, recalls.

On arrival at No. 10, to his great regret he was advised to get rid of his elderly Rolls-Royce which he loved driving: Central Office thought that such a symbol of wealth would damage Mrs Thatcher's image. Ironically it was practically the only car that was British-made at the time, but he exchanged it for a modest battered Ford Cortina: 'Gave us nightmares. Denis wasn't always abstemious and now and again the damn thing would appear with dents in it and Special Branch would set out to investigate what he might have hit on the way,' says Charles Powell. Denis adamantly rejected security protection, except for one brief period of high alert, because 'he refused to accept that he was a proper public figure, and it would look as if he was exaggerating himself,' Powell says. When the security gates were erected at Downing Street, he was furious: 'It was as though he was being put in prison, being locked up,' Tim Bell says. At Chequers, 'he used to walk through the "magic eyes" quite deliberately and set the alarms off. He'd go and practise his pitch and putting and deliberately do it so that the ball would break all the security barriers.'

Another escape from No. 10 was his golf. With Bill Deedes and a couple of old friends from Lamberhurst days, he played as often as possible, and twice a year they took him on golfing holidays abroad to France, Germany, Portugal, America – 'almost anywhere, to get him away from Number Ten. We thought that a week of golf was very important for him.' They never talked about politics – the point was to escape from it in sympathetic company. Bill Deedes was 'certain that he did go through passages of loneliness and feeling that he was right out of it . . . There were weekends when she would be at Chequers and he was not required.'

It is a fact of life at No. 10 that the Prime Minister, or his wife, is expected to cook for themselves – no staff are provided. 'People find it incredible that there was nobody, not even a cleaner, provided for the flat at No. 10, that prime ministers are expected to provide all that themselves,' Robin Butler observes. In the flat, which did not greatly appeal to Denis – 'the only time the sun comes in – if at all – is at seven o'clock in the evening' – Margaret introduced floral sofas, lots of flowers and lamps, and made it brighter. She brought her cleaner from Flood Street, but preferred to sort out the cooking herself, despite the admonitions of her son, Mark: 'We never had full-time staff. She still had to look after the family. That was a huge issue. I thought [she should have somebody to help]. But she wouldn't have it. I think it was something to do with her Methodist upbringing.' Either she or one of her assistants cooked in bulk for the freezer, or she bought pre-cooked meals, usually lasagne or shepherd's pie. 'It was all very informal, not structured,' Mark says. Denis was used to fending for himself from the freezer – it was the arrangement she had adopted at Flood Street: 'It was all a bit meals-on-wheels type thing. And Dad was very good about that, never got flustered by it, never got irritated by it', though it 'drove me scatty'.

When meetings with officials or aides spanned a mealtime, Mrs Thatcher would prepare the meal herself, interrupting their flow as she served out the peas. 'We had these speech-writing sessions up in the little flat up there in No. 10, and we used to break for supper at about nine o'clock in the dining room and she would dish up these monotonous shepherd's pies she got from Marks and Spencer, and at the end of supper she would rise smartly and say, "All right, come on, back to work. Denis will clear away and wash up." And Denis was left with this mound of crockery and dead shepherd's pie which he then stacked in the dishwasher and put away in the fridge,' Charles Powell remembers.

Carol, now 26, was carving out a career for herself as a journalist in Australia, but Mark lived at No. 10 to begin with. Everybody 're-ordered themselves to support the greater good', he says. At first, as with all incumbents, 'the family were feeling their way, finding out how the system works best, what it's possible to change, what it's not possible to change'. With his father, he adjusted to being part of a machine which revolved round the Prime Minister: 'If I wanted to talk to my mother, 10.30 in the evening, after she's back from the House, she'll come and sit down and she'll have a drink, and we'll talk about anything except politics for twenty minutes, and then it's boxes,' Mark remembers.

In their marriage, Denis was a solid, undemanding presence: 'He always kept saying what a wonderful Prime Minister she was. He was just so devoted to her: if she wanted something then he would just do it,' says an adviser. 'I think he was also very aware that she was a great figure on the world stage, and she deserved nothing less.' Margaret reciprocated with 'huge respect for Denis as a person. She never dismissed his view,' and, according to Tim Bell, they were 'very, very affectionate – a sort of 1950s affection. They didn't kiss and cuddle, but they touched hands and they would sit close together and walk with each other and he'd put his arm through hers and she'd put her arm through his.'

His common sense and irreverence provided a safety valve: 'She would say, "Well, Denis, he is the Prime Minister of France, I do have to . . .", and he'd reply, "It doesn't alter the fact that he is a complete pain in the arse," and that was a relief to her,' Tim Bell says. Margaret once told a reporter: 'When I'm in a state, I have no-one to turn to except Denis. He puts his arm round me and says, "Darling, you sound just like Harold Wilson." And then I always laugh.'[45]

His influence made a great difference to the level of tension. Her colleague Douglas Hurd was 'always glad to notice that he was there. He had a way of handling her which was unique. No one else could do that. He knew her absolutely backwards and he could assess every mood.' It quite often happened that arguments with Margaret got out of hand, but 'with Denis there, that was less likely to happen'. Robin

Butler was one of many officials who knew his value during tense late-night sessions: 'When there was real trouble and she was rampaging about something,' and it would go on till two in the morning, 'Denis would sit there in the corner of the room, when he'd obviously clearly love to be in bed. And he was the only person who could say, at just the right moment – he always knew the right moment to say it – "Now, my dear, I don't think this is going to get any easier tonight, why don't we pack it up now and have a look at it in the morning?" And she would say, "All right, then."'

Denis was interested in politics, though not in the intricacies of policy, and he kept in close touch with events, reading the papers every morning over breakfast in the flat's small dining room. With his aversion to socialism, nationalisation, taxation and bureaucracy and his down-to-earth, patriotic, sometimes xenophobic attitudes, he was often seen as the touchstone for 'saloon bar' British opinion: 'If she wanted to know what the backbone of the Tory Party was thinking, she only had to ask Denis,' says Charles Powell; though according to adviser Grey Gowrie his opinions were 'almost identical to the Queen Mother's, who adored him. She used to say "Denis is such a splendid and sensible man. A National Treasure."'

He had 'rather a gut reaction to things' and 'he would give you it in pretty colourful terms', says Robin Butler. Even in front of the secretaries, he was 'never shy of speaking his mind, however controversial it was at the time, and Mrs T wouldn't interrupt him, just saying "yes dear",' secretary Suzanne Reinholt remembers. But he never intervened in policy or day-to-day business, according to Butler. Though he often sat in on meetings in the flat, an unobtrusive presence in the background 'listening to it with half an ear', he never offered his opinion, and 'I don't think he ever influenced her very much, and he certainly never tried to influence her in my presence about anything. He would just stay there to be useful in whatever way he could.' 'He was an echo-chamber for her,' reinforcing her views, says Charles Powell. On marathon planning sessions, he did sometimes chip in: 'You'd sit there for *hours* debating and discussing a strategy and what shall we do about this . . . and just as you got to the end he'd say, "Not a vote in the box!" It was his killer comment,' Tim Bell recalls.

He was an observant judge of people, who could spot when someone was trying to manoeuvre him, and wasn't easily taken in. 'He had an instinct for a "wrong 'un",' Robin Butler says. Every now and again, Bill Deedes remembers, Denis would be 'pretty abrupt: "I wouldn't take any further notice of that idiot, if I were you, he's this, that and the other thing."' And 'if he thought well of somebody then his praise was extravagant: "Ahh! One of the best fellows on earth!" But there weren't a lot in that category.'

Undoubtedly he discussed events with Margaret in the privacy of 'upstairs'. Denis 'was a fund of shrewd advice and penetrating comment. And he very sensibly saved these for me rather than the outside world,' wrote Margaret. She particularly respected his knowledge of business and finance: 'His industrial experience was invaluable to me. He was also a crack cost and management accountant. Nothing escaped his professional eye – he could see and sense trouble before anyone else.' His experience in the oil industry gave her 'immediate access to expert advice when in 1979 the world experienced the second sudden oil price increase. Indeed, through him and our many friends I was never out of touch with industry and commerce.'[46] One diplomat, Antony Acland, remembers her expressing doubts, as she prepared for a meeting in Luxembourg to discuss the hike in oil prices, about whether the other European leaders really understood the oil business: 'And with a real shine in her eyes she said, "*I* really understand it because of Denis. Denis has always talked to me, and I *really* know about the oil industry because of Denis."' In the early days at No. 10 he was present at meetings with businessmen, where he was 'very constructive, very well-informed', Alistair McAlpine, Party Treasurer and later Deputy Party Chairman, recalls. 'He was in the boardroom probably at least once a month, so he'd have really a great practical knowledge,' an adviser adds. 'So if the Treasury came and presented her with a paper saying [for instance] the future's really rosy, Denis would say to her, "Nonsense. This isn't happening in my company. I talk to other businesses, it's not happening in their company – how does their model know what's happening?"'

Several advisers found Denis a helpful conduit: 'If there was a problem, you'd go and speak to Denis and you'd get it through to Margaret,' adviser Philip Harris says. Margaret could often be peremptory with colleagues and advisers, believing in 'the force of argument . . .

It was for her a voyage of discovery,' Alistair McAlpine says. If an idea was put to her and she disagreed straight away, says Philip Harris, 'you would go and speak to Denis, and say, "Denis, I think she's got this completely wrong," and you kept going at Denis. I think he listened. I wouldn't know for sure if he took a view, but he listened to a lot of people, whereas she wouldn't listen. That's probably one of her faults.' Then, 'Denis would come back to you and say, "Yes, I've spoken to Maggie." He'd give you feedback, because the Prime Minister didn't have time to give you feedback.' Another device irregularly employed by one adviser was to post notes to Denis under the door of the flat with a version of what he thought should be done.

Though Mrs Thatcher was commanding with colleagues, with whom she could be merciless if they were not properly briefed, she seems rarely to have argued with Denis, and certainly not in public, though occasionally Denis was seen to storm out of No. 10 in a state of furious agitation. Several observers noticed that, though never deferential, she was 'softer' in his presence. With him, 'she became much more passive. Downstairs she was the chairman, so to speak, whereas upstairs she was more like the company secretary,' says one colleague, who 'came to the conclusion that he was really her most powerful and closest adviser'.

At official functions, Denis established a reputation as 'the prince of hosts. If he saw wallflowers, he was frightfully good at picking them up and saying, "You haven't met the Chancellor of the Exchequer, have you? No, well meet him. Here he is." In that sense he jolly well earned his keep here, he really did,' Bill Deedes thinks. He was a good conversationalist and an entertaining companion; he particularly enjoyed the company of former Prime Minister's spouse, Mary Wilson: 'She's a very, very nice lady. One of the most lovely ladies I've ever sat next to at dinner parties,' he told us. He was noted for treating women with an old-fashioned courtesy – kissing their hand and pulling back their chair, which they found charming. If there were any misunderstandings, or people were left out, he would notice: 'He was simply there to lubricate, make things come and go smoothly,' Douglas Hurd says. At receptions they circulated separately, Denis going round with his cigarette and a stiff drink (normally gin and tonic or gin and 'French' – a mixture of red and white martini) and including everyone. Nobody outside the inner circle ever saw Denis inebriated, despite his consumption and his reputation. 'He, I think naturally, had a strong head and he liked his drink, but he was never *ever* the worse for drink. And if he saw someone, particularly an official, who was the worse for wear, they were struck off the list immediately. There was one official, I remember, on a trip abroad, who over-indulged at lunch and became rather bellicose and stupid. Denis was absolutely furious, and the aide was excluded from other gatherings,' Antony Acland recalls.

He got genuine pleasure out of going to the big public events, like the Lord Mayor's banquet, state banquets at Buckingham Palace, and the Diplomatic Reception, though 'there's a lot of chatting there, that's jolly tiring. Lot of standing about', he said. At the Commonwealth Heads of Government meetings, Denis played host to the leaders' wives, and was the sole male in the procession of wives at the opening session, looking, according to Charles Powell, 'slightly forlorn' and 'thoroughly sheepish, hands behind his back', until Pakistan leader Benazir Bhutto got married, and her husband and Denis 'happily brought up the rear'. He did not generally take part in the ladies' programme and would go off for the day unless he was needed to support Mrs Thatcher.

Though he sometimes looked over the guest list, it was Mrs Thatcher who oversaw the menu and preparations at No. 10, liaising with Government Hospitality through Social Secretary Sue Goodchild. In an area which would normally be the preserve of the spouse, Mrs Thatcher took charge, arriving beforehand to check the flowers and table arrangements. 'She was fond of making everything look nice, she liked everything to look plentiful,' says Cally Blennerhasset, one of the caterers who worked on rotation at No. 10.

Denis was usually at the larger functions involving anything from dinner for around sixty people in the State Dining Room to receptions of up to 200, when they greeted guests in a receiving line. As always, he kept a watchful eye on procedures. When an inexperienced new butler, David Allen, was assigned to announce the guests, Denis came up during a lull and 'got hold of me by the shoulders and he said, "Look old chap, she can't hear what you're saying, you're not speaking clearly enough, and you've got to stop hopping around when you speak", and I thought, "right!" – I'd been doing it totally wrong.' For lunch at Trooping the Colour, Denis by tradition carved the beef or ham and was always 'chatty'. Staff soon learned that he could not abide pink meat: 'Cally, we want it almost black – nothing pink about it at all,' he told Cally Blennerhasset. Once when served pink lamb chops in France, he sent them back to the kitchen complaining 'I'll still be able to taste the wool.' At dinner in the later years, 'he'd occasionally nod off towards the end of her speech. I'd have to give him a little tap – pretend to pour a drop more wine and just touch his shoulder as I leaned across,' David Allen remembers.

The standard of entertaining was upgraded during the Thatcher period at No. 10. After Denis's first official function at Downing Street, a dinner for German Chancellor Helmut Schmidt, Denis had protested to Margaret: 'Look love, the so-called silver was so awful it wasn't true. It nearly had the broad arrow on it. In the name of God, what goes on here? It was appalling. It looked as if it had come out of the Sergeant's Mess!'[47] No. 10 did not have its own silver – it was brought in by Government Hospitality for each dinner and then removed, leaving everything bare. Mrs Thatcher wanted a permanent collection for important occasions. After Denis's comments she borrowed from the collections of patrons – Lord Brownlow loaned her some from his Belton House collection. 'She didn't want us to be seen to be poor. She went to all these wonderful places – the White House, the Kremlin – and she didn't want us to look like the poor relations,' her personal assistant Cynthia Crawford recalled.[48] At that time, there was a collection of the Treasury silver some of which – Georgian candlesticks, penholders, etc. – was used in the Cabinet Room. Margaret 'set about trying to get it. She came to the Treasury, and we had a great consultation about what we should do. We decided it was no good concealing it. We had it in a display cabinet, locked, and we sent the chap with the key off for a very long lunch – she never got that,' Robin Butler recalls.

Later, a Silver Trust was set up by a group of patrons, some surprised that the nation's leaders, unlike their counterparts in France, America and other countries, had to beg and borrow silver for formal occasions. They saw an opportunity to encourage and publicise the work of practising silversmiths and artists by providing a collection to be made available on loan to Downing Street and embassies abroad. First suggested by Mary Henderson, wife of diplomat Nicko Henderson, in 1985, the silver collection was ready in 1993 and the pieces are now on loan to Downing Street for use at state and other formal occasions.

Mrs Thatcher was keen to improve the appearance of No. 10 and Denis backed her. When she arrived, she thought it 'looked rather like a "furnished house to let", which in a way, I suppose, it was'. The National Portrait Gallery was persuaded to lend some pictures and 'she raided embassies around the world for things. Rather like Queen Mary,' Butler recalls. 'She'd go in and say, "Oh, that's a nice carpet. Now that would just do for the Small Dining Room in Number 10. That's just what I'm looking for. And the Ambassador would say, "Oh well, all right then."' In 1982, she also cannily managed to get hold of two extra bedrooms belonging to No. 11, by swiftly partitioning them before her new Chancellor realised. Later, from 1988 to 1989, Margaret oversaw the complete refurbishment of the three state rooms, when architect Quinlan Terry restored the Pillared Room, the White and the Green (formerly Blue) Drawing Rooms. She wanted the rooms 'to look more imposing. She felt that, after the Falklands War, the time had come to do something mildly triumphant and confident.'[49] She kept the original Kent fireplaces, door surrounds and cornices, added a Palladian over-mantel and other features in the Green Room, and the ceilings of the main state rooms were enriched with ornate decoration, picked out in gold, in the Baroque style.

Chequers was a different and, for Denis, wholly pleasurable experi-ence: 'I loved Chequers. I think it's a magnificent house and an ideal house to entertain in. And it's a lovely part of the world – Buckinghamshire was a new stamping area for me,' he told us. They travelled down most weekends on Friday and returned on Sunday. A keen reader of biographies and military history, Denis appreciated its historical associations, particularly its use as a convalescent home for officers in the First World War. Though often there alone, they some-times entertained for lunch: 'We de-pompousised it. I used to say to people coming to lunch on Sunday that if they were early they shouldn't sit in that lay-by in the lane but come in because my woman didn't like me to start drinking before the guests arrived,' he told Carol. (He frequently referred to Margaret as 'My woman'.)

While Mrs Thatcher got on with her boxes, he would play golf or practise on the lawn, though he could be protective towards her there.

Suzanne Reinholt recalls turning up with the red boxes one Friday and 'tapping on the study door and hearing DT shout "Who is it", and him positively barking at me to "Go away, go away, she's got far too much already." I'm not sure what trembled more, me or the door.' Denis was, however, popular with the staff, whom he addressed by rank: 'He never got my rank right. I was always promoted. When I became corporal he called me sergeant, and when I became sergeant he called me flag sergeant, though I never got that far! But he'd never call you by your name,' a member of the Chequers staff says. At Chequers and at No. 10, Margaret took care of staff and remembered their first names. She 'was like a mother hen. She knew everyone, she knew everybody's children. She was very nice. Two types of people. One you saw on television, and one you saw in here,' says a No. 10 messenger.

On Christmas Eve, Denis played the genial host at drinks for the estate staff and people from Stoke Mandeville hospital. After church on Christmas Day there was champagne followed by traditional lunch with the family, close friends and the 'waifs and strays' – those who were single, alone, or recently divorced. Everything stopped for the Queen's speech in the Churchill Library, and on Boxing Day they held a larger buffet lunch for around forty friends, political colleagues and businessmen, when the Great Hall, with its towering Christmas tree, was cleared and the guests sat at round tables on gold chairs.

They held dinners and lunches for visiting heads of state, who rarely stayed overnight. King Hussein of Jordan, whom Denis thought was 'a terribly, terribly nice chap' – they shared a military background – paid several visits, as did President Ronald Reagan and Nancy. Denis had admired Reagan since hearing him speak at the Institute of Directors in London in 1969: he had enthusiastically shown the speech to Margaret, though it was only later that she warmed to him.[50] Denis thought Reagan 'a super chap and excellent host. He has a natural affinity for putting people at their ease. You're not short of a sentence when you're talking to him.'[51] When Nancy Reagan visited Chequers, a glittering party packed with stars, including Sir Laurence Olivier and Michael Caine, welcomed her.

During the Falklands War in 1982, after Argentina invaded the British dependency of the Falkland Islands, War Cabinet meetings were frequently held there. 'Denis was [there] but he disappeared discreetly into the background and took no part in the discussion,' Michael Palliser, Mrs Thatcher's special adviser, says. Even so, he held strong views. After he'd looked in the atlas ('and I wasn't the only one') to establish where they were, 'as an ex-soldier, I thought, "How the hell are we going to get a force 8,000 miles away?" I looked at the time and the distances – it was a logistical nightmare,' but he was in no doubt that action was necessary: 'From the word go, I said, "Get them off!"'[52] but he confined his role at Chequers to calming nerves and raising the morale of the personnel gathered there. After the war, he went with Margaret to the Falklands, which was festooned with Union Jacks in her honour. Though moved by the tour, he commented to Carol later, 'We sure as hell didn't go there for the real estate; it's miles and miles of bugger all.'

The war was a turning point. Before it, after two years in office, Mrs Thatcher had the lowest rating of any prime minister since polls began. Even within her Cabinet, some colleagues thought that the price of 'Thatcherism' in unemployment, worsening economic recession, and the abandonment of 'consensus politics', was too high. Criticism from within and outside the Party was relentless. Denis took a robust view of attacks, then and later: 'If Maggie had any problem – "Bugger 'em all! Bugger 'em all!" That would be it. "I don't know why she does this job. I don't know why any of you do it,"' Philip Harris remembers. What upset Denis more than press criticism was disloyalty in the Tory Party, as Bill Deedes recalls: 'He belonged to the Thatcher party not the Tory Party. As far as he was concerned, they were there to serve her interests, and if they didn't do what he expected them to do, they were four-letter fellows – "Useless! Useless! Those Tories!"'

The Falklands War saved Mrs Thatcher. Her victory as war leader stirred deep seams of patriotism – 'We have ceased to be a nation in retreat,' she declared. By the time of the 1983 general election, with support flowing her way and the opposition divided and in disarray, the Conservatives won with an overwhelming majority of 144.

Denis was always on parade for the annual Party Conferences and the regular events in the Conservative Party calendar. In 1984, he was staying at the Grand Hotel in Brighton when an IRA bomb tore through the building at 2.54 a.m. Denis was asleep and Margaret had just finished polishing her speech with Robin Butler. When the large thud shook the room, both realised it was a bomb: 'Before I could stop her, she said, "I must see if Denis is all right." She opened the door and plunged into the gloomy corridor. By now, the sound of falling masonry was deafening,' Robin Butler recalled. Woken by the blast, Denis put his head round the bedroom door to see that Margaret was all right. The bathroom in the suite had collapsed, and glass covered the sitting-room carpet. Advised against going back into the bedroom, he declared, 'Do be reasonable. I can't go around in my pyjamas',[53] and went back to get dressed: 'For some reason neither of us quite understands he took a spare pair of shoes with him,' Margaret remembers.[54]

They were ushered out of the hotel, a huge front section of which had completely collapsed, and were driven off to Brighton police station, where they found the American Ambassador, Charles Price, wandering without shoes. Denis gave him his spare pair. They were driven in almost complete numbed silence to Lewes police station, where Denis shared a room with the detectives as Margaret and her personal assistant Crawfie bedded down as best they could along the corridor.

The decision was taken to continue the conference at the scheduled time. Denis sat beside Margaret as, struggling to contain her emotions, she delivered a speech which got a standing ovation from the half-full conference, many dressed in clothes from the local Marks and Spencer branch which Alistair McAlpine had persuaded to open up early. Afterwards, Denis gave her a present of a watch with a rare note: 'Every minute is precious.'

In his dealings with the press, Denis formulated his own guidelines. He had early on decided to keep his head below the parapet and never to give interviews. He thought it 'better to keep my mouth shut and be *thought* a fool rather than open it and remove all doubt'.[55] Rarely did reporters catch him out. 'Be careful,' was his watchword. 'You've got to be on your toes. If you've got a press woman or press man within ten feet of you – watch your step!' To Denis, 'the BBC were the Reds and the press were the vipers, nothing circumlocutory about that!' Deedes reported, but he had 'always taken the view that they've got a living to earn taking their pictures and asking their silly question, and nothing is gained by being rude to them . . . There's everything to be gained by saying "no" politely,' he told us. Another maxim was: 'Avoid telling them to "sod off". It makes them cross,' and 'Never appear *speaking* on TV.

This is the short road to disaster.'[56] When he was upset about attacks on his wife, he didn't show it, but took the view, according to Alistair McAlpine, that '"You should take no notice of these people whatsoever, treat them with utter contempt." If you can dismiss it and say, "Bloody fool, doesn't know a thing", you can overcome it.' The press 'liked him, because he was pretty blunt with them,' McAlpine says. Occasionally he lunched with chosen journalists, but they rarely reported on him. He was 'out of bounds. No one on tour had a go at the Prime Minister through Denis,' Bernard Ingham, the Downing Street press chief, wrote. Perhaps they thought him a decent chap, perhaps they were careful not to provoke sanctions by No. 10 if they 'misbehaved', or perhaps it was because he was a man among (mostly) chaps. Once while travelling to Canada, he wandered into the press area at the back of the VC10 plane and fell into conversation with Michael Jones, *Sunday Times* political editor: '"And what," DT says to Michael, "do you think Northern Canada is full of?" Michael confesses ignorance . . . "Northern Canada", says DT with all the whispered emphasis at his command, "is full of eff all."'[57] Far from reporting this blatant indiscretion, Jones roars with laughter. Jones's definition of the rules regarding this Prime Minister's spouse was: 'DT was off limits. He wasn't a paid official, he wasn't a civil servant. He was a private person living at No. 10.'[58] This definition clearly lost its currency after Denis left No. 10.

In order not to embarrass Mrs Thatcher, Denis confined his speeches 'to sports occasions. Not more than thirty seconds or perhaps a minute or two. You can make a big black in a minute, can't you?' he told us. He had learned this in 'an unfortunate incident' in 1979 during the controversy over sanctions against apartheid South Africa: 'This one I learned *hard*. I was making a speech at a rugby football dinner. And going on at the same time was a great argument about the Lions, the rugby football side, going to South Africa. And what we in rugby football referred to as "the other game", Association, I think an England side, was in fact playing in Russia. And in the course of my speech, I said, "if those chaps who are playing the other game can go to Russia, as sure as hell we can go to South Africa". And that blew up in my face! A simple thing – [you have to be] so careful.' Margaret 'didn't say a word. Front page of the *Daily Telegraph* – she didn't say a word. She didn't say, "Well, I can do without that, can't I?"'

Several months later, he was again in hot water for writing on his Downing Street headed notepaper a letter to the Welsh Secretary about planning delays on a housing scheme in Snowdonia, for which he was a part-time consultant. Denis had a reputation for being scrupulous about separating his business affairs from his prime ministerial consort role. But according to Charles Powell he took the line: 'Well, No. 10 Downing Street is my address, I live here. How do you expect me not to write my letters here?' But he was more careful after that.

When his son Mark attracted press attention over some of his business dealings, Denis, though reportedly not pleased, remained in the background. 'Margaret was blind to any defects in Mark, and he was alert to them,' Grey Gowrie says. In January 1982, when Mark went missing during a car rally in the Sahara desert, Margaret was distraught and Denis was reluctantly dispatched in a private plane to look for him, with the press in tow. Within 24 hours Mark was picked up. On their return to London, after a briefing from Bernard Ingham, Mark faced the nation's press to explain his mishap while Denis sat tight-lipped beside him, holding in his temper. To Denis, Mark had let the side down.

After an IRA bomb hit Harrods just before Christmas 1983, killing five people, Denis was caught by press outside Downing Street. The previous evening he had visited the horrific scene: 'The day after, I went to Harrods. It was empty, obviously. I'd always gone to Harrods at Christmas time, and I came back, got out of the car and there were one or two press men there. One of them shouted out to me, "Where have you been?", so I said, "I've been to Harrods. I always go to Harrods at Christmas time and no whatnot Irishman – murdering Irishman – is going to keep me away." That was a mistake. "Murdering Irishmen." Naturally it wasn't being insulting, it was a natural [reaction]. I saw bodies on the ground when we went there, you see. And did I get some press? Did I get some letters? "We're not all murdering Irishmen. We're against murdering Irishmen." It's always the same.' Denis once expressed to an adviser his private view: 'It's always seemed to me that if the Irish want to kill each other, that should be strictly their own affair.'

Much of the heat was taken off him by the 'Dear Bill' column in *Private Eye*, which cast him as a rather befuddled, golf-playing, drinking and smoking archetype of unreconstructed Tory Britain, frequently sozzled, thoroughly right-wing, wildly politically incorrect and forever being summoned back to duty by 'M.' or 'the Boss'. Writer John Wells had immediately spotted in Denis a very attractive, sympathetic comic character. The 'Dear Bill letters' meant that people felt they knew him and removed any suspicion that he might have influence over Margaret as an *eminence grise* – the endearing character was clearly not up to it. It had enough truth in it – his lexicon of 'snifters', 'copious snorts', 'tinctures' was particularly accurate – for Downing Street insiders to suspect someone from within was leaking to *Private Eye*. 'He always took it pretty manfully . . . I think he recognised that it was warm fun, not spiteful fun. It used to horrify me sometimes, the detail they had,' Charles Powell says. Sometimes Denis seemed to enjoy living up to his image. Asked by a woman at a charity how he spent his time, he is alleged to have replied, 'Well, when I'm not completely pissed I like to play a lot of golf.' When a woman asked sympathetically whether he might have a drink problem, Denis waved his glass: 'Yes, Madam, I have. There is never enough of it.'[59] On Denis's 80th birthday, his cake, which the family proudly displayed, was a model of *Private Eye*, with a front cover photo of him holding up a jeroboam of champagne.

Attending a charity performance of the much cruder stage version, *Anyone for Denis?* at the suggestion of Tim Bell (who hadn't seen it) was a 'serious error': 'He was horrified by the whole thing. He was disinclined to forgive me at first . . . They were very polite, very charming, they met all the stars, said all the right things – I mean, gritted teeth, wanting to kill me most of the time,' Tim Bell recalls.

On official trips abroad with Margaret, Denis was considered a positive asset by her officials. 'He was a quiet presence,' Charles Powell says. 'If things went wrong or she was getting over-tired, if she got too hot – she hated the heat, because it sort of melted the make-up – Denis was the only person who could scrape her off the ceiling, get her feet back on the ground.' She was known for her incessant work and amazing stamina and Denis would, to the relief of all the team, suggest gently that it was time to retire to their suite and let the others sleep or write up their reports or briefings for the next day, 'and off they'd go, and you'd think, God bless Denis!' Antony Acland, then Ambassador to Washington, recalls.

Denis saw his role as 'showing the flag' – in the arena of business rather than the humanitarian and charity projects which most prime ministers' wives visited: 'When we got notice of the thing, then Charles Powell, mostly, would get in touch and arrange a separate programme of my own, visiting factories, particularly British factories or British interests. I was interested in all sorts of manufacturing industry – car factories in China, pharmaceutical in Japan, and that sort of thing,' he told us. He imposed strict limits: 'I used to say to Powell "no hospitals". I'm not very keen on hospitals, I never know what to say in hospitals.' He gladly laid wreaths at war memorials, visited local British businessmen and attended any sort of sporting event: 'Always went, particularly in places like Canada, and met a lot of people who had been players there. We had a lot of fun.'

Clothes were not a problem for Denis, who adopted some simple rules. Prime ministerial spouses (and indeed prime ministers) do not normally have any personal help when travelling: 'I'm an expert at hanging 'em all up and ironing it all!' Denis said. 'I don't like them unpacking my suitcases, and I put a large notice, "Please Do NOT Unpack", so I know when I unpack – it doesn't take long to unpack it – I know where I've hung it up. So when it comes to changing for dinner, I know exactly what I've done with it, instead of finding they've put your evening dress shoes in some place where you wouldn't expect to see 'em. Otherwise you can get in a muddle.' Naturally, there was no press comment on his dress – all the attention focused on Margaret.

Mishaps were a source of frustration and some colourful language. Staying at the Presidential palace in Sri Lanka, Denis 'came down to breakfast and there were forty Sri Lankan servants all lined up. He asked for some milk with his cereal and a nervous Sri Lankan arrived and somehow poured it all over his trousers. With a look of great saint-hood, Denis said to me, "You know, the only problem about this country – the buggeration factor's too high,"' Charles Powell recalls. (According to Mark, this was known in private as the 'e-factor' – 'e' for embuggerance.) When he once asked Jeffrey Archer if he had ever been to Saudi Arabia and Archer said no, he warned: 'Well don't have dinner with them'. Archer said, 'What do you mean?' Denis said, 'Well, it starts at six and ends at three in the morning.'

Inevitably Denis spent time with leaders' wives. American President

Reagan's wife, Nancy, 'was rather intrigued by him, and he was always very polite and courteous to her' in his slightly old-fashioned way. Denis got on with Barbara Bush, after an initial hitch on their first encounter before her husband became President, when she found Denis 'rather rude, especially when he made several disparaging remarks to me about Americans'. When she was First Lady, she learned 'that he has a wonderful sense of humour and is steady as a rock, plus, he's a good sport. Many times he found himself the only male in a room full of "spouses".' Denis thought the down-to-earth Barbara (who once declared: 'Politics consists of rushing and then waiting') 'a great chum and very nice . . . Sitting next to her was no hardship.'[60]

He also established a rapport with President Gorbachev's wife Raisa, when Gorbachev, who was not yet the Russian leader, paid his first visit to Chequers in December 1984. Denis sensed that it was 'one of the lunches that change history . . . At the time one doesn't say that it is "history in the making", but I realised in my dim-witted way that this was something pretty special,' he told Carol. Gorbachev struck a chord with the woman the Russians had dubbed 'The Iron Lady', and Mrs Thatcher saw Gorbachev as a man she could 'do business with' in the long process of breaking down East–West tensions and ending the Cold War. 'Gorbachev fell in love with her [Margaret] and I like to think that Raisa got on well with me.'[61] Denis took Raisa on a tour of Chequers, stopping in the library, where she browsed through English classics. Later she recalled discussing with Denis and an official which of their two countries had the most recipes for potatoes.

By the 1987 general election, though his admiration was undimmed, Denis was concluding that this should be Margaret's last campaign. He shared the team's nervousness about the outcome. The economy had recovered during the previous twelve months but unemployment was still high, and Mrs Thatcher's personal popularity was faltering. She had taken on the unions and won by refusing, during their year-long strike, to give in to Arthur Scargill's National Union of Mine-workers, but in so doing had incurred deep bitterness, and her 'conviction' politics had alienated significant sectors of the community, including the Church and the educational establishments.

In April the previous year, her popularity rating had dipped to its lowest since 1981 (28 per cent in April 1986); she was perceived as 'uncaring' and her government was thought to have 'lost its way'.[62] In addition, simmering resentment among her Cabinet colleagues at her leadership style surfaced publicly with the resignation of Michael Heseltine over the Westland Helicopters issue. However, a new strategy offensive and an upturn in the economy meant that by December the Tories had regained a clear lead over Labour. In the March 1987 Budget, Chancellor Nigel Lawson cut income tax and increased spending on health and other services, which added an essential 'feel-good factor' in the run-up to the election.

Even so, the outcome of the June election was uncertain. The Labour Party, rebranded with a red rose symbol under its leader since 1983, Neil Kinnock, mounted a strong campaign in the early days, presenting Neil and his wife, Glenys, as young, idealistic and somewhat glamorous. It was only in the last week that the Tories surged ahead. An injection of £3 million into the campaign budget for newspaper ads, on the principle, Alistair McAlpine reasoned, that 'It was better to be a Party in power with an overdraft than a rich opposition', helped the Tories win with an overall majority of 102.

It was a decisive mandate for Mrs Thatcher to continue her radical 'revolution', but it did not remove Denis's fears. A few days after polling, he and Carol were in the No. 10 flat watching Margaret as she acknowledged cheers from the crowd: 'Denis turned to get himself a refill and said, "In a year she'll be so unpopular you won't believe it,"' Carol recalled. His words were prescient. The collapse of the stock market on 'Black Monday', 19 October 1987, brought a halt to the 1980s boom and fuelled inflation, and Mrs Thatcher's insistence on introducing the deeply unpopular Community Charge ('poll tax' to its opponents) soon divided the Party and the country. Denis's doubts sharpened as he detected, as Jim Callaghan had in 1979, that a 'time for a change' momentum was gathering. In the last few years, 'he would often say "Oh, she should pack up, you know, we should go." It was quite a refrain,' says Alistair McAlpine.

As Mrs Thatcher passed the anniversary of her ten years in office, Denis 'actually thought she'd done enough and it was time for her to move on', Tim Bell says. 'And he did several times say to me, and to her, "You know, you really have done enough, actually, dear. I think you've done enough. Time to stop now." He thought it was damaging her health. He thought she was beginning to reach the down curve, so she was going to be less successful rather than more. He thought that she had earned the right to go. But there was always that caveat, "But if that's what you want to do, pet, I'm with you."'

At Chequers over Christmas 1989, Denis, now aged 71 and fourteen years into his formal 'retirement', broached the subject with Margaret: 'I didn't want to see her lose. I wanted her to go out at the top. She could say that she never lost – she was never defeated or humiliated; with her reputation entirely intact and after ten years she would hand it on to the next person,' he told Carol. But when her supporter Willie Whitelaw said, 'You can't do that, there'll be blood on the walls when choosing your successor. It will split the Party', Denis did not pursue it.[63]

He observed closely as opposition to the poll tax mounted, divisions deepened within and outside Cabinet over Britain's application to join the ERM and erupted over her handling of economic policy, where she was increasingly at odds with her Chancellor, Nigel Lawson, who resigned suddenly in October 1989. She still commanded a strong position on the world stage. She was staying with President Bush in August 1990 when Iraq invaded Kuwait, and played a key role in backing his decision to take military action against Saddam Hussein. 'George, this is no time to go wobbly,' she memorably told Bush.

When the little-known backbencher, Anthony Meyer stood as the stalking horse candidate for the leadership in November 1989 and gained 33 votes against Mrs Thatchar's 314, with 27 abstentions, Carol said to her mother, 'Oh well, that's over then.' 'Oh no,' she said, that's just the beginning.' Denis noted, 'We had too many people voting against.'[64] But to every question about whether she should continue, Mrs Thatcher insisted she would go on – her job was uncompleted and, like Churchill, she felt it was her duty to stay. At the Party Conference in October 1990 the cry of 'Ten more years!' from the loyal audience was deafening.

Events then moved fast. In a measured speech in the House of Commons on 13 November, her former Foreign Secretary, then Leader of the House of Commons, Geoffrey Howe, announced his resignation due to differences over Europe. It was the second resignation of a major front-bench figure in twelve months, and Howe's speech contained a

devastating attack on Mrs Thatcher's style of government and her treatment of colleagues, which he characterised as 'sending your opening
batsman to the crease only for them to find, the moment the first balls
are bowled, that their bats have been broken before the game by the
team captain'. By declaring that 'The time has come for others to
consider their own response to the tragic conflict of loyalties with which
I have wrestled for perhaps too long', he paved the way for a leadership challenge. Michael Heseltine, who had been in the wilderness since
his own resignation in 1986, instantly put in his bid.

Mrs Thatcher's position had been undermined, and the question
was – how fatally? The first leadership ballot was set for a week later,
Tuesday 20 November. Mrs Thatcher refused to canvass for support
by ringing up MPs and spending time in the Tea Room: 'That's not
for me after eleven years,' she told Party Chairman Kenneth Baker.[65]
'She took the view that she'd been leader of the Conservative Party for
God knows how many years, and she didn't need to go round pleading
for their votes,' Alistair McAlpine says. She also refused advice that
she put off her visit to Paris to join Bush, Gorbachev, Kohl and
Mitterand in the formal ceremonies at the CSCE conference marking
the end of the Cold War. Though it reinforced her status as a world
leader, it meant she would be out of the country on the day of the count.

On the weekend before the ballot, Denis and Margaret were at
Chequers with a group of the inner circle. After dinner, Denis sat in
as discussion turned to the ballot. Tim Bell recalls: 'Kenneth Baker
had written a list of who would vote for her and who wouldn't and
who would vote for Heseltine – and he was 100 per cent correct. She
absolutely refused to accept what he'd written down. Peter Morrison
[Margaret's PPS and nominal campaign manager] stood there saying,
"You've won by 120 votes" – or something ridiculous. And Kenneth
Baker, rather boldly, I thought, because Kenneth was never prone to
boldness, said, "Well I'm sorry, but I don't agree with that. Here's my
list" and he gave it to Margaret, and Margaret [was saying] "Why is
he – why wouldn't he vote for me?"' When 'she got grumpy and was
clearly very confused because two sets of people she trusted were telling
her opposite things', Denis intervened. 'He said, "Listen to them, pet!"
What I think he was saying is: "You're going to lose, dear, don't muck
about, make a decision, get on with it."'

When the group dispersed, the inner core, including Gordon Reece and Tim Bell, remained: 'We got into a conversation about what to do if she lost, what to do in different scenarios. And she went through complete denial – she *absolutely* refused to accept that there was any real problem, that this was just Heseltine, who was a complete pain in the arse and waste of space and everybody would see through that . . . [and] Denis said "You should go. You should go." "What?!" "You should go. You're among friends, you can talk here, you should go." "Is that what you think, Gordon?" "No, no, certainly not. You must fight, you must fight, all day, every day. Always fight, fight, fight, fight!" Denis chided them: "Let me down badly, Gordon. And you, Tim. We agreed. We agreed you'd tell her. And you haven't. You're encouraging her to go on fighting and she's going to lose. You think you're doing her a service and you're not," he said. And I remember those words, engraved on my soul. And he knew it was the end. He knew that whatever happened, even if she won by twenty or thirty votes, it wasn't enough. Unless she won by a thumping great 150 or whatever. And he knew that she would – in the end – come to that view, I think. But we were all too emotionally involved in the whole thing.'

Next evening, as Margaret prepared to leave for Paris, Crawfie said to Denis, 'Well, Mr Thatcher, hopefully we will come back with the right vote.' He turned and said, 'Crawfie, she is done for now.'[66] In Paris next day, as Mrs Thatcher was preparing to go to a splendid banquet at Versailles, the results of the first ballot came through. She had gained 204 to Heseltine's 152, a majority of 52, but four votes short of the 56 she needed by the Party rules. She went downstairs, 'breathing the fire of purpose', Bernard Ingham recorded, walked straight to the waiting press in the courtyard of the British Embassy and interrupted John Sergeant in the middle of a BBC news report to announce that she was disappointed that the result was not quite enough to win, but she intended to let her name go forward for the second ballot. Then she went upstairs and phoned Denis. He 'was fabulous: "Congratulations, sweetie pie, you've won; it's just the rules," he said, as tears trickled down his face. He was crying for her, not for himself,' Carol remembered.[67]

A sympathetic President Mitterand had delayed the start of the banquet. When Mrs Thatcher arrived, Barbara Bush 'gave her a big hug and told her that we had been waiting all day for the news. She said, "Not to worry" and went on to say she'd get it on the second ballot. George and I took Margaret by the arm and ran the gamut of the press.'[68]

On her return to Downing Street at lunchtime next day, she 'went straight up to the flat to see Denis. Affection never blunted honesty between us. His advice was that I should withdraw. "Don't go on, love," he said. But I felt in my bones that I should fight on,' she wrote. 'My friends and supporters expected me to fight, and I owed it to them to do so as long as there was a chance of victory. But was there?'[69] She was ebullient when asked by the press outside Downing Street for a comment: 'I fight on. I fight to win.' But with her authority damaged, her support was crumbling. As she sounded out opinion among her Cabinet that evening, she was told by one after another in individual meetings that, though they would support her if she stood, they did not think she could win in a second ballot, and they did not want to see her humiliated by standing and losing. Paradoxically, they perceived that the only way to defend her legacy was for her to give up. John Major, who remained at home in Huntingdon following a wisdom tooth operation, was waiting in the wings.

On Wednesday evening, after seeing each of the Cabinet in turn, she moved to a decision. 'I had lost the Cabinet's support. I could not even muster a credible support team. It was the end,' she wrote.[70] Denis knew the score, even as supporters arrived to encourage her to stay on: 'He said to me, "it's all over",' Robin Butler recalls. Denis had gone to supper with Carol, Mark and Alistair McAlpine at Mark's club. On the way back, Carol walked with Denis across Horse Guards' Parade to avoid the glow of television lights and cameras massed outside No. 10's front door. Carol remembered: 'Halfway across Horse Guards Denis stopped and turned to look at me. He pushed up his glasses and I could see tears in his eyes. "Oh, it's just the disloyalty of it all," he whispered and we hugged.[71] Alistair McAlpine was in the flat with Denis when Margaret went up after seeing her Cabinet: 'it was the only time I heard him express anything really forcibly. When she told us what had happened, Denis said, "Well, they don't bloody well deserve you", you know – "Go".' By then Charles Powell was drafting a resignation speech and Tim Bell had been summoned at 11.15 from a restaurant in

Hampstead – 'I've decided to go. Can you come and see me?' With Gordon Reece, he helped her write her resignation speech. Denis went to bed.

Next morning, 22 November, she announced her resignation to the Cabinet, while Denis breakfasted upstairs. 'He looked relieved in a quietly subdued way. He could see that this whole long interminable saga was over . . . he might have been quietly seething underneath at the way in which it was done, but I don't think he was actually sorry that it was over', Bernard Ingham told Carol.[72] As the manoeuvring began for the leadership, Denis, dressed in black, left to attend the memorial service for Elizabeth Home at Westminster Abbey. There he paid homage to a former prime ministerial spouse who, though only six years older than him, seemed to hail from a bygone age of Conservative politics. Margaret drove to the Palace to tender her resignation to the Queen, and returned to face a No Confidence debate in the House of Commons, watched on television by Denis, who told her, 'That was wonderful . . . brilliant . . . magnificent.'[73]

Their last weekend at Chequers was poignant. Both Denis and Margaret loved the place which for eleven years they had treated as their country home. For Denis, Chequers was one of the best aspects of the job. They walked hand in hand one last time through the rooms 'as the light faded on that winter afternoon'. Saying goodbye to the staff was among the most difficult of their farewells.

Unusually for a departing prime minister, they had a week to pack up at No. 10 while the leadership issue was resolved. John Major, her chosen successor, emerged as the victor. On the day they departed, after they had walked past the staff and officials who lined the hall, Denis stood expressionless outside the door of No. 10 as Mrs Thatcher addressed the waiting press corps, then got into the car. Fighting back tears, she waved through the window, and they sped away.

From Downing Street the Thatchers moved to the house which they had bought in Dulwich when they sold the Flood Street house in 1986. Though it had presented some advantages then, not least that it backed on to a golf course, it rapidly proved a nightmare for security, and they soon moved out and eventually settled in a house in Chester Square.

For a while Margaret was consumed by her sense of betrayal. Denis shared her deep hurt at her colleagues' behaviour – 'Treachery with a smile on its face,' as she described it. She never forgave them. Even her closest allies tired of the same refrain – 'How could they do this to me? Do you know the names of the traitors?' – each time they visited. The 'saintly Denis' 'went out a lot, and saw a lot of friends and he just avoided too much of it because he said, "there's nothing I can do about it, and I can't change what happened",' Tim Bell recalls.

To begin with, Margaret was lost: 'From total communication and contact and constant events taking place to nothing. It must have been *absolutely* horrific,' says Tim Bell. He and others ensured that the Thatchers went out to theatres and restaurants, the Ritz for example, where 'the entire restaurant would get up and clap when she came in, which was so good for her because her self-esteem had been completely battered'.

Denis pursued his business commitments from an office in Victoria, spoke at charity functions and went out to business lunches and dinners. 'He absolutely loved all that because that was *his* world, he could now return to it,' Tim Bell says. 'He was finally back in control – although he didn't actually say it – and he had his life back.' He also had his Rolls-Royce after eleven years: 'He was picking me up for a game of golf and suddenly this Rolls came round the corner. "Denis I see you're back behind the wheel",' Bill Deedes said, cheerfully.

Margaret was much in demand for lectures (at $50,000) in America and the Far East, and she began working on her memoirs, the first volume of which was completed during 1992. Denis accompanied her round the world on her speaking engagements and book tours, delighted that she was again in the limelight. He moved his office to the Chesham Place headquarters of the Thatcher Foundation, set up in 1991 to propagate her ideas worldwide, though he played little part in its running.

In 1990 he received a hereditary baronetcy and became Sir Denis Thatcher, and in 1992 Margaret gave up her parliamentary seat and was elevated to the House of Lords with a life peerage. Denis remained in reasonable health, continuing to play golf, despite troubles with arthritis. When she showed signs of short-term memory loss, he was invariably on hand to ease her path. But in January 2003 he underwent a heart bypass operation. When he went to South Africa to recuperate, she missed him terribly: 'Without him, she's really a changed person. Denis was always the real stable person in her life,' Alistair McAlpine said.

Though he seemed to recover, five months later he was taken ill again. On 26 June 2003, Denis died from pancreatic cancer. He was 88. Margaret was holding his hand, and Carol, Mark and Crawfie were by his bedside. Tributes to the man who had so expertly negotiated the uncharted role of male prime ministerial spouse filled the national press. 'The perfect consort who gave his "Blessed Margaret" half a century of love and loyalty,' as the *Daily Telegraph* put it, was, said Lord Tebbit, 'a great gentleman and a very decent man who put his interests second to that of his wife and country'. To former Conservative leader Edward Heath, 'his outstanding quality was an ability to create good fellowship and enjoy it among all those with whom he mixed'.[74]

As family, friends and colleagues gathered to pay tribute at his memorial service on 30 October 2003 another drama in the Conservative Party's fortunes was unfolding. In an eerie echo of Elizabeth Home's memorial service, which took place on the day Mrs Thatcher resigned, the Party had just ousted its leader, Iain Duncan Smith, and the new leader, former Thatcher supporter Michael Howard, took his place. Gathered there, Tim Bell says, were 'All those people I'd seen two days ago in the House of Commons, fighting and abusing each other, suddenly there they all were, close bosom pals, totally united – extraordinary!'

Denis Thatcher was the first man to occupy No. 10 in the role of prime ministerial spouse. He was a man of integrity with no personal agenda, who found himself unexpectedly at the centre of power. His strong views, leavened by his often self-deprecating humour and common sense, were well known in private, though not in public. Throughout his life he was immensely proud of his wife and her achievements, and utterly loyal. It was in his nature to accept being two steps behind his wife, a woman who always stole the show. At No. 10, for eleven years he worked on behalf of her interests, smoothing her path and making himself useful, while also being able to stand aside from the storm – an invaluable asset appreciated by all those around her. In her memoirs, Mrs Thatcher wrote: 'Being Prime Minister is a lonely job. In a sense it ought to be: you cannot lead from a crowd. But with Denis there I was never alone. What a man. What a husband. What a friend.'[75]

Chapter Seven

Norma Major

1990–97

During the crisis that culminated in Mrs Thatcher's resignation in November 1990, John Major, her Chancellor of the Exchequer, was outside the fray. On Saturday morning, 17 November, he was with his wife, Norma, in their Huntingdon constituency opening the Grand Charity Fair in aid of Mencap, of which Norma was President. Norma stayed on at the fair while John's agent drove him to a long-standing appointment in hospital to have a wisdom tooth removed. He was warned it would put him out of action for a week. As it turned out, it was the most crucial week in their entire political life together.

Three days earlier, Michael Heseltine had challenged Margaret Thatcher for the Party leadership. When Norma and their 19-year-old daughter Elizabeth visited John as he recovered from the anaesthetic on Saturday evening, Norma recalls (though John does not remember the conversation) that they speculated on whether Mrs Thatcher would survive, and if John should stand if she lost: 'And I remember Elizabeth saying to him, "go for it, Dad,"' said Norma, who agreed with her.[1] Meanwhile, over at Chequers, Margaret Thatcher was weighing up the odds with her inner circle of advisers while Denis Thatcher, who feared her possible humiliation, looked on.

John Major supported Thatcher and seconded her nomination. He had left his Treasury office the day before believing that she would win in the first round, despite speculation over the previous few days that she might lose. Several of his close colleagues suggested that if she lost John would be in the frame as her successor, but he was noncommittal. Asked by his agent Peter Brown if he would put his name forward, he replied 'I won't oppose Mrs Thatcher, but I've been asked, and if there is the chance there I shall let my name go forward. It may not happen again.'[2] He told Graham Bright, his Parliamentary Private Secretary, that he wanted no canvassing on his behalf before the result of the first ballot was declared.

John spent much of Sunday at home asleep or drowsy from painkillers while Norma fielded phone calls from people offering their support if he decided to stand. Major 'still thought she would win on the first round' and would do nothing unless she withdrew.[3] Among the calls that Norma took was one from Mrs Thatcher: 'I've had "Mother" on the phone', she told a friend. 'She was just about to leave for Paris. She asked how he was. "No, don't disturb him," she said, "don't do that. He's my favourite son; give him my best wishes."'[4]

On Monday, Jeffrey Archer, Major's neighbour and former MP, joined Norma and John for lunch, when Archer expressed the view, now wide-spread in the Party, that he wanted Mrs Thatcher to survive, but thought 'her chances were bleak'. As the conversation turned to what might follow the ballot next day, Norma was taken aback, suddenly exclaiming: 'Do you realise we're sitting here talking about you becoming Prime Minister?'[5] John, however, had not made up his mind to stand. He believed it was too soon. So far, his rise had been meteoric. He had been appointed as Chancellor of the Exchequer only a year before. It was just three years since he had entered the Cabinet, and he doubted he was thought experienced enough to get sufficient support. At 47 he thought he might be next but one in line. He remained loyal to Mrs Thatcher.

When Margaret Thatcher failed to get the overall majority she required on 20 November, Norma and John watched on television as she strode down the steps of the British Embassy in Paris and seized the microphone from a BBC reporter to announce that she would stand in the second ballot.

With speculation raging that John was in line as the successor (though Douglas Hurd was the front-runner), Norma had her first taste of a press siege of their house. Appalled, she phoned her friend Emily Blatch, a prominent member of the constituency and later leader of Cambridge-shire County Council: 'We're just completely surrounded,' she said. 'They're hanging in the trees,' John added, 'they're out here and they've got ladders and they've got ropes and they're up in the trees.' The phone rang constantly as colleagues pressed him to put his name forward. When Mrs Thatcher called him that afternoon to confirm his support, she claimed 'there was a moment's silence. The hesitation was palpable.'[6] John recalled: 'She was brisk. "Douglas is going to nominate me and I want you to second me," she burst out before I could say a word.' Though he would have liked to discuss her prospects and strategy, 'she simply assumed that she had my support. Her approach was a classic example of her management style. Taken aback, I paused before replying: "If that is what you want, I will."'[7]

By the evening, John, who had been in touch with Downing Street, knew that the cards were collapsing. In single interviews with her Cabinet, most had offered Mrs Thatcher their support, but told her they believed she could not win. Jeffrey Archer's chauffeur was dispatched to John's house to get his signature as seconder on Mrs Thatcher's nomination papers. As he signed them, John 'knew it was becoming less likely that the document would ever be used'. Prompted by Graham Bright, Norma typed out a second document declaring that he was prepared to let his name go forward for the second round if she withdrew.[8] By the time Archer delivered the nomination papers to Downing Street at 1.30 a.m., Mrs Thatcher had decided to resign.

John agreed to stand. Norma saw clearly the political imperative which launched him into the leadership: 'It was an opportunity. The pressures were there. I don't think he could have turned away from it. I'm a great one for going with the flow. I would never have stopped John doing anything he wanted to do.' Next morning, Norma drove John down to Westminster, arriving just before the deadline for nominations. He walked into a crowded office filled with colleagues eager to back him and he immediately launched his campaign. Mrs Thatcher let it be known that Major was her favoured successor, though it was the view of her wise counsel, William Whitelaw ('Every Prime Minister needs a Willie,' she had memorably commented), that: 'Many will vote for him thinking that he is on the right wing. They'll be disappointed and soon find out that he isn't.'[9] 'It was never entirely clear why she regarded him as her philosophical Dauphin, because John was never like that,' Chris Patten, Party chairman, confirms. Major, who had bridled at Mrs Thatcher's saying that she was 'a very good back-seat driver', had no wish to be seen 'as son of Margaret Thatcher. I am running as myself, with my own priorities and my own programme,' he told an interviewer.[10]

Norma drove back to Huntingdon as the five-day campaign swung into action. She had scant time to consider the full implications for her life and that of her family if he won, which seemed increasingly likely. She wanted John to win, though she knew he was nervous. Norma recalls. 'He had one sleepless night at No. 11 during the leadership campaign. He said he hadn't been able to sleep and I said, "Oh, are you afraid you're going to lose?" And he said, "No, I'm afraid I'm going to win." It was very exciting.' Norma returned to a crowded No. 11 'with a car full of food that I'd cooked, because we had so many people at the flat to feed'. On Tuesday 27 November, John put his arms round Norma as they watched the results on a flickering TV screen: 185 for Major, 131 for Heseltine and 56 for Hurd. Norma was delighted, but 'it was sad, too. It was sad taking over from someone in those circumstances. I was a fan of Margaret's, and I think what the Party did was shocking. I guess with hindsight there was a certain inevitability. It was always going to end in tears.'

Shortly after the declaration, Mrs Thatcher arrived in No. 11 through the interconnecting door from No. 10, and went up to John: 'Well done, John, well done,' she said. She went to Norma. 'It's what I've always wanted, she told her.'[11] As the press were milling outside, friends and supporters gathered upstairs in the kitchen. The phone rang. A friend, Peter Golds, picked it up: 'and it was the White House – "We have President Bush for Mr Major." That is the second you realise you are in the presence of power.'

Next morning, Norma and John drove to the Palace, where John 'kissed hands' as Norma waited in an ante-room. On their arrival at Downing Street, as Mrs Thatcher watched from an upstairs window, he made a brief speech to the press, then he and Norma turned into No. 10 where the hall was lined, by tradition, with applauding staff and officials. John was whisked off to the Cabinet Room. Norma went upstairs to the No. 10 flat.

It had been Norma's hope, in the brief time she had had to think about this unexpected turn of events, that her life would not change dramatically. From the day she became an MP's wife on John's election to the Huntingdon seat in 1979, she had ordered her life to fit her political obligations to him around her family and her own interests. The glare of publicity which suddenly focused on this relatively unknown couple was a revelation and a shock to her. Her occupation of No. 10, which seemed to her an unwelcoming environment, taxed her considerable resourcefulness. 'There was absolutely no guidance at all. There was nobody there to say "This is what you have to do and this is what we're going to do to help you do it." Which I think was absolutely staggering,' Norma says.

When Norma Johnson met John Major on polling day for the GLC election in 1970, she knew that his life already revolved around politics. She was 28, a warm, attractive, independent woman with a career as a domestic science teacher, her own flat and a Mini car. Though she had joined the Young Conservatives, she was not particularly interested in politics. She was sensitive, cultured and a fanatical opera fan. It was at the request of a fellow fan, Peter Golds, that she arrived that day with her car to help bring in the votes on behalf of her friend and candidate Diana Geddes, and met John Major, then Chairman of Brixton Conservative Association and of Lambeth Council's Housing Committee. John first saw Norma in a committee room at election headquarters in Brixton Road: 'She was slender, a little above average height, with mid-brown hair, shining brown eyes and a beautiful, curving, glamorous smile. Dressed in a beige checked suit, fawn blouse and white, knee-length boots, she was stunningly attractive,' he recalls.[12] Norma saw John 'and thought, "What a gorgeous man!"'[13] She says: 'It was a deeply mutual thing . . . It's rather strange to discover love and politics at the same time.' John made sure that Norma was smuggled into the Town Hall for the count. The Conservatives lost their seats on the GLC, 'but I had found Norma', John wrote.

She invited him to a party, which he turned down, then to the opera, which he accepted (though he fell asleep). John, who 'knew from the moment we met that I wanted to marry Norma', proposed ten days later. 'It's probably the only impetuous thing he's ever done, really. It might be the only impetuous thing I've ever done. It was exciting, brilliant and right,' she says. 'He was good-looking. He was exciting. I think a sense of humour stood us in good stead – to be able to laugh at the ridiculous and even to laugh at ourselves and see the funny side . . . He had purpose in life, too. There was something driving him and I liked that because I like somebody to have purpose.' Six months later, on a sunny day in October, they were married at St Matthew's Church, Brixton, with Norma dressed in a bodice of guipure lace sewn with crystal drops merging into a velvet skirt and train. Norma's friend, opera singer June Bronhill, sang 'Ave Maria'. After a honeymoon in Ibiza, they returned to John's spartan flat in Primrose Court, Brixton.

Norma was not only attractive and warm, she was also efficient and unusually resourceful. Born in Shropshire on 12 February 1942, she had been brought up alone by her mother, Edith ('Dee') after her father, Norman Wagstaff, was killed in a motorcycle accident in Belgium only days after the Second World War ended. Norma was three. Dee had lost her baby son only four months earlier. Dee took Norma back to Bermondsey, where she herself had been brought up, but which was now bomb-scarred from the war. To keep them, Dee took on up to three bookkeeping and accounting jobs at a time. She was 'very independent, very determined, and disciplined', Norma says. 'She just loved figures', and was keen on self-improvement. While her mother earned a living, with the help of Royal Artillery Charities (in which her father had served in the war), Norma was sent at the age of four to boarding-school in Bexhill. Dee visited each weekend and they went on the pier at Hastings, ate buttered toast, listened to the Palm Court orchestra and went shrimping. When she was seven Norma moved as a weekly boarder to Oakfield School in Dulwich, and then went as a day pupil to a school in Camberwell which was moved into one of the first purpose built comprehensives to become Peckham Girls School.

Though her circumstances were tough, Norma remembers a secure childhood, surrounded by relations and friends. Life was frugal. 'There wasn't a lot of money,' and with rationing still in place, there was 'a great shortage of everything and you had to make do. I grew up learning the value of money' – as everyone did, she says. 'I still don't like waste. It runs deep.' Like her mother, she was self-reliant, though she was more practical about making and fixing things in the home. Her grandmother, a tailor, taught her to use a sewing machine. From the age of 12, like many others of her day, she made her own clothes, helped by an uncle, who brought back fabrics from the fashion house where he worked.

At Peckham School, when most girls left at 16, she stayed on after taking seven O levels to study for A-level exams in English, Needlework and Geography and was appointed Head Girl – she wasn't sure why. 'I'm quite good, I suppose, at administration, and I'm good at charts and time sheets so I was quite good at organising the prefects. I'm not pushy,' she says. She also had 'a sense of duty and sense of obligation. A sense of responsibility,' though she was not ambitious, except 'in anything I did, to do it well'. Later, a friend commented on Norma's meticulousness: 'She worries. She wants to do everything 100 per cent right.'

In common with an increasing number of young women of her generation, she decided to continue her education. She was the first person in her family to do so, and she met some resistance, though not from her mother: 'The idea of further education was difficult for some members of the family to grapple with. "You're going to get married and have children, what do you need all this expensive education for?" But that's hardly the point!' she says. She enrolled at Battersea Training College of Domestic Science in 1960, and left home to live in college. She qualified as a home economist, and, since she had always expected to have a full-time career, she then taught domestic science for the next ten years.

Although the 'swinging sixties' was happening in places like the King's Road and Carnaby Street, it had little impact in Penge, where Norma then lived. Norma, who was well read and had a wide range of interests, discovered that her real passion was for opera. In 1965 she went with a friend to see singer June Bronhill in the musical *Robert and Elizabeth* at the Lyric Theatre, and met her backstage. June Bronhill became a friend; Norma helped her out with babysitting, and took care of her house and child during school summer holidays. Soon Norma was borrowing opera records wherever she could, and when she discovered Joan Sutherland she was completely hooked. Two or three times a week, after queuing for tickets, sometimes overnight, she sat in the 'gods' at Covent Garden with a growing group of like-minded friends. 'It was relatively cheap then, only eight shillings. And we used to sleep on the pavement as a matter of course to get tickets,' Norma says. Peter Golds recalls how she would stroll into a nearby hotel to wash and brush up with such elegance and panache that no one ever stopped her or asked if she was a guest. With Peter she went to almost every one of Sutherland's performances during one Covent Garden season, turning up at the stage door to see her afterwards. Such was her enthusiasm that she drove across Europe to see Sutherland's performances with three friends squashed into her Mini ('Crazy. With your foot on the floor you couldn't do more than forty miles an hour'). Their journey took them to Holland, and once by cheap car ferry to Hamburg.

When she met John, Norma was supply teaching in Norwood and worked for Simplicity Patterns making up designs for fashion shows which she continued after they married. John worked as a junior in Standard Chartered Bank, studied for his banking exams and continued his political activities in the evening. There was not much money – her housekeeping was £8 a week. Norma grew accustomed to John's absences. 'The fact that I was relatively independent and actually I don't get lonely, helped,' she says. She had other things to get on with, and 'the idea of being married to a man who came home every night and put his slippers on and sat and watched the television would drive me to distraction'. She went to the opera and enjoyed going to civic functions connected with John's council activities, though these ceased in spring 1971 when he lost his seat and Lambeth reverted to traditional Labour control.

By then Norma was pregnant with Elizabeth, who was born that November, and John – unusually for the time – was present at the birth. Norma gave up teaching but continued her freelance dressmaking, and they soon moved out of Lambeth to the suburb of Beckenham, where her mother lived and she was surrounded by friends who also had small children. Norma accepted that John's ambition was now for a parliamentary seat: 'It never bothered me at all, if that's what he wanted to do. Anything he wanted to do was all right by me.' Norma 'realised I was trying to get into Parliament, but I don't think she realised what might follow from that', John says. He was selected as candidate for St Pancras North in 1971 and in the February 1974 general election, which the Conservatives lost to Labour after four years in power, she went out canvassing, made tea, attended rallies and was swept up in the excitement. When Major stood, again unsuccessfully, in the election that October, she did less because she was by then pregnant with their son James, born in January 1975.

John tried and was rejected for several seats – 'eventually he didn't even tell me what he was applying for'14 – until he was selected as candidate for the Huntingdon constituency, a safe Conservative stronghold, in 1976. Norma was delighted: 'It was really very exciting. And a marvellous place to live.' She knew the area, as she had stayed with an aunt and had played on a farm nearby during her childhood. It was a mixed constituency, with the local squirearchy and its agricultural population swelled by the arrival of London 'overspill' – people of similar backgrounds to theirs who were attracted to the area by its rapid commercial expansion. It was also not too far from London – and the Opera House. In 1977 they bought a three-bedroomed detached house in the village of Hemingford Grey (John had by then moved up to a marketing job at Standard Chartered Bank) and Norma was soon heavily involved in local constituency activities which she fitted in with her growing children, Elizabeth, now aged six, and James, who was three.

In the 1979 general election which brought Mrs Thatcher to power, Major won the Huntingdon seat with an increased majority. When it came to the decision which faces all MPs about where to live, Norma and John agreed that she would remain in the constituency and provide a stable home for the children while John stayed from Monday to Friday in London in a series of rented furnished apartments. They could not afford to keep up two houses, one in London and another in Huntingdon. Norma rarely attended political events in London, and she turned down invitations to meetings of the parliamentary wives' groups – 'I didn't see the need . . . I never felt isolated' – so she did not become part of the Westminster wives' circle. Norma felt at ease in the constituency and, like John, saw it as home.

For her, the hub of political activity lay in Huntingdon rather than in Westminster. In this, she was the inheritor of a long tradition of Conservative wives whose indispensable role in the Party is to mobilise voluntary support and social activity, particularly among women, at local level. During elections, she enjoyed 'getting out and about with the Party workers, visiting people in the committee rooms and generally encouraging them and wishing them well . . . She would do anything, whatever she was called upon to do,' Emily Blatch recalls. While she was a prominent presence, she never spoke at meetings. Every Friday and Saturday, when John returned she drove him on a busy schedule round the constituency – 'he was better at talking and I was better at driving', she says.

She was conscientious, popular and well regarded: 'I did everything I could possibly have done. I went with John to almost everything he did.' She was happy to carry out what was required of her, giving the Party 'two for the price of one', as she puts it. 'I'm practical, so I'd rather sit down with a group of people and actually organise something than just sit down and talk. I'm a doer, I think,' she says. 'Norma operates fantastically at a personal level, so meeting people in the room and talking to people and empathising – she's really very good at that. It was a very warm personality that came across,' Emily Blatch says. 'She was an activist for the community,' according to John. She quickly got to know people and was always there to help with the local Entertainments Committee, which arranged fundraising lunches or dinners, the Conservative Women's Committee, and 'endless wine and cheese parties', openings of fêtes, village halls, bazaars, flower shows, and the rota for Meals on Wheels. Her particular interest was working with charities, and she became deeply involved with Mencap – 'she has a marvellous way with mentally handicapped people', Emily Blatch says – among other charities.

Though Norma was absorbed in her family, and shared with other parents the school run, swimming, riding and babysitting, she always knew that she needed to 'keep a grip on a bit of life outside the children. I liked to have something of my own.' In her spare time she began compiling a catalogue of all Joan Sutherland's performances, which, she thought at first, might be a useful reference for somebody else's archive. In 1977 she 'started writing to the opera houses . . . but gradually people started sending me more than I'd asked for, and were saying it's time somebody wrote another book [about her]'.

With no previous experience of writing, she began to write a biography. 'It was a solitary thing, which appeals to me as well. Something that I can do in my own way in my own time,' which also demanded that she be self-disciplined and 'pretty single minded'. Even so, it took several years to write and she often thought of abandoning it. In 1981, she took herself on a three-week research visit to Australia, the country of Sutherland's birth, leaving the children in the care of a friend, though she suspects the book 'was just an excuse to go to Australia'. When it was finished, she was relieved; writing books is 'worse than giving birth', she concluded. Joan Sutherland paid her tribute in the introduction: 'Norma's diligence and stamina in accomplishing such an enormous project have been admirable', and the book was well received; *Opera* magazine called it 'one of the best books about the diva. It allows Sutherland's good nature, her humour and her lack of self-importance to shine through.'

But when it came to the date of the launch in 1987, politics threatened to intervene: 'Every big moment of my life has been subsumed by something else,' Norma declares. A general election was announced: 'I remember sitting in our drawing room with John and his agent, discussing the date of [his] adoption meeting, and I said, "Do you realise what you've just said? It's the day of my book launch." I couldn't believe it.' John put back his adoption meeting by a day. Norma held a launch party in the constituency. Instead of touring the country publicising her book, within two days she was swept up in the 1987 general election campaign, which ended with the Tories gaining a majority of 102.

As John moved steadily up in his career, Norma adjusted to each change. He joined the Whip's Office in 1983, became a senior whip in 1984, and a minister at the Department of Health and Social Security the following year. After the 1987 election victory, he was made Chief Secretary to the Treasury with a demanding brief. 'Step by step you move up the ministerial ladder, so you get used to each step quite gradually,' Norma recalls. 'I don't think it made much difference to me. John was living in London all week so it didn't affect the weeks very much. It affected the weekends a bit, because there was more work – all the red boxes came home with him.'

Norma's life was centred on her home, Finings in Great Stukeley, a large detached four-bedroomed house built in the 1930s in two and a half acres of grounds, which they bought when they fell in love with it in 1983. Norma 'is a superb home-maker', says Barbara Wallis (later Oakley), John's constituency secretary. 'Their house is lovely, a very warm house, a very relaxed home. You walk in the door and you feel at home.' Home was John's escape, where he relaxed, away from the pressures of Westminster. Their teenage children were their priority, and Norma's life still revolved largely around their welfare and everyday activities. When Norma visited John's office at the Treasury, where she would chat with the staff who found her kind and surprisingly unassuming, she usually drove back to Huntingdon to be there for the children next morning. Every Friday and Saturday night were taken up with their joint activities in the constituency.

Norma supported John in all he did, though 'we weren't a *political* couple in the sense that that was our prime joint interest', says John. Norma talked about what he was doing and they discussed 'the personalities of politics and the drift of politics and the prospects of winning a seat and what was happening locally'. John 'relies tremendously on Norma's judgement', Barbara Wallis thinks. 'He's always had the utmost respect for her ability to cut through pretentiousness and get to the heart. Norma is very aware of what really matters. There's a core of good judgement and values, and John is very much aware of that. I think he consults her more than people recognise. People think she's politically naïve, but she's not. She's very well informed politically.' In public she tended to keep her counsel: 'She's self-contained and she doesn't feel the need to express her opinion,' John says, but it didn't mean that she didn't have a view.

When John was unexpectedly promoted to Foreign Secretary in July 1989, it was a shock and a change of pace for them both. This was the first stage of their rollercoaster progress to No. 10: 'It was the biggest domestic upheaval,' Norma says. 'I thought it was the one job that he was never likely to get. It was announced on the Monday and we got wind of it on the Friday. I was saying, "I don't believe it. I'm sure you've got it wrong." We didn't see it coming at all.' John didn't feel at first that he was prepared (though he enjoyed it later), and it meant constant travel at an inconvenient time in the children's lives when they were coming up to exams.

Norma's own plans were interrupted. That very weekend, she had been asked to follow up her Joan Sutherland book with a biography of opera singer Jessye Norman. Now there was no question of doing that project and she never had time to consider the prospect again. Norma realised immediately that this post would demand more of her as spouse than any of John's previous jobs. She took the view, as 'an acceptivist', that 'if something's going to happen it may be a struggle to begin with but you get on and do it, you don't back off'. Even so, she was alarmed at being plunged into a 'huge' job 'with no qualifications, no training, and you're expected to put a smile on your face and say, "Well this is absolutely great." It wasn't because you've got to go through this period of adjustment, which you can't do in private.'[15] She had only one briefing – with the Protocol Officer at the Foreign Office – 'but that was mostly about dress code, the sort of kit that I needed to buy' (for which there is no allowance).

They lost their privacy as Finings was disrupted overnight with the arrival of security. A caravan housing police officers 'disfigured' their garden: 'They moved in with their caravan and hung their tea towels on my trees. Amazing! I used to come up the drive and think, "Oh God, it looks like a gypsy encampment",' Norma remembers. Electronic devices invaded the house and the perimeter fences, and John was accompanied on his every move, which he hated. Later the officers became part of an extended family; Norma became fond of the policemen and appreciated their help. But it intruded on their time together. 'We used to do much of our talking in the car because you're undisturbed, you're together, and that was good', but with protection there, 'you actually can't have a proper conversation in the back of the car about anything that's meaningful' and 'you can't do anything spontaneously any more'. With John's busier schedule and the pressure on their home life there was speculation that the marriage might be going through a period of difficulty, though not, Norma said, 'to a degree that was insupportable or insurmountable',[16] and there was never any question of divorce then, or at any stage in their marriage.[17]

Family life was disrupted as Norma travelled more often to London and on trips abroad, including to the United Nations in New York in September. 'The Foreign Office demands as much of a wife – maybe even more – than No. 10, and suddenly these demands came banging on the door,' John recalls. She attended all the social events: 'standing around with a drink in my hand, you can't have a proper conversation with anybody, you can't hear. No, it's not my idea of heaven,' Norma says. Up till then, she could take it or leave it, but now she was expected to be there. She feels that: 'one ought to be able to take it or leave it, anyway. I think the expectations of Foreign Secretaries' wives – all these diplomatic receptions and dinners and God knows what – I think actually it's wrong.' John, too, thinks it wrong that 'someone who has not been elected or appointed to anything should suddenly be regarded as a soldier in the battle, to be deployed as the

Department thinks fit'. 'Maybe it will take somebody to say, "No, I'm not doing it all",' Norma suggests.

In the ninety-four days that John was in the post, she went only once to Carlton Gardens, the Foreign Secretary's official residence. She was appalled. 'I spent one weekend cleaning it. It was absolutely disgraceful.' No government provision was made for cleaners in any official government residence, she discovered. Emily Blatch says, 'It was the first time that I became angry on her behalf about the lack of help. There wasn't a system in Whitehall for thinking about how the wife adjusts. Not just the husband. There wasn't a cleaning lady that went with the house. Nobody can run a house of this size in addition to a commitment to home in the constituency, constituency obligations, going here, there and everywhere with her husband to foreign climes – and not need help. It was just extraordinary.'

Looking back, Norma sees one advantage of this period: 'It was actually quite valuable in so many ways for what was to come. It was a good three months' training. If there is such a thing.' Everything changed again in October 1989, when John was appointed Chancellor of the Exchequer after Nigel Lawson resigned. It was the job he had always wanted. Norma was delighted for him, but another upheaval threatened – the move to the Chancellor's official home at No. 11 Downing Street. Norma continued to base herself in the constituency. The children were at Kimbolton, the nearby independent school and had important exams coming up – Elizabeth at 17 was doing A levels, and James, 14, was coming up to his GCSEs. Both had full social lives which Norma did not want to disrupt by moving them to London, and she had her own agenda of regular constituency commitments. 'I didn't see any mileage in being in London and getting dinner on the table every night that he wasn't going to come home and eat. There's nothing more soul destroying. And I didn't want him to have that burden. If he wanted to go and do something in the House of Commons in the evening, I didn't want him thinking, "Oh, crikey, I'd better get home before another dinner's ruined". So I think it gave him the freedom to engage in politics,' Norma says.

There were fewer social commitments as Chancellor, and Norma agreed that, as before, she would be available when required in London and she joined him for part of every week. On Budget Day, as John held aloft his dispatch box, she smiled as she faced the photographers outside No. 11 Downing Street: 'I worked out we'd be one and a half minutes on the steps showing the budget box and all I had to do was stand there, shut up and smile. That one and a half minute smile seemed to last a lifetime. It was like going to the dentist,' she told journalist Jean Rook.[18] With her daughter Elizabeth and son James she watched from the Strangers Gallery in the House of Commons as John made his Budget speech.

Norma had her first experience of press intrusion when Elizabeth, who had just passed her driving test, was tail-gated by a car as she drove to work: 'She came back home and she was in floods of tears. I got on the phone [to the newspaper editor]. I was so *angry*. I thought, "This poor kid." And it's dangerous. It's dangerous,' Norma says. Barbara Wallis remembers that it was 'the one time I have seen Norma really, really angry. She can be a tigress if she's really roused on the children. She gave him the most tremendous blistering. It was – "How would you feel if it were your daughter that somebody else was doing this to?"' Norma recalls, 'I got a letter of apology. I was appalled. I'd no idea it was going to get worse.'

Norma had just settled into the routine when, in November 1990, the leadership crisis shook the Tory Party. In the short week between Mrs Thatcher's resignation and John becoming Prime Minister, she had little time to prepare herself, though she acknowledged, as John said, that 'When the ball comes your way, you have to grab it and get on with the job.'

It was a short move from No. 11 to No. 10 Downing Street, but a huge adjustment for Norma. A few hours after she arrived, she told an interviewer, 'Nothing's sunk in. I'm still reeling. Every time you mention "the Prime Minister" I think you're talking about Mrs Thatcher, not John.' When she and John returned from Buckingham Palace and faced the press outside Downing Street, she looked 'worried', she thought, but it was exaggerated in the later legend that she had looked 'like a frightened rabbit in the spotlight'. She confessed that she was not sure what her job was 'but I've always taken things one step at a time, and I keep telling myself this is just another huge step'.[19] The Downing Street machine clicked into action the night she arrived. Norma had booked tickets months before for herself and Elizabeth at Covent Garden – in the 'gods' as usual, and she decided to go: 'We got into a taxi with this rather dishy young man, and I think it was a while before I realised he was actually a policeman. Nobody told you this. It was extraordinary how everything falls into place but nobody actually tells you what's happening.'

The early days at No. 10 were not easy. There had not been a prime ministerial wife for eleven and a half years. Denis Thatcher had carved out a successful role as the male spouse, but the expectations of a wife were uncertain. 'They hadn't had a wife at No. 10 for so long that I think nobody had the faintest idea what was involved,' Norma says. She soon realised that everything that she did would be noticed and commented on far more than for her predecessors. Her privacy diminished, as did her options. Though Norma gave the impression of being self-effacing, she was clear about her priorities and, like many of the new generation of women, she was not prepared stoically to accept circumstances she found unacceptable. Her apparent shyness concealed a will of steel. 'Norma is quite determined. Once she's decided to do something, she's not easily put off, and once she's decided not to do something, she's not easily persuaded to the contrary either,' Mary Archer, wife of Jeffrey Archer, surmises.

On one thing she was certain: she would carry on with their existing routine and not move their family base. She had no intention of exposing her teenage children to life at No. 10 Downing Street. Though Elizabeth had now left school, James had his A levels ahead and they did not want, nor could they afford, to send him to boarding-school. She knew that John would be even busier. 'You want to be supportive, but actually you haven't got much contribution to make. You can't interfere in policy-making or how to tackle a particular problem. If asked, I would have said what I thought, but I don't know how valid that was, really,' she says. She was often torn between her competing commitments. She came up to Downing Street when she was needed, about two or three times a week for the first eighteen months, sometimes staying overnight but often driving herself back after a function. Her decision not to live full-time at No. 10 provoked press comment and misrepresentation – 'They chose to say that I wasn't going to have anything to do with the fact that he was Prime Minister and I'd be scuttling back to the country all the time, which of course wasn't true,' she says, but it did not alter her resolve.

There were other factors. When John was swept off by the officials to the Cabinet Room on that first day in office, Norma was taken up to the flat. She was not impressed: 'Margaret [Thatcher] said to me, "Don't move in until the new carpet's been put down." And I took one look at it and thought, "Well, how can you put new carpet down when the skirting boards and the doors and everything are in such a state?" So we tried to make a start. We didn't make a start at all until '93 or so. We lived with the holes in the ceilings and the torn curtains – the result of the IRA mortar attack in 1991 – for eighteen months. You obviously wouldn't walk in and expect to change it just because it wasn't to your taste, but it ought to at least be a suitable residence for the Prime Minister.' She drew up plans to alter the kitchen, but 'it wasn't allowed, so in the end we did a little bit at a time, economically', because 'when you do something and it looks like you're spending taxpayers' money, you're in trouble for it'.

She was also astonished to find that there was no official help with cleaning, cooking or any other domestic tasks: 'Surely we ought to require our head of government to live in pleasant surroundings, have a certain status . . . And that there's a housekeeper and that they don't have to pay for their own cleaner. It's an official residence after all, you pay tax on it, for God's sake. I think half the population will think, if they give it any thought at all, that it comes as a package – though the other half will [say] "Why should she have this, that and the other when I haven't",' Norma concedes.

Immediately, she was plunged into the schedule of engagements normal for a prime minister's spouse. There were no guidelines about her responsibilities or about the workings of this wholly new environment – an omission which Norma feels strongly should be rectified in future. Though each spouse brings something different to the job, there are expectations and duties which have to be fulfilled and routines to be observed. As with those before her, no secretarial help was provided, so John called in Barbara Wallis to help with Norma's suddenly enlarged agenda and correspondence. Norma could not afford a secretary of her own. It was an 'absolute ruddy nightmare. She had no back-up staff at all and nobody had even thought about it, apparently,' says Barbara

Wallis. Cars, again, were a problem. 'If she went out on an official engagement on her own, there was no car. Nobody told me, but eventually I discovered that I could go down and book a government car,' Barbara says. Norma was billed for its use on the basis of a three-way split between official, Party and private.

At first Norma was overwhelmed by the volume of letters: 'I'm quite independent so I'm not good at asking for help . . . I carted this stuff backwards and forwards to Huntingdon and Chequers with me for six months and I just couldn't get to the bottom of these letters. It wouldn't have dawned on me to go down to the Garden Room and say, "Here, look, I need some help", because as far as I was concerned the people there were looking after John and they weren't there to look after me . . . That first six months was quite hard,' Norma recalls. Barbara was typing on average twenty-five letters a day for Norma – far more than for Denis Thatcher – and, as she was the first woman in that position for years, there were not only invitations but letters from people who saw her as a person of influence, a social worker, an MP or a confidante as well as someone with youngish children who was similar to millions of wives around the country. For Barbara, who also had her constituency work for John, it was beginning to get too much. It took six months before a part-time secretary, Barbara Booth, came in from the House of Commons. It was another two years before their campaign to get proper paid secretarial help produced any result.

Nor was the situation helped by the unforthcoming attitude of the officials – it was 'If they ask the right question, we'll tell them the answer,' says Barbara Wallis. A senior civil servant later confessed that they had paid too little attention to Norma's needs. It was not a welcoming atmosphere. Norma is not naturally inclined to push herself forward: 'I didn't make waves. My whole life's ethos, I suppose, is not to make waves. I like to get on with people. I like to be positive, but I don't like to stir up trouble and dramas.' Perhaps because of this, and because she was not in residence full-time, they felt that they didn't have to make any real changes, Barbara Wallis says. 'The whole attitude was, "Well, the next general election is only eighteen months away, so we'll just get through it as best we can."' Barbara, who spoke up for Norma, often had 'the feeling that you were actually a flaming nuisance and they would much rather you weren't around'. She felt that they also had to contend with the strong personal loyalty which Mrs Thatcher still commanded among some of the Political Office staff, who remained bitter about the manner of her downfall: 'The place was stashed with Mrs T's supporters and the Political Office had the most enormous photograph of her hanging over the door, and it wasn't taken down for a year. And when you went in you could actually feel the hostility,' Barbara Wallis recalled. 'Though some civil service officials were helpful, the top ones were perfectly correct in the way that they treated the incomers, but there's a difference between being perfectly correct and actually being helpful and friendly. We came into an Establishment at its "best" – total, icy politeness.'

When Norma and John arrived at No. 10 they were little-known figures on the political stage. Norma's adjustment to Downing Street took place in the glare of unfamiliar press attention to a degree which Denis Thatcher never had to cope with. For over a decade there had been no prime ministerial wife to anatomise; the last time there had been such a young wife – Norma was 48 – was when Mary Wilson took up residence back in 1964. During the 1980s the voice of the image consultant, along with the shoulder pads, had gained the ascendancy. How the Prime Minister's wife looked now mattered to an unprecedented degree. The press had changed. More competitive and intrusive, a capacity had been unleashed, in the words of one journalist, to 'destroy with a pitiless and awesome brutality'.[20]

Norma was apprehensive about her role but reassured that Denis Thatcher had set no precedent for her 'except keeping out of the way, and that suits me very well'.[21] She was unprepared for the media storm: 'The media formed an instant impression of what we were like and in that first 24 hours or so, which is not really a good basis for judgement, we got ourselves painted into a corner that was quite hard to get out of,' Norma says. The press played up their 'ordinariness'. Much was made of John's humble origins and his lack of university education, or possibly even O levels, which provoked patronising and snobbish comments in the upmarket press, perhaps reflecting sentiments among Tory grandees as well as disaffected Thatcher supporters. Norma was portrayed as 'just a housewife' – 'a mumsy hausfrau' was how she interpreted it, who was, according to the *Daily Mirror*, the 'reluctant celebrity, a shy woman thrust blinkingly into the limelight'[22] or, as the

Daily Express sneered, 'the Everywoman of the classless Britain', though the same paper's Jean Rook called her 'totally likeable, thoroughly sensible, utterly genuine'.[23] Because she had admitted to being nervous about the prospect of No. 10, she was cast as tentative, shy, tearful, and sometimes terrified, rather than capable, charming, and confident that, given time, she would take new things in her stride. Those who knew her were astonished and angry at the huge gap between the image and the real person.

One of her 'biggest mistakes', she admits, was to wear the same blue suit to go to the Palace as she wore on the day of John's victory – 'that ghastly blue suit', she later called it. She left few clothes at No. 11 and had only two suits to hand when John won. He did not like the second suit, so she wore the first one twice, having decided against going shopping for another outfit. The press had a field day, and piled in with advice on her clothes, her hair, her make-up – 'Norma has to get a cleaner, crisper and generally smarter image,' intoned one.[24] Ten days later she wore the second suit, and they all thought she'd had a makeover. But the damage was done. Not only was she portrayed as a 'self-effacing housewife', but, horror, she wore the same dress – 'drab and perhaps home-made' more than once, which rendered her 'dowdy'. All this happened in three short days. 'I think she decided after that, "well, I'm just going to remain private", which is why they never saw the Norma that her friends see,' John says.

Only later did she come over as an authoress in her own right, elegant, intelligent and strong – 'Norma is nobody's fool,' the *Sunday Times* pointed out in December 1990. After a while she stopped reading the papers: 'I never read diary columns or gossip. It's the only way you can insulate yourself from it, really. Every time you get through a difficult situation you come through it and you're still OK, you think, "OK, well, I survived that." I don't like to think it's developing a thick skin, but I suppose it's just getting used to it.' Of *Spitting Image*, the television satire programme in which Norma was portrayed as the long-suffering 'little wife' to an entirely grey John who was forever counting peas, Norma was dismissive: 'I watched it just once. It was stupid. It became too cruel to be funny. Long before we featured on it I thought it was beyond the pale.'[25]

They had made a point of keeping their children out of the public gaze in an attempt to protect their privacy and Norma still had hopes of retaining a reasonably normal family life. She was furious when her children were trailed by newspaper reporters, including one who stood on the sidelines during a school football match taunting James into a rash reaction: 'Are we not entitled to any private life at all?' she once exploded.[26] 'It used to make me angry. I'd sort of go into a lift and scream,' or go into the Press Office and moan – 'at least you could get it out of your system'. James attracted increasing attention. Once on his way from work he 'happened to subliminally notice that there was a guy in black leather lying on the grass by a motorbike, and James got into the car and realised that this guy was following him. So he took lots of evasive action and this guy stuck with him all the way into the Cambridge Constabulary area when James rang our police at home and they intercepted him.' He was a reporter from the *News of the World*, Norma says, 'but usually they're stringers, just after a photograph or story that they can sell to the highest bidder'.

In her role as hostess at Downing Street, Norma enjoyed official functions and was interested in the people she met. The Majors favoured a more informal style and preferred smaller dinners to the lavish functions of the Thatcher era. Norma frequently hosted receptions on her own if John was late arriving. Usually they had a receiving line at such events. Walking into a room full of strangers soon ceased to be 'quite awe-inspiring', she recalls, even though she would think, 'I've got to talk to three hundred people tonight.' Barbara Wallis says, 'She's a very good hostess. She puts her guests first, so her guests automatically relax. At big receptions, she moved around a great deal and talked to people and made them laugh. And every single person who came in she repeated their name to them – like "Hello, Mary" – making them feel that they were slightly special.' State visits went smoothly after an early hiccup when nobody was on hand to advise her: 'I was told, "You go down to the front door, you greet the wife." Then six cars roll up and dozens of women get out and nobody knows who the principal is. This happened to me twice. There was nobody who was standing beside me who could tell me who I was supposed to be greeting. And you like to look outgoing, not looking around a bit shifty with the press on the other side of the road. And I said, "OK, if we can't sort this out, if you can't have somebody with me who knows who I'm supposed to be greeting, then I'll do it upstairs in the drawing room and you can bring whoever it is up to meet me. I'll do it my way.'"

Norma oversaw the menus and liaised with the Social Secretary and the Government Hospitality Service about arrangements for official functions. She was less interfering than Mrs Thatcher, but 'always noticed everything. She'd be absolutely sweet' when the caterers had gone to a lot of trouble, such as arranging ice flowers for a Trooping the Colour lunch. One problem was establishing what John, who liked plain, unfussy food, would eat: 'I love food, but John isn't so enthusiastic, so I was quite careful, I was trying to choose something that John liked.' When a meal was being served at No. 10, he would sometimes refuse it all and ask for an omelette instead. Catering staff got used to this: 'Whenever we did a meal for him we'd have a soup, we'd have eggs, we'd have a piece of fish, we'd have several things, just in case,' Government Hospitality Service butler David Allen remembers. After one particularly splendid banquet at the European Summit in Cannes in 1995, John emerged and said to his Political Secretary, Howell James: '"I'm absolutely starving." I said, "How can you be starving? You've just had a nine-course dinner," and he said, "No, I didn't eat a thing." And we got back to the suite in the Carlton Hotel and ordered room service.'

From the outset, Norma, who had always been very active in charities, decided to use her higher profile to promote their work. 'It would have been madness not to have made the most of the opportunities to help people who needed it,' she says, echoing Audrey Callaghan before her. She used Downing Street for receptions for the charities of which she was patron – Mencap, Crossroads, John Grooms, and the International Spinal Research Trust – as well as many others who could apply to have receptions there and who then paid for the event. Both she and John were keen that No. 10 should be made accessible to many more people and the number of charity events increased to more than one a month. Norma's work often went unnoticed, but she took great pride in it, was very effective and was popular because of her easy warmth and sympathy with people. Later she was the driving force behind an entirely new initiative – four sponsored evenings of opera at Chequers. After drinks in the Long Gallery, the performance in the splendour of Great Hall was followed by dinner in a marquee outside. The events raised £2.5 million spread between four charities including Mencap and Chickenshed Theatre and Norma followed this up by setting up the Challenge Fund with her colleague Pauline Harris which administered grants and funds for special projects connected with Mencap's activities.

She was much in demand, and had her own agenda of engagements, visiting Tory constituencies, hospitals, schools, and so on round the country. 'The diary became so full that you just couldn't accept anything else, so that it became easier to say no, and then you were able to focus a bit more on the things that you felt you could make an impression on,' she says. She never made speeches: 'I just hated doing it. It used to worry me too much and I didn't think it was worth putting everybody else around me through the atmosphere I would create because I was so wound up. I didn't want to get wound up. And it's dangerous territory. I just thought it was a minefield in all kinds of ways, so – maybe a bit cowardly, but I thought it was safer.' With her busy schedule, there was little time for leisure at No. 10: 'When we moved in, Peter Taylor, the house manager at the time, said to me, "If you want a cup of tea you've only got to pick up the phone and ask a messenger." And I thought, "Peter, if the day comes when I haven't got time to put a kettle on and make myself a cup of tea then I'm going to be in dire straits." But he was absolutely right. It was just so hectic all the time. There was one crisis after another. I don't think there was ever a period of tranquillity.'

The first eighteen months were taxing on all fronts. Major was immediately plunged into preparations for the Gulf War which followed Saddam Hussein's invasion of Kuwait in August 1990. Just before Christmas, he and Norma stayed with President George and Barbara Bush at Camp David, when the leaders established a rapport: 'There was no hesitation. No unease. No holding back,' John recorded, as they discussed plans for the military offensive 'Desert Storm' to reverse the Iraqi occupation of Kuwait. After their talks, 'George and Barbara Bush gave us a delightful weekend, full of log fires, good food, Christmas songs with a small male-voice army choir, and the occasional film.'[27] Norma got on well with Barbara Bush: 'I don't think it does to underestimate Barbara Bush. When I first observed her I thought this isn't your cuddly granny. I have huge admiration for her. She's sharp. She's observant and I've never heard her say anything spiteful. And he's gorgeous. They're very easy company.' Of all the leaders she met, Norma formed the closest bond with the Bushes.

When Major took over the leadership, the country was in the first stages of a recession and inflation was rising. He had distanced himself from Mrs Thatcher almost immediately by declaring his belief in a 'one nation' Conservatism, and his aim to 'build a country that is at ease with itself . . . confident . . . prepared and willing to make the changes necessary to provide a better quality of life for all our citizens'. He signalled policy changes on the two most divisive issues of the previous regime – the unpopular Poll Tax, and Europe – but there were continuing tensions within the Party over the manner of Mrs Thatcher's downfall, generated by those who wished to see her legacy continued. Most of Major's Cabinet colleagues welcomed his more collegiate style of leadership. 'The first Cabinet meeting when John was Prime Minister was like the prisoner's chorus in *Fidelio* – people staggering into the light after all these years when the conclusion of the meeting was set out at the beginning,' Chris Patten remembers. Though the Maastricht Treaty was initially hailed as a success and the government regained temporary control of the economy, fissures in the Party would widen as Europe came to dominate the agenda.

The problem of Northern Ireland did not go away. The Cabinet was in session on 7 February 1991 when an IRA mortar exploded outside the Cabinet Room window. Norma was in Huntingdon, speaking on the phone to Barbara Wallis in Downing Street when she heard it down the line: 'I suddenly heard this bang and I said "Is that a bomb?" and she said, "I think it's a bomb. I'll call you back,"' Norma recalls. Barbara could not get out of her office at first because the door was jammed with the blast. She went downstairs where, she says, 'with unbelievable intelligence we were all assembled in the hall directly under the main chandelier'. For Norma: 'That was quite an anxious ten minutes. The first thing I did was go out to the police to see if they could get any news. Barbara called me back within ten minutes. I realised that nobody had been hurt and John was all right and everybody was OK, that was all that mattered.' Norma carried on with her schedule for the day. John too was undeterred. 'I think we'd better start again somewhere else,' he said as he emerged from under the Cabinet table where he had been pushed by his adviser, Charles Powell, as the windows buckled in.[28] The Cabinet reassembled below ground while sirens screamed outside. The IRA had launched three mortars from a stolen van parked in Whitehall, only one of which exploded in the garden, 20 metres from the Cabinet Room.

The 1992 general election a year later was a watershed for both Norma and John. The uncertainty about their future at No. 10 dissolved as, against all expectations, the Conservatives were returned, with a reduced majority of 21. John now had his own mandate as leader. Norma had travelled with John every day as he toured the country in the Battle Bus. She was 'with me throughout, easy-going and tremendously popular at every stop', John wrote. 'The image of her as a shy, home-loving woman keen to shun the limelight is, at best, only a fragment of the truth. She fiercely wanted us to win, and carried with her the cheery aura of someone in no doubt about the result.'[29]

With the Tories behind Neil Kinnock's Labour Party in the opinion polls, Norma was an invaluable confidence booster. She enjoyed the excitement of the campaign, despite the eggs and other missiles thrown at John and frequent scuffles in the crowd, and made herself available to do anything that was asked of her. She had resisted the civil servants' suggestion that she pack up at No. 10. 'You have, of course, ordered a removal van?' one senior civil servant had asked. After the declaration of the result at Huntingdon, they drove to London: '"It looks as though we've got another five years, I remember saying to Norma as the car radio ground out late results. "Good," she replied. "I can take it if you can." I turned to reply but she was asleep.'[30]

Norma benefited from having a sense of secure tenure. She was by now familiar with the workings of the Downing Street machine and took a more active role and was there more often after James left school. She grew rapidly in confidence: 'She developed a different persona at No. 10. She came into her own,' Barbara Wallis observed. 'You grow into it in the sense that you get used to what's required,' Norma explains. 'You develop a cycle. It's a rolling programme, and the charity stuff gets fitted in between.' Without having a 'makeover', she subtly altered her dress style, favouring Frank Usher and Windsmoor, with Louisa Tyler as her dressmaker. It was noticed. Her understated elegance was now widely remarked upon. But there were pitfalls. During a

Conservative annual conference, Norma decided she needed a new pink jacket so went out to buy one at a local Brighton shop. Someone tipped off a tabloid that Mrs Major had bought a foreign jacket – by a German designer – and a furore ensued, which upset Norma. Only later did a textile industry representative point out that the jacket fabric was Scottish. There is no clothes allowance for prime ministers' wives, even though ambassadors' wives on foreign posting are entitled to one.

After the election Norma pressed again for changes to the flat. During extensive repairs to No. 10 after the mortar attack (including to the Main Hall ceiling which had fallen down) work began on the flat renovations, though Norma still worked in a small study which she had converted from an 'old-fashioned pantry with white wooden cupboards and a white sink – *circa* 1900!' her secretary Lorne Roper-Caldbeck recalls. Over two years, on a tight budget, Norma managed to re-order things, putting the kitchen at the centre rather than the end of the 'railway carriage', improving the 'rather squashed' dining room and decorating it in her taste to make it more homely. The three bathrooms in 'real sixties style, with all that floral wallpaper' and no showers, Lorne remembers, remained untouched for another few years. Budgetary restrictions and being accountable to Parliament for such expenditure are paramount considerations. Alterations throughout Downing Street are expensive, partly because of the need for strict security clearance on contractors.

Until 1992 Norma had survived with minimal back-up support, but after Barbara Wallis's long campaign she was finally allowed to have a secretary/assistant for four days a week. She employed Lorne Roper Caldbeck, who had earlier worked for Elizabeth Douglas-Home – and who was amazed to walk into the flat and find that it hadn't changed since 1964. In a major breakthrough, it was agreed that Lorne should be paid by the Cabinet Office (though she was not paid for the first three months, and she had to prompt them to pay the annual increment due in her contract, 'which was not exactly welcoming'). Lorne organised Norma's diary and correspondence and accompanied her on engagements. Under her firm but persuasive control, guidelines were worked out on the tricky territory between what was official business and what was not. For instance, when Norma was appearing in her capacity as Prime Minister's wife at an interview, the Downing Street

Press Office would come along. If it was a Conservative Party matter, or personal, they would not. It was another aspect of there being no defined role – or perhaps even status – for the Prime Minister's spouse.

On official trips abroad, Norma had travelled without any helper. Though she was briefed by the Foreign Office and guided by ambassadors' wives through the programme for spouses, in the course of hectic schedules she was often left to her own devices. On a trip to Malaysia two years after Lorne arrived, Norma sat next to John Coles, Permanent Under Secretary at the Foreign Office: 'He said, "What are you doing here on your own?" And I said, "Well, it's the way it's always been." And he was absolutely appalled that I was travelling on my own. It was from then on that they decided that Lorne would travel with me. It made a huge difference,' Norma says. The organisation worked more smoothly when Lorne was there taking Norma's interests into account, so that she did not, as had once happened in Kuala Lumpur, get stranded in a great cavalcade and have to be rescued. The duty clerks appreciated the arrangement, according to Lorne: 'They said, "We're so relieved you're here, because there'd been moments when there was a crisis or something's happened and everybody's got to drop everything to look after the Prime Minister – because he is, after all, the focus – and we suddenly realise there's poor Mrs Major not knowing what she's meant to be doing or where she's meant to be."'

Though she felt it was her duty to go on most trips where wives were expected, after a while she reassessed her priorities. Unable to go to the Munich G7 economic summit in 1992 because of other commitments, Norma wrote to Hillary Clinton and Hannelore Kohl to apologise for her absence. Foreign trips had always been difficult for her since she suffered from intense, potentially embarrassing travel sickness – and having not gone to Munich, she 'began to think there were other things to do. I don't honestly think it serves a lot of purpose. They're supposed to be meetings with some substance, they're not joy-rides.' Then, 'having crossed that barrier of not doing one and realising that I could get away with it, I didn't see the point,' Norma says. She enjoyed hosting the spouses' programme at the G7 in London in 1991, however, and was particularly impressed when she went to the celebrations commemorating D-Day in 1994: 'That's part of one's living history. To sit on Arromanches Beach and all these veterans. They said there was supposed to be five thousand – there were more than five thousand, they just kept coming, and it was so moving. It really was tremendous.'

The Majors retreated whenever possible to their 'secure and organised base' at Finings where Norma could reclaim her territory. 'I'm sure it helped to keep us sane, having our own place with our own things around us,' she says. 'John genuinely liked to be in his own house,' Howell James thinks. 'He just felt more comfortable at home. And Norma recognised that he relaxed better, so he got more of a break from all the nonsense.'

At first they went only rarely to Chequers. Norma 'thought it was fantastic, actually. It was like a country house hotel where you were spoiled to bits!' but John preferred not to be so tied to the routine of the house, and not to have to tell staff when he was coming and going. 'I chilled out better in Huntingdon, I was a bit more cut off,' he told us. The first Christmas at Chequers, John had wanted to go for a walk: 'So he opened the doors and walked out, and nobody had told us that you couldn't do that, so before you could blink there were dogs barking everywhere and a helicopter overhead,' Norma remembers. A senior staff member, Jane Uff (a former Naval Commander), 'sat us down and said, "Didn't anyone give you any rollover notes?" And I said "What are rollover notes?"'

The fact that they used the house less than the Thatchers, who had gone every weekend, created a problem. 'We actually lost staff at Chequers because it wasn't being used as often,' Linda Lalley, later Chequers house-keeper says, and it was likely that more would have to go. At the same time there was concern that John's catering arrangements at No. 10 needed adjustment, since he was sometimes making his own meals (*not* eating take-aways, except very occasionally, he says – that was yet another fiction). To solve both problems staff came up on a rota basis from Chequers to No. 10 during the week to cook and 'do' for John. They arrived on Sunday with meals prepared at Chequers, shopped when needed during the week, and prepared meals for which the Majors were charged the cost of the food.

Later, they fitted Chequers more into their agenda. Their 25th wedding anniversary, Norma's 50th and Elizabeth's 21st birthdays were held there, but it was more often used for seminars, conferences, dinners and entertaining heads of government. These included German Chancellor Helmut Kohl and President Clinton and his wife Hillary, who arrived on a flying visit for lunch during the D–Day commemorations in the 'sleek and gleaming Marine One helicopter' (plus two armoured limousines in an accompanying Chinook). Russian President Yeltsin and his wife Naina stayed for a weekend in 1994, along with a large retinue who brought copious supplies of black bread, water and Russian Coke – 'that was a nightmare for the staff,' says Norma. A carpenter had to lengthen the four-poster bed to accommodate Yeltsin's size – 'He was a great bear of a man, but I don't think he had the charisma of Gorbachev,' Norma says. Yeltsin's 'protection officers and so-called doctors moved in with their bags of kit. They were a bit of a law unto themselves.' The Majors took them on a long walk which was rather too strenuous exercise for Boris and landed up in the local pub, the Bernard Arms, for a pint. (When told it was Boris Yeltsin, the landlord quipped cheerfully, 'Oh yes, and I'm the Kaiser.')[31] Yeltsin was very taken with Princess Alexandra and changed the place names himself so that he could sit next to her at dinner: 'What do you do when the President of Russia picks up the name tags, moves them round, and plonks himself over there?' John reflects. Later the British Youth Opera gave a concert of operatic items, including an aria in Russian from *Eugene Onegin*, in the Great Hall.

Norma took No. 10 in her stride after 1992: 'It wasn't home. I don't think it ever could be home. Perhaps because I wasn't there all the time I enjoyed it rather more. It was quite fun to be there when something exciting was happening.' She got on well with No. 10 staff, knew people's names and 'she was very pleasant to everybody. Just quiet and pleasant,' a custodian, Ray Penny, remembers. Shortly after one Chequers staff member's father died, Norma took her to a concert she knew she'd enjoy and sat with her in the royal box, then took her to the meal afterwards, and 'made sure I got home safe and sound'. Suzanne Reinholt, who worked as a secretary in the Garden Room, found Norma 'always very serene. She was very easy to talk to. She was very hospitable.' Once Norma drove her home after a weekend shift in Huntingdon, and one Sunday while delivering red boxes, Norma invited her 'to try her carrot and coriander soup' and 'chatted away quite happily while I waited for the Prime Minister to come off the telephone. She did not have to do this. She could have just left me alone – I was "staff" after all,' Suzanne says.

Like other spouses Norma got used to intrusions on her privacy. The Majors were rarely alone together: 'The social life was pretty killing. You'd go out to perhaps a reception and then a dinner and get back to No. 10 at eleven o'clock or later, and he'd be handed tomorrow's papers, and then he'd go upstairs and have to do his boxes. There was always a meeting over breakfast or lunch – we hardly ever had a private breakfast or lunch together,' but Norma found it 'nice to be part of what was going on, like being a fly on the wall, really' – a spectator to history.

When officials and advisers arrived in the flat first thing in the morning, Norma did not complain: 'One became very tolerant of things because you know how difficult the job is and how trying life is so to make a fuss about trivia didn't seem worth it. You tend to think, "OK, it's a difficult job. So I won't make life hard for you."' Howell James and others regularly turned up before 8 a.m. to 'grab him before the day started . . . On several occasions I went in and he would be sitting in his towelling dressing robe at the end of the bed. And sometimes Norma was in bed, asleep and he would be working and he'd say, "Yes, yes, come in", and he'd be surrounded by all these papers. Or she'd appear from the bathroom while you were sitting at the end of the bed, or on the blanket box, or on the floor. She was very patient about it. Remarkably good humoured about it. I think she'd got used to it.' Christopher Meyer, John's Press Secretary, remembers: 'Every now and then she would fling in a remark. She would come in and just say something of such astounding common sense and you'd sit there thinking, "Well, yes, exactly." It was the real world talking to the inbred claustrophobic political world.'

Norma was swept up by events as one crisis followed another. A brief period of tranquillity after the 1992 election ended abruptly on 'Black Wednesday', 16 September, when a sterling crisis forced Britain out of the ERM and severely damaged Major's authority. The economy went into down-turn, and from then on the Party and the Cabinet were torn apart by divisions – between 'One Nation' Tories and economic liberals over the handling of the economy, over social policy with the collapse of Major's 'Back to Basics' initiative, and over Europe. Eurosceptic and right-wing rebels fought a more or less continuous rearguard action against his leadership, backed up by significant sections of the press.

Mrs Thatcher joined in the sniping from the sidelines. Allegations of 'sleaze' among leading Tories multiplied. Rumours of an affair between Major and a Downing Street caterer, Claire Latimer, ceased when Major successfully sued the *New Statesman* which published them. Despite Major's attempts to hold the Party together, polls showed the Tories consistently behind.

With only an occasional respite, every day there was a fight. It was warfare all the time, as Norma remembers: 'It's difficult enough fighting the opposition without fighting your own people, too,' and John Major says, 'There was never a moment when we weren't fighting on both fronts, both in front of us with an opposition who sensed a government in trouble and a party behind who thought it was more important to damage our policy on Europe than to sustain the government. [It] was the worst philosophical split in the Conservative Party that we have had since the Corn Laws of the 1840s.' Norma was now at No. 10 most of the time, 'supporting John, being more visible. She could see that he was under a lot of stress and I think she felt it was right for her to be around. They were very close,' says Howell James.

Norma was upset for John, who got to the stage where he could trust almost nobody in his Cabinet. 'She has an instinctive sense of decency which must have made her pretty angry about the way he was treated,' Chris Patten says. 'She's pretty smart, and a great sort of lioness in defending him.' On the whole, though, Norma says, she was 'a bit disinclined to put my head above the parapet. It wouldn't have been helpful. I don't care much for confrontation,' but she concedes: 'If I did get an opportunity in a subtle way to put the knife into anybody, I did.' Sometimes she tackled John, as Howell James recalls: 'She was good at challenging him. She would perfectly cheerily say, "Well, why don't you do something about them?" "Do you have to put up with these wretches?" She would provoke occasionally. She can be quite quick and quite pointed about things, and particularly about people.' Chris Patten thinks 'she would have brought out what he should have let loose more frequently, which was a "get stuffed" dash and *élan* about things'.

Norma was appalled at the betrayals and the dissembling that went on. Once she spotted the name of one rebel on the list for a reception at No. 10: 'He was such a traitor. I saw him on the list and I said,

"John, why are you – why?" And he came in and shook hands. I couldn't have done that.' But she was always guarded about what she said in public: 'You could never guarantee that you weren't going to be repeated or misreported.' What Norma found astonishing about the politicking was that 'they couldn't actually see the damage that they were doing. I thought it was unbelievable. I suppose they didn't care. No, they didn't care. It was extraordinary to see everyone jockeying for position. And as it is, between them all, they managed to destroy the Party.'

A leadership challenge which threatened in November 1994 failed to materialise, but when the sniping continued Major decided to throw down the gauntlet: 'Norma was the first person I talked to about that, and Norma was the only person who knew that I was *actually* going to do it,' John told us. 'If she had said "No, I think this is a daft idea, you really shouldn't do it," then I probably wouldn't have done it,' he says, but her view was the reverse, 'that although this might not work, a jolt like that might be the best way of putting things on an even keel'.

On 22 June 1995 he made the dramatic announcement to press assembled in the No. 10 Rose Garden that he intended to resign the leadership and stand again for re-election. 'I enjoyed that. That was really exciting. We corralled them in the No. 10 Rose Garden and nobody had a clue what was going to happen. So he stole a march on the press,' Norma says. Despite having almost no support from the press, in the ballot on 4 July Major won with a sound majority: 218 against 89 for the right-wing candidate John Redwood, with 20 abstentions. As they waited for the result at No. 10, John stood with his back to the fireplace and his arm round Norma. When a note of the result came through, he handed it to Norma. 'Well, that's all right then,' she said, and 'there were kisses for Norma, hugs and handshakes' as the tension relaxed.[32]

It was not only at times of crisis that John relied on Norma. 'I always got the feeling that John was much happier and more secure to have her around. She was a real stabilising force, a quiet force,' who 'could sometimes see things a damn sight more clearly than all of us saw them in the hothouse of Downing Street', Christopher Meyer says. Norma had a wide range of interests, and in some areas of policy she 'influenced my thinking', John says. There were times when, in the course of discussion 'she convinced me that part of a policy would probably not meet a particular problem or there was something else that we could do'.

Her practical experience was very useful, he says, particularly on issues concerning the disabled, 'because she would talk to me about what she'd seen practically'. He also listened to her about family matters, like family credit, 'because she would have had much greater contact with the people who were at the other end of those policies than I did', and over lottery funding: 'she had a lot to say about the funding short-fall in the arts, not just to places like Covent Garden, but to the grass-roots of art'. She was also, according to sometime Party Deputy Chairman Jeffrey Archer, a great asset in the Conservative Party: 'The party *adored* her. I would say they identified with her. John Major had a standing joke about it. When we did speeches before the Conference, I remember him saying, "How many times have we mentioned Norma?" And Sarah Hogg (his political adviser) said, "Three times. Three is sensible." "Good, we'll get three rounds of applause then" – it was a lovely comment.'

With the Party divided and in constant crisis, and almost every national newspaper opposed to his leadership, press attacks on Major were relentless. Norma took a calmer view than John: 'She would tell him to ignore it. She was much more pragmatic and tougher about those things – "Oh, for God's sake, why do you care what they say? I wouldn't read it,"' while John 'remained thin-skinned. He took too much interest in what was written about him,' Howell James says. 'It got under his skin in a big way, particularly the patronising sneering about him not having been to university.' Chris Patten recalls: 'I remember having breakfast with him and saying to him, "John, you really mustn't read the newspapers. Get a summary made, don't be waiting for the first edition at half-past ten at night." And he said, "I know you're right. I know it".' It was Patten's view that 'They're bullies. If you show you're too sensitive, they come after you. It's like sharks in the water.'

Norma became a target herself, and disliked always being in the public gaze. As she went out of No. 10, 'She used to say to me, "Is the press outside?" So I'd have to look out of the window and make sure they weren't there. [And she'd say] "Am I looking all right?" And I'd say, "Yes. You're fine,"' one staff member recalls. The press was a night-mare, historian and friend Martin Gilbert remembers. Once when he was visiting them in the flat, John picked up a newspaper 'and there was a picture of Norma looking depressed. And underneath was a story about how Norma Major has told her husband she's never going to be in Downing Street, she hates Downing Street. And there she was, sitting in Downing Street. And he looked at this and he just blew his top. I just felt sorry – for him and for her. What did they need it for?'

Norma objected to the way the press perpetuated an invariably distorted image of her, and was even more upset when the children were involved: 'I've seen her pretty angry, sometimes because of what the press were saying about her, which simply was not true,' Emily Blatch says. 'And as the wife of the Prime Minister you're not looked after in that respect, you don't have the female version of a Bernard Ingham [Mrs Thatcher's Press Secretary] looking after your interests, who can fend off some of this criticism or put the other side. Those of us who knew her, we did our bit, but it's a drop in the bucket when you're trying to correct a distortion. On a number of occasions I said, "Do you want me to do something publicly?" and the answer was, "No, because it just makes matters worse."' However, Norma was once so incensed that she phoned the *Sun* editor, Kelvin MacKenzie when he had published a double-page spread of their summer holiday destination after journalists had tricked the owners into gaining access to the house. Norma was 'hopping mad' about the invasion of the owner's privacy, and pointed to the extra security costs that identifying the location would entail: 'Are we not entitled to any privacy?' she asked, to which the editor replied – none at all.

Although Norma's schedule was more tied in to Downing Street, she still needed something of her own. When it was suggested that she write a book about Chequers, she readily agreed because she liked Chequers and was fascinated by its associations and also because, Lorne Roper-Caldbeck says, 'with all the engagements she was expected to do here, and the charities, [the book] was *her* space, that was *her* time. She had to do that for herself.' *Chequers: The Prime Minister's Country House and its History* is a history of the house and of the prime ministers who have occupied it since it was made over to the government by Lord Lee in 1921. Norma enjoyed her four years of research and writing. As the deadline approached, she spent stretches of time working at Chequers in the Great Parlour or at the big table in the Great Hall, typing the whole book herself. She paid for her residence there.

Chequers was well received. Simon Jenkins, former *Times* editor and an authority on Britain's architectural heritage, thought it 'a serious work . . . one of the best country house histories on the shelf'. On the political life of Chequers, Norma was 'neither sentimental nor over-awed. The joy, the sadness and the sheer exhaustion of high office race across her screen . . . The well-known stories stay fresh under Mrs Major's pen.'[33] *Good Housekeeping* headlined it A MAJOR ACHIEVEMENT.

A surge of articles and interviews, most portraying a 'new' Mrs Major, followed. She 'cut a relaxed, confident figure, very different from the shy housewife who stood with her husband outside No. 10 Downing Street six years ago', according to *The Times*.[34] 'Mrs M grows on you. She's very poised and rather regal, where you were expecting awkwardness, and unexpectedly chatty and charming, where you thought you'd meet reluctance. Her face is softer and prettier than photographs allow . . . and she fixes you, once she's relaxed a bit, with a frank, enquiring gaze . . . you'd trust her completely as a confidante and problem-solver,' declared John Walsh in the *Independent*.[35] In an interview with David Frost filmed in the conservatory at Finings she was authoritative and poised as she spoke up for curbs on intrusive photographers (who had taken long lens shots of them on their private holiday). 'I don't think the public has a right to know everything and be everywhere,' she declared.

Her book publication in September coincided with the launch of the Conservatives' 'Life's Better' campaign which was seen as the opening shot in the run-up to the election, due at the latest in 1997. Norma, it was announced, would join the two-week countrywide tour with John. His off-the-cuff comment that Norma had been 'his secret weapon for twenty-six years' fuelled speculation that Norma was being fielded as the Tories' secret weapon – an idea she repeatedly dismissed – whose 'modest-but-supportive First Lady role' appealed to the older woman voter. CONSERVATIVES UNLEASH ORDINARY NORMA ON CAMPAIGN TRAIL screamed the headlines; 'Stormin' Norma' was striding in as a 'campaign trooper' – as if she hadn't done the same in the 1992 election. She was now enlisted as a 'positive electoral asset' to the team as all the leaders' wives found themselves minutely scrutinised and compared – to their mutual discomfort. A minor frenzy followed Norma's reply to a reporter's question: 'Did she have any advice for Cherie Blair? Mrs Major emits a charming peal of laughter. "Oh, I wouldn't presume." Her sweet, suddenly animated face is all kindly benignity. "I think we all have to make of this job what we can. But I've no brief. She'll do it her way."'[36]

She loyally asserted throughout the six-week general election campaign that the Conservatives would win, though it was soon clear to most of the team that their chance of victory was remote. Opinion polls, with one rogue exception, showed a Labour lead of between 18 and 25 points.[37] 'We didn't really have any illusions about how things were going,' Norma says. 'There was no hostility. People were reserved, you sensed that everybody knew that this was all going to turn out badly for us.'

Norma 'kept going', says Lorne Roper-Caldbeck. What few knew at the time was that her mother, Dee, had been undergoing chemotherapy for several months, and was ill at the beginning of the campaign. 'That was grim . . . I did keep diving off to see how she was. So it was quite difficult, emotionally and logistically,' Norma says. It was another poignant instance of politics intervening at a crucial moment in her life. When *The Times* commented that Norma's 'finely-honed celebrity smile vanished yesterday to reveal a persistently glum expression', which 'did little to lighten the Tory campaign mood', an outraged press officer was dispatched by John to counter this 'churlish and cruel remark'.[38] Sadly, Dee died a month after the election.

There was another worry for Norma. She discovered a mole on her back which was possibly malignant, and agreed to an immediate operation. To avoid her attracting attention by going into hospital, Ian McColl, John's Parliamentary Private Secretary, who was an eminent surgeon, operated on it at No. 10. Next day, Norma was determined to return to the campaign trail, but in a crowded square, a clap on the back from a supporter opened the wound and she nearly fainted from the pain. She retreated to the Battle Bus, but her departure was noticed and construed as a sign of her losing interest in the campaign. A few days later the biopsy showed that the mole was benign.

On polling day, 1 May, the forecasts were getting gloomier by the hour. As Norma and John, surrounded by photographers, approached the polling booth to vote, Norma warned, 'Don't pause by the exit sign.' By evening, the true picture was emerging. 'John Major and I went for a walk around the carp pond in the garden, and he said, "It's going to be a very, very difficult evening. It's going to be much, much worse than we anticipated",' Howell James recalls. Norma and John sat alone in one room at Great Stukeley and watched the results on television as the scale of the defeat became clear: 'We said little, except to express sadness at particular results,' John wrote. 'It was like being in a house with someone dying upstairs who was terminally ill,' Howell James says. 'There was a sort of hush, but you didn't talk about the death. Norma is not an emotional, teary [person]. She was very, very pragmatic that evening. It was, "Right, when are we leaving? When have we got to be at Huntingdon? When's the count coming through?" . . . None of us went around saying, "Chin up, it's not as bad as it seems." We were all pretty short of script, is the honest truth. You'd say, "Does anyone want a cup of tea?" – these prosaic things.' The defeat of so many colleagues distressed John, even those who 'had tormented the government from within the party'.

At 2 a.m., John called Tony Blair to congratulate him on his success. John 'can remember little of what was said, I was so exhausted, but we were both friendly enough'.[39] They talked for a few minutes. According to Howell James, who was beside him, 'He said, "I'm about to go to my count, I'm going to be asked. I'm going to say you've won a splendid victory. I just wanted to phone and tell you I'm going to say that. I didn't want you to be blind-sided. Good luck. You'll find it's a lonely job."'

They left for his constituency count – 'a subdued affair' where John was re-elected as MP with a majority of over 18,000. He expressed his gratitude to Norma: 'It was heartfelt. Such grace and charm through all the highs and lows of over a quarter of a century. I had always been proud of her. She had married a young councillor, and fate had taken this shy woman into a public role she had never sought, but had carried out so well,' he wrote.[40]

On the way to London, they listened to the results, shocked and saddened by news of defeat after defeat. They parked on the Embankment, waiting for the other cars to catch up. 'As dawn broke, the sounds of revelry floated across the river from the Royal Festival Hall, where Labour was celebrating its triumph,' John recalled. They

went on to Central Office – 'a mixture of long faces etched with tired-
ness and enforced jollity' – then returned to Downing Street. Unlike
1992, they had packed all their belongings, which were stored in No.
10. They did not want the indignity of having their possessions loaded
into vans in full view of the press – 'so the pictures that the press
managed to get of a big pantechnicon with all sorts of boxes and stuff
being moved into it certainly wasn't our stuff,' Norma says.

They said goodbye to the officials and staff in the Pillared Room
upstairs, rather than in the downstairs hall where No. 10 staff tradi-
tionally 'clap out' the Prime Minister: 'That was the saddest part,
saying goodbye to the people. Not the house and not the role, but saying
goodbye to the people. There were several people in the room who I
had something specific to say to, which I think kept me focused. It kept
my head above the emotion, really, because there were a lot of people
crying in the room, and I did not want to go through that door with
tears in my eyes,' Norma says. 'John made a very gracious speech. That
was quite hard for him. Elizabeth was a bit tearful, and I just said,
"Don't go out on that step with tears in your eyes. You just think about
anything, think about something else, don't even think about what's
going on here."'

John and Norma left the room hand in hand, then John went upstairs
to the flat: 'I left a bottle of champagne for Tony and Cherie Blair with
a brief note saying, "It's a great job – enjoy it." In such a mood, I left
No. 10,' he wrote. On the steps outside, flanked by Norma and his
family, he said it had been an 'immense privilege to serve as Prime
Minister over the past six and a half years', and declared, 'When the
curtain falls it is time to get off the stage, and that I propose to do.'[41]
They got into the waiting car, and as they drove away, Norma flicked
a finger across her cheekbone – 'which was the picture they had of Mrs
Thatcher, and I thought, "bugger!" Because that was not how I felt at
all!'

After John handed in his resignation to the Queen at Buckingham
Palace they drove straight to the Oval where they spent the day watching
a cricket match with Elizabeth and James and their partners. That
evening at Finings, with no red boxes and no immediate crises, John
'felt a huge surge of relief that my life was my own again, and that I
could once again control it'. When photographers were invited in next

day, Norma recognised one who had harassed James: 'He was ejected as she showed her steel,' John wrote. Norma's view was: 'We are not public property now . . . and we would co-operate only on our own terms.'[42]

It took time to adapt to the change of pace in their lives. After Dee's death in June Norma needed time to recover. She continued her work in the constituency at first, but they had agreed that when they left No. 10 they would put a ring fence round politics; after John gave up his parliamentary seat in 2001 he had no wish to enter the House of Lords. When John started lecture tours, Norma went with him for the first two years until she found that 'it got to be a bit like politics, with endless receptions and dinners and listening to the speech, [and] nothing else was getting done', so she went less, but together they have travelled round the world, enjoying life outside politics. Their marriage remains close. John still travels for the various companies of which he is consultant or chairman, and as they always have done, they phone each other every day. John, according to Chris Patten, 'is so happy now. It's extraordinary. Like a man liberated.'

Norma has continued her active involvement in charities and until recently was on the board of the Welsh National Opera. She was the one who kept up with their old friends when they were at No. 10, and now she has more time for them and for her family, including their young grandson. Norma had provided for John 'a hinterland outside the frenzied world of politics', reminding him that 'beyond politics there was a real world to which I could return at any stage', he says. But after being prime minister, he adds, 'you never have the privacy that once you may have hoped for. You're always public property.'

One instance, six years after their departure from No. 10, was the publication in 2003 of Edwina Currie's version of an affair with John in the mid-1980s. It took John's closest colleagues and friends completely by surprise; none knew anything about it at the time. The publication was, for Norma, yet another example of politics intervening in an important event in her life. It broke on the day she was due to speak at a major fundraising event for Mencap which she had spent an entire year organising. When concerned friends rang to send their love and support and ask if she was still going, she firmly declared that she would go ahead with it, and did. 'You can imagine what a night it was.

Everybody there was fantastic. It went well, there was no problem, but it's sod's law, isn't it?' Norma says. In the only comment Norma and John made at the time, they made it clear that they regarded the matter as 'long over, and long forgiven'.

Norma is a resilient and self-sufficient woman. She grew into her role at No. 10 after an uneasy start, when she had commitments to her young family, and the Downing Street machine appeared – as it has to so many spouses – to take little account of her. Though the spouse is expected to play an important role on the national and international stage and is constantly in the public spotlight, Norma found that little was provided in the way of back-up support. She now believes that a set of guidelines should be available for all future spouses.

For a couple without the private income enjoyed by the Thatchers and their much earlier predecessors, the expense of being at No. 10 stretched available resources. The lack of privacy, being constantly noticed and commented on, was also difficult for someone who, by nature, shunned the limelight, and Norma's plea – 'do we have no right to privacy *at all*?' – became more insistent as the years went on, though she learned to deal with the often blatant misrepresentations by largely ignoring them.

Once she got accustomed to the machine and sorted out the rhythm of life in Downing Street, Norma's confidence grew. She used her position to open up No. 10 for the benefit of a wider range of charitable causes than any of her predecessors. A popular hostess, she enjoyed the privilege of being there and carrying out the role that was increasingly called 'First Lady'. The job description, however, remains unclear: like all the spouses before her, Norma Major brought to it her own qualities and made of it what she could. She thinks it unlikely, despite the pressures she experienced, that any spouse will in future put her or his foot down and opt out of the duties that come with that undefined, often misunderstood, though also in so many ways rewarding role.

Conclusion: The Goldfish Bowl

There is no job description for the Prime Minister's spouse because there is no job. But there is a unique position that provides for each holder an opportunity and a challenge. The opportunity is to support and, if possible, add value to the work of the Prime Minister; the challenge is to live up to the public's expectations of the role without doing any harm. For myself, I don't believe that any person has ever cast a vote for a party on the basis of whether they liked or disliked the leader's wife. In history and in the polls, the Prime Minister and his or her party stand or fall on their record. But particularly in the modern media age, a wife or husband can and does contribute to the overall image of the premiership.

Nothing can prepare you for the sense of excitement and apprehension when the front door of No. 10 closes behind you for the first time. Once inside, too, you find there are no guidelines, no template, no lists of dos and don'ts. Each of our spouses has defined their own role according to their time, personality and the circumstances they encountered. Each has had to find their own path. As Norma Major once said in an interview about her [potential] successor, 'she'll do it her way'. Like all my predecessors, I had no choice. But while each of our seven prime ministerial spouses is unique, there are common threads that weave their way through all of their stories. The spouses understood it was a privilege to live here in No. 10 but one that required many adjustments. They each saw that their main role was to be a support and comfort to the Prime Minister. They all responded, as well, with a strong sense of public service. But they found, too, that life at No. 10 can be all-embracing and worked hard to find their own way to preserve their sense of identity and personal space.

Nor, of course, was No. 10 the start or end of each couple's life together. These stories began before they entered through the black door and carried on after they left. Their relationships may have been intensified in No. 10 but the basic parameters were already set. For example, Clarissa married Anthony Eden when he was already a respected international statesman: to this day she remains the principal guardian of his reputation, protecting it with the style and intelligence for which she was renowned as a young woman in the 1940s. For Clarissa, the time at No. 10 came in the early years of what was to be a long and successful marriage.

Very few relationships are entirely harmonious. There is no doubt that the affair with Boothby cast a shadow over the marriage of Dorothy and Harold Macmillan, but theirs was a close partnership, which survived the impact of the affair. Perhaps because of her background in a political family (where women supported the men and provided a social back-up), she was familiar with the ropes of political office. Even when she was first intensely involved with Boothby, she was still there in the constituency playing the role that she excelled in – indeed, she was much better at working in the constituency than he was. That was where her duty lay, and, despite her passions, she always backed Harold up politically. Her grandson told us that the affair with Boothby – which devastated Harold personally – may have been the spur that made him all the more determined to succeed in the career which was so important to both of them. In his twenty years as a widower Harold constantly talked about Dorothy and how much she meant to him.

In a different way, the close bond between Elizabeth and Alec Home was deepened during the Second World War when Elizabeth, then a young mother with three daughters, saw her energetic husband struck down by an illness that left him helpless in her care. That closeness continued to sustain them throughout his long political career, both when they were together in Downing Street and afterwards.

It is not always easy defining the right balance between private and public life, but most of these people have managed it, juggling the roles in different ways. From an early stage Mary and Harold Wilson drew a firm line between their private family life and Harold's life as a politician. They continued that division in No. 10, where Mary supported Harold without ever pretending that she shared his fascination with politics. There is no doubt that during his political career it was Harold's consuming passion, and the family had to live with the consequences of that. But after politics, the family was the only other fixed point in his life and in their later years together, as in the beginning, Mary got her husband back. She remains fiercely proud of his achievements and performs her obligations in public life as his widow just as she did when she was the Prime Minister's spouse.

Edward Heath is one of only two unmarried prime ministers in the twentieth century. The other was Balfour who succeeded his uncle Lord Salisbury in mid-term, and like Heath, did not win a second term. In fact both bachelor leaders lost three elections, but not, I think, because they did not have a wife! Indeed the story goes that when Balfour was asked if he was going to marry Margot Tennant (later Asquith), he said, 'No. I'm rather thinking of having a career of my own!' Ted did not have a confidante, someone he could totally trust and who had no other agenda in politics but to back him, which other prime ministers found in their spouses. But this was something that was settled well before he entered No. 10. He sought relaxation in his music and sailing, in his family, and in a circle of male and female friends. When we asked him if he ever felt the lack of a spouse he said that it made no difference to his ability to carry out the role of Prime Minister. He did not try to draft in a female friend to help out as that would have caused more trouble and jealousy and it was easier to do the job himself with the help of his officials. He noticed that on foreign summits the officials went to a great deal of trouble to get rid of the wives and felt that he had the advantage, as he did not have to worry about keeping a spouse happy! Others may have perceived him as a bit of a loner but from his own point of view, you do not miss what you have never experienced.

Jim and Audrey Callaghan shared an interest in politics that began with their early discussions and carried on during a long courtship. They continued to exchange ideas all their lives and no one who has spoken about them has doubted Jim's devotion to and respect for Audrey. Many of our interviewees stressed the importance he placed on her opinions, particularly in relation to policies affecting children. Theirs was a real personal and political partnership.

This was also true of the Thatchers. Denis Thatcher might have expected to marry a stay-at-home wife, like so many of his business associates, yet he enabled Margaret to pursue her own career, first in the law and later in politics. He was her number one fan from the start and his influence over her cannot be overestimated. The tie between them ran so deep that she is still struggling to adjust to life without him.

The Majors too worked out their own style. Like the families of so many MPs, they had long ago decided to make their home in the constituency, and that pattern of spending Monday to Thursday in town and the weekends in the constituency continued into No. 10. While Norma supported John in the political career that he had already embarked on when they met, at the same time she built up an independent life as an author and charity worker, although the family was the centre of her concerns. I think it may have helped that Norma was forced to be self-sufficient from infancy, living as she did with her widowed mother struggling to make ends meet. She carries that strength with her today.

In all the spouses, I detected a strong sense of duty often coupled with a religious faith; moreover this duty was an obligation that they sensed they owed to the position they were in, which was wider than their love for their spouse. It is striking that both Mary Wilson and Audrey Callaghan were brought up in the Nonconformist tradition, which imbues lives with the ideal of service and with a certain stoicism, particularly marked in Mary's case. Religious belief was also important to Elizabeth Home, who was the daughter of a cleric and perhaps the most openly Christian of the spouses, a regular churchgoer with a deep religious faith. Dorothy Macmillan too came from the Anglican tradition and brought with her the sense of social obligation that was expected of a daughter of a duke in her generation. In much the same way, Clarissa Eden came from a family which had a long history of duty to country.

Denis Thatcher was not overtly religious, but his upbringing gave him certain values of duty to God and country. He came from a comfortable, middle-class family with a traditional Church of England background reinforced by public school and military service in the Second World War. He had strong right-wing beliefs tempered by a romantic, Kipling-inspired view of his role as an English gentleman. His personal courtesy and his ability to hold his tongue (and his drink) in public meant that he came to personify the old-fashioned English gentleman for many people both in the UK and abroad. He was a baronet in character long before he received the honour from the Queen.

Norma Major comes from a different generation from the other spouses and her sense of duty and social conscience is more contemporary, reflecting our more secular times. Her self-reliance and public service typify the attitudes of women born at the beginning of the Second World War who grew up during the period of rationing and pulling-together that characterised 1940s and 1950s Britain, the land which her husband once famously described as 'the country of long shadows on county [cricket] grounds, warm beer, invincible green suburbs, dog lovers and old maids bicycling to Holy Communion through the morning mist'.[1] This was more the image of Huntingdon where they made their life together than the London suburbs where they both had underprivileged beginnings.

Even more striking than this shared faith or sense of duty is the clear class divide between our first three spouses and those who come after them. Both Clarissa and Dorothy were from upper-class families with long-standing political connections. It is difficult to imagine that the relatives of any future prime minister could say, 'when Uncle Winston was replaced as Prime Minister by Uncle Anthony . . .' And although Elizabeth Home was not an aristocrat, she too belonged to the traditional Establishment. Her father was a clergyman who ended his career as Dean of Durham, her mother a member of the Lyttelton family, her uncles included a general, a bishop and a colonial administrator, and she married into the Scottish nobility.

There was a real sea-change in 1964, when the Wilsons, both from respectable lower middle-class families, moved into No. 10. This departure from aristocratic rule was a trend that was to continue in both political parties so that in 1990 Douglas Hurd had to try to play down his upper-class origins when he was contesting the Tory leadership with the distinctly non-patrician John Major. If there is still a ruling class in Britain, it is certainly no longer found on the grouse moors or in the drawing rooms of the upper classes, its natural element before the profound social changes of the 1960s. Before the Wilsons the spouses had all moved in the same broad social milieu. After them, although the spouses may well have met each other, they did so in the political world rather than in society.

The received wisdom about all the prime ministers' wives in the books and articles previously written about them or their husbands is that they had no careers of their own. This ignores their history before they came to Downing Street and often the important and successful jobs they did when they were here. Norma Major had been a teacher and a dressmaker and is the author of two well-received books, a biography of Joan Sutherland and a book about Chequers. Audrey Callaghan also started as a teacher and then had a long career as a local politician before finally, while her husband was Prime Minister, holding down the very demanding role of chairman of Great Ormond Street Hospital. Mary Wilson wrote successful poetry books during and beyond her time at No. 10 (her most recent poem was written last year to celebrate the marriage of her granddaughter). Both Elizabeth Home and Dorothy Macmillan played a large part in running their family estates, while Clarissa Churchill earned her own living during the war and later had her own review column, 'Spotlight' in *Vogue*. They were all capable, talented women whose roles reflected the changing expectations of women throughout the twentieth century.

We can see these changing patterns for all women in the bare outlines of the education and relation to the world of work of our women spouses. Dorothy Macmillan was born in 1900 when Queen Victoria was still on the throne. As the daughter of one of the leading aristocratic families in the land she was not expected to have a career, indeed she barely had an education as we would define it today. Elizabeth Home, born in 1909, was unusual for her time: as the daughter of the then headmaster of Eton, her education was better than that of the daughter of a duke. While she took a secretarial course, two of her younger sisters went to Oxford. Clarissa Eden was born in 1920. Her education was not as haphazard as Dorothy's and she went voluntarily to several courses at Oxford. She had a vivid intellectual curiosity and showed remarkable independence for her time – both in living alone and in supporting herself well into her thirties when most of her contemporaries would have regarded her as 'on the shelf'.

Mary Wilson (1916) and Audrey Callaghan (1913) were both born into the middle class at a time of great change, with the Great War opening up more opportunities for women, leading to the 1920s when women got the vote, the first female MP was elected and women started to enter the professions in very small numbers. Audrey and Mary did receive a formal education and were expected to earn a living, at least up until the time they were married. It was still very unusual for women to go to university then, although both of them would almost certainly have gone today. Instead we find Mary, whose brother became a university professor, taking a secretarial course while Audrey qualified as a domestic science teacher (like Norma Major later) but in her spare time pursued a wider education in politics and social policy.

From their first meeting, Denis Thatcher admired Margaret for her intelligence and determination: as an older man already established in his family business he did not find this off-putting. By the time Margaret went to university in the 1940s a new breed of career woman was becoming established, but what marked her out was the fact that, unlike most of those women, she did not remain single and childless. Thanks to Denis, she was able to have a supremely successful career and a family life with a supportive spouse and two children. As someone who sat the Bar exams myself, I know just how determined she must have been to give birth to twins and then within a couple of months take and pass those exams. What is more intriguing to me is how Denis was able to give her that wholehearted support, when the very idea of having a working wife must have been antipathetic to his background and ideas. It was clear when we asked him about it that it had never crossed his mind that this was contradictory. To him she was just Margaret, his remarkable and determined wife, and he was happy to back her as someone who was so very different from the crowd. It did not seem to occur to either of them, however, that what Margaret was able to achieve should be generally available to all women. In her eleven years in office, Britain's first woman prime minister failed to put another woman into her Cabinet of twenty or so males, with the short-lived exception of Baroness Young. Her ministerial appointments amounted to only eight women, only one of whom rose higher than the rank of junior minister.

Norma Major is part of the post-war generation. She was born in 1942 and is more the age of her predecessors' daughters. By the time she married in 1970, more and more women were continuing to work after marriage. Norma's career as a teacher ended when she became pregnant with her first child, although she continued with dressmaking for a while after that. But in 1971 it was unusual for married women with young children to work. In 1972, when I was doing my A levels, the nuns at my school acknowledged that all the girls would have to work initially but suggested teaching as a career which could occupy our time usefully before we retired to become good Catholic mothers. As a result I was determined to do anything but teach, and became a lawyer instead.

For much of the twentieth century there was a clear division of labour between men and women, at least in the middle and upper classes which was reflected in No. 10 Downing Street as much as in the country as a whole. The wives supported their husbands' careers by working in the home and, by extension, in the constituency. Denis, by providing Margaret with the financial independence to nurture her political career, contributed to their joint enterprise in a comparable manner to the wives. Everyone we interviewed agreed it was fortuitous that Denis was ready to retire from full-time business when his wife became Prime Minister, allowing him to take on the traditional supportive role without any conflicts with his own career. This pattern of married women giving up their careers to support their husband's career is no longer the norm. Today, the UK has the third-highest rate of female employment in Europe, with a record 70 per cent of women at work. This includes 65 per cent of women with dependent children. We can expect in the future that more prime ministerial spouses will have careers of their own.

People ask me all the time, 'What is it like living in No. 10?' and it was one of the things I wanted to ask my fellow spouses when we interviewed them. Living in No. 10 is of course an enormous privilege but it can also impose unique stresses on family life. Time and again in the interviews we did there was a feeling that family life was sacrificed to the machine. Even in the more leisurely pace of the 1950s, we find Clarissa remarking that, even at weekends, they were surrounded by the Private Office. This has increased in intensity with the development of technology and the phenomenon of 24-hour-a-day communications – television, emails, faxes and satellite phones. In the fifties and early sixties, the Macmillans and the Homes were able to spend long holidays at their country homes, grouse-shooting and attending house parties, but in recent years it has become axiomatic that the Prime Minister has to be available around the clock, fifty-two weeks a year. Today, even when climbing in the Pyrenees on holiday, the Prime Minister is accompanied by a satellite phone and is expected to and does receive calls. At least it is not as bad as being President of the USA, where the electronic monitoring of the President inside the White House means that they are even aware of when he goes to the bathroom.

Although we are the only family at No. 10 in the twentieth century since the Asquiths to have young children, we are not the only ones to have family commitments. It can in no way be described as a normal family home but our own children have found the staff here like a large extended family. The Macmillans had young grandchildren whose para-phernalia could be seen lying around the front hall. Dorothy would encourage them to run around the corridors and play games with the No. 10 custodians. Elizabeth Douglas-Home's first grandchild spent her first few months living at No. 10. Giles Wilson was a teenage schoolboy when his parents first moved in and Mary was moved to tears because of the difficulties he experienced just getting in and out of the house. Julia Callaghan lived at No. 10 until she married and the Callaghan grandchildren visited No. 10 and Chequers. Carol and Mark Thatcher both spent some time living 'above the shop'. The Majors had teenage children, and the system had to make adjustments to the fact that they preferred to base their family in their own home at Huntingdon, although Norma spent many hours going back and forth between the two, often late at night after official engagements.

There is no clear-cut demarcation between the office at No. 10 and the private quarters. Officials can and do come in and out of the private accommodation at all times of day and night. It is not possible to lock the door, take the phone off the hook and escape. Clarissa Eden spoke of officials coming into their bedroom in the 1950s, Mary Wilson would wake up at 3 a.m. and find secretaries taking dictation in their bedroom in the 1960s and Norma Major found officials in their bedroom first thing in the morning in the 1990s. For the Prime Minister, this lack of privacy is mitigated by the fact that they live above the shop and can pop back home if they have a break in their duties. But the downside is that they never escape the office. All our spouses had their own strategies to cope with this. Dorothy Macmillan would spend as much time as she could in the place she felt most at home, Birch Grove. Mary Wilson, who did not have a bolt-hole of her own during their first period in No. 10, used to cry out her frustrations on the shoulders of friends in Hampstead Garden Suburb. She refused to move back into No. 10 for the second period, preferring to keep her personal space completely private. Above all she valued her haven, her bungalow in the Scilly Isles. For Denis Thatcher, there were times when the strain of waiting for his spouse to leave the excitement of the issues of the day became too much. He was a familiar figure in his black opera cape striding down Downing Street escaping for an evening with his business and sporting friends. For a longer respite he enjoyed his golfing holidays with Bill Deedes and others. Norma Major made it clear that she was not going to be always available and chose to return to her own home as much as she could. For all the spouses it was important to have other interests, something to keep them from being sucked too closely into the maelstrom of life at No. 10. This is not just a question of individual personalities. None of them could be described as a doormat, nor were they wholly wrapped up in their spouses. They all had lives and views of their own and were tough independent characters. Yet they all found the constraints of the system frustrating.

It may seem trivial to turn from affairs of state to the layout of a flat but in fact this is intimately tied up with the feeling that many spouses had, that they did not have control over their environment or their lives. The character of the No. 10 flat contributes to this. Unlike the house at No. 11, which was rebuilt in the early 1960s, the flat above the state rooms at No. 10 was adapted on an *ad hoc* basis rather than specifically planned. Mrs Thatcher is known to have contrasted her own accommodation with the far more spacious accommodation provided to Lady Howe at No. 11, into which our family were fortunate to move after the 1997 election. The No. 10 flat is laid out in a haphazard fashion and is furnished at a level below that of most of our ambassadors' residences. Norma quite rightly described it as 'a loft conversion'. She said it was in an appalling state. Margaret Thatcher told her not to move in until a new carpet had been laid and Norma had to live for the first eighteen months after moving in with holes in the ceiling and torn curtains. The popular myth of the press that the various spouses have been anxious to measure up the curtains at

No. 10 does not reflect the reality. For many of the wives, being parked in accommodation not to your taste, without your own furniture and with little privacy, contributed to the feeling of isolation.

This has been exacerbated over the years by the fact that while before 1964 the state rooms were often used as part of the living accommodation at No. 10 – Clarissa and Elizabeth both used the White Drawing Room and the Small Dining Room – after that the family was confined to the flat itself. Dorothy Macmillan spent the years from 1960 to 1963 at Admiralty House while No. 10 was being refurbished and preferred the former as a home. Mary Wilson had a long battle to change the decoration from the country house chintz favoured by Dorothy to a more modern look. Everyone who visited the flat in the Thatchers' time remarked on how small and inconvenient the kitchen was. It took Norma Major several years after the 1992 election finally to instal a modern and pretty kitchen together with a decent bathroom for the main bedroom. Even so, when I saw the flat in 1997, the other two bathrooms were museum pieces. The No. 11 flat next door did not have a shower when we first moved in.

If there is little room for discretion in the private quarters, the spouse is even more restricted in relation to the public areas. Although Dorothy did have a large say in the refurbishment, choosing the fabrics and wallpaper, she was limited by budgetary constraints, which meant that after all the building works were completed there was very little money left for decoration. Clarissa before her had hoped to restore the state rooms at No. 10 to William Kent's original concept but had been prevented from doing so by the credit squeeze. Mary will proudly tell you that the carpet in the White Drawing Room was chosen by her and that she was able to change the look of No. 10 by returning the portraits of the prime ministers to the main staircase and displaying the official gifts that the Wilsons received.

More recently the major changes have been undertaken because the Prime Minister, rather than any spouse, took a personal interest. It was the bachelor Prime Minister Ted Heath who started to change the look of No. 10 almost immediately he moved in, wanting to restore it to its original grandeur. Severe dry rot provided the opportunity to redecorate. He started with the State Dining Room and then found like any other householder that once you do up one room, the others look worse and he ended up redecorating all the state rooms. He hung new pictures, some from the Government Art Collection but many others lent by generous benefactors. He displayed porcelain in cupboards and installed a grand piano in the White Drawing Room overlooking St James's Park. Every lunchtime, when he could, he would pop in there from his next door study to play his beloved classical music.

It is perhaps not surprising that the next prime minister who significantly altered the appearance of No. 10 was Margaret Thatcher. It is even less of a surprise that Denis took little interest in the house's appearance. Although the colour schemes have changed, the gilding and moulding that she installed remain there to this day, as does the silver brought in by the Silver Trust. Today these matters are dealt with by a committee of civil servants and an architect who initiate and control all major changes. During the recent redecoration works I was allowed to express a view about which of two or three colour schemes should be used but quite rightly was not allowed to dictate how a historic public building should look – although we have installed a climbing frame, swing and a trampoline in the garden.

At Chequers, there is even less scope for the Prime Minister to make changes. The house belongs to the Chequers Trust and it is the Trustees who take the decisions on refurbishment, not the Prime Minister. Until her death in 1967 Lady Lee of Fareham, whose husband set up the Trust, held strong views against alterations and again it was left to Ted Heath to initiate major improvements there, including stripping all the panelling – transforming a once dark house – and installing a swimming pool.

Everybody I meet imagines that there is a large personal staff in No. 10 to look after the Prime Minister. In fact, this was the basis for one of the storylines in the recent British film *Love, Actually* in which Hugh Grant plays the Premier. It is, however, way off the mark. People often laugh when, at the end of functions at No. 10, I tell them I have to rush off to cook Tony's dinner. But each of the spouses featured in this book knows that the reality of life here is that strange mixture of the grand and the humdrum.

While the Government Hospitality Fund provides the caterers, waiters and butlers for all official entertaining it does not provide, and never has provided, personal services to the Prime Minister in his or her flat. No. 10 has a house manager but his role is to look after the public parts of the building and to ensure that the fabric of the house is preserved. But that doesn't include the private flat. Once you pass that door, the family themselves – as in every other home – are responsible for ensuring the cooking, cleaning and other household chores are done. Until the Majors' time, the Prime Minister paid rent for living in No. 10; since then the Prime Minister has paid additional tax based on the cost of the accommodation and its upkeep.

Ted Heath told us of his first evening in No. 10 when after a busy day settling into government he and Willie Whitelaw asked one of the Private Secretaries for something to eat, only to be told, 'Well, we haven't got any food here.' So Willie said to him, 'Well then, go out and get some food for us' and he came back with some very old, stale sandwiches. The Thatchers relied on Margaret's personal assistant Cynthia Crawford and on the staff at Chequers to stock up on frozen lasagne and other easy meals to sustain them during the week. When the Majors first moved into No. 10 and Norma was spending much of her time looking after the family in Huntingdon, it was a while before the Private Office realised John was looking after himself and decided to get some of the Chequers staff to come and help. Chequers, on the other hand, is staffed by members of the armed forces and it provides a welcome respite from the stresses of No. 10. All of our subjects enjoyed Chequers, though they used it in different ways.

The official system has not always been quick to respond to the role of the spouse in No. 10. So we find both Clarissa in the 1950s and Norma in the 1990s having to drive themselves to official functions until they suddenly discover that help is available. Or Mary Wilson having to ask that she receive a copy of the Prime Minister's diary, marked with the engagements she is expected to attend, as a matter of course rather than by specific request, something which happened again to Norma Major. As for secretarial help, all our spouses needed this, all had to struggle to get it and it was only under Norma that the practice of the state paying for such help came to be accepted. All future prime ministerial spouses have cause to thank Norma for that. Yet it is not as if the other spouses before her did not have letters, invitations and public engagements. On the contrary, as I hope we have shown, they all made a contribution to public life. But their work was simply not recognised as worthy of support by the state until she made her stand. There is still a real need for Norma's idea of an induction paper for all new spouses.

The explanation, of course, is that the system is designed to serve the office of Prime Minister, not the person with possibly a family and a hinterland. This is not to say that the Private Office and No. 10 staff do not show great personal loyalty and dedication. They work extraordinarily long hours, often at the expense of their own private lives, with good humour. But despite many individual kindnesses, the system still makes little allowance for the needs of the Prime Minister as a person, let alone the needs of his or her family life.

There has always been more awareness of these needs when prime ministers travel abroad with their spouses. Foreign Office officials whom we interviewed acknowledged the importance of the spouse's role as a back-up, support, hostess (or host) and observer. This may be because they tend to get to know the Prime Minister on a more informal basis on foreign trips, or it could reflect the fact that, as ambassadors, their own personal experience has given them an insight into the role of the family in official life.

There is one area, however, where as a matter of course the machine of government expects and indeed demands that the spouse should play a role. This is in the official entertaining at No. 10 and Chequers and in the meeting and greeting of foreign dignitaries. Over the years the kind of entertaining which has taken place behind the familiar black door has reflected the personalities and preferences of the different inhabitants. Clarissa Eden took pride in making the formal dinners served at No. 10 more sophisticated and imaginative. Mary and Harold Wilson presided over a new kind of general reception at No. 10 with fewer members of the Establishment and more ordinary people as well as representatives of popular culture, sport and show business. The formal white tie and long glove dinners of the fifties were replaced by dinner jackets and cocktail dresses, all designed to reinforce the idea that there was a new kind of Britain.

Edward Heath transformed the entertaining at No. 10 by introducing music at every opportunity. He provided chamber music at his receptions and had a sung grace at the beginning of every formal dinner and an eight-person choir who would sing while coffee was served. At one dinner for Sir William Walton's seventieth birthday, in March 1972, which the Queen Mother attended, there was a musical performance in the Pillared Room which lasted until one o'clock in the morning. Heath also introduced the idea of a social secretary who arranged the entertainment. It was under Audrey Callaghan that the idea of the spouse giving specific charity receptions began, through her interest in Great Ormond Street Hospital. The Callaghans also introduced the Hugh Casson print on the No. 10 menus which we still use to this day.

The redecoration of No. 10 in the late 1980s under Margaret and Denis Thatcher lent a grandeur to their receptions and dinners, which was meant to signify the re-establishment of British prestige in world affairs. Margaret took a great deal of interest in the official entertaining, and the standard of catering went up. There would be traditional English food with four courses with different wines and liqueurs served at the end; green chartreuse was a particular favourite. Denis did not preside over many events at No. 10 on his own, although he kept the receptions going with his geniality and gin and tonics. He did host a few sporting receptions, including a memorable one for Chris Bonington and the other Everest mountaineers. Norma and John Major had a less grand style with smaller more informal groups, although long dresses and dinner jackets were still *de rigueur*. The drinks served at receptions changed from spirits to wine. Norma also introduced the idea of using Chequers for grand charitable events.

Throughout the years all the spouses had the chance to meet with and entertain foreign visitors. Although they all found it interesting this is not always an easy task, especially if there is no common language and interpreters have to be used. Clarissa, Elizabeth and Audrey each had the benefit of a period as wife to the Foreign Secretary to prepare them for this role. The odd man out, literally, was Denis, who was often the only man on the 'spouses' programme' arranged on official summits to keep the spouses busy while official talks and business were being conducted. He must have found it quite a challenge to keep up the conversation at times. I doubt whether his business training had really prepared him for the discussion with Raisa Gorbachev over dinner on the use of the potato in British and Russian cooking!

The other acceptable role for the spouse has been as a patron and supporter of charities and good causes. In the fifties and sixties, their charity work tended to be a continuation of their personal preferences before they came into No. 10. But as the media spotlight intensified, and as the previous class structures crumbled and the charity world became more and more professional, so too there grew up an expectation that the co-inhabitant of No. 10 could and should play a public role in the broader charitable world. This applied less to Denis as a man than to Mary, Audrey and Norma, although he played a significant role in supporting sports and military charities. It also reflects a growing trend in the wider world for 'first ladies', usually wives of presidents, to set up charitable foundations. I too have tried to respond to the growing number of requests from charities by hosting a reception at No. 10 each Tuesday for different charitable causes. As a self-employed lawyer, I have some control over my work diary. How far it will continue to be feasible in the future to expect the consort to undertake this role, if he or she has a full-time job, remains to be seen.

Above all, life in No. 10 is life in the eye of the media. What was surprising was that all our spouses identified this as a problem, even though press intrusion was far less for our first three than for the later ones. Perhaps the explanation is that living in No. 10 brings with it an inevitable media attention greater than anyone has experienced before. There is no doubt that this is something that not only the spouse but the whole family has to learn to cope with and that the pressure is very unlikely to diminish.

The media in the 1950s, however, was quite a different animal from the media today. The newspapers were mainly staid affairs with fewer pictures, and black and white television was only just starting to make an impact on the public. Pre-recorded newsreels in cinemas rather than the 24-hour-a-day live news in your own living room were the order of the day. Even so, the media mattered. Clarissa Eden herself smiles at the naïvety that led them to conclude that by marrying in the 'quiet' month of August she and Anthony could escape media scrutiny: in fact in the 'silly season' their marriage became the main story. And if at first the fact that it was a second marriage led to criticism from those who opposed divorce, that was soon replaced with a focus on the glamour of the couple. Later on Clarissa was subjected to an early example of 'spin' when the *Daily Mirror* wrongly accused her of arrogance over Maud Butt's washing line at Chequers. Clarissa's experience was just an early example of how over the years prime ministers and their families have become the subject of intense press scrutiny. Their private lives have become public property and they are seen as a legitimate focus of press interest. This was not so much of an issue in the fifties. Dorothy Macmillan was famously uninterested in her appearance in a way, perhaps, that only the daughter of a duke can be. I doubt, however, if she would have remained so unconcerned if it had been suggested by the press that she was letting her husband and the country down. I wonder whether Dorothy, who cared passionately about her husband's career, would then have minded more about how she was viewed.

In contrast, there is no doubt that the appearance of Mary at 48, dressed in the new shorter look of the sixties, added to the image that the Wilsons were more 'modern' than the 'old-fashioned' Homes even if Elizabeth was actually only seven years older than Mary. Elizabeth herself attracted little publicity but was worried about the unflattering way her husband appeared on television. Their children did find the press attention irksome and comments about their social life and activities started a trend that has continued. Increasingly the Prime Minister's family have found they too are in the public eye. Jim Callaghan may have been able to prevent the *Daily Mirror* publishing photographs of his family's belongings as they moved into No. 11, but Norma Major had limited success in keeping her family out of the press.

Political satire became much more accessible in Mary's time. Hers was the era of 'Mrs Wilson's Diary', which presented a wholly fictional character to the public. This was followed in the eighties by the 'Dear Bill' letters of *Private Eye* which – rather than proving a problem for Denis – created a useful, generally sympathetic image which protected him from further scrutiny. At no time, however, were these images presented as the real person. By Norma's time the more biting satire of *Spitting Image*, rather than illuminating the truth, was actually obscuring it. No one who has met Norma could mistake her for the downtrodden, uninteresting and dowdy woman portrayed in that programme.

If 1964 represented a sharp change in the kind of people who lived in No. 10 then 1990 marked another change – this time in the way the media treated the spouse of the Prime Minister. This reflects a change in the media itself which certainly started in the 1980s: more competitive; more news-hungry; more gossip-driven. There were two reasons why Norma rather than Denis fell victim to this. Firstly she was a woman, and for the first time in eleven years, the press could talk about the appearance of the consort at a time when image and pictures were becoming more and more important as a way of selling papers. Secondly, sections of the Tory Party and the press could not forgive the manner of Mrs Thatcher's leaving No. 10 and almost from the start felt that everything in the new regime must be worse than before. Once it became apparent that the new Prime Minister did pay attention to the newspapers and was hurt by them, the temptation to attack was overwhelming. This trend could be seen from the beginning, with the widespread scorn about Norma's blue suit, and it intensified in carping remarks about her appearance throughout the Major premiership, to a far larger extent than had ever been seen before. Not for her the sentiment expressed about Denis by the mainly male journalists who followed the prime ministerial visits – that it was not legitimate to target him as he was a private person who happened to live at No. 10. Just a few years later the attitude had changed to: you are a public person so our readers have a right to know about you.

This raises the question: how far is the Prime Minister's spouse a political figure? Is she/he and the wider family a legitimate object for comment? After all, although the prime ministers all volunteered for the job, the families did not. Apart from Clarissa Eden, none of the others could possibly have expected that their partner would become Prime Minister. All our subjects spoke of helplessness in the face of inaccurate or misleading statements and of feeling unable to reply. They all steered clear of expressing their views in public. This is partly because of the ambiguity of the spouse's position with no defined role, and indeed, no formal support structure. In future anyone entering No. 10 as Prime Minister will have to expect that it is not just his or her policies that will be critically examined but the personality and behaviour of the whole family. This is harder to accept in practice than in principle and little can prepare you for its sometimes harsh reality. I conducted a number of the interviews for this book in the middle of a media storm of my own. Talking to others who had been in a similar position helped me to keep a sense of proportion and to realise that these things do pass.

Meeting the families of past prime ministers at our No. 10 Golden

Jubilee dinner for the Queen, I was struck by how profoundly each family had been affected by their time at No. 10 and their sense of pride in what *their* Prime Minister had been able to achieve. Crossing that threshold for the first time does bring home how much the history of our country has been shaped by what goes on in the house. But No. 10 is also a home, where normal family life has to be conducted under the glare of the media spotlight. Each time I walk into the house, I am amazed that I am actually living there and conscious that it will not last for ever. For me, as for all the spouses in the book, there will come a time when the black door is closed for the last time. I will be left with a sense of tremendous pride and privilege at having been there at all and at having followed in the footsteps of such a remarkable group of people.

Cherie Booth

Acknowledgements

We would like to express our warm thanks to all those who have helped us with the preparation of this book. We have greatly appreciated the generosity of those who agreed to be interviewed and who gave us their time, insights and reflections on the lives of prime ministers' spouses spanning over half a century.

Our particular thanks go to the Countess of Avon (Clarissa Eden), Dame Norma Major, Sir Denis Thatcher and Lady Wilson (Mary Wilson), each of whom was generous with their support for the project, despite some reservations about returning to the spotlight after their often treasured years of relative privacy since leaving No. 10. It has been a great privilege and a pleasure to talk to them at length over several interviews, and we have greatly valued their patience and help. It was with sadness that we heard in 2003 of the death of Sir Denis Thatcher, who had impressed us with his charm and personality during our interview with him. In March 2005 we learned that Audrey Callaghan had died, followed eleven days later by the death of her husband, Jim Callaghan, whose devotion to Audrey shone through as he talked to us about her.

Many members of the families of former prime ministers' spouses gave us interviews and access to family archives and private papers and diaries. We owe thanks to: Lady Ashburton, niece of the Countess of Avon, and Lady Mary Soames; the relatives of Lady Dorothy Macmillan: Lady Carol Faber, the Earl of Stockton (Alexander Stockton), their Graces the late Duke and (now) Dowager Duchess of Devonshire (Andrew and Debo Devonshire), the Hon. Adam Macmillan; Viscountess Macmillan of Ovenden (Katharine Macmillan) and Lady Anne Tree; the Countess of Home, Lady Caroline Douglas-Home and

Lady Meriel Darby; Lady Wilson's son and daughter-in-law Professor Robin Wilson and Joy Crispin-Wilson; the late James (Lord) Callaghan, Margaret (Baroness) Jay, Julia Hubbard and Michael Callaghan; Mark Thatcher; and John Major. Our thanks also, to Sir Edward Heath for his hospitality and for kindly giving us an interview.

We would also like to acknowledge the help of friends, associates, No. 10 staff, and political colleagues: Sir Antony Acland, Robert Alexander, David Allen, Jeffrey (Lord) Archer and Lady Archer (as Mary Archer), Hugh and Roger Barrell, Tim (Lord) Bell, Baroness Blatch (as Emily Blatch), Lady Cally Blennerhasset, Gordon and Ursula Bowyer, Tom (Lord) Bridges, Robin (Lord) Butler, Peter (Lord) Carrington, Lady Charteris (as Gay Charteris), Shelagh Collingwood, Lady Margaret Colville, William (Lord) Deedes, Gordon and Helen Denniss, Devonshire), Bernard (Lord) Donoughue, Grey (Lord) Gowrie, the Dowager Lady Egremont (as Pamela Egremont), Lady Falkender (as Marcia Williams or Marcia Falkender), Lady Antonia Fraser, Peter Golds, Sue Goodchild, Philip (Lord) Harris and Lady Harris (Pauline Harris), Sir Nicholas Henderson, Anthony Holden, Douglas (Lord) Hurd, Howell James, Peggy Jay, Dame Jennifer Jenkins, Gerald Kaufman, Marja and John Kinsella, Linda Lalley, Sir Trevor and Lady Lloyd-Hughes, Alistair (Lord) McAlpine, Tom (Lord) McNally, Colleen (Lady) Merlyn-Rees, Sir Christopher Meyer, Len Michel, Sir Derek Mitchell, Barbara Oakley (Barbara Wallis), the Reverend Julian Ould, The Earl of Oxford and Asquith (Julian Oxford), Sir Michael Palliser, Chris Patten, Ray Penny, Charles (Lord) Powell, Suzanne Reinholt, Lady Ann Riches, Lorne Roper-Caldbeck, Brenda Shepherd, Anne Shevas, Shirley Taylor, Quinlan Terry, Harvey Thomas, Lady Anne Tree, Eric (Lord) Varley, George (Lord) Weidenfeld, Sir Oliver Wright and Lady Wright (as Marjorie Wright), Patrick (Lord) Wright.

We are grateful to D.R. Thorpe for his advice on the chapters on the Countess of Avon and the Countess of Home, and for sweeping up any errors of fact or interpretation when he read the draft of the whole book, and to Sir Alistair Horne for his counsel on Lady Dorothy Macmillan and for reading the draft of that chapter, and to Peter Hennessy for his early enthusiasm for the project. We owe thanks to Sir Martin Gilbert and Lord Thomas (Hugh Thomas) for sharing both their personal experience and their political perspective on people and events.

In the course of research we have consulted a number of archives and other historical sources, and we thank for their co-operation: the Countess of Avon for access to her private letters and for permission to quote from these and other documents held at the Avon Archive in the Special Collections, University of Birmingham, and to reproduce photos from her private collection; the Earl of Home for permission to quote from the Scrapbooks of Hester Alington and The Countess of Home's Scrapbooks, Diary for 1955, and 1956 'Suez Diary', and to reproduce photographs from the Hirsel Archive; Lord Callaghan for access to his Private Archive; Christine Penney at the Avon Archive, Special Collections section at the University of Birmingham; Helen Langley at the Bodleian Library, Oxford; Emily Tarrant at Conservative Party Archives at the Bodleian Library, Oxford and Sheridan Westlake at Conservative Central Office; Stephen Bird of the Labour Party Archive and Phil Dunn at the People's History Museum, Manchester; Rhys Griffith at the London Metropolitan Archives; staff at the archives of Great Ormond Street Hospital; Antonia Byatt and staff at the Women's Library, London; and the staff of the London Library.

We are most grateful to our researchers: Sue McConachy, whose knowledge of the period as well as her advice and support were greatly valued, and Catherine Haddon, and the assistance of Ben Taylor. Julia Matheson did a sterling job with transcripts over many months, casting aside other projects to make us her priority. Our editor at Chatto, Jenny Uglow, has been constantly encouraging and positive; her suggestions for changes including cuts were always delivered with exquisite charm, and she was a joy to work with, as was our agent, Faith Evans, who spent much time beyond the call of duty casting her eye over successive drafts and keeping us on track. Also at Chatto, we thank Poppy Hampson for assistance at all stages, and our copy-editor Beth Humphries. And we would like to acknowledge and thank those who have supported us privately during the preparation of this book, including Angela, Jackie and Maureen, and Melvyn, Alice and Tom.

In addition to the private collections named above, we would also like to thank the following for permission for quotations: Lady Wilson and Hutchinson Ltd., for her poems 'After the Bomb' , 'The House at the Edge of the Hill' and 'Reply to the Laureate' from *Selected Poems* (1970) and *New Poems* (1976); John Betjeman's 'A Mind's

Journey to Diss', from Mary Wilson, *New Poems* (1976), reproduced by permission of John Murray Publishers; quotations from Carol Thatcher's *Below the Parapet: The Biography of Denis Thatcher* (1996), reprinted by permission of HarperCollins Publishers Ltd. © Carol Thatcher 1996. We are also most grateful to all the individuals, institutions and agencies for permission to reproduce illustrative material, as acknowledged in the 'List of Illustrations'.

Select Bibliography

Place of publication is London unless otherwise specified.

Mark Amory, Ed., *The Letters of Ann Fleming* (1985)

Mark Amory, *Lord Berners: The Last Eccentric* (1998)

Bruce Anderson, *John Major: The Making of the Prime Minister* (1991)

Lucy Archer, *Raymond Erith: Architect* (1985)

Cynthia Asquith, *Remember and Be Glad* (1952)

Sidney Aster, *Anthony Eden* (1976)

Kenneth Baker, *The Turbulent Years: My Life in Politics* (1993)

Denis Bardens, *Portrait of a Statesman: The Personal Life Story of Sir Anthony Eden* (1955)

Joel Barnett, *Inside the Treasury* (1982)

Cecil Beaton, *The Happy Years: Diaries 1944–48* (1972)

——*The Strenuous Years: Diaries 1948–55* (1973)

Tony Benn, *Out of the Wilderness: Diaries 1963–1967* (1987)

——*Office Without Power: Diaries 1968–72* (1988)

——*Against the Tide: Diaries 1973–1977* (1989)

——*The Benn Diaries* (1995)

Lewis Broad, *Sir Anthony Eden: The Chronicles of a Career* (1955)

Richard Buckle, Ed., *Self Portrait with Friends: The Selected Diaries of Cecil Beaton 1926–74* (1979)

Barbara Bush, *A Memoir* (New York, 1994)

David Butler & Gareth Butler, *Twentieth Century British Political Facts 1900–2000* (8th Edition, 2000)

Lord Butler, *Art of the Possible: The Memoirs of Lord Butler* (1971)

Beatrix Campbell, *The Iron Ladies: Why do Women Vote Tory?* (1987)

James Callaghan, *Time and Chance* (1987)

John Campbell, *Margaret Thatcher: Volume One: The Grocer's Daughter* (2000)

——*Margaret Thatcher: Volume Two: The Iron Lady* (2003)

——*Edward Heath: A Biography* (1993)

David Carlton, *Anthony Eden: A Biography* (1981)

Lord Carrington, *Reflect on Things Past* (1988)

Barbara Castle, *The Castle Diaries 1974–76* (1980)

——*The Castle Diaries 1964–7* (1984)

Winston S. Churchill: *The Life of Randolph Churchill* (1996)

William Clark, *From Three Worlds* (1986)

John Colville, *The Fringes of Power: Downing Street Diaries 1939–1955* (1985)

Diana Cooper, *Trumpets from the Steep* (1960)

Patrick Cosgrave, *Margaret Thatcher: A Tory and Her Party* (1978)

Susan Crosland, *Tony Crosland* (1982)

Richard Crossman, *The Diaries of a Cabinet Minister Volume Two: Lord President of the Council and Leader of the House of Commons* (1976)

Richard Davenport Hines, *The Macmillans* (1992)

John Dickie, *The Uncommon Commoner: A Study of Sir Alec Douglas-Home* (1964)

Bernard Donoughue, *The Heat of the Kitchen* (2003)

——*Prime Minister. The Conduct of Policy under Harold Wilson and James Callaghan* (1987)

William Douglas-Home, *Mr Home Pronounced Hume. An Autobiography* (1979)

——*Old Men Remember* (1991)

Anthony Eden, *The Memoirs of Sir Anthony Eden: Full Circle* (1960)

Lord Egremont, *Wyndham and Children First* (1968)

Harold Evans, *Downing Street Diary: The Macmillan Years, 1957–1963* (1981)

Diana Farr, *Five at Ten: Prime Ministers' Consorts since 1957* (1985)

Nigel Fisher, *Harold Macmillan: A Biography by Nigel Fisher* (1982)

George Gardiner, *Margaret Thatcher: From Downing Street to Leadership* (1975)

Lord Home, *The Way the Wind Blows* (1976)

Paul Halloran and Mark Hollingsworth, *Thatcher's Gold: The Life and Times of Mark Thatcher* (1995)

Alethea Hayter, Ed., *A Wise Woman: A Memoir of Lavinia Mynors from her Diaries and Letters* (1996)

Edward Heath, *The Course of My Life: My Autobiography* (1998)

Nicholas Henderson, *Mandarin: The Diaries of an Ambassador* (1994)

——*The Private Office Revisited* (2001)

Peter Hennessy and A. Seldon, Ed., *Ruling Performance: British Governments from Attlee to Thatcher* (1987)

Peter Hennessy, *Muddling Through: Power, Politics and the Quality of Government in Postwar Britain* (1996)

——*The Prime Minister: The Office and its Holders Since 1945* (2000)

Elizabeth Hodder, *Hats off! To Conservative Women: Conservative Party of Great Britain Annual Women's Conferences 1921–1990* (Conservative Political Centre, 1990)

Sarah Hogg and Jonathan Hill, *Too Close to Call: Power and Politics – John Major in No. 10* (1995)

Alistair Horne, *Macmillan 1894–1956 Volume One of the Official Biography* (1988)

——*Macmillan 1957–1986 Volume Two of the Official Biography* (1989)

Douglas Hurd, *Memoirs* (2003)

——*The Search for Peace* (1997)

Bernard Ingham, *Kill the Messenger* (1991)

W. Eric Jackson, *Achievement: A Short History of the LCC* (1965)

Peggy Jay, *Loves and Labours* (1990)

Miles Jebb, Ed., *The Diaries of Cynthia Gladwyn* (1995)

Penny Junor, *Margaret Thatcher, Wife, Mother and Politician* (1983)

——*The Major Enigma* (1993)

Ernest Kay, *Pragmatic Premier: An Intimate Portrait of Harold Wilson* (1967)

Peter Kellner and Christopher Hitchens, *Callaghan: The Road to Number Ten* (1976)

Tessa Keswick, *Second Among Equals: Women and the Conservative Party* (Centre for Policy Studies Lecture to Conservative Party Conference, 2000)

Nigel Lawson, *The View from No. 11: Memoirs of a Tory Radical* (1992)

Russell Lewis, *Margaret Thatcher: A Personal and Political Biography* (1975)

Robert Lusty, *Bound to be Read* (1975)

Candida Lycett Green, Ed., *John Betjeman: Letters, Volume Two: 1951–1984* (1995)

Selwyn Lloyd, *Suez 1956: A Personal Account* (1978)

Alistair McAlpine, *Once a Jolly Bagman* (1997)

Harold Macmillan, *Winds of Change 1914–1939* (1966)

——*The Blast of War 1939–45* (1967)

——*Tides of Fortune 1945–1955* (1969)

——*Riding the Storm 1956–1959* (1971)

——*Pointing the Way* (1972)

——*At the End of the Day* (1973)

——*War Diaries: Politics and War in the Mediterranean, January 1943–May 1945* (1984)

Peter Catterall, Ed., *The Macmillan Diaries: The Cabinet Years 1950–1957* (2003)

Brenda Maddox, *Maggie: The First Lady* (2003)

G.E. Maguire, *Conservative Women: A History of Women and the Conservative Party, 1874–1997* (1998)

John Major, *John Major: The Autobiography* (1999)

Norma Major, *Joan Sutherland: The Authorised Biography* (1987)

——*Chequers: The Prime Minister's Country House and its History* (1996)

Ronald Millar, *A View from the Wings* (1993)

Ernle Money: *Margaret Thatcher: First Lady of the House* (1975)

Austen Morgan, *Harold Wilson* (1992)

Patricia Murray, *Margaret Thatcher: A Profile* (1980)

Christopher Ogden, *Maggie* (1990)

Kenneth O. Morgan, *Callaghan: A Life* (1997)

Ben Pimlott, *Harold Wilson* (1992)

Nigel Hamilton, *JFK: Life and Death of an American President. Volume One: Reckless Youth* (1992)

James Pope-Hennessy, *London Fabric* (1940)

Mark Pottle, Ed., *Daring to Hope, The Diaries and Letters of Violet Bonham-Carter 1946–1969* (2000)

Robert Rhodes James, *Anthony Eden* (1986)

——*Bob Boothby: A Portrait* (1991)

Andrew Roth, *Harold Wilson: A Yorkshire Walter Mitty* (1977)

Anthony Sampson, *Macmillan: A Study in Ambiguity* (1967)

Evelyn Schuckburgh, *Descent to Suez: Diaries 1951–56* (1986)

Anthony Seldon, *10 Downing Street The Illustrated History* (1999)

Anthony Seldon with Lewis Barton, *Major: A Political Life* (1997)

Dudley Smith, *Harold Wilson: A Critical Biography* (1964)

Mary Soames, *Clementine Churchill* (2002)

——Ed., *Speaking for Themselves: The Personal Letters of Winston and Clementine Churchill* (1998)

Nicholas Taylor, 'The Downing Street Story', in *The Architect & Building News*, 25 December, 1963

Carol Thatcher, *Below the Parapet: The Biography of Denis Thatcher* (1996)

——*Diary of an Election: With Margaret Thatcher on the Campaign Trail* (1983)

Margaret Thatcher, *The Path to Power* (1995)

——*The Downing Street Years* (1993)

Harvey Thomas with Judith Gunn, *In The Face of Fear* (1985)

Hugh Thomas, *The Suez Affair* (1967)

D. R. Thorpe, *Alec Douglas-Home* (1996)

——*Selwyn Lloyd* (1989)

——*Eden: The Life and Times of Anthony Eden, First Earl of Avon, 1897–1977* (2003)

George Urban, *Diplomacy and Disillusion at the Court of Mrs Thatcher: An Insider's View* (1996)

Nicholas Wapshott and George Brock, *Thatcher* (1983)

Phillip Whitehead, *The Writing on the Wall: Britain in the Seventies* (1985)

Marcia Williams, *Inside Number 10* (1972)

——(Marcia Falkender), *Downing Street in Perspective* (1983)

Harold Wilson, *The Labour Government 1964–1970: A Personal Record* (1971)

——*A Prime Minister on Prime Ministers* (1977)

——*Final Term: The Labour Government, 1974–76* (1979)

——*Memoirs: The Making of a Prime Minister 1916–1964* (1986)

Mary Wilson, *Selected Poems* (1970)

——*New Poems* (1977)

——*Poems I Like* (1983)

Woodrow Wyatt, *The Journals of Woodrow Wyatt* (1998–2000)

Nesta Wyn Ellis, *John Major* (1991)

Hugo Young, *One of Us: A Biography of Margaret Thatcher* (1989)

Kenneth Young, *Sir Alec Douglas-Home* (1970)

Philip Ziegler, *Wilson: the authorised life of Lord Wilson of Rievaulx*
  (1993)

Notes

Place of publication is London unless otherwise stated.

Introduction

1   Kati Marten, *Hidden Power: Presidential Marriages That Shaped Our History*, Pantheon Books, New York, 2001.

Chapter One Clarissa Eden, 1955–57

The principal interviews for this chapter were with the Countess of Avon (as Clarissa Eden) who was most generous with her time, as were relations, friends and colleagues, including: Lady Ashburton (as Sally Ashburton), Lady Charteris (as Gay Charteris), Lady Margaret Colville, Lady Antonia Fraser, Sir Martin Gilbert, Sir Nicholas Henderson, the Earl of Oxford and Asquith (as Julian Oxford), Lady Mary Soames, Hugh (Lord) Thomas, D.R. Thorpe, George (Lord) Weidenfeld. We are grateful for the Countess of Avon's co-operation in giving us access to her private letters, and to the Avon Archive at the Special Collections of the University of Birmingham.

1   D.R. Thorpe, *Eden: The Life and Times of Anthony Eden, First Earl of Avon, 1897–1977*, 2003, 377.
2   Richard Buckle (ed.), *Self Portrait with Friends: The Selected Diaries of Cecil Beaton 1926–74*, 1979, 234.
3   Thorpe, *Eden*, 377.
4   Cynthia Asquith, *Remember and Be Glad*, 1952, 88.
5   Mary Soames, *Clementine Churchill*, 2002, 62.
6   Mark Amory, *Lord Berners, the Last Eccentric*, 1998, 189.
7   James Pope-Hennessy, *London Fabric*, 1940, 12, 5.
8   Letters to Cecil Beaton, 20 April 1942; 7 April 1944; 8 May 1944, Countess of Avon Private Collection.
9   Letter to Cecil Beaton, 23 Feb. 1944, ibid.
10   Letter to Cecil Beaton, 15 Nov. 1947, ibid.
11   Letter to Cecil Beaton, n.d., 1946, ibid.
12   Buckle (ed.), *Self Portrait with Friends*, 233.
13   Thorpe, *Eden*, 48.

14 Evelyn Shuckburgh, *Descent to Suez: Diaries 1951–56*, 1986, 34 (15 Feb. 1952).

15 Avon Archives, Birmingham University: AP2/2/3–6.

16 Ibid., AP20/1/24–28, Anthony Eden Diary, 1952, 29 Dec. 1952.

17 Buckle (ed.), *Self Portrait with Friends*, 235.

18 Cited in Robert Rhodes James, *Anthony Eden*, 1986, 414; 387 (5 Sept. 1954).

19 Avon Archives, AP 20/45/16–38.

20 Ibid., AP/20/45/16–38, 18 Sept. 1952.

21 Mark Amory (ed.), *The Letters of Ann Fleming*, 1985, 128.

22 Thorpe, *Eden*, 387.

23 Cited, Ibid., 388.

24 Ibid., 415, 418, 421.

25 Avon Archives, AP 20/45/16–38, 2 Dec. 1953; 6 Dec. 1953.

26 Shuckburgh, *Descent to Suez*, 188 (1 May 1954); 189 (3 May 1954).

27 Rhodes James, *Anthony Eden*, 398.

28 Thorpe, *Eden*, 427.

29 Ibid., 425.

30 John Colville, *The Fringes of Power: Downing Street Diaries 1939–1955*, 1985, 708.

31 Winston S. Churchill, *The Life of Randolph Churchill*, 1996, 332–3 (5 April 1955).

32 *Evening Standard*, 21 April 1955.

33 Anthony Eden, *Full Circle*, 1960, 282.

34 Lewis Broad, *Sir Anthony Eden. The Chronicles of a Career*, 1955, 225.

35 Cited, Alan Thompson, *The Day before Yesterday*, 1971, 122.

36 Avon Archives, AP3/2/3, 5, 6, 7.

37 Amory (ed.), *The Letters of Ann Fleming*, 170 (13 Jan. 1956).

38 *Daily Telegraph*, 13 Jan. 1956.

39 Peter Hennessy, *The Prime Minister: The Office and its Holders since 1945*, 2000, 212.

40 William Clark, *From Three Worlds*, 1986, 156.

41 Eden, *Full Circle*, 361.

42 Ibid., 419.

43 Avon Archives, AP/3/2/1–3, Speech at the opening of Gateshead Conservative Association Headquarters, 20 Nov. 1956.

44 Cited in Thorpe, *Eden*, 507–8 (Countess of Avon Diary, 27 August 1956).

45 Clark, *From Three Worlds*, 157.

46 Miles Jebb (ed.), *The Diaries of Cynthia Gladwyn*, 1995, 191–2 (14 Nov. 1956).

47 Thorpe, *Eden*, 524.

48 Selwyn Lloyd, *Suez 1956: A Personal Account*, 1978, 207.

49 David Butler and Gareth Butler, *Twentieth-Century British Political Facts 1900–2000*, 8th edition, 2000, 268.

50 Thorpe, *Eden*, 520.

51 Hirsel Archives, Countess of Home, Suez Diary.

52 Amory (ed.), *The Letters of Ann Fleming*, 190.

53 Jebb (ed.), *The Diaries of Cynthia Gladwyn*, 192–3 (25 Nov. 1956).

54 *Daily Mirror*, 1 Dec. 1956.

55   Thorpe, *Eden*, 544.
56   Ibid., 546.
57   Ibid., 559 (10 Jan. 1957).
58   Mark Pottle (ed.), *Daring to Hope: The Diaries and Letters of Violet Bonham-Carter 1946–1969*, 2000, 184 (10 Jan. 1957).
59   Letter to Cecil Beaton, Otekai Bay, 16 March 1957, Countess of Avon Private Collection.
60   Jebb (ed.), *The Diaries of Cynthia Gladwyn*, 253 (1 May 1961).
61   Buckle (ed.), *Self Portrait with Friends*, 384.
62   Thorpe, *Eden*, 589, 591.

Chapter Two Dorothy Macmillan, 1957–63

The principal interviews for this chapter were with members of Lady Dorothy's family: the Earl of Stockton (as Alexander Stockton), Lady Carol Faber, the Hon. Adam Macmillan, their Graces the Duke and Duchess of Devonshire (as Andrew and Debo Devonshire), Viscountess Macmillan of Ovenden (as (Dame) Katharine Macmillan), and Lady Anne Tree. Also Sir Alistair Horne, the Dowager Lady Egremont (as Pamela Egremont), Lady Antonia Fraser, Lady Soames.

1   Quoted in Alistair Horne, *Macmillan 1957–1986: Volume Two of the Official Biography*, 1989, 513 (22 June 1963).
2   Harold Macmillan, *At the End of the Day*, 1973, 474, 472, 473.
3   Cited in Horne, *Macmillan 1957–1986 Vol. Two*, 290.
4   Macmillan, *At the End of the Day*, 474.
5   Cited in Horne, *Macmillan 1957–1986 Vol. Two*, 514.
6   *East Grinstead Gazette*, 5 July 1963.
7   Alistair Horne, *Macmillan 1894–1956 Volume One of the Official Biography*, 1988, 56.
8   Ibid., 57 (20 April 1920).
9   Harold Macmillan, *Winds of Change 1914–1939*, 1966, 118.
10   Horne, *Macmillan 1894–1956 Vol. One*, 73.
11   Ibid., 73.
12   Cited in Richard Davenport Hines, *The Macmillans*, 1992, 184.
13   Cited in Robert Rhodes James, *Bob Boothby: A Portrait*, 1991, 116 (to Cynthia Mosley, 14 Sept. 1932).
14   Horne, *Macmillan 1894–1956 Vol. One*, 87 (Interview with Lord Boothby).
15   Ibid., 88; *Daily Mail*, 10 May 1978.
16   Cited in James, *Bob Boothby*, No. 115 (Robert Boothby to Cynthia Mosley, 14 Sept. 1932; Dorothy Macmillan to Cynthia Mosley, n.d., 1932; Robert Boothby to Cynthia Mosley, 14 Sept. 1932).
17   Ibid., 118 (Letter to John Strachey, 7 Nov. 1933).
18   Cited in Hines, *The Macmillans*, 1992, 192.
19   Horne, *Macmillan 1894–1956 Vol. One*, 88–9.
20   Ibid., 98.
21   Macmillan, *Winds of Change*, 276, 278.
22   Horne, *Macmillan 1894–1956 Vol. One*, 90.
23   Cited in Ibid., 177.

24   Harold Macmillan, *War Diaries: Politics and War in the Mediterranean, January 1943–May 1945*, 1984, 422 (16 April 1944).
25   Ibid., 432 (28 April 1944).
26   Ibid., 136 (27 June 1943).
27   Harold Macmillan, *Tides of Fortune 1945–1955*, 1969, 298.
28   Peter Catterall (ed.), *The Macmillan Diaries: The Cabinet Years 1950–1957*, 2003, 259 (27 Aug. 1953); 23(12 Oct. 1950).
29   Ibid., 113 (28 October 1951).
30   Macmillan, *Tides of Fortune*, 365.
31   Ibid., 603.
32   Ibid., 690, 697.
33   Harold Macmillan, *Riding the Storm 1956–1959*, 1971, 20.
34   Ibid., 184.
35   Ibid., 201–2.
36   Ibid., 22, 208.
37   Ibid., 208.
38   Catterall (ed.), *Macmillan Diaries*, 214 (21 Feb. 1953).
39   *Newcastle Journal*, 12 Jan. 1959.
40   Horne, *Macmillan 1957–1986 Vol. Two*, 286.
41   Harold Macmillan, *Pointing the Way*, 1972, 31.
42   Ibid., 25.
43   *Times*, 2 June 1960.
44   *Daily Mail*, 15 Jan. 1959.
45   *News Chronicle*, 14 Jan. 1959.
46   *Bury Times*, 25 April 1959.
47   *Times*, 2 June 1960.
48   Cited in Horne, *Macmillan 1957–1986 Vol. Two*, 244.
49   Macmillan, *Riding the Storm*, 412, 411.
50   Harold Evans, *Downing Street Diary, The Macmillan Years, 1957–1963*, 1981, 92 (10 Jan. 1960); 99 (23 Jan. 1960); 106 (11 Feb. 1960).
51   Macmillan, *Pointing the Way*, 395.
52   Nicholas Taylor, 'The Downing Street Story', *Architect and Building News*, 25 Dec. 1963.
53   *Times*, 6 Oct. 1960.
54   Macmillan, *Pointing the Way*, 415–16, 417.
55   *Daily Sketch*, 7 Oct. 1963.
56   Horne, *Macmillan 1957–1986 Vol. Two*, 52.
57   Macmillan, *At the End of the Day*, 86.
58   Ibid., 487.
59   Horne, *Macmillan 1957–1986 Vol. Two*, 470.
60   Evans, *Downing Street Diary*, 247 (20 Jan. 1963).
61   Horne, *Macmillan 1957–1986 Vol. Two*, 474.
62   Macmillan, *At the End of the Day*, 439.
63   Ibid., 441.
64   Ibid., 444, 442.
65   Evans, *Downing Street Diary*, 283 (14 July 1963).
66   Horne, *Macmillan 1957–1986 Vol. Two*, 484, 478, 495.
67   Ibid., 514.
68   *Daily Sketch*, 7 Oct. 1963.

69   Macmillan, *At the End of the Day*, 500.
70   Evans, *Downing Street Diary*, 296–7 (13 Oct. 1963).
71   Ibid., 123 (8 Oct. 1960).
72   Ibid., 303.
73   Ibid., 303.
74   Horne, *Macmillan 1957–1986 Vol. Two*, 586.

Chapter Three Elizabeth Home, 1963–64

The principal interviews for this chapter were with the family of the Countess of Home (as Elizabeth Home): the Earl of Home (as David Home), Lady Caroline Douglas-Home and Lady Meriel Darby, all of whom were generous with their time, as were her friends, colleagues and associates, who include: Sir Antony Acland, Tom (Lord) Bridges, Shelagh Collingwood, Lorne Roper-Caldbeck, D.R.Thorpe, Sir Oliver Wright and Lady Wright (as Marjory Wright). We are grateful to Lord Home and the Home family for giving us access to the Hirsel Archive, which contains the important scrapbooks and diaries of the Countess of Home and the scrapbooks of her mother, Hester Alington.

1   Lord Home, *The Way the Wind Blows*, 1976, 182, 181, 183.
2   Lord Butler, *Art of the Possible: The Memoirs of Lord Butler*, 1971, 246.
3   D. R. Thorpe, *Alec Douglas-Home*, 1996, 293–4.
4   Ibid., 8.
5   Elizabeth Home, Scrapbook, No. 33: 1964, Hirsel Archive.
6   Home, *The Way the Wind Blows*, 55.
7   Thorpe, *Alec Douglas-Home*, 26.
8   Home, *The Way the Wind Blows*, 56.
9   William Douglas-Home, *Mr Home Pronounced Hume. An Autobiography*, 1979, 46.
10   Hester Alington, Scrapbook: 1913, Hirsel Archive.
11   Ibid.
12   Home, *The Way the Wind Blows*, 56.
13   Hester Alington, Scrapbook: 1914.
14   Hester Alington, Scrapbook: 1915.
15   Cited in Thorpe, *Alec Douglas-Home*, 17.
16   Home, *The Way the Wind Blows*, 25, 24.
17   Thorpe, *Alec Douglas-Home*, 31.
18   Cited in Diana Farr, *Five at Ten: Prime Ministers' Consorts since 1957*, 1985, 74.
19   Home, *The Way the Wind Blows*, 57.
20   William Douglas-Home, *Old Men Remember*, 1991, 14.
21   Thorpe, *Alec Douglas-Home*, 81, 86.
22   Ibid., 89 (Chamberlain to Lady Home, 22 Oct. 1938, Hirsel Archive).
23   Home, *The Way the Wind Blows*, 72.
24   John Colville, *The Fringes of Power: Downing Street Diaries 1939–1955*, 1985, 122.
25   John Dickie, *The Uncommon Commoner: A Study of Sir Alec Douglas-Home*, 1964, 67.
26   Cited in Thorpe, *Alec Douglas-Home*, 111.

27   Ibid., xvii.
28   Kenneth Young, *Sir Alec Douglas-Home*, 1970, 81.
29   *Daily Mail*, 28 May 1974.
30   Thorpe, *Alec Douglas-Home*, 213.
31   *Daily Mail*, 28 May 1974.
32   Elizabeth Home, 1955 Diary, 22 Oct. 1955; 26 Oct. 1955, Hirsel Archive.
33   Ibid., 22 Oct. 1955; 19 Oct. 1955, 25 Oct. 1955.
34   Elizabeth Home, 1955 Diary, 17 Nov., Hirsel Archive.
35   Thorpe, *Alec Douglas-Home*, 175, Elizabeth Home Diary, 26 July 1956, Hirsel Archive.
36   Elizabeth Home Diary, 2 Nov. 1956.
37   Ibid., 10 Nov. 1956.
38   Lady Home to Lady Avon, 10 Jan. 1957, Avon Archive, University of Birmingham, AP 31/1/40–68.
39   *Daily Mirror*, 28 July 1960.
40   *Daily Express*, 27 July 1960.
41   *Daily Mail*, 10 Aug. 1963.
42   Thorpe, *Alec Douglas-Home*, 213 (Elizabeth Home to Antony Acland, Sept. 1961).
43   William Douglas-Home, *Mr Home Pronounced Hume*, 29.
44   Cited in Farr, *Five at Ten*, 67.
45   Thorpe, *Alec Douglas-Home*, 258.
46   Home, *The Way the Wind Blows*, 216.
47   Thorpe, *Sir Alec Douglas-Home*, 193.
48   Elizabeth Home, Scrapbook No. 29, Oct.–Nov. 1963.
49   Cited in Farr, *Five at Ten*, 69–70.
50   Alethea Hayter (ed.), *A Wise Woman: A Memoir of Lavinia Mynors from her Diaries and Letters*, 1996, 145 (22 Oct. 1963).
51   Elizabeth Home, Scrapbook No. 35, May–July 1964.
52   Home, *The Way the Wind Blows*, 187.
53   *Woman and Home*, 5 Nov. 1963.
54   Elizabeth Home, Scrapbook No. 32, Feb.–Mar. 1964.
55   Elizabeth Home, Scrapbook No. 35, May–July 1964.
56   *Daily Mail*, 19 Nov. 1963.
57   Home, *The Way the Wind Blows*, 197, 198.
58   Elizabeth Home, Scrapbook No. 35, May–July 1965.
59   Ibid.
60   Elizabeth Home, Scrapbook No. 31, Feb. 1964; No. 33 April 1964.
61   *Spectator*, 17 Jan. 1964 (David Watt, *The Gladiators*).
62   *Newcastle Journal*, 21 Oct. 1963.
63   Elizabeth Home, Scrapbook No. 35, June 1964.
64   Home, *The Way the Wind Blows*, 203.
65   Ibid., 200.
66   Ibid.
67   Thorpe, *Sir Alec Douglas-Home*, 209.
68   David Butler and Gareth Butler, *Twentieth-Century British Political Facts 1900–2000*, 8th edition, 2000, 270.
69   Cited in Farr, *Five at Ten*, 77.
70   Thorpe, *Alec Douglas-Home*, 372.

71 Ibid., 370.
72 Ibid., 222.
73 Ibid., 390.
74 Ibid., 391 (Lord Home's speech at Church House, Westminster, 2 Aug. 1965).
75 Alistair Horne, *Macmillan 1957–1986 Volume Two*, 1989, 687.

Chapter Four Mary Wilson, 1964–70, 1974–76

The principal interviews for this chapter were with Mary (Lady) Wilson and with her son Professor Robin Wilson and daughter-in-law Joy Crispin-Wilson. Friends, colleagues and political aides who gave us interviews include: Robin (Lord) Butler, James (Lord) Callaghan, Bernard (Lord) Donoughue, Lady Falkender (as Marcia Williams or Marcia Falkender), Sir Martin Gilbert, Sue Goodchild, Dame Jennifer Jenkins, Gerald Kaufman, Sir Trevor and Lady Lloyd-Hughes, Tom (Lord) McNally, Sir Derek Mitchell, Sir Michael Palliser, and, on the Scilly Isles, Len Michel, the Reverend Julian Ould and Shirley Taylor.

1   Ben Pimlott, *Harold Wilson*, 1992, 317.
2   Andrew Roth, *Harold Wilson: A Yorkshire Walter Mitty*, 1977, 307.
3   Marcia Williams, *Inside Number 10*, 1972, 15.
4   Ibid., 28.
5   *Guardian*, 10 May 1976.
6   Diana Farr, *Five at Ten: Prime Ministers' Consorts since 1957*, 1985, 85.
7   Ibid., 88.
8   Harold Wilson, *Memoirs: The Making of a Prime Minister 1916–1964*, 1986, 29–30.
9   E. Kay, *Pragmatic Premier: An Intimate Portrait of Harold Wilson*, 1967, 18.
10 Wilson, *The Making of a Prime Minister*, 29–30.
11 *Observer*, 17 Jan. 1965.
12 *Daily Record*, 24 March 1966.
13 *Daily Mirror*, 13 Sept. 1947.
14 *Evening News*, 11 Dec. 1964.
15 Wilson, *The Making of a Prime Minister*, 119.
16 *Observer*, 17 Jan. 1965.
17 Wilson, *The Making of a Prime Minister*, 119–20.
18 *Observer*, 16 June 1963.
19 *Observer*, 17 Jan. 1965, 7 Feb. 1965.
20 *Woman's Own*, 22 May 1976.
21 Pimlott, *Harold Wilson*, 203.
22 *Observer*, 7 Feb. 1965.
23 Ibid.
24 Mary Wilson, *Selected Poems*, 1970.
25 *Observer*, 17 Jan. 1965.
26 Pimlott, *Harold Wilson*, 337.
27 *Observer*, 7 Feb. 1965.
28 David Butler and Gareth Butler, *Twentieth-Century British Political Facts 1900–2000*, 8th edition, 2000, 270.

Ursula Bowyer, Gordon and Helen Denniss, Bernard (Lord) Donoughue, Sir
Nicholas Henderson, Anthony Holden, Peggy Jay, Dame Jennifer Jenkins, Marja
and John Kinsella, Tom (Lord) McNally, Colleen (Lady) Merlyn-Rees, Lady Ann
Riches, Brenda Shepherd, Eric (Lord) Varley and Patrick (Lord) Wright. We are
grateful to Lord Callaghan for giving us access to his private archive, including
testimonies from Audrey's colleagues, Caroline Bond and Sir Anthony Tippet.

1   James Callaghan, *Time and Chance*, 1987, 387.
2   Ibid., 40, 43.
3   Ibid., 49.
4   Ibid., 50.
5   Diana Farr, *Five at Ten: Prime Ministers' Consorts since 1957*, 1985, 138, 137.
6   Callaghan, *Time and Chance*, 94.
7   *Daily Mirror*, 21 May 1976.
8   Minutes of proceedings of London County Council meeting, 14 Nov.
    1961: Children's Committee Periodical Report, 1 April–30 Sept. 1961,
    741, London Metropolitan Archives.
9   Farr, *Five at Ten*, 144–5.
10 Callaghan, *Time and Chance*, 162.
11 *South Wales Echo, and Evening Express*, 30 March 1966.
12 Susan Crosland, *Tony Crosland*, 1982, 188.
13 Farr, *Five at Ten*, 149.
14 Callagan, *Time and Chance*, 233.
15 Caroline Bond testimony; Sir Anthony Tippet testimony, Callaghan
    Private Archive.
16 *Western Mail*, 5 June 1970.
17 Farr, *Five at Ten*, 152.
18 Callaghan, *Time and Chance*, 392.
19 *Times*, 6 April 1976.
20 *Western Mail*, 6 April 1976.
21 *Daily Telegraph*, 6 April 1976.
22 *Daily Mirror*, 21 May 1976.
23 Farr, *Five at Ten*, 153.
24 *Evening Standard*, 30 Nov. 1976.
25 *Daily Mirror*, 21 May 1976.
26 *Daily Telegraph*, 14 April 1977.
27 Farr, *Five at Ten*, 156.
28 Ibid., 158
29 Nicholas Henderson, *Mandarin, The Diaries of an Ambassador*, 1994, 144–5.
30 Farr, *Five at Ten*, 154.
31 *Sun*, 11 Jan. 1979.
32 *Daily Express*, 27 Oct. 1978.
33 *Daily Express*, 2 Feb. 1979.
34 Joel Barnett, *Inside the Treasury*, 1982, 175; Peter Hennessy, *The Prime
    Minister: The Office and its Holders since 1945*, 2000, 394.
35 *Daily Express*, 1 March 1979.
36 Bernard Donoughue, *The Heat of the Kitchen*, 2003, 270.
37 Bernard Donoughue, *Prime Minister. The Conduct of Policy under Harold
    Wilson and James Callaghan*, 1987, 191.

30 C. Thatcher, *Below the Parapet*, 52.
31 *Spectator*, 7 May 1988.
32 C. Thatcher, *Below the Parapet*, 72.
33 *Sunday Graphic*, 17 Feb. 1952.
34 George Gardiner, *Margaret Thatcher: From Childhood to Leadership*, 51.
35 C. Thatcher, *Below the Parapet*, 91–2.
36 Russell Lewis, *Margaret Thatcher, A Personal and Political Biography*, 1975, 146.
37 Patricia Murray, *Margaret Thatcher, A Profile*, 1980, 60.
38 C. Thatcher, *Below the Parapet*, 98.
39 *Times*, 27 June 2003.
40 Ronald Millar, *A View from the Wings*, 1993, 236.
41 Ibid., 257, 258.
42 C. Thatcher, *Below the Parapet*, 118.
43 Millar, *A View from the Wings*, 268, 269.
44 C. Thatcher, *Below the Parapet*, 123.
45 Hugo Young, *One of Us: A Biography of Margaret Thatcher*, 1989, 38; *Financial Times*, 8 March 1976.
46 Margaret Thatcher, *The Downing Street Years*, 1993, 22–3.
47 C. Thatcher, *Below the Parapet*, 125.
48 Brenda Maddox, *Maggie: The First Lady*, 2003, 129.
49 Anthony Seldon, *10 Downing Street: The Illustrated History*, 1999, 36.
50 *The Times*, 7 June 2004.
51 C. Thatcher, *Below the Parapet*, 182.
52 Ibid., 190, 192.
53 Ibid., 219, 220.
54 M. Thatcher, *The Downing Street Years*, 220.
55 *Times*, 27 June 2004.
56 Letter to J.B. Hoskinson, 15 May 1992, Private Collection.
57 Bernard Ingham, *Kill the Messenger*, 1991, 248, 249.
58 Interview for *Married to Maggie*, Brook Lapping Productions, 2003.
59 C. Thatcher, *Below the Parapet*, 148.
60 Ibid., 252.
61 Ibid., 222.
62 John Campbell, *Margaret Thatcher Volume Two: The Iron Lady* (2003), 499.
63 C. Thatcher, *Below the Parapet*, 254.
64 Ibid., 256.
65 Kenneth Baker, *The Turbulent Years: My Life in Politics* (1993), 390.
66 *Sunday Telegraph*, 29 June 2003.
67 C. Thatcher, *Below the Parapet*, 263.
68 Barbara Bush, *A Memoir* (New York 1994), 376–7.
69 M. Thatcher, *The Downing Street Years*, 846–7.
70 Ibid., 855.
71 C. Thatcher, *Below the Parapet*, 266.
72 Ibid., 267.
73 Ibid., 268.
74 *Daily Telegraph*, 27 June 2003; *Daily Mirror*, 27 June 2003.
75 M. Thatcher, *The Downing Street Years*, 23.

Chapter Seven Norma Major, 1990–97

The principal interviews for this chapter were with Dame Norma Major whose generosity we have greatly appreciated, with John Major, and with friends, associates and colleagues, including: Robert Alexander, David Allen, Jeffrey (Lord) Archer and Lady Archer (as Mary Archer), Baroness Blatch (as Emily Blatch), Lady Cally Blennerhasset, Robin (Lord) Butler, Anne Chevas, Sir Martin Gilbert, Peter Golds, Sue Goodchild, Philip (Lord) Harris and Lady Harris (as Pauline Harris), Douglas (Lord) Hurd, Howell James, Linda Lalley, Sir Christopher Meyer, Barbara Oakley (as Barbara Wallis), Chris Patten, Ray Penny, Harvey Thomas, Charles (Lord) Powell, Lorne Roper-Caldbeck, Harvey Thomas, Patrick (Lord) Wright, and correspondence with Suzanne Reinholt.

1   John Major, *John Major: The Autobiography*, 1999, 184.
2   Penny Junor, *The Major Enigma*, 1993, 194.
3   Major, *John Major: The Autobiography*, 184.
4   Junor, *The Major Enigma*, 195.
5   Major, *John Major: The Autobiography*, 184, 185.
6   Margaret Thatcher, *The Downing Street Years*, 1993, 850.
7   Major, *John Major: The Autobiography*, 187.
8   Ibid., 188.
9   Kenneth Baker, *The Turbulent Years*, 1993, 396.
10 Anthony Seldon with Lewis Baston, *Major: Political Life*, 1997, 126; *Times*, 26 Nov. 1990.
11 Major, *John Major: The Autobiography*, 199.
12 Ibid., 45.
13 Nesta Wyn Ellis, *John Major*, 1991, 210.
14 Ibid., 229.
15 Junor, *The Major Enigma*, 168, 169.
16 Ibid., 168.
17 Private information.
18 *Daily Express*, 29 Nov. 1990.
19 Ibid.
20 Peter Oborne, *Alastair Campbell: New Labour and the Rise of the Media Class*, 1999, 119; cited in Peter Hennessy, *The Prime Minister: The Office and its Holders since 1945*, 2000, 471.
21 *Daily Express*, 29 Nov. 1990.
22 *Daily Mirror*, 28 Nov. 1990.
23 *Daily Express*, 28 Nov.; 29 Nov. 1990.
24 *Daily Mirror*, 29 Nov. 1990.
25 *Sunday Times*, 2 Dec. 1990; *Radio Times*, 5–11 Oct. 1996.
26 *Times*, 19 March 1992.
27 Major, *John Major: The Autobiography*, 225, 227.
28 Ibid., 238.
29 Ibid., 299.
30 Ibid., 306.
31 Norma Major, *Chequers: The Prime Minister's Country House and its History*, 1996, 267.
32 Major, *John Major: The Autobiography*, 644, 645.

33 *Times*, 28 Sept. 1996.
34 *Times*, 16 Sept. 1996.
35 *Independent*, 21 Sept. 1996.
36 *Times*, 5 Sept. 1996; *Guardian*, 3, 4 Sept. 1996; *Independent*, 21 Sept. 1996.
37 A. Seldon with L. Baston, *Major: A Political Life*, 713.
38 Major, *John Major: The Autobiography*, 719.
39 Ibid., 723.
40 Ibid., 724.
41 Ibid., 726.
42 Ibid., 727, 728.

Conclusion The Goldfish Bowl

1 Speech to the Conservative Group for Europe, 22 April 1993.

Index